T0331683

PROGRAM LOGICS FOR CERTIFIED COMPILERS

Separation logic is the twenty-first-century variant of Hoare logic that permits verification of pointer-manipulating programs. This book covers practical and theoretical aspects of separation logic at a level accessible to beginning graduate students interested in software verification. On the practical side it offers an introduction to verification in Hoare and separation logics, simple case studies for toy languages, and the Verifiable C program logic for the C programming language. On the theoretical side it presents separation algebras as models of separation logics; step-indexed models of higher-order logical features for higher-order programs; indirection theory for constructing step-indexed separation algebras; tree-shares as models for shared ownership; and the semantic construction (and soundness proof) of Verifiable C. In addition, the book covers several aspects of the CompCert verified C compiler, and its connection to foundationally verified software analysis tools. All constructions and proofs are made rigorous and accessible in the Coq developments of the open-source Verified Software Toolchain.

Andrew W. Appel is the Eugene Higgins Professor and Chairman of the Department of Computer Science at Princeton University, where he has been on the faculty since 1986. His research is in software verification, computer security, programming languages and compilers, automated theorem proving, and technology policy. He is known for his work on Standard ML of New Jersey and on Foundational Proof-Carrying Code. He is a Fellow of the Association for Computing Machinery, recipient of the ACM SIGPLAN Distinguished Service Award, and has served as Editor-in-Chief of *ACM Transactions on Programming Languages and Systems*. His previous books include *Compiling with Continuations* (1992), the *Modern Compiler Implementation* series (1998 and 2002), and *Alan Turing's Systems of Logic* (2012).

PROGRAM LOGICS FOR CERTIFIED COMPILERS

ANDREW W. APPEL

Princeton University, Princeton, New Jersey

ROBERT DOCKINS

Portland State University, Portland, Oregon

AQUINAS HOBOR

National University of Singapore and Yale/NUS College, Singapore

LENNART BERINGER

Princeton University, Princeton, New Jersey

JOSIAH DODDS

Princeton University, Princeton, New Jersey

GORDON STEWART

Princeton University, Princeton, New Jersey

SANDRINE BLAZY

Université de Rennes 1

XAVIER LEROY

INRIA Paris-Rocquencourt

CAMBRIDGE
UNIVERSITY PRESS

CAMBRIDGE
UNIVERSITY PRESS

32 Avenue of the Americas, New York NY 10013-2473, USA

Cambridge University Press is part of the University of Cambridge.

It furthers the University's mission by disseminating knowledge in the pursuit of education, learning and research at the highest international levels of excellence.

www.cambridge.org
Information on this title: www.cambridge.org/9781107048010

© Andrew W. Appel 2014

First published 2014

A catalogue record for this publication is available from the British Library

ISBN 978-1-107-04801-0 Hardback

This book is typeset in the Bitstream Charter font.
Font Copyright © 1989–1992, Bitstream Inc., Cambridge, MA.

in memory of

Kenneth I. Appel
1932–2013

a pioneer in computer proof

Contents

Road map

Readers interested in **the theory of separation logic** (with some example applications) should read Chapters 1–21. Readers interested in **the use of separation logic to verify C programs** should read Chapters 1–6 and 8–30. Those interested in **the theory of step-indexing** and **indirection theory** should read Chapters 35–39. Those interested in building models of **program logics** proved sound **for certified compilers** should read Chapters 40–47, though it would be helpful to read Chapters 1–39 as a warm-up.

Acknowledgments

I thank Jean-Jacques Lévy for hosting my visit to INRIA Rocquencourt 2005–06, during which time I started thinking about the research described in this book. I enjoyed research collaborations during that time with Francesco Zappa Nardelli, Sandrine Blazy, Paul-André Melliès, and Jérôme Vouillon.

I thank the scientific team that built and maintains the Coq proof assistant, and I thank INRIA and the research funding establishment of France for supporting the development of Coq over more than two decades.

Mario Alvarez and Margo Flynn provided useful feedback on the usability of VST 0.9.

Research funding for some of the scientific results described in this book was provided by the Air Force Office of Scientific Research (agreement FA9550-09-1-0138), the National Science Foundation (grant CNS-0910448), and the Defense Advanced Research Projects Agency (agreement FA8750-12-2-0293). The views and conclusions contained herein are those of the authors and should not be interpreted as necessarily representing the official policies or endorsements, either expressed or implied, of AFOSR, NSF, DARPA, or the U.S. government.

Chapter 1

Introduction

An exciting development of the 21st century is that the 20th-century vision
of mechanized program verification is finally becoming practical, thanks
to 30 years of advances in logic, programming-language theory, proof-
assistant software, decision procedures for theorem proving, and even
Moore's law which gives us everyday computers powerful enough to run all
this software.

We can write functional programs in ML-like languages and prove them
correct in expressive higher-order logics; and we can write imperative
programs in C-like languages and prove them correct in appropriately
chosen program logics. We can even prove the correctness of the verification
toolchain itself: the compiler, the program logic, automatic static analyzers,
concurrency primitives (and their interaction with the compiler). There
will be few places for bugs (or security vulnerabilities) to hide.

This book explains how to construct powerful and expressive program
logics based on separation logic and Indirection Theory. It is accompanied
by an open-source machine-checked formal model and soundness proof, the
Verified Software Toolchain[1] *(VST)*, formalized in the Coq proof assistant.
The VST components include the theory of *separation logic* for reasoning
about pointer-manipulating programs; *indirection theory* for reasoning
with "step-indexing" about first-class function pointers, recursive types,

---

[1]http://vst.cs.princeton.edu

recursive functions, dynamic mutual-exclusion locks, and other higher-order programming; a *Hoare logic* (separation logic) with full reasoning about control-flow and data-flow of the C programming language; theories of *concurrency* for reasoning about programming models such as Pthreads; theories of *compiler correctness* for connecting to the CompCert verified C compiler; theories of *symbolic execution* for implementing foundationally verified static analyses. VST is built in a modular way, so that major components apply very generally to many kinds of separation logics, Hoare logics, and step-indexing semantics.

One of the major demonstration applications comprises certified program logics and certified static analyses for the *C light* programming language. C light is compiled into assembly language by the CompCert[2] certified optimizing compiler. [62] Thus, the VST is useful for verified formal reasoning about programs that will be compiled by a verified compiler. But Parts I, II, and V of this book show principles and Coq developments that are quite independent of CompCert and have already been useful in other applications of separation logics.

PROGRAM LOGICS FOR CERTIFIED COMPILERS. Software is complex and prone to bugs. We would like to reason about the correctness of programs, and even to prove that the behavior of a program adheres to a formal specification. For this we use program logics: rules for reasoning about the behavior of programs. But programs are large and the reasoning rules are complex; what if there is a bug in our proof (in our application of the rules of the program logic)? And how do we know that the program logic itself is sound—that when we conclude something using these rules, the program will really behave as we concluded? And once we have reasoned about a program, we compile it to machine code; what if there is a bug in the compiler?

We achieve soundness by formally verifying our program logics, static analyzers, and compilers. We prove soundness theorems based on foundational specifications of the underlying hardware. We check all proofs by machine, and connect the proofs together end-to-end so there are no gaps.

---

[2] http://compcert.inria.fr

DEFINITIONS. A *program* consists of instructions written in a *programming language* that direct a computer to perform a task. The *behavior* of a program, *i.e.* what happens when it executes, is specified by the *operational semantics* of the programming language. Some programming languages are *machine languages* that can directly execute on a computer; others are *source languages* that require translation by a *compiler* before they can execute.

A *program logic* is a set of formal rules for *static* reasoning about the behavior of a program; the word *static* implies that we do not actually execute the program in such reasoning. *Hoare logic* is an early and still very important program logic. *Separation logic* is a 21st-century variant of Hoare logic that better accounts for pointer and array data structures.

A compiler is *correct* with respect to the specification of the operational semantics of its source and its target languages if, whenever a source program has a particular defined behavior, and when the compiler translates that program, then the target program has a *corresponding* behavior. [38] The correspondence is part of the correctness specification of the compiler, along with the two operational semantics. A compiler is *proved correct* if there is a formal proof that it meets this specification. Since the compiler is itself a program, this formal proof will typically be using the rules of a program logic for the implementation language of the compiler.

Proofs in a logic (or program logic) can be written as derivation trees in which each node is the application of a rule of the system. The validity of a proof can be checked using a computer program. A *machine-checked proof* is one that has been checked in this way. Proof-checking programs can be quite small and simple, [12] so one can reasonably hope to implement a proof-checker free of bugs.

It is inconvenient to construct derivation trees "by hand." A *proof assistant* is a tool that combines a proof checker with a user interface that assists the human in building proofs. The proof assistant may also contain algorithms for proof automation, such as *tactics* and *decision procedures.*

A *certified compiler* is one proved correct with a machine-checked proof. A *certified program logic* is one proved sound with a machine-checked proof. A *certified program* is one proved correct (using a program logic) with a machine-checked proof.

A *static analysis* algorithm calculates properties of the behavior of a program without actually running it. A static analysis is *sound* if, whenever it claims some property of a program, that property holds on all possible behaviors (in the operational semantics). The proof of soundness can be done using a (sound) program logic, or it can be done directly with respect to the operational semantics of the programming language. A *certified static analysis* is one that is proved sound with a machine-checked proof—either the static analysis program is proved correct, or each run of the static analysis generates a machine-checkable proof about a particular instance.

In Part I we will review Hoare logics, operational semantics, and separation logics. For a more comprehensive introduction to Hoare logic, the reader can consult Huth and Ryan [54] or many other books; For operational semantics, see Harper [47, Parts I & II] or Pierce [75]. For an introduction to theorem-proving in Coq, see Pierce's *Software Foundations*[76] which also covers applications to operational semantics and Hoare logic.

THE VST SEPARATION LOGIC FOR C LIGHT is a higher-order impredicative concurrent separation logic certified with respect to CompCert. *Separation logic* means that its assertions specify heap-domain footprints: the assertion $(p \mapsto x) * (q \mapsto y)$ describes a memory with exactly two disjoint parts; one part has only the cell at address p with contents x, and the other has only address q with contents y, with $p \neq q$. *Concurrent* separation logic is an extension that can describe shared-memory concurrent programs with Dijkstra-Hoare synchronization (e.g., Pthreads). *Higher-order* means that assertions can use existential and universal quantifiers, the logic can describe pointers to functions and mutex locks, and recursive assertions can describe recursive data types such as lists and trees. *Impredicative* means that the $\exists$ and $\forall$ quantifiers can even range over assertions containing quantifiers. *Certified* means that there is a machine-checked proof of soundness with respect to the operational semantics of a source language of the CompCert C compiler.

A separation logic has assertions $p \mapsto x$ where p ranges over a particular address type A, x ranges over a specific type V of values, and the assertion as a whole can be thought of as a predicate over some specific type of "heaps" or "computer memories" M. Then the logic will have theorems such as $(p \mapsto x) * (q \mapsto y) \vdash (q \mapsto y) * (p \mapsto x)$.

We will write down *generic* separation logic as a theory parameterizable by types such as A, V, M, and containing generic axioms such as $P * Q \vdash Q * P$. For a particular instantiation such as CompCert C light, we will instantiate the generic logic with the types of C values and C expressions.

Chapter 3 will give an example of an informal program verification in "pencil-and-paper" separation logic. Then Part V shows the VST tools applied to build a foundationally sound toolchain for a toy language, with a machine-verified separation-logic proof of a similar program. Part III demonstrates the VST tools applied to the C language, connected to the CompCert compiler, and shows machine-checked verification C programs.

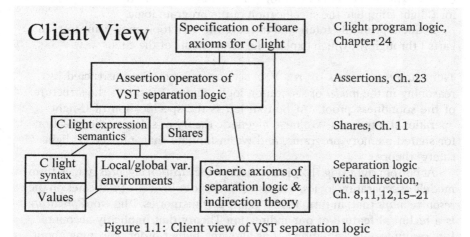

Figure 1.1: Client view of VST separation logic

FIGURE 1.1 SHOWS THE *client view* of the VST separation logic for *C light*— that is, the specification of the axiomatic semantics. Users of the program logic will reason directly about CompCert values (integers, floats, pointers) and C-light expression evaluation. Users do not see the operational semantics of C-light commands, or CompCert memories. Instead, they use the axiomatic semantics—the Hoare judgment and its reasoning rules—to reason indirectly about memories via assertions such as $p \mapsto x$.

The modular structure of the *client view* starts (at bottom left of Fig. 1.1) with the specification of the C light language, a subset of C chosen for its compatibility with program-verification methods. We have C values (such as integers, floats, and pointers); the abstract syntax of C light, and the mechanism of evaluating C light expressions. The client view treats statements such as assignment and looping *abstractly* via an axiomatic semantics (Hoare logic), so it does not expose an operational semantics.

At bottom right of Figure 1.1 we have the operators and axioms of separation logic and of indirection theory. At center are the assertions of our program logic for C light, which (as the diagram shows) make use of C-light expressions and of our logical operators. At top, the Hoare axioms for C light complete the specification of the program logic.

Readers primarily interested in *using* the VST tools may want to read Parts I through III, which explain the components of the client view.

THE SOUNDNESS PROOF OF THE VST SEPARATION LOGIC is constructed by reasoning in the *model* of separation logic. Figure 1.2 shows the structure of the soundness proof. At bottom left is the specification of C-light operational semantics. We have a generic theory of safety and simulation for shared-memory programs, and we instantiate that into the "C light safety" theory.

At bottom right (Fig. 1.2) is the theory of *separation algebras*, which form models of separation logics. The assertions of our logic are predicates on the *resource maps* that, in turn, model CompCert memories. The word *predicate* is a technical feature of our Indirection Theory that implicitly accounts for "resource approximation," thus allowing higher-order reasoning about circular structures of pointers and resource invariants.

We construct a semantic model of the Hoare judgment, and use this to prove sound all the judgment rules of the separation logic. All this is encapsulated in a Coq module called SeparationLogicSoundness.

Parts IV through VI explain the components of Figure 1.2, the semantic model and soundness proof of higher-order impredicative separation logic for CompCert C light.

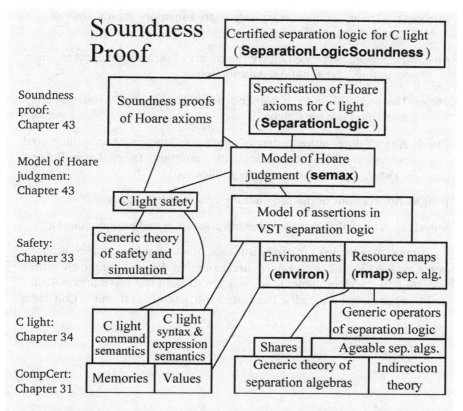

Figure 1.2: Structure of the separation-logic soundness proof

The Coq development of the Verified Software Toolchain is available at vst.cs.princeton.edu and is structured in a root directory with several subdirectories:

compcert: A few files copied from the CompCert verified C compiler, that comprise the specification of the C light programming language.

sepcomp: Theory of how to specify shared-memory interactions of CompCert-compiled programs.

msl: Mechanized Software Library, the theory of separation algebras, share accounting, and generic separation logics.

veric: The program logic: a higher-order splittable-shares concurrent separation logic for C light.

floyd: A proof-automation system of lemmas and tactics for semiautomated application of the program logic to C programs (named after Robert W. Floyd, a pioneer in program verification).

progs: Applications of the program logic to sample programs.

veristar: A heap theorem prover using resolution and paramodulation.

A proof development, like any software, is a living thing: it is continually being evolved, edited, maintained, and extended. We will not tightly couple this book to the development; we will just explain the key mathematical and organizational principles, illustrated with snapshots from the Coq code.

Part I

Generic separation logic

SYNOPSIS: *Separation logic is a formal system for static reasoning about pointer-manipulating programs. Like Hoare logic, it uses assertions that serve as preconditions and postconditions of commands and functions. Unlike Hoare logic, its assertions model anti-aliasing via the disjointness of memory heaplets. Separation algebras serve as models of separation logic. We can define a calculus of different kinds of separation algebras, and operators on separation algebras. Permission shares allow reasoning about shared ownership of memory and other resources. In a first-order separation logic we can have predicates to describe the contents of memory, anti-aliasing of pointers, and simple (covariant) forms of recursive predicates. A simple case study of straight-line programs serves to illustrate the application of separation logic.*

Chapter 2

Hoare logic

Hoare logic is an axiomatic system for reasoning about program behavior in a programming language. Its judgments have the form $\{P\}\, c\, \{Q\}$, called *Hoare triples*.[1] The command c is a statement of the programming language. The precondition P and postcondition Q are assertions characterizing the state before and after executing c.

In a Hoare logic of *total correctess*, $\{P\}\, c\, \{Q\}$ means, "starting from any state on which the assertion P holds, execution of the command c will safely terminate in a state on which the assertion Q holds."

In a Hoare logic of *partial correctness*, $\{P\}\, c\, \{Q\}$ means, "starting from any state on which the assertion P holds, execution of the command c will either infinite loop or safely terminate in a state on which the assertion Q holds." This book mainly addresses logics of partial correctness.[2]

---

[1] Hoare wrote his triples $P\{c\}Q$ with the braces quoting the commands, which makes sense *when quoting program commands within a logical statement.* Wirth used the braces as comment brackets in the Pascal language to encourage assertions as comments, leading to the style $\{P\}c\{Q\}$, which makes more sense *when quoting assertions within a program.* The Wirth style is now commonly used everywhere, regardless of where it makes sense.

[2] Some of our semantic techniques work best in a partial-correctness setting. We make the excuse that total correctness—knowing that a program terminates—is little comfort without also knowing that it terminates in less than the lifetime of the universe. It is better to have a *resource bound,* which is actually a form of partial correctness. Our techniques do extend to logics of resource-bounds [39].

THE INFERENCE RULES OF HOARE LOGIC include,

$$\text{seq}\frac{\{P\}\,c_1\,\{P'\} \qquad \{P'\}\,c_2\,\{Q\}}{\{P\}\,c_1;c_2\,\{Q\}} \qquad\qquad \text{assign}\frac{}{\{Q[e/x]\}\,x := e\,\{Q\}}$$

$$\text{consequence}\frac{P \Rightarrow P' \qquad \{P'\}\,c\,\{Q'\} \qquad Q' \Rightarrow Q}{\{P\}\,c\,\{Q\}}$$

The notation $P[e/x]$ means "the logical formula P with every occurrence of variable x replaced by expression e." A natural-deduction rule $\frac{A\ B}{C}$ derives conclusion C from premises A and B.

Using these rules, we can derive the validity of the triple $\{a \geq b\}\,(c := a + 1;\ b := b - 1)\,\{c > b\}$, as follows:

$$\text{seq}\frac{\text{con}\dfrac{a \geq b \Rightarrow a+1 > b-1 \qquad \text{ass}\dfrac{}{\{a+1 > b-1\}\,c := a+1\,\{c > b-1\}}}{\{a \geq b\}\,c := a+1\,\{c > b-1\}} \qquad \text{ass}\dfrac{\vdots}{\{c > b-1\}\,b := b-1\,\{c > b\}}}{\{a \geq b\}\,(c := a+1;\ b := b-1)\,\{c > b\}}$$

(Here we use a 1-sided version of the rule of consequence, omitting the trivial $c > b - 1 \Rightarrow c > b - 1$.)

Writing derivation trees in the format above is unwieldy. Hoare-logic proofs can also be presented by interleaving the assertions with the commands; where two assertions appear in a row, the rule of consequence has been used:

```
assert {a ≥ b}
assert {a + 1 ≥ b − 1}
c:=a+1;
assert {c > b − 1}
b:=b-1;
assert {c > b}
```

MANY OF THE STEPS in deriving a Hoare logic proof can be completely mechanical, with mathematical insight required at only some of the steps. One useful semiautomatic method is "backward proof", that takes advantage of the way the **assign** rule derives the precondition $Q[e/x]$ from the postcondition Q.

Read the following proof from bottom to top:

$\{(a \geq b)\}$ (by mathematics)
$\{(a + 1 > b - 1)\}$ (by substitution)
$\{(c > b - 1)[a + 1/c]\}$ (by **assign**)
c:=a+1;
$\{(c > b - 1)\}$ (by substitution)
$\{(c > b)[b - 1/b]\}$ (by **assign**)
b:=b-1;
$\{c > b\}$ (the given postcondition)

Working backwards, every step labeled "by **assign**" or "by substitution" is completely mechanical; only the step "by mathematics" might require nonmechanical proof—although in this case the proof is easily accomplished by any of several automated semidecision procedures for arithmetic.

SOMETIMES FORWARD PROOF IS NECESSARY. Especially in separation logic (which we will see later), one must establish the a memory-layout precondition before even knowing that a command is safe to execute, so backward proof does not work well. Forward proof can be accomplished with Hoare's assignment rule, but working out the right substition can feel clumsy. Instead we might use Floyd's assignment rule,

$$\text{floyd} \frac{}{\{P\} \ x := e \ \{\exists x', x = e[x'/x] \wedge P[x'/x]\}}$$

whose postcondition says, there exists a value x' which is the *old* value of x before the assignment, such that the *new* value of x is the evaluation of expression e but using the old value x' instead of x, and the precondition P holds (but again, substituting x' for x).

We can try a forward proof of the same program fragment:

$\{(a \ge b)\}$ (the given precondition)
c:=a+1;
$\{\exists c'.\ c = ((a+1)[c'/c]) \wedge (a \ge b)[c'/c]\}$ (by **floyd**)
$\{c = ((a+1)[c'/c]) \wedge (a \ge b)[c'/c]\}$ (by $\exists$-elim)
$\{c = a+1 \wedge (a \ge b)\}$ (by substitution)
b:=b-1;
$\{\exists b'.\ b = ((b-1)[b'/b]) \wedge (c = a+1 \wedge a \ge b)[b'/b]\}$ (by **floyd**)
$\{b = b'-1 \wedge c = a+1 \wedge a \ge b'\}$ (by $\exists$-elim and substitution)
$\{c > b\}$ (by mathematics)

All the steps except the last are quite mechanical, and the last step is such simple mathematics that many algorithms will also solve it mechanically.

TO REASON ABOUT PROGRAMS WITH CONTROL FLOW, we use the if and while rules.

$$\text{if} \frac{\{P \wedge e\}\, c_1\, \{Q\} \quad \{P \wedge \neg e\}\, c_2\, \{Q\}}{\{P\}\, \text{if } e \text{ then } c_1 \text{ else } c_2\, \{Q\}} \qquad \text{while} \frac{\{I \wedge e\}\, c\, \{I\}}{\{I\}\, \text{while } e \text{ do } c\, \{I \wedge \neg e\}}$$

We can use these to prove correctness of an (inefficient) algorithm for division by repeated subtraction. To compute $q = \lfloor a/b \rfloor$, count the number of times b can be subtracted from a:

q:=0; **while** (a>b) **do** (a:=a-b; q:=q+1)

To specify this algorithm, we write a precondition and a postcondition; what should they be? We want to say that the quotient q equals a divided by b, rounded down. But when the loop is finished, it will *not* be the case that $q = \lfloor a/b \rfloor$, because a has been modified by the loop body. So we make up *auxiliary variables* a_0, b_0 to represent the original values of a and b. Auxiliary variables are part of the specification or proof but not actually used in the program.

So we might write a precondition $a = a_0 \wedge b = b_0$ and a postcondition $q = \lfloor a_0/b_0 \rfloor$. This looks convincing, but during the proof we will run into trouble if either a or b is negative. This algorithm requires a strengthened precondition, $a = a_0 \wedge b = b_0 \wedge a \ge 0 \wedge b > 0$.

We will use the loop invariant $I = (a_0 = a + bq \wedge b = b_0 \wedge a_0 \geq 0 \wedge b_0 > 0)$. Now the (forward) proof proceeds as follows.

$\{a = a_0 \wedge b = b_0 \wedge a \geq 0 \wedge b > 0\}$
q := 0;
$\{q = 0 \wedge a = a_0 \wedge b = b_0 \wedge a \geq 0 \wedge b > 0\}$
$\{I\}$
while (a≥b) **do** (
   $\{a \geq b \wedge I\}$
   $\{a \geq b \wedge a_0 = a + bq \wedge b = b_0 \wedge a_0 \geq 0 \wedge b_0 > 0\}$
   a:=a-b;
   $\{a = a' - b \wedge a' \geq b \wedge a_0 = a' + bq \wedge b = b_0 \wedge a_0 \geq 0 \wedge b_0 > 0\}$
   q:=q+1
   $\{q = q' + 1 \wedge a = a' - b \wedge a' \geq b \wedge a_0 = a' + bq' \wedge b = b_0 \wedge a_0 \geq 0 \wedge b_0 > 0\}$
   $\{a_0 = a + bq \wedge b = b_0 \wedge a_0 \geq 0 \wedge b_0 > 0\}$ (2)
   $\{I\}$
)
$\{I \wedge \neg(a \geq b)\}$
$\{a_0 = a + b_0 q \wedge a_0 \geq 0 \wedge b_0 > 0 \wedge a < b_0\}$
$\{q = \lfloor a_0/b_0 \rfloor\}$ (3)

The only nonmechanical steps in this proof are (1) finding the right loop invariant I, and the two rule-of-consequence steps labeled (2) and (3).

It turns out that this algorithm also computes the remainder in variable a, so we could have easily proved a stronger postcondition, $a_0 = qb_0 + a \wedge 0 \leq a < b_0$ characterizing the quotient q and remainder a.

That algorithm runs in time proportional to a/b, which is exponential in the size of the binary representation of a.

A more efficient algorithm is *long division*, in which we first shift the divisor b left enough bits until it is greater than a, and then repeatedly subtract z from a, shifting right after each subtraction. This is a linear time algorithm, assuming that each primitive addition or subtraction takes constant time. It relies on the ability to shift z right by one bit, which we write as $z := z/2$.

$\{a \geq 0 \wedge b > 0\}$
n:=0;
z:=b;
while (z≤a)
   do (n:=n+1; z:=z+z);
q:=0; r:=a;
while (n>0) **do** (
     n:=n-1;
     z:=z/2;
     q:=q+q;
     if (z≤r)
     then (q:=q+1; r:=r-z)
     else skip
)
$\{a = qb + r \wedge 0 \leq r \leq b\}$

This algorithm is complex enough that it really is useful to have a proof of correctness. The precondition and postconditions are shown here. We avoid the need to mention a_0 and b_0 because the algorithm never assigns to a and b, so of course $a = a_0 \wedge b = b_0$. One could prove this formally by adding $a = a_0 \wedge b = b_0$ to both the precondition and the postcondition.

There are two loops here, and their invariants are,

$$I_0 = z = b2^n \wedge n \geq 0 \wedge a \geq 0 \wedge b > 0$$

$$I_1 = a = qz + r \wedge 0 \leq r < z \wedge z = b2^n \wedge n \geq 0$$

The reader is invited to work though the steps of the proof, or to consult the detailed proof by Reynolds [81].

Chapter 3

Separation logic

In Hoare logic it is difficult to reason about mutable data structures such as arrays and pointers. One can model the statement $a[i] := v$ as an assignment to a of a new array value, $\text{update}(a, i, v)$, such that $\text{update}(a, i, v)[i] = v$ and $\text{update}(a, i, v)[j] = a[j]$ for $j \neq i$. One cannot simply treat $a[i]$ as a local variable, because assertion P may contain references such as $a[j]$ that may or may not refer to $a[i]$. Instead, one can use a variant of the Hoare assignment rule to model array update:

$$\text{Hoare-array-assign} \frac{}{\{P[\text{update}(a, i, v)/a]\}\ a[i] := v\ \{P\}}$$

But this is clumsy: it looks like a global update to all of a, instead of a local update to just one slot. For example, consider this judgment:

$$\{a[i] = 5 \wedge a[j] = 7\}\ a[i] := 8\ \{a[i] = 8 \wedge a[j] = 7\}$$

To prove this we "simply" apply the Hoare array-assignment rule and the rule of consequence:

$$
\begin{aligned}
\text{let } P = &\ a[i] = 5 \wedge a[j] = 7 \\
Q = &\ \text{update}(a, i, 8)[i] = 8 \wedge \text{update}(a, i, 8)[j] = 7 \\
R = &\ a[i] = 8 \wedge a[j] = 7
\end{aligned}
$$

$$\text{consequence} \frac{P \Rightarrow Q \qquad \text{H-a-a} \frac{}{\{Q\}\ a[i] := 8\ \{R\}}}{\{P\}\ a[i] := 8\ \{R\}}$$

Proving $P \Rightarrow Q$ requires keeping track of the fact that $i \neq j$ so that we can calculate $(\text{update}(a, i, 8))[j] = a[j]$. But wait! We are not told $i \neq j$, so this step is invalid. The correct precondition should have been, $i \neq j \wedge a[i] = 5 \wedge a[j] = 7$.

This illustrates the difficulty: a proliferation of antialiasing facts $(i \neq j)$ and tedious rewritings $(i \neq j \Rightarrow \text{update}(a, i, v)[j] = a[j])$. Modeling the pointer update $p.f := v$, on similar principles, is even more clumsy: it looks like a global update to the entire heap.

THE IDEA OF SEPARATION LOGIC is to better support the principle of *local action*. An assertion (precondition or postcondition) holds on a particular *subheap*, or *heaplet*. In Hoare logic we might say $\{P \wedge R\} c \{Q \wedge R\}$ to mean that P and R both hold on the initial state, Q and R both hold on the final state. In separation logic we say $\{P * R\} c \{Q * R\}$, meaning that the initial state comprises two disjoint heaplets satisfying P and R, and the final state comprises two disjoint heaplets satisfying Q and R.

One can think of an assertion P as describing a certain set of addresses, and characterizing the values stored there. The "maps-to" assertion $p \mapsto e$ describes a single-word heaplet whose domain is just address p, and says that the value e is stored there. The expression p must be an *l*-value, an expression of the programming language that can appear to the left of an assignment statement. For example, $a[i]$ is an *l*-value in,

$$\{a[i] \mapsto 5 * a[j] \mapsto 7\}\ a[i] := 8\ \{a[i] \mapsto 8 * a[j] \mapsto 7\}$$

The assertion $a[i] \mapsto 5 * a[j] \mapsto 7$ means that $a[i] \mapsto 5$ and $a[j] \mapsto 7$ hold on two disjoint parts of the heap, and therefore $i \neq j$.

INFERENCE RULES OF SEPARATION LOGIC include the Hoare rules *assignment, sequence, if, consequence* exactly as written on page 11. But we must now understand that each assertion characterizes a particular subheap of the global heap. Furthermore, expressions e can refer only to local variables; they cannot refer to the heap at all. That is, the assignment rule can describe $x := y + z$ but it *does not cover* $x := a[i]$; and assertions can describe $x > y + z$ but *cannot say* $a[i] = v$.

Instead of the assignment rule, we use a *load* rule to fetch $a[i]$, and the *maps-to* assertion $a[i] \mapsto v$. The existential $\exists x'$ in the load rule serves the same purpose as in the Floyd assignment rule (page 12).

$$\text{load-array} \frac{}{\{a[e_1] \mapsto e_2\}\, x := a[e_1]\, \{\exists x'. x = a[e_1[x'/x]] \wedge (a[e_1] \mapsto e_2)[x'/x]\}}$$

$$\text{store-array} \frac{}{\{a[e] \mapsto e_0\}\, a[e] := e_1\, \{a[e] \mapsto e_1\}}$$

$$\text{frame} \frac{\{P\}\, c\, \{Q\} \qquad \mathrm{modv}(c) \cap \mathrm{fv}(R) = \emptyset}{\{P * R\}\, c\, \{Q * R\}}$$

THE FRAME RULE IS THE VERY ESSENCE of separation logic. The triple $\{P\}\, c\, \{Q\}$ depends *only* on the part of the heap described by P, and modifies *only* that part of the heap (into some state described by Q). Any other part of the heap—such as the part described by R—is unchanged by the command c. In contrast, in an ordinary Hoare logic with ordinary conjuction $\wedge$, the triple $\{P\}\, c\, \{Q\}$ does *not* imply $\{P \wedge R\}\, c\, \{Q \wedge R\}$ (where P and R describe the *same* heap). It is for this reason that separation-logic proofs are more modular than Hoare-logic proofs.

The condition $\mathrm{modv}(c) \cap \mathrm{fv}(R) = \emptyset$ states that the modified variables of the command c must be disjoint from the free variables of the assertion R. The command $a[i] := 8$ modifies no variables—storing into one slot of array a does not modify the value of a considered as an address.

The proof of our array store $a[i] := 8$ is then,

$$\text{frame} \frac{\text{store-array} \dfrac{}{\{a[i] \mapsto 5\}\, a[i] := 8\, \{a[i] \mapsto 8\}} \qquad \emptyset \cap \{a, i\} = \emptyset}{\{a[i] \mapsto 5 * a[j] \mapsto 7\}\, a[i] := 8\, \{a[i] \mapsto 8 * a[j] \mapsto 7\}}$$

IT IS OBLIGATORY IN AN INTRODUCTION TO SEPARATION LOGIC to present a proof of the in-place list reversal algorithm. Here's some C code that reverses a list (treating 0 as the NULL pointer):

```
/* v points to a linked list */
w=0;
while (v != 0) { t = v.next; v.next = w; w = v; v = t; }
/* w points to the in-place reversal of the list. */
```

It can be understood using these pictures. At the beginning:

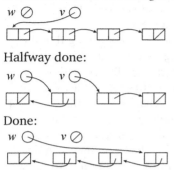

Halfway done:

Done:

Now we prove it in separation logic. The first step is to define what we mean by a list.

$$\text{listshape}(x) = \quad (x = 0 \land \text{emp}) \lor$$
$$(x \neq 0 \land \exists h \, \exists t. \; x.\text{head} \mapsto h * x.\text{next} \mapsto t * \text{listshape} \, t)$$

That is, listshape(x) is a recursive predicate, that says either x is nil—the pointer is 0 and the heaplet is empty—or x is the address of a cons cell with head h, tail t, where t is a list. Furthermore, the head cell is disjoint from all the other list cells. (The predicate emp describes the heap with an empty footprint; it is a unit for the $*$ operator.)

What does that mean, a recursive predicate? There are different choices for the semantics of the recursion operator, as Chapters 10 and 17 will explain. Here we can just use our intuition.

Program analyses in separation logic often want to reason not about the whole list from x to nil, but with *list segments*. The segment from x to y is either empty ($x = y$) or has a first element at address x and has a last element whose tail-pointer is y. Written as a recursive predicate, this is,

$$\text{listsegshape}(x, y) = \quad (x = y \land \text{emp}) \lor$$
$$(x \neq y \land \exists h \, \exists t. \; x.\text{head} \mapsto h * x.\text{next} \mapsto t$$
$$* \text{listsegshape}(t, y))$$

For example, the list $p \rightarrow \boxed{1 \mid a} \quad \boxed{2 \mid b} \quad \boxed{3 \mid c} \quad \boxed{4 \mid 0}$ contains the segments $p \rightsquigarrow 0$ (the whole list with contents [1,2,3,4]), $p \rightsquigarrow c$ (the segment with contents $[1, 2, 3]$), $a \rightsquigarrow c$ (the segment with contents $[2, 3]$), $b \rightsquigarrow b$ (an empty segment with contents $[]$), and so on. When we use 0 to represent nil, then listsegshape$(x, 0)$ is the same as listshape(x).

Some proofs of programs focus on *shape* and *safety*—proving that data structures have the right shape (list? tree? dag? cyclic graph?) and that programs do not dereference nil (or otherwise crash). But sometimes we want proofs of stronger correctness properties. In the case of list-reverse, we may want to prove not only that the result is a list, but that the elements now appear in the reverse order. For such proofs we need to relate the *linked-list* data structure to abstract mathematical *sequences*.

Instead of an operator listsegshape(x) saying that x points to a list segment, we want to say listrep$(\sigma)(x, y)$ meaning that x points to a list segment ending at y, and the contents (head elements) of that segment are the sequence σ. That is, the chain of list cells $x \rightsquigarrow y$ is the *representation in memory* of σ.

$$\text{listrep}\,\sigma\,(x, y) = \quad (x = y \land \sigma = \epsilon \land \text{emp})$$
$$\lor (x \neq y \land \exists \sigma' \, \exists h \, \exists t. \sigma = h \cdot \sigma'$$
$$\land \, x.\text{head} \mapsto h * x.\text{next} \mapsto t * \text{listrep}\,\sigma'\,(t, y))$$

We will notate listrep$\sigma\,(x, y)$ as $x \overset{\sigma}{\rightsquigarrow} y$.

Now we are ready to prove the list-reversal program. The precondition is that v is a linked list representing σ, and the postcondition is that w represents rev(σ):

assert$\{v \overset{\sigma}{\rightsquigarrow} 0\}$
w=0; **while** (v != 0) {t = v.next; v.next = w; w = v; v = t; }
assert$\{w \overset{\text{rev}\,\sigma}{\rightsquigarrow} 0\}$

As usual in Hoare logic, we need a loop invariant:

$$\exists \sigma_1, \sigma_2. \; \sigma = \text{rev}(\sigma_1) \cdot \sigma_2 \land v \overset{\sigma_2}{\rightsquigarrow} 0 * w \overset{\sigma_1}{\rightsquigarrow} 0$$

This separation-logic formula describes the picture in which the original sequence σ can be viewed as the concatenation of some σ_1 (reversed) and some σ_2—we use $\cdot$ to denote se-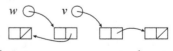

quence concatenation—and where the list segment from v to nil represents σ_2, and the list segment from w to nil represents σ_1.

To prove this program we need the inference rules of separation logic; the ones shown earlier, plus rules for loading/storing of record fields and for manipulating existential quantifiers. The rule for while is just like the Hoare-logic while rule; as usual, all expressions e (including the while-loop condition) must be *pure*, that is, must not load from the heap directly.

$$\text{load-field} \frac{}{\{e_1.\mathsf{fld} \mapsto e_2\}\, x := (e_1.\mathsf{fld})\, \{\exists x'.\; x = e_2[x'/x] \wedge (e_1.\mathsf{fld} \mapsto e_2)[x'/x]\}}$$

$$\text{store-field} \frac{}{\{e.\mathsf{fld} \mapsto e_0\}\, (e.\mathsf{fld}) := e_1\, \{e.\mathsf{fld} \mapsto e_1\}}$$

$$\text{while} \frac{\{e \wedge P\}\, c\, \{P\}}{\{P\}\, \text{while } e \text{ do } c\, \{\neg e \wedge P\}}$$

$$\text{generalize-exists} \frac{}{P \vdash \exists x.P} \qquad \text{extract-exists} \frac{\{P\}\, c\, \{Q\}}{\{\exists x.P\}\, c\, \{\exists x.Q\}}$$

Our rules for the existential are written in a semiformal ("traditional") mathematical style, assuming that x may be one of the free variables of a formula P. In later chapters we will treat this more formally.

Figure 3.1 presents the program annotated with assertions, where each assertion leads to the next. The proof is longer than the program! Checking such a proof by hand might miss some errors. Automating the application of separation logic in a proof assistant ensures that there are no gaps in the proof. Better yet, perhaps parts of the *construction*, not just the *checking*, can be automated.

Let us examine some of the key points in the proof. Just before the while loop (line 3), we have $\{w = 0 \wedge v \overset{\sigma}{\leadsto} 0\}$, that is, the initialization of w and the program precondition that the sequence σ is represented by the list starting at pointer v. We must establish the loop invariant (line 5), $\{\exists \sigma_1, \sigma_2.\; \sigma = \mathrm{rev}(\sigma_1) \cdot \sigma_2 \wedge v \overset{\sigma_2}{\leadsto} 0 * w \overset{\sigma_1}{\leadsto} 0\}$. To do this we let σ_1 be the empty sequence and $\sigma_2 = \sigma$.

1   assert$\{\mathbf{v} \overset{\sigma}{\rightsquigarrow} 0\}$

2   w=0;

3   assert$\{\mathbf{w} = 0 \wedge \mathbf{v} \overset{\sigma}{\rightsquigarrow} 0\}$

4   assert$\{\text{let } \sigma_1 = \epsilon,\ \sigma_2 = \sigma \text{ in } \sigma = \text{rev}(\sigma_1) \cdot \sigma_2 \wedge \mathbf{v} \overset{\sigma_2}{\rightsquigarrow} 0 * \mathbf{w} \rightsquigarrow 0\}$

5   assert$\{\exists \sigma_1, \sigma_2.\ \sigma = \text{rev}(\sigma_1) \cdot \sigma_2 \wedge \mathbf{v} \overset{\sigma_2}{\rightsquigarrow} 0 * \mathbf{w} \overset{\sigma_1}{\rightsquigarrow} 0\}$

6   **while** (v != 0) with loop invariant$\{\exists \sigma_1, \sigma_2.\ \sigma = \text{rev}(\sigma_1) \cdot \sigma_2 \wedge \mathbf{v} \overset{\sigma_2}{\rightsquigarrow} 0 * \mathbf{w} \overset{\sigma_1}{\rightsquigarrow} 0\}$

7     $\{$ assert$\{\mathbf{v} \neq 0 \wedge \exists \sigma_1, \sigma_2.\ \sigma = \text{rev}(\sigma_1) \cdot \sigma_2 \wedge \mathbf{v} \overset{\sigma_2}{\rightsquigarrow} 0 * \mathbf{w} \overset{\sigma_1}{\rightsquigarrow} 0\}$

8   assert$\{\mathbf{v} \neq 0 \wedge \sigma = \text{rev}(\sigma_1) \cdot \sigma_2 \wedge \mathbf{v} \overset{\sigma_2}{\rightsquigarrow} 0 * \mathbf{w} \overset{\sigma_1}{\rightsquigarrow} 0\}$

9   assert$\{\exists \rho, h, p.\ \sigma = \text{rev}(\sigma_1) \cdot (h \cdot \rho) \wedge \mathbf{v}.\text{head} \mapsto h * \mathbf{v}.\text{next} \mapsto p * p \overset{\rho}{\rightsquigarrow} 0 * \mathbf{w} \overset{\sigma_1}{\rightsquigarrow} 0\}$

10   assert$\{\sigma = \text{rev}(\sigma_1) \cdot (h \cdot \rho) \wedge \mathbf{v}.\text{head} \mapsto h * \mathbf{v}.\text{next} \mapsto p * p \overset{\rho}{\rightsquigarrow} 0 * \mathbf{w} \overset{\sigma_1}{\rightsquigarrow} 0\}$

11   t = v.next;

12   assert$\{\sigma = \text{rev}(\sigma_1) \cdot (h \cdot \rho) \wedge \mathbf{v}.\text{head} \mapsto h * \mathbf{v}.\text{next} \mapsto t * t \overset{\rho}{\rightsquigarrow} 0 * \mathbf{w} \overset{\sigma_1}{\rightsquigarrow} 0\}$

13   v.next = w;

14   assert$\{\sigma = \text{rev}(\sigma_1) \cdot (h \cdot \rho) \wedge \mathbf{v}.\text{head} \mapsto h * \mathbf{v}.\text{next} \mapsto w * t \overset{\rho}{\rightsquigarrow} 0 * \mathbf{w} \overset{\sigma_1}{\rightsquigarrow} 0\}$

15   assert$\{\exists q.\ \sigma = \text{rev}(\sigma_1) \cdot (h \cdot \rho) \wedge \mathbf{v}.\text{head} \mapsto h * \mathbf{v}.\text{next} \mapsto q * t \overset{\rho}{\rightsquigarrow} 0 * q \overset{\sigma_1}{\rightsquigarrow} 0\}$

16   assert$\{\sigma = \text{rev}(h \cdot \sigma_1) \cdot \rho \wedge t \overset{\rho}{\rightsquigarrow} 0 * \mathbf{v} \overset{h \cdot \sigma_1}{\rightsquigarrow} 0\}$

17   assert$\{\exists \sigma_1, \sigma_2.\ \sigma = \text{rev}(\sigma_1) \cdot \sigma_2 \wedge t \overset{\sigma_2}{\rightsquigarrow} 0 * \mathbf{v} \overset{\sigma_1}{\rightsquigarrow} 0\}$

18   assert$\{\sigma = \text{rev}(\sigma_1) \cdot \sigma_2 \wedge t \overset{\sigma_2}{\rightsquigarrow} 0 * \mathbf{v} \overset{\sigma_1}{\rightsquigarrow} 0\}$

19   w = v;

20   assert$\{\sigma = \text{rev}(\sigma_1) \cdot \sigma_2 \wedge t \overset{\sigma_2}{\rightsquigarrow} 0 * \mathbf{w} \overset{\sigma_1}{\rightsquigarrow} 0\}$

21   v = t;

22   assert$\{\sigma = \text{rev}(\sigma_1) \cdot \sigma_2 \wedge \mathbf{v} \overset{\sigma_2}{\rightsquigarrow} 0 * \mathbf{w} \overset{\sigma_1}{\rightsquigarrow} 0\}$

23     $\}$

24   assert$\{\mathbf{v} = 0 \wedge \exists \sigma_1, \sigma_2.\ \sigma = \text{rev}(\sigma_1) \cdot \sigma_2 \wedge \mathbf{v} \overset{\sigma_2}{\rightsquigarrow} 0 * \mathbf{w} \overset{\sigma_1}{\rightsquigarrow} 0\}$

25   assert$\{\exists \sigma_1, \sigma_2.\ \sigma = \text{rev}(\sigma_1) \cdot \sigma_2 \wedge \sigma_2 = \epsilon \wedge \text{emp} * \mathbf{w} \overset{\sigma_1}{\rightsquigarrow} 0\}$

26   assert$\{\mathbf{w} \overset{\text{rev}\,\sigma}{\rightsquigarrow} 0\}$

Figure 3.1: List reverse. 4: $\text{rev}(\epsilon) \cdot \sigma = \epsilon \cdot \sigma = \sigma$ 5: by *generalize-exists*   7: by *while* 8: by *extract-exists*   9: by unfolding $\mathbf{v} \overset{\sigma_2}{\rightsquigarrow} 0$, then removing the disjunct inconsistent with $v \neq 0$.   10: by *extract-exists*   12: by *load-field*, then eliminating variable p 14: by *store-field*   15: by *generalize-exists*   16: $\text{rev}(\sigma_1) \cdot (h \cdot \rho) = \text{rev}(h \cdot \sigma_1) \cdot \rho$, then fold the definition of $\mathbf{v} \overset{\sigma_2}{\rightsquigarrow} 0$ 17: by *generalize-exists*   18: by *extract-exists*   20: by *assign*   22: by *assign*   24: by *while*   25: by folding the definition of $\mathbf{v} \overset{\sigma_2}{\rightsquigarrow} 0$, given $\mathbf{v} = 0$ 26: by *extract-exists*, $\text{emp} * P = P$, $\text{rev}(\epsilon) \cdot \sigma_2 = \sigma_2$, then discarding inconsistent conjuncts.

First thing inside the loop body (line 7), we have the loop invariant and the additional fact $v \neq 0$, and we must *rearrange* the assertion to *isolate* a conjunct of the form $v.\text{next} \mapsto p$ (at line 10), so that we can load from v.next. (Both *rearrange* and *isolate* are technical terms in the symbolic execution of programs in separation logic—see Chapter 46.) The loop invariant says that σ_1 and σ_2 exist, so we instantiate them using the *extract-exists* rule.

Then (line 9) we can unfold the definition of list-segment $v \overset{\sigma_2}{\rightsquigarrow} 0$; but the nil case is inconsistent with $v \neq 0$ so we can eliminate it. The non-nil case of $v \overset{\sigma_2}{\rightsquigarrow} 0$ is

$$(v \neq 0 \wedge \exists \sigma' \exists h \exists t. \sigma = h \cdot \sigma' \wedge v.\text{head} \mapsto h * v.\text{next} \mapsto t * \text{listrep } \sigma \, (t, 0))$$

so we use that, extracting σ', h, t by *extract-exists*. Now we can rearrange this assertion into $v.\text{next} \mapsto p * other \; stuff$, which serves as the precondition for the load rule.

At line 14 after the store command, we have $\text{rev}(\sigma_1) \cdot (h \cdot \rho)$. By the algebra of sequence-reversal and concatenation, this is equivalent to $\text{rev}(h \cdot \sigma_1) \cdot \rho$. We will let the *new* σ_1 be $h \cdot \sigma_1$, and the *new* σ_2 be ρ. We can fold the definition of $v \overset{h \cdot \sigma_1}{\rightsquigarrow} 0$ to make (in effect) the same change at the representation level.

The extract-exists rule justifies the transition from line 17 to line 18, that is, from $\text{assert}(\exists \sigma_1.P)$ to $\text{assert}(P)$. It's not that $\exists \sigma_1.P$ entails P in isolation, it's that the Hoare triple $\{\exists \sigma_1.P\} \, c \, \{Q\}$ is provable from $\{P\} \, c \, \{Q\}$. In this case, the Hoare triple $\{\exists \sigma_1.\exists \sigma_2.P\} \, w = v; v = t \, \{Q\}$ (lines 17–22) is provable from $\{P\} \, w = v; v = t \, \{Q\}$ (lines 18–22).

At line 24 after the loop, we have the loop invariant *and* the fact that the loop condition is false, therefore $v = 0$. We can extract the existentially quantified σ_1 and σ_2, then notice that $v = 0$ implies σ_2 is empty. Thus $\sigma = \text{rev}(\sigma_1)$, and we're done.

For a longer tutorial on separation logic, the reader might try Reynolds [80] or O'Hearn [72].

ARE THE AXIOMS OF SEPARATION LOGIC, as presented in this chapter, really sound—especially when applied to a real programming language, not an idealized one? Building their soundness proof within a proof assistant will ensure that when we prove properties of programs using separation logic, those properties really hold of their execution. Can this separation logic be used to reason about function-pointers or concurrent threads? All such questions are the subject of the rest of this book.

Chapter 4

Soundness of Hoare logic

A program logic is *sound* when, if you can prove some specification (such as a Hoare triple $\{P\}\, c\, \{Q\}$) about a program c, then when c actually executes it will obey that specification.

What does it mean to "actually execute"? If c is written in a source language L, then we can formally specify an operational semantics for L. Then we can give a formal model for the program logic in terms of the operational semantics, and formally prove the soundness of all the inference rules of the logic.

Then one is left trying to believe that the operational semantics accurately characterizes the execution of the language L. But many source languages do not directly execute; they are compiled into lower-level languages or machine language that executes it its own operational semantics. Fortunately, at this point in the 21st century we can rely on formal compiler correctness proofs, that execution in the operational semantics of the source language corresponds to execution in the operational semantics of the machine language. And the machine languages tend to be well specified; machine language is already a formal language, and it is even possible to formally prove that the logic gates of a computer chip correctly implement the instruction set architecure (ISA), that is, the machine language.

So, we prove the program correct using the program logic, we prove the program logic sound with respect to the source-language operational semantics, and prove the compiler correct with respect to the source- and machine-language semantics. Then *we don't need to worry about whether the program logic and source-level operational semantics are the right ones,* because—as long as each proof goes through and all the proofs connect—the end-to-end composition of proofs guarantees program correctness.

Here we will give a brief introduction to some standard techniques of operational semantics, and show how a soundness proof of separation logic!soundness separation logic is built.[1] Consider a language L with local variables x, y, z, expressions e built from variables and arithmetic operators, and a memory-dereferencing operator written with square brackets $[e]$.

Opers	op	::=	$+ \mid - \mid >$
Exprs	e	::=	$x \mid n \mid e_1 \, op \, e_2$
Commands	c	::=	$\text{skip} \mid x := e \mid x := [e] \mid [e_1] := e_2 \mid c_1 ; c_2$
		$\mid$	$\text{if } e \text{ then } c_1 \text{ else } c_2 \mid \text{while } e \text{ do } c$

The *values* of the variables are integers that (in this simple language) can be interpreted as memory addresses. The *expressions* are variables x, constants n, or the addition, subtraction, or comparision of subexpressions. The *commands* are assignment $x := e$, load $x := [e]$, store $[e_1] := e_2$, sequencing $c_1 ; c_2$, if statements, and while loops.

Each execution state of L has three components $\langle \rho, m, c \rangle$ where

ρ is a local variable environment, a partial function mapping variables to values; in separation-logic parlance this is often called a *stack*;

m is a memory, mapping values to values;

c is a command, saying what to do next.

In operational semantics of expressions e or commands c one can use a *small-step* style $e \longmapsto e'$ saying that e does just one primitive operation to get to e'; the Kleene closure $e \longmapsto^* e_n$ describes multiple steps. Or one can use a *big-step* style $e \Downarrow v$ saying that the entire evaluation of e results

---

[1]Everything in this chapter is proved in Coq, in examples/hoare/hoare.v.

in a value v. Both for this little example and for our full-scale C-language system we will use big-step for expressions and small-step for commands.[2]

A big-step operational semantics for our expressions looks like this:

$$\frac{\rho(x) = v}{\rho \vdash x \Downarrow v} \qquad \rho \vdash n \Downarrow n \qquad \frac{\rho \vdash e_1 \Downarrow v_1 \qquad \rho \vdash e_2 \Downarrow v_2}{\rho \vdash (e_1 \, op \, e_2) \Downarrow (op \, v_1 \, v_2)}$$

Note that $e_1 \, op \, e_2$ refers to the syntax expression tree with two subexpressions and an operator-function $op : V \to V \to V$, while $op \, v_1 \, v_2$ is the application of that operator-function to two values.

We have carefully designed the programming language and its semantics so that expressions do not directly access the memory m; instead, this is done via special load and store commands. This arrangement is typical of languages designed for use with separation logic.

Figure 4.1 gives the operational semantics for commands. A state $\langle \rho, m, c \rangle$ small-steps to another state by executing the first piece of command c.

The meaning of an entire program c (in this toy language) is to execute the Kleene closure of the small-step relation, starting from the empty stack ρ_0, the empty memory m_0, and the initial command $(c; \text{skip})$. Then we examine the contents of variable a (for "answer") in the final stack.

$$\frac{\langle \rho_0, m_0, (c; \text{skip}) \rangle \longmapsto^* \langle \rho, m, \text{skip} \rangle \qquad \rho(a) = v}{\text{program } c \text{ results in answer } v}$$

Let us say that ρ_0 maps every identifier to nothing (has an empty domain), so an expression attempting to use an uninitialized variable is "stuck" (does not big-step evaluate); and m_0 has an empty domain, so a command trying to load from an uninitialized location is stuck.

---

[2]The reason is that we are interested in reasoning about well-synchronized concurrent programs using the Dijkstra-Hoare style of locking, for example in the Pthreads system for Verifiable C. In such programs we don't need to know what order subexpressions of an expression are evaluated—because expressions cannot read from memory—but on the other hand we cannot assume that a thread executes its commands to completion "all at once."

$$\langle \rho, m, ((c_1; c_2); c_3) \rangle \longmapsto \langle \rho, m, (c_1; (c_2; c_3)) \rangle$$

$$\langle \rho, m, (\text{skip}; c) \rangle \longmapsto \langle \rho, m, c \rangle$$

$$\frac{\rho \vdash e \Downarrow v}{\langle \rho, m, (x := e; c) \rangle \longmapsto \langle \rho[x := v], m, c \rangle}$$

$$\frac{\rho \vdash e \Downarrow v \qquad m[v] = v'}{\langle \rho, m, (x := [e]; c) \rangle \longmapsto \langle \rho[x := v'], m, c \rangle}$$

$$\frac{\rho \vdash e_1 \Downarrow v_1 \qquad \rho \vdash e_2 \Downarrow v_2}{\langle \rho, m, ([e_1] := e_2); c \rangle \longmapsto \langle \rho, m[v_1 := v_2], c \rangle}$$

$$\frac{\rho \vdash e \Downarrow v \qquad v \neq 0}{\langle \rho, m, (\text{if } e \text{ then } c_1 \text{ else } c_2); c \rangle \longmapsto \langle \rho, m, (c_1; c) \rangle}$$

$$\frac{\rho \vdash e \Downarrow 0}{\langle \rho, m, (\text{if } e \text{ then } c_1 \text{ else } c_2); c \rangle \longmapsto \langle \rho, m, (c_2; c) \rangle}$$

$$\frac{\rho \vdash e \Downarrow v \qquad v \neq 0}{\langle \rho, m, ((\text{while } e \text{ do } c_1); c) \rangle \longmapsto \langle \rho, m, (c_1; (\text{while } e \text{ do } c_1); c) \rangle}$$

$$\frac{\rho \vdash e \Downarrow 0}{\langle \rho, m, ((\text{while } e \text{ do } c_1); c) \rangle \longmapsto \langle \rho, m, c \rangle}$$

Figure 4.1: Small-step rules

Hoare logic. Before tackling the difficulties of memory, pointers, aliasing, and so on, we will specify a Hoare logic for the local-variable subset of the language without load and store. Then every state contains memory m_0 which is in any case irrelevant to the evaluation of expressions.

The assertions P, Q of our Hoare triples $\{P\} c \{Q\}$ can be just predicates on stacks ρ; or in the notation of the Coq proof assistant, $P : \rho \to \mathrm{Prop}$. In previous chapters we mentioned program expressions e rather informally within assertions, and used substitution $e[v'/x]$ rather informally to mean, the expression e with every use of x replaced by v'. Now we write $e \Downarrow v$ as a predicate on ρ, meaning that e big-step evaluates to v: that is, $\rho \vdash e \Downarrow v$. We will write substitution $P[v'/x]$ to mean $\lambda \rho . P(\rho[x := v'])$, meaning that $P[v'/x]$ holds on state ρ whenever P holds on the state $\rho[x := v']$ in which variable x has been assigned value v'— note here that x is a program variable while v' is a value, not a variable.

Our Hoare logic for this language has a Floyd-style assignment rule,

$$\frac{\forall \rho . P\rho \to \exists v . \rho \vdash e \Downarrow v}{\{P\} x := e \{\exists v, v'. \ x \Downarrow v \wedge (e \Downarrow v)[v'/x] \wedge P[v'/x]\}}$$

This is uglier than our Floyd rule of section 2, because we don't know that the expression e will safely evaluate (without getting stuck). Thus, we require an extra hypothesis above the line (that P is a guarantee that e will evaluate to something) and an extra existential variable v (to stand for a value that e evaluates to, since we can't simply say "*the* value of e"). But see Chapter 25 for another way to express "the value of e".

To prove soundness of our Hoare logic, we first model the meaning of $\{P\} c \{Q\}$. Intuitively, this means that on any state in which P holds,

1. c is safe to execute—it cannot get stuck, and

2. if c finishes (without infinite-looping), then Q will hold.

The definition of our model proceeds in stages. First, we say that a state $\langle \rho, m, c \rangle$ is *immediately safe* if it is safely halted ($c = \mathrm{skip}$) or if it can small-step to another state. A state s is *safe* if, whenever $s \longmapsto^* s'$ then s' is immediately safe. A predicate P *guards* command c, written $\{P\}c$, when:

$$\{P\}c \ = \ \forall \rho.\, P\rho \to \text{safe}\, \langle \rho, m_0, c \rangle.$$

P guards c means that, in any state ρ that satisfies P, it is safe to execute c. Finally, the meaning of the Hoare triple is,

$$\{P\}c\{Q\} \ = \ \forall k.\, \{Q\}k \to \{P\}(c;k).$$

What does this mean? If Q is a good enough precondition for running the command k, then P is a good enough precondition for running $(c; k)$. This is partial correctness twisted into *continuation-passing style*.

One might think that this definition talks only about safety, not correctness; but since it quantifies over all continuations k, we must think about all possible observations of the state that the program k might make. The postcondition Q must guarantee that no matter what can possibly be observable in the state after executing c, the program k must not get stuck. This means, in effect, that if the command c terminates in a post-state, then that state actually satisfies Q. For example, if Q is $\exists i, v \Downarrow 2i$, that is, "$v$ is even", we can build a program that tests v for evenness, and deliberately gets stuck if not. We claim that any reasonable whole-program specification is computably testable. Therefore, *although our soundness proof seems to guarantee just safety, in fact it guarantees partial correctness for any reasonable specification.*

The point of having such a semantic model of the Hoare triple is that we can use it to prove the soundness of each of the Hoare-logic inference rules. We prove the soundness of the Floyd assignment rule as an ordinary lemma in Coq (see examples/hoare/hoare.v).

Lemma floyd_assign:
  ∀ (P: h_assert) (x: var) (e: expr),
  (∀ ρ, P ρ → ∃v, eval e v ρ) →
  Hoare P (Cassign x e)
  (fun ρ ⇒ ∃v, ∃v',
    eval (Evar x) v ρ ∧ subst x v' (eval e v) ρ ∧ subst x v' P ρ).

Compare this lemma to Floyd's assignment rule shown on page 29. To prove it, we unfold the definition of Hoare and guard to obtain the proof goal,

```
P : h_assert
x : var
e : expr
H : ∀ρ : stack, P ρ → ∃v : val, eval e v ρ
k : command
H0 : guard (fun ρ : stack ⇒
                ∃v : val, ∃v' : option val,
                    eval (Evar x) v ρ ∧
                    subst x v' (eval e v) ρ ∧ subst x v' P ρ) k
ρ : stack
H1 : P ρ
-------------------------------------(1/1)
safe (State ρ m0 (Cseq (Cassign x e) k))
```

Now, we can use H ρ H1 to find v such that $ρ ⊢ e ⇓ v$. Therefore by the small-step rule for assignment, the state $⟨ρ, m_0, (x := e; k)⟩$ can step to state $⟨ρ[x := v], m_0, k⟩$. A lemma about safety says that if $s ⟼ s'$ then safe(s) ⟷ safe(s'), so all we have to prove is,

safe (State (upd rho x (Some v)) m0 k)

But this is the conclusion of $\{Q\}k$, that is, hypothesis H0; so we apply H0 yielding the proof goal,

```
H : eval e v rho
H1 : P rho

--------------------------------------(1/1)
∃v0 : val, ∃v' : option val,
    eval (Evar x) v0 (upd rho x (Some v)) ∧
    subst x v' (eval e v0) (upd rho x (Some v)) ∧
    subst x v' P (upd rho x (Some v))
```

We instantiate the existentials with v and $\rho(x)$, respectively. Now it turns out that $\rho[v/x][\rho(x)/x] = \rho$, and that is enough to finish the proof.

Readers who want to see this one step at a time should step through the proof in examples/hoare/hoare.v.

WHY DO WE NEED THE "CONTINUATION PASSING" MODEL of the Hoare triple? A more intuitive model is to say something like,

$$\{P\}\,c\,\{Q\} \stackrel{?}{=} \forall \rho, c, \rho'.\, P\rho \wedge (\langle \rho, m_0, (c;\mathsf{skip})\rangle \longmapsto^* \langle \rho', m_0, \mathsf{skip}\rangle) \;\rightarrow\; Q\rho'$$

but unfortunately this does not work: an unsafe program (in which $\langle \rho, m_0, (c;\mathsf{skip})\rangle$ gets stuck) satisfies this definition of the Hoare triple. We can attempt to correct for this by requiring safety, but by then it becomes simpler to use the continuation-passing version. And finally, in languages where the command c can *escape* by breaking out of loops, returning from functions, or go-to, the continuation-passing definition of the Hoare triple [9] works much better than "direct-style" models.

SEPARATION LOGIC is a variant of Hoare logic in which assertions P, Q are not simply predicates on states: they characterize a *footprint*, a subset of memory locations of a heaplet. Over the next five chapters, we will show how to construct general models of separation logics and prove soundness of their inference rules. The basic idea is the same—define assertions as predicates on states, and the Hoare judgment as a relation between predicates, commands, and states.

Chapter 5

Mechanized Semantic Library
by Andrew W. Appel, Robert Dockins, and Aquinas Hobor

In constructing program logics for particular applications, for particular languages, 20th-century scientists had particular difficulty with *pointers*—aliasing and antialiasing, updates to state, commuting of operators; and *self-reference*—recursive functions, recursive types, functions as first-class values, types and predicates as parameters to functions. The combination of these two was particularly difficult: pointers to mutable records that can contain pointers to function-values that operate on mutable records.

Two strains of late-20th-century logic shed light on these matters.

- Girard's 1987 *linear logic* [43] and other *substructural logics* treat logical assertions as *resources* that can be created, consumed and (when necessary) duplicated. This kind of thinking led to the Ishtiaq/O'Hearn/Reynolds invention in 2001 of separation logic [56, 79], which is a substructural Hoare logic for reasoning about sharing and antialiasing in pointer-manipulating programs.

- Scott's 1976 *domain theory* [84] treats data types as *approximations*, thereby avoiding paradoxes about recursive types and other recursive definitions/specifications: a type can be defined in terms of more approximate versions of itself, which eventually bottoms out in a type that contains no information at all. These ideas led to the

Appel/McAllester/Ahmed invention in 2001 of *step-indexing* [10, 2] which is a kind of practical domain theory for computations on von Neumann machines.

Many 21st-century scientists have generalized these methods for application to many different program logics (and other applications); and have formalized these methods within mechanical proof assistants.

THE MECHANIZED SEMANTIC LIBRARY (MSL) is a formalization in Coq of the general theory of separation logic (and its models) and indirection theory (and its step-indexed models). The MSL can serve as a basis for a wide variety of logical applications; there is no "baked in" programming language, memory model, or assertion model.

The software distribution of the MSL is the msl subdirectory of the VST. *One* application of the MSL is the *Verifiable C* program logic (the veric subdirectory of vst). But the MSL is not specific to (or specialized to) the VST, and has many other potential applications.

Chapters 6–14 and 21 of this book describe MSL components that build models of separation logic. Chapters 15–17 and 35–39 describe MSL components that build step-indexed models. Then the rest of the book describes application of the MSL to the Verified Software Toolchain.

Chapter 6

Separation algebras

Separation logics have assertions—for example $P * (x \mapsto y) * Q$—that describe objects in some underlying model—for example "heaplets"—that *separate* in some way—such as "the heaplet satisfying P can join with (is disjoint from) the heaplet satisfying $x \mapsto y$." In this chapter we investigate the objects in the underlying models: what kinds of objects will we have, and what does it mean for them to *join?*

This study of *join* relations is the study of *separation algebras*. Once we know how the underlying objects join, this will explain the meaning of the $*$ operator (and other operators), and will justify the reasoning rules for these operators.

In a typical separation logic, the state has a *stack* ρ for local variables and a *heap m* for pointers and arrays. Typically, m is a *partial function* from addresses to values. The key idea in separation logic is that that each assertion characterizes the domain of this function as well as the value of the function. The separating conjunction $P * Q$ requires that P and Q operate on subheaps with disjoint domains.

In contrast, for the stack we do not often worry about separation: we may assume that both P and Q operate on the entirety of the stack ρ.

For now, let us ignore stacks ρ, and let us assume that assertions P are just predicates on heaps, so $m \models P$ is simply $P(m)$. Then we can give a simple model of the separating conjunction $*$ as follows:

$$(P * Q)(m) = \exists m_1, m_2.\ m_1 \oplus m_2 = m \ \wedge\ P(m_1) \ \wedge\ Q(m_2)$$

where the *join operator* $m_1 \oplus m_2 = m$ for these heaplets means that the domain of m is the disjoint union of the domains of m_1 and m_2, that wherever $m_1(p)$ is defined, $m_1(p) = m(p)$, and wherever $m_2(p)$ is defined, $m_2(p) = m(p)$. So, that is one kind of $\oplus$ operator: disjoint union.

BUT WE WILL SOON WANT to generalize the notion of $\oplus$. For example, in concurrent separation logic we want concurrent-read, exclusive-write access—that is, two threads should be able to have shared read-only access to a location, or at other times a single thread should be able to have exclusive read/write access to that location. We achieve this with *permission shares*: a *partial* share gives enough access to read, and several threads can each hold partial shares at the same location. If a single thread can reclaim all the partial shares (by synchronization operations) to obtain a *full* share, this is a guarantee that no other thread can hold a nonempty partial share at that location. Thus, no other thread can be reading the location right now, and (with a *full* permission) it is safe to do a write.

In this model, the domain of a heap is not just a set of addresses, but a mapping from locations to shares, and the join operator $\oplus$ no longer means *disjoint* but *share-compatible*.

We may have a variety of join relations, but we do not wish to rederive separation logic many times. So we factor the model of separation logic into two layers: First, we define a *join relation* $\oplus$ satisfying certain laws (for example, commutativity); this is a *separation algebra*. Then, we define separation logic whose $*$ operator is defined in terms of the separation algebra's $\oplus$. We prove inference rules for $*$ derived from the laws of separation algebras (independently of any particular join relation).

What are the laws of separation algebra that $\oplus$ must satisfy? Calcagno *et al.* [32] propose one set of axioms; Dockins *et al.* [40] propose an inequivalent set; Pottier [78] proposes a different one; Jensen and Birkedal [58] propose yet another.

A FRAMEWORK FOR SEPARATION ALGEBRAS. We can fit all these variants into a unifying framework that starts with the essential properties, then adds laws as needed for specific applications (see the file msl/sepalg.v).[1]

A *join relation* $\oplus$ is a three-place relation over a type A.

$$\text{join} : A \to A \to A \to \text{Prop}$$

Informally we write $x \oplus y = z$ to mean join $x\,y\,z$, but do not be misled by the notation: $x \oplus y$ might not exist! This is really a three-place relation, not a two-place function.

We can define a join_sub relation as,

$$x \prec z \;:=\; \exists y.\, x \oplus y = z$$

A join relation over A forms a *permission algebra* (Perm_alg) when it is an associative commutative partial function with the property of *positivity*:

join_eq :	$x \oplus y = z \;\to\; x \oplus y = z' \;\to\; z = z'$
join_assoc[2] :	$a \oplus b = d \to d \oplus c = e \to \Sigma f.\, b \oplus c = f \wedge a \oplus f = e$
join_comm :	$a \oplus b = c \;\to\; b \oplus a = c$
join_positivity :	$a \prec b \;\to\; b \prec a \;\to\; a = b$

The join_assoc axiom expresses associativity of a relation. If d and e exist, then so must f in this diagram:

Positivity ensures that there are no "negative" elements. It would be a very bad thing in separation logic if an empty resource could be split into a positive resource and a (negative) anti-resource. For if that were possible, then a thread with no access at all to a location l could split its empty permission into a positive permission and a negative permission; then it

---

[1] I thank Jonas Jensen for an illuminating e-mail discussion and Robert Dockins for an acoustic discussion that helped derive this framework.

[2] $\Sigma f.\, b \oplus c = f \wedge a \oplus f = e$ is a *dependent sum*, a constructive version of the existential $\exists f.\, b \oplus c = f \wedge a \oplus f = e$. When representing the axioms of separation algebras in a constructive logic, it is often helpful for join_assoc to be constructive. In a classical logic with the axiom of choice, the ordinary existential will suffice.

could use the frame rule to hide the negative permission, and access the resource!

Demonstration that positivity prevents negative elements. Suppose we have three elements suggestively named $a, -a, 0$. Suppose indeed a joins with $-a$ to make 0, and 0 is a unit for a:

$$a \oplus -a = 0 \qquad 0 \oplus a = a$$

So $a \prec 0$ and $0 \prec a$; thus by positivity $a = 0$.

UNITS AND IDENTITIES. We say that an element e is a *unit for a* if $e \oplus a = a$, and i is an *identity* if it is a unit for anything that it happens to join with:

$$\text{unit\_for}\, e\, a \;:=\; e \oplus a = a$$
$$\text{identity}\, e \;:=\; \forall a, b.\ e \oplus a = b \;\rightarrow\; a = b$$

A *separation algebra* (Sep_alg)[3] is a permission algebra augmented with a function[4] core $: A \to A$, written as $\hat{x}$, with these properties:

$$\text{core\_unit} : \quad \text{unit\_for}\, \hat{x}\, x$$
$$\text{join\_core} : \quad a \oplus b = c \;\rightarrow\; \hat{a} = \hat{c}$$

Thus, every element of a separation algebra has at least one unit. But units can contain nontrivial information. An element of a separation algebra may contain "separable" information (such as the contents of heap cells) and "pure" information (such as facts about local variables). The core of an element contains all the pure information, with an empty separable part. Cores obey the following lemmas (proofs are all supplied in the Coq development):

$$\text{core\_duplicable} \frac{}{\hat{a} \oplus \hat{a} = \hat{a}} \qquad\qquad \text{core\_self\_join} \frac{a = \hat{a}}{a \oplus a = a}$$

$$\text{core\_idem} \frac{}{\hat{\hat{a}} = \hat{a}} \qquad \text{core\_hom} \frac{a \oplus b = c}{\hat{a} \oplus \hat{b} = \hat{c}} \qquad \text{split\_core} \frac{a \oplus b = \hat{c}}{\text{unit\_for}\, a\, a}$$

---

[3]We will often write *SA* for *separation algebra*.
[4]The notion of *core* is from Pottier [78].

THE CONCEPT OF SEPARATION has many applications. In some models, $\_ \oplus b = c$ has at most one way of filling in the blank, in others more than one way. In some models, $a \oplus a = b$ forces $a = b$; in others not. In some models $\hat{a} = \hat{b}$ necessarily; in others not. Our general theory of separation algebras permits all of these models. To specialize for specific applications with extra axioms, we use type-classes such as Canc_alg, Disj_alg, Sing_alg, and so on, as we now describe.

CANCELLATION. A join relation is *cancellative* (Canc_alg) if,

$$\text{join\_canc} : a_1 \oplus b = c \;\rightarrow\; a_2 \oplus b = c \;\rightarrow\; a_1 = a_2.$$

Both Calcagno *et al.* [32] and Dockins *et al.* [40] assume that separation algebras must be cancellative, while Jensen *et al.* [58] and Pottier [78] do not assume cancellation.

The following lemmas hold in cancellative separation algebras:

$$\text{unit\_identity} \frac{\text{unit\_for } e\, b}{\text{identity } e} \qquad\qquad \text{core\_identity} \frac{}{\text{identity } \hat{a}}$$

$$\text{unit\_core} \frac{\text{unit\_for } a\, a}{a = \hat{a}} \qquad \text{same\_unit} \frac{\text{unit\_for } e_1\, a \qquad \text{unit\_for } e_2\, a}{e_1 = e_2}$$

$$\text{split\_identity} \frac{a \oplus b = c \qquad \text{identity } c}{\text{identity } a}$$

CLASSICAL VS. INTUITIONISTIC SEPARATION LOGIC. For reasoning about languages with explicit deallocation, one wants rules such as $\{p \mapsto x\}\text{free}(p)\{\text{emp}\}$, and one often thinks of an assertion Q as holding on a heaplet with a precise domain; this is called *classical separation logic*. For reasoning about languages with automatic garbage collection, there is no rule for free, and one often thinks of Q as holding on any heaplet with *at least* a certain domain; this is called *intuitionistic separation logic*. In the intuitionistic style, one has $Q * \text{true} = Q$, which is not true in classical style; and emp is not a useful concept in the intuitionistic style (because it is equivalent to true).

If a join relation is cancellative, then it naturally leads to a classical separation logic. That is, in Chapter 8 we will define the operators emp and $*$ based on the notions of identity and join (respectively), and with a cancellative (Canc_alg) separation algebra we can prove the characteristic axiom of classical separation logic, $P * \mathsf{emp} \leftrightarrow P$.

DISJOINTNESS. A join relation has the *disjointness* (Disj_alg) property if no nonempty element can join with itself:

$$\mathsf{join\_self} : a \oplus b = b \;\rightarrow\; a = b$$

Dockins *et al.* [40] require disjointness of their separation algebras (see Chapter 11); other authors do not.

If a separation logic over program heaps lacks disjointness then unusual things can happen when defining predicates about inductive data in a program heap. For example, without disjointness, the "obvious" definition of a formula to describe binary trees fails: it occasionally permits shared subtrees [27].

Disjointness solves another problem that had been identified by Bornat *et al.* [27] It appeared that no one share model was expressive enough to model two useful patterns of exclusive-write-concurrent-read (the *fork-join* and the *token factory*). Chapter 11 of this book explains that the problem was that Boyland's fractional shares [28] lack disjointness, and Dockins's *tree shares* solve the problem.

SINGLE-UNIT. In a *single-unit* (Sing_alg) separation algebra, every element has the same core:

$$\mathsf{the\_unit\_core} : \forall a.\; \hat{a} = \mathsf{the\_unit}$$

Calcagno *et al.* [32] assume single-unit separation algebras. But many useful SAs do not have a single unit. The disjoint-product SA has two sets of elements, each with its own (different) unit (see Chapter 7). Step-indexed SAs (in indirection theory) have a different unit for each index class. [5] An extreme case is the *discrete separation algebra* on a base type A, in which each element is its own unit, and each element joins only with

---

[5] Indirection theory: Chapter 35; combined with separation: Chapter 38

itself. In all these cases, elements divide into equivalence classes, each represented by its own unit.

The monotonic counter of Jensen and Birkedal [58] is a quite different multi-unit SA. Here, the elements are natural numbers, and $a \oplus b = c$ when $c = \max(a, b)$. An element e is a unit for a whenever $e \leq a$. Thus, there are six different units for 5, and 0 is a unit for everything.

CROSS-SPLIT. Some join relations have the *cross-split* (Cross_alg) property:

$$\text{cross\_split}: \quad a \oplus b = z \ \rightarrow \ c \oplus d = z \ \rightarrow$$
$$\Sigma ac, ad, bc, bd.\ ac \oplus ad = a \wedge bc \oplus bd = b \wedge ac \oplus bc = c \wedge ad \oplus bd = d$$

That is, suppose a single resource can be split in two different ways; then one should be able to divide the original resource into *four* pieces that respect the original splittings. This can be expressed graphically as,

$$\forall \ \left(\boxed{a \mid b} \right) \ \left(\frac{c}{d} \right) \ \exists \ \left(\frac{ac \mid bc}{ad \mid bd} \right)$$

This property does not follow from the other axioms. It is required to reason about natural definitions of data structures with intrinsic sharing, such as graphs [53].

HERE IS A SUMMARY of some of the separation algebras mentioned above. The properties are **Sing**le-unit, **Canc**ellative, **Dis**joint, **Cross**-split.

	Type	$a \oplus b = c$ when,	properties
Heaplets	$\mathbb{N} \rightharpoonup \mathbb{N}$	see page 36	Sing,Canc,Disj,Cross
Booleans	bool	$(c = a \vee b) \wedge \neg(a \wedge b)$	Sing,Canc,Disj,Cross
Counter	$\mathbb{N}$	$c = \max(a, b)$	Sing
Discrete	any	$a = b = c$	Canc,Disj,Cross
Rational shares	$\mathbb{Q}$	$a + b = c$	Sing,Canc,Cross
Parkinson shares	$\mathscr{P}(\mathbb{N})$	$c = a \cup b \ \wedge \ a \cap b = \emptyset$	Sing,Canc,Disj,Cross
Tree shares	⬣	see Chapter 11	Sing,Canc,Disj,Cross

The (rational, Parkinson, tree) share models are described in Chapter 11.

POSITIVE PERMISSION ALGEBRAS. Sometimes we want to say that an execution thread owns a *nonempty* share of some resource. To reason about join relations of nonempty resources, we take a separation algebra and remove all the units. More straightforwardly, a *positive permission algebra* (Class Pos_alg) is a permission algebra with the additional axiom that there are no units:

$$\text{no\_units} : \quad \forall e, a. \; \neg \text{unit\_for} \, e \, a$$

Positive permission algebras may be cancellative or disjoint, depending on the underlying join relation.

Type classes for separation algebras

We summarize all layers (permission algebras, separation algebras, etc.) and their axioms as a set of type classes in Coq, as shown in Figure 6.1.

Class Join (t: Type) : Type := join: t $\to$ t $\to$ t $\to$ Prop.

Class Perm_alg (t: Type) {J: Join t} : Type := mkPerm {
  join_eq: $\forall$ {x y z z'}, join x y z $\to$ join x y z' $\to$ z = z';
  join_assoc: $\forall$ {a b c d e}, join a b d $\to$ join d c e $\to$
                            {f : t & join b c f $\wedge$ join a f e};
  join_comm: $\forall$ {a b c}, join a b c $\to$ join b a c;
  join_positivity: $\forall$ {a a' b b'}, join a a' b $\to$ join b b' a $\to$ a=b
  }.

Definition unit_for {t}{J: Join t} (e a: t) := join e a a.
Definition identity {t}{J: Join t} (e: t) := $\forall$ a b, join e a b $\to$ a=b.

Class Sep_alg A {J: Join A} : Type := mkSep {
  core: A $\to$ A;
  core_unit: $\forall$ t, unit_for (core t) t;
  join_core: $\forall$ {a b c}, join a b c $\to$ core a = core c
  }.
Class Sing_alg A {J: Join A}{SA: Sep_alg A} := mkSing {
  the_unit: A;
  the_unit_core: $\forall$ a, core a = the_unit
  }.
Class Canc_alg (t: Type) {J: Join t} :=
  join_canc: $\forall$ {a1 a2 b c}, join a1 b c $\to$ join a2 b c $\to$ a1 = a2.

Class Disj_alg (t: Type) {J: Join t} :=
  join_self: $\forall$ {a b}, join a a b $\to$ a = b.

Class Pos_alg {A} {J: Join A} := no_units: $\forall$ e a, $\sim$unit_for e a.

Figure 6.1: Type classes for permission algebras and separation algebras, found in the file msl/sepalg.v.

Chapter 7

Operators on separation algebras

A new separation algebra can be built by applying operators to other SAs. Recall that $x \oplus y = z$ is our shorthand for $\oplus(x, y, z)$, and a *permission algebra* (PA) $\langle A, \oplus \rangle$ comprises an element type A and a join relation $\oplus$ of type $A \to A \to A \to$ Prop that satisfies the properties join_eq, join_assoc, join_comm, and join_positivity.

A separation algebra (SA) has, in addition, a core operator satisfying core_unit and join_core. But if a core operator exists, then it is unique. To state this lemma formally it is best to use Coq notation that makes explicit all the parameters that the mathematical notation $\hat{\cdot}$ leaves implicit:

Lemma \idef{core_uniq} {A} {J: Join A}:
 ∀ (SA1 SA2: @Sep_alg A J), ∀x, @core A J SA1 x = @core A J SA2 x.
Proof. *(* see msl/sepalg.v *)* **Qed**.

The uniqueness of cores justifies (informally) writing $\langle A, J \rangle$ for a separation algebra with element type A and join operator J, without needing to explicitly mention the core operator.

SA PRODUCT OPERATOR. Let $\langle A, J_A \rangle$ and $\langle B, J_B \rangle$ be SAs. Then the product SA is $\langle A \times B, J \rangle$, where J is defined componentwise:

$$J((x_a, x_b), (y_a, y_b), (z_a, z_b)) := J_A(x_a, y_a, z_a) \wedge J_B(x_b, y_b, z_b) \qquad (7.1)$$

If J_A and J_B are permission algebras, then J is a permission algebra; if J_A and J_B are separation algebras, then J is a separation algebra; if J_A and J_B are cancellative then J is cancellative; if J_A and J_B satisfy disjointness, then so does J. These statements are expressed as typeclass-instances in Coq (in msl/sepalg_generators.v):

Instance Join_prod : Join (A∗B) :=
    fun(x y z:A∗B)⇒ join(fst x)(fst y)(fst z) ∧ join(snd x)(snd y)(snd z).
Instance Perm_prod : Perm_alg (A∗B).
Instance Sep_prod (SAa: Sep_alg A)(SAb: Sep_alg B) : Sep_alg (A∗B).
Instance Canc_prod{CAa:Canc_alg A}{CAb:Canc_alg B}: Canc_alg (A∗B).
Instance Disj_prod{DAa: Disj_alg A}{DAb: Disj_alg B}: Disj_alg (A∗B).

A similar litany will apply to all the operators in this section; we will not repeat it each time. Of course, each of these **Instance** declarations must be followed by a **Proof** (omitted here) that Join_prod really has the specified properties.

SA function operator. Let A be a set and let $\langle B, J_B \rangle$ be a SA. Then the *function SA* is $\langle A \to B, J \rangle$, where J is defined pointwise:

$$J(f, g, h) := \forall a \in A.\ J_B(f(a), g(a), h(a)) \tag{7.2}$$

(Instances Join_fun, Perm_fun, Sep_fun, etc.)

Lovers of dependent types will enjoy the observation that the SA product and the SA function operators are isomorphic to special cases of the general indexed product (*i.e.*, dependent function space) operator:

SA indexed product operator. Let I be a set, called the index set, and let P be a mapping from I to separation algebras. Then the indexed product SA is $\langle \Pi x : I.\ P(x), J \rangle$ where J is defined pointwise:

$$J(f, g, h) := \forall i \in I.\ J_{P(i)}(f(i), g(i), h(i)) \tag{7.3}$$

(Instances Join_pi, Perm_pi, Sep_pi, etc.)

The disjoint union operator illustrates the need for multi-unit separation algebras; it cannot be constructed in Sing_alg. For suppose we have two single-unit SAs $\langle A, J_A \rangle$, $\langle B, J_B \rangle$. We would like to define $\langle A + B, J \rangle$ such that J is the smallest relation satisfying:

$$J_A(x, y, z) \rightarrow J(\text{inl } x, \text{inl } y, \text{inl } z) \qquad \text{for all } x, y, z \in A \qquad (7.4)$$
$$J_B(x, y, z) \rightarrow J(\text{inr } x, \text{inr } y, \text{inr } z) \qquad \text{for all } x, y, z \in B \qquad (7.5)$$

Here $A + B$ is the disjoint union of A and B with inl and inr as the left and right injections. This structure cannot be a single-unit separation algebra, for if u_A and u_B are the units of A and B, then core(inl u_A) and core(inr u_B) must be equal, by the_unit_core. However, this is a contradiction as the injection functions for disjoint union always produce unequal elements. (Instances Join_sum, Perm_sum, Sep_sum, etc.)

INDEXED SUM OPERATOR. Disjoint union is is a special case of indexed (dependent) sums. Let I be a set, called the index set. Let S be a mapping from I to separation algebras. Then the indexed sum SA is $\langle \Sigma i : I. S(i), J \rangle$ such that J is the least relation satisfying:

$$J_{S(i)}(x, y, z) \rightarrow J(\text{inj}_i(x), \text{inj}_i(y), \text{inj}_i(z)) \qquad \forall i \in I; x, y, z \in S(i) \quad (7.6)$$

Here inj_i is the injection function associated with i. If $|I| = 2$, the indexed sum is isomorphic to the disjoint union operator. (Instances Join_sigma, Perm_sigma, Sep_sigma, etc.)

DISCRETE SA. Let A be a set. Then the discrete SA is $\langle A, J \rangle$ where J is defined as the smallest relation satisfying:

$$J(x, x, x) \qquad \text{for all } x \in A \qquad (7.7)$$

(Instances Join_equiv, Perm_equiv, Sep_equiv, etc.)

The discrete SA has a join relation that holds only when all three arguments are equal: *every* element of the discrete SA is a unit. The discrete SA is useful for constructing SAs over tuples where only some of the components have interesting joins; the other components can be turned into discrete SAs. Note the *compositionality* of this construction using the discrete and product operators together.

The discrete-SA construction is incompatible with the Sing_alg axiom (single-unit SAs). With single-unit SAs, one would instead have to "manually" construct an appropriate tupling operator. This is an important reason not to assume the single-unit axiom for all separation algebras.

IN SOME APPLICATIONS we need to relate positive permission algebras (PAs with no units) to separation algebras (PAs with units) that have the same elements (aside from the unit) [50]. We define the *lifting* operator that removes all the units from a SA, leaving a positive PA; and we define the *lowering* operator that and adds a unit to a positive PA, yielding a (single-unit) SA. (Instances Join_lift, Perm_lift, Sep_lift, etc.)

As an example of their use, consider heaplets in which each address contains either DATA with a permission share π and integer i, or NONE with no value at all. Permission shares will be described in Chapter 11, but for now it suffices to know that they form a separation algebra with a full share •, an empty share ∘, and various partial shares in between.

The values DATA • 3 and DATA • 4 are clearly unequal: one is "a full share of 3" and the other is "a full share of 4". But an empty share of a data value is really the same as NONE; that is, DATA ∘ 3 = DATA ∘ 4 = NONE. If we want to enforce the rules that

$$i \neq j \;\rightarrow\; \text{DATA}\,\pi_1\, i \;\neq\; \text{DATA}\,\pi_2\, j \qquad\qquad \text{DATA}\,\pi_1\, i \;\neq\; \text{NONE},$$

one way is to prohibit the use of empty shares in DATA constructors. We can do this by apply Join_lift to the share SA.

To complete this example in full, we apply Join_equiv to the type $\mathbb{Z}$ of integers, yielding the *discrete* separation algebra in which 3 does not join with 4 (and every integer is its own core). Then we apply the product operator Join_prod to these two constructed permission algebras, to make the cartesian product algebra over (nonempty) shares and integers. Finally, to accomplish the disjoint union of DATA $\pi\, i$ and NONE, we simply apply the lowering operator, Join_lower.

Parameter Join_sh: Join share.
Definition pshare := lifted Join_sh. (∗ *positive shares* ∗)
Definition Join_pshare : Join pshare := @Join_lift _ Join_sh.

Definition heaplet := address → option (pshare * Z).
Definition Join_heaplet: Join heaplet :=
   Join_fun address (option (pshare * Z))
      (Join_lower (Join_prod pshare Join_pshare Z (Join_equiv Z))).

THE OPERATORS OF THIS CHAPTER can construct many kinds of separation algebras. The associated Coq development includes a number of additional operators (*e.g.*, lists, subsets, bijections, etc.) that we have also found useful.

Chapter 8

First-order separation logic

A separation algebra (SA) is a set of elements $x, y, \ldots$ on which there is a *join* relation $x \oplus y = z$. A separation logic is a system of assertions P, Q with a *separating conjunction* operator such that $z \models P * Q$ just when there exist x, y such that $x \models P$, $y \models Q$, and $x \oplus y = z$.

The axioms and inference rules of separation logics are sufficiently generic that we can induce most of them just from the definition of the join relation and the axioms of separation algebras. To these we add application-specific axioms, depending on the element type.

IN THIS CHAPTER WE WILL FOCUS PARTICULARLY on the representation of generic separation logics *in Coq*. We use the convenient parametrizability of typeclasses. That is, we want to write $P * Q$, so we define Notation:

Notation "P '*' Q" := (sepcon P Q) : pred.

This means that $*$ stands for the sepcon operator. But what is sepcon, and to what separation algebra does it belong?

The answer depends on whether we are constructing *first-order* separation logics (the "traditional" kind); or *higher-order* separation logics, in which assertions can predicate over assertions. Higher-order separation logics permit smoother reasoning about higher-order functions, or about the resource invariants of first-class locks and threads. To achieve such predication, we must use some form of step-indexing, indirection theory, ultrametric spaces, or domain theory (all of which are related techniques). In our Verified Software Toolchain we use higher-order separation algebras, whose construction will be described in later chapters.

For many applications, ordinary first-order SAs will suffice. In this chapter[1] we present the construction of generic first-order separation logics from separation algebras. These "first-order" SAs do permit *quantification* over predicates (a higher-order concept), but they do not support fully higher-order features such as contravariant recursive predicates or impredicative predication over predicates.

Definition pred (A:Type) := A → Prop.

Delimit **Scope** pred **with** pred.
Bind **Scope** pred **with** pred.

The **Scope**-related commands specify that (1) the mark (...)%pred henceforth indicates that text between the parentheses should be parsed using the **Notation** operators we are about to introduce, and (2) expressions of type pred should also be parsed that way.

We can begin a logic of predicates with the entailment operator ⊢, pronounced derives:

Definition derives (A:Type) (P Q:pred A) := ∀ a:A, P a → Q a.

Notation "P '|--' Q" := (derives P Q) (at level 80, no associativity).

Here are some very generic lemmas that follow from the definition of derives:[2]

$$\text{equiv\_eq} \frac{P \vdash Q \qquad Q \vdash P}{P = Q} \qquad \text{derives\_trans} \frac{P \vdash Q \qquad Q \vdash R}{P \vdash R}$$

[1]The Coq definitions in this chapter are in the file msl/predicates_sa.v.
Warning! If you will be needing the step-indexed predicates of a higher-order separation logic, the definition pred(A) := A→Prop will not suffice. In that case, we use a different definition of pred(A) introduced in Chapter 38. However, most of the ideas and concepts of this chapter still apply to higher-order separation logics.
[2]We can write $P = Q$ for the equivalence of assertions because we use the axioms of functional extensionality and proof irrelevance.

Even before we populate the logic with "interesting" operators, we can write down the basic connectives such as true, false, and, or, implication.

Definition TT {A}: pred A := prop True.   *(* see page 52 *)*
Definition FF {A}: pred A := prop False.

Definition imp {A} (P Q:pred A) := fun a:A $\Rightarrow$ P a $\rightarrow$ Q a.
Definition orp {A} (P Q:pred A) := fun a:A $\Rightarrow$ P a $\vee$ Q a.
Definition andp{A} (P Q:pred A) := fun a:A $\Rightarrow$ P a $\wedge$ Q a.

Now we add notation for these operators:[3]

Infix "||" := orp (at level 50, left associativity) : pred.
Infix "&&" := andp (at level 40, left associativity) : pred.
Notation "P '-->' Q" := (imp P Q) (at level 55, right associativity) : pred.
Notation "P '<-->' Q" := (andp (imp P Q) (imp Q P))
                            (at level 57, no associativity) : pred.

One can prove the usual inference lemmas on the propositional connectives; there is no need to show more than a couple of examples here:

$$\text{modus\_ponens}\frac{}{P \mathbin{\&\&} (P \rightarrow Q) \vdash Q} \qquad \text{andp\_right}\frac{X \vdash P \qquad X \vdash Q}{X \vdash P \mathbin{\&\&} Q}$$

Our logic has existential and universal quantifiers. Since the assertion language is embedded in a logical framework (the Calculus of Inductive Constructions) with quantifiers and variables of its own, we can we avoid constructing an entire theory of variable binding and substitution by the usual trick of "higher-order abstract syntax." That is, we use the variable-binding machinery of the enclosing logical framework to implement binding in our embedded logic.

Definition allp{A B: Type} (f: B $\rightarrow$ pred A): pred A := fun a $\Rightarrow$ $\forall$b, f b a.
Definition exp{A B: Type} (f: B $\rightarrow$ pred A): pred A := fun a $\Rightarrow$ $\exists$b, f b a.

---

[3]We use the horrible || and && instead of \/ and /\ because we will want "and" and "or" at a similar precedence level to "separating conjunction" ∗, but Coq's predeclared precedence for these operators is quite different. Here, level 40 precedence binds tighter than level 50.

Notation " 'ALL' x ':' T ',' P " := (allp (fun x:T ⇒ P%pred))
                            (at level 65, x at level 99) : pred.
Notation " 'EX' x ':' T ',' P " := (exp (fun x:T ⇒ P%pred))
                            (at level 65, x at level 99) : pred.

Now we can write such formulas as (ALL x:nat, P x && Q x) where P is a function from nat → pred A. We can even write (ALL x: pred A, P || x), that is, nothing stops us from instantiating the type T with the very pred type itself. Another way of saying this is that our logic is *impredicative*.

We define a prop operator for embedding Coq propositions into our assertion language:

Definition prop {A: Type} (P: Prop) : pred A := (fun _ ⇒ P).
Notation "'!!' e" := (prop e) (at level 25) : pred.

The utility of prop is in how it combines with the quantifiers. For example, in our assertion language we may have an operator eval e i saying that (in the current program state) a program expression e evaluates into an integer i. We might write,

Parameter eval : expression → Z → pred state.

Definition eval_gt_zero (e: expression) : pred state :=
                    EX i:Z, eval e i && !!(i>0).

Notice how the embedded Coq proposition i>0 has a free variable i that is bound by the existential quantifier.

WE ADD THE OPERATORS OF SEPARATION LOGIC (such as *) to our Hoare logic. When we write the notation $P \land Q$ we mean that P and Q are predicates over an element type A. For separation $P * Q$ there must also be a join relation {JA: Join A}; the Coq typeclass system will automagically search for a JA of the right type.

Definition sepcon {A} {JA: Join A} (p q:pred A) := fun z:A ⇒
  ∃x:A, ∃y:A, join x y z ∧ p x ∧ q y.

Notation "P '*' Q" := (sepcon P Q) : pred.

Lemmas about the operators of separation logic will need the typeclass-instance parameters JA to access the join relation, will need PA to access the axioms of permission algebras, and sometimes SA for separation algebras. For example, the associativity of $*$ relies on the associativity of join, which is found in Perm_alg:

Lemma sepcon_assoc {A} {JA: Join A}{PA: Perm_alg A}:
 $\forall$ p q r, $(((p * q) * r) = (p * (q * r)))$.
Proof. ... **Qed**.

Although in this text we will present many of these lemmas in a more "mathematical" style,

$$\text{sepcon\_assoc} \frac{}{(P * Q) * R = P * (Q * R)} \qquad \text{sepcon\_comm} \frac{}{P * Q = Q * P}$$

one must remember that they are typeclass-parametrized, which will cause Coq proof-scripts to fail if the required typeclass instances do not exist.

The unit for separating conjunction is emp:

Notation "'emp'" := identity.

Here we define $x \models$ emp whenever x is an *identity*, that is, whenever $\forall y, x \oplus y = z \rightarrow y = z$. Identities are not exactly the same as units, i.e. something can be an identity without being a unit for anything (vacuously, if it fails to join with anything), and a unit might not be an identity. We do not directly define "unit for separating conjunction" in terms of "unit in the underlying separation algebra" because (in our possibly multi-unit separation algebras) we can't simply say *unit*, we have to say what elements it is a unit *for*.

But in a *cancellative* separation algebra, every identity is a unit (for at least itself), and every unit is an identity. The separation-logic emp really is only useful in cancellative systems, and most of the lemmas about emp require cancellation. For example,

Lemma emp_sepcon {A}{JA: Join A}{PA: Perm_alg A}{SA: Sep_alg A}{CA: Canc_alg A}:
 $\forall$ P, (emp$*$P) = P.

Provided that the reader remembers that Canc_alg is implicit whenever emp appears, we can write,

$$\text{emp\_sepcon} \frac{}{\text{emp} * P = P} \qquad \text{sepcon\_emp} \frac{}{P * \text{emp} = P}.$$

We have both universal and existential magic wands. The (universal) magic wand $P \twoheadrightarrow Q$ is a kind of "separating implication;" if you add P to it, you get Q. The existential wand $P \multimap Q$, also called *septraction*, says that you *can* add P and get Q.

Definition wand $\{A\}$ $\{JA:$ Join $A\}$ (p q:pred A) := fun y $\Rightarrow$
$\forall x\, z,$ join x y z $\rightarrow$ p x $\rightarrow$ q z.

Definition ewand $\{A\}$ $\{JA:$ Join $A\}$ (P Q: pred A) : pred A :=
fun w $\Rightarrow$ $\exists$ w1, $\exists$ w2, join w1 w w2 $\wedge$ P w1 $\wedge$ Q w2.

They satisfy many of the expected axioms, needing only Perm_alg (permission algebras)—they do not require Sep_alg (existence of units) or cancellation.

$$\text{wand\_sepcon\_adjoint} \frac{}{(P * Q \vdash R) = (P \vdash Q \twoheadrightarrow R)}$$

$$\text{modus\_wand} \frac{P * (P \twoheadrightarrow Q)}{Q} \qquad \text{sepcon\_cut} \frac{P \vdash Q \twoheadrightarrow R \qquad S \vdash Q}{P * S \vdash R}$$

$$\text{ewand\_sepcon} \frac{}{(P * Q) \multimap R = P \multimap (Q \multimap R)}$$

Intuitionistic predicates. In an intuitionistic separation logic, whenever P holds on x, then it must also hold on $x \oplus y$. But even in a classical separation logic where this is not true in general, sometimes we find it useful to say a predicate holds in every extension of the current state. This is written %P, and we have $x \models \%P$ whenever $\forall y, z, x \oplus y = z \rightarrow (x \models P)$. The % sign is notation for the modal operator box extendM, just as $\triangleright$ is notation for the modal operator box laterM.

Chapter 9

A little case study

To demonstrate the use of separation algebras and separation logic, consider this tiny little programming language (see examples/sep/language.v).

Variables	$x, y, z, \ldots$		**Definition** var := nat.
Commands	c	::= skip	**Inductive** command :=
		| $x := y$	| Skip: command
		| $x := [y]$	| Assign: var $\to$ var $\to$ command
		| $[x] := y$	| Load : var $\to$ var $\to$ command
		| $c_1; c_2$	| Store: var $\to$ var $\to$ command
			| Seq: command$\to$command$\to$command.

Each state of the operational semantics comprises a stack (partial function from variable name to pointer) and a heap (partial function from pointer to pointer). We use natural numbers for variables and for pointers, and we represent stacks and heaps as table, a list of ordered pairs with duplicates. Here we define get and set operators on tables:

Definition table (A B : Type) := list (A$*$B).

Fixpoint table_get {A B}{H: dec_eq A} (rho: table A B) (x: A) : option B :=
  match rho **with**
  \| (y,v)::ys $\Rightarrow$ **if** eq_dec x y **then** Some v **else** table_get ys x
  \| nil $\Rightarrow$ None
  end.

Definition table_set {A B}{H: dec_eq A}
                        (x: A) (v: B) (rho: table A B) : table A B
    := (x,v)::rho.

Lemma table_gss {A B}{H: dec_eq A}:
    ∀ rho x (v: B), table_get (table_set x v rho) x = Some v.

Lemma table_gso {A B}{H: dec_eq A}:
    ∀ rho x y (v:B), x≠y → table_get (table_set x v rho) y = table_get rho y.

The lemma table_gss stands for "get-set-same," and table_gso stands for "get-set-other." Now we define variables and addresses (both nat), and stacks and heaps (both represented as table):

Definition var := nat.
Definition adr := nat.
Definition stack := table var adr.
Definition heap := table adr adr.
Definition state := (stack * heap)%type.

WE PRESENT THE SEMANTICS of program execution as a small-step operational semantics. The rules for Assign, **Load**, and Store are straightforward. There are different ways to describing control sequencing. A direct method is this:

$$\text{Assign} \frac{\sigma(y) = v}{([\![x := y]\!], \sigma, h) \longmapsto ([\![\text{skip}]\!], \sigma[x := v], h)}$$

$$\text{Load} \frac{\sigma(y) = v \qquad h(v) = v'}{([\![x := [y]]\!], \sigma, h) \longmapsto ([\![\text{skip}]\!], \sigma[x := v'], h)}$$

$$\text{Store} \frac{\sigma(y) = v \qquad \sigma(x) = p}{([\![[x] := y]\!], \sigma, h) \longmapsto ([\![\text{skip}]\!], \sigma, h[p := v])}$$

$$\text{Seq0} \frac{}{([\![\text{skip}; c]\!], \sigma, h) \longmapsto ([\![c]\!], \sigma, h)} \qquad \text{Seq1} \frac{([\![c_1]\!], \sigma, h) \longmapsto ([\![c_1']\!], \sigma', h')}{([\![c_1; c_2]\!], \sigma, h) \longmapsto ([\![c_1'; c_2]\!], \sigma', h')}$$

The inductive definition step (in examples/sep/language.v) encodes these rules.

We can abstract and combine the Seq0/Seq1 rules by describing syntactic *execution contexts* [47, §5.3], that is:

$$E ::= [\,] \mid E;c$$

where the context $[\,]$ means "right here" and $E;c$ means "within the left side of a Seq command, as specified by the subcontext E." Using execution contexts, we can express the Seq0 and Seq1 rules as a single rule:

$$\text{Seq} \frac{([\![c]\!], \sigma, h) \longmapsto ([\![c']\!], \sigma', h')}{([\![E[c]]\!], \sigma, h) \longmapsto ([\![E[c']]\!], \sigma', h')}$$

The natural inductive definition for E has two constructors—it is isomorphic to list(command), and we will represent it as such. If E is an execution context represented as a list, we can represent $E[c]$ by the list $c :: E$. In our operational semantics for C light (Chapter 34) we have a the *control stack* $c :: \kappa$, which amounts to the same thing; henceforth we will write κ instead of E.

If we reformulate all the rules to small-step in an execution context, we obtain this semantics—which is the inductive definition of the step' relation in examples/sep/language.v:

$$\text{Skip'} \frac{}{([\![\text{skip}]\!] :: \kappa, \sigma, h) \longmapsto (\kappa, \sigma, h)}$$

$$\text{Assign'} \frac{\sigma(y) = v}{([\![x := y]\!] :: \kappa, \sigma, h) \longmapsto (\kappa, \sigma[x := v], h)}$$

$$\text{Load'} \frac{\sigma(y) = v \qquad h(v) = v'}{([\![x := [y]]\!] :: \kappa, \sigma, h) \longmapsto (\kappa, \sigma[x := v'], h)}$$

$$\text{Store'} \frac{\sigma(y) = v \qquad \sigma(x) = p}{([\![[x] := y]\!] :: \kappa, \sigma, h) \longmapsto (\kappa, \sigma, h[p := v])}$$

$$\text{Seq'} \frac{(c_1 :: c_2 :: \kappa, \sigma, h) \longmapsto (\kappa', \sigma', h')}{([\![c_1; c_2]\!] :: \kappa, \sigma, h) \longmapsto (\kappa', \sigma', h')}$$

We want to define an axiomatic semantics and prove it sound with respect to the operational semantics. *Sound* means, if a program satisfies an appropriate Hoare triple, then it is *safe* in the operational semantics—the $\longmapsto^*$ relation will not get stuck. But which operational semantics, the direct small-step (with Seq0/Seq1) or the one with execution contexts κ? It's easier to build a soundness proof with the execution contexts (small-step relation step'). For readers who prefer the direct relation step, the theorem step'_equiv (in examples/sep/language.v) shows that execution in step' implies execution in step.

SINCE THIS IS A LANGUAGE OF POINTER-UPDATE, a separation logic seems called for. However, we cannot make a separation algebra (Perm_alg and Sep_alg) directly on states or tables, because tables do not have *unique representations*. The positivity rule (join_positivity) requires, among other things, that if two elements are equivalent, then they are equal. But the representation of tables as unsorted lists of pairs means that unequal elements can be equivalent. (a is equivalent to b if each is a join_sub of the other, that is, $a \oplus x = b$ and $b \oplus y = a$.)

One solution to this problem would have been to avoid equality and use equivalence relations (or *setoids*). We have chosen not to do that in our formulation of separation algebras, because we want the convenience and efficiency of Leibniz equality. Another solution would be to insist that the data structure for environments have unique representations, but this solution is not very general.

We solve the problem as follows. Instead of building a separation algebra directly on tables, we write a *denotation function* from tables to their denotations, and we build the separation algebra on denotations. The denotation of a table is a function nat $\rightarrow$ option nat, and any equivalent environments must have equal denotations.[1]

---

[1] To reason about equal functions, we will need the axiom of extensionality. The pure calculus of inductive constructions (CiC) does not have extensionality, but extensionality is consistent with CiC. Almost any application of our type-classes for separation algebras will need extensionality, so it is assumed right at the beginning of the MSL, in the file msl/Axioms.v.

We call the denotation of a state a *world*, and it is easy to write the denotation function:

Definition world := ((var → option adr)∗(adr → option adr))%type.
Definition den (s: state) : world := (table_get (fst s), table_get (snd s)).

TO BUILD A SEPARATION ALGEBRA OVER WORLDS,[2] we must specify a join relation. We want $P * Q$ to mean that predicates P and Q both see the same stack (they can both refer to the same local variables), but see disjoint subheaps (they cannot both refer to the same memory-cell contents). Thus we do,

Instance Join_world: Join world :=
    Join_prod
        (var → option adr) (Join_equiv (var → option adr))
        (adr → option adr) (Join_fun adr (option adr)
                            (Join_lower (Join_discrete adr))).

By using Join_equiv as the join relation for stacks, we say that any stack joins with itself, so that P and Q can see it simultaneously.

Now consider the join relation for heaps. A *heap* is a function from addresses to memory cells, and we may consider each cell separately. In a given heap, each cell is either present (Some v) or absent (None), and we want $\text{None} \oplus c = c$ for any c.

The relation Join_discrete adr is the empty relation: $J(a, b, c) = \bot$. Thus it has no units: it is a positive permission algebra (Pos_alg).

If J is a join relation on type τ, the relation Join_lower(J) is a join relation on option(τ), with None as the unit:

$$\text{None} \oplus \text{None} = \text{None} \qquad \text{None} \oplus \text{Some}\, a = \text{Some}\, a$$

$$\text{Some}\, a \oplus \text{None} = \text{Some}\, a \qquad \frac{a \oplus b = c}{\text{Some}\, a \oplus \text{Some}\, b = \text{Some}\, c}$$

---

[2]The separation logic is presented in two versions: examples/sep/fo_seplogic.v, using separation algebras *without* indirection theory, and examples/sep/seplogic.v, using the higher-order separation algebras with indirection theory. Because this simple example makes no essential use of indirection theory, the proofs are almost identical.

Considering a heap as a partial function from addresses to addresses, equivalently a total function from addresses to address-options, then the join relation we want for the *range* of that function is just Join_lower(Join_discrete adr). Two heap-cells join if at least one is empty, yielding the other one. That is what *disjointness* really means.

We lift this from option(adr) to adr→ option(adr) pointwise, by Join_fun. Two heaps join if each of their cells joins.

Hence the definition of Join_world, above. Then we prove that worlds form a permission algebra and a cancellative disjoint separation algebra:

Instance Perm_world : Perm_alg world := _.
Instance Sep_world : Sep_alg world := _.
Instance Canc_world : Canc_alg world := _.
Instance Disj_world : Disj_alg world := _.

These theorems are proved automagically by the type-class system,[3] using lemmas about the join operators from which we constructed Join_world.

Now that the separation algebra is constructed, we automatically have the basic operators (∗, emp) of separation logic just by **Import** msl.msl_direct.[4] But we also need application-specific operators,[5] such as *maps-to* ($x \mapsto y$), *subst* ($P[y/x]$), and *equal* ($x = y$) which tests whether the variables x and y have the same contents in this world.

Definition fun_set (f: nat → option nat) (x: nat) (y: option nat) :=
  fun i ⇒ **if** eq_dec i x **then** y **else** f i.

Definition subst (x y: var) (P: pred world) : pred world :=
  fun w ⇒ P (fun_set (fst w) x (fst w y), snd w).

Definition mapsto (x y: var) : pred world :=
  fun w ⇒ ∃ ax, fst w x = Some ax ∧ ∃ ay, fst w y = Some ay ∧
    ∀ a, **if** eq_dec a ax **then** snd w a = Some ay **else** snd w a = None.

---

[3] See the Instance lemmas in the msl/sepalg_generators library.

[4] For separation algebras with indirection theory, **Import** msl.msl_standard.

[5] Many applications will need *maps-to, equal*, and *subst*, but the details of each will depend on the underlying representations of heaps and local-variable environments ("stacks"), so we consider these operators application-specific.

Definition equal (x y: var) : pred world :=
         fun w ⇒ fst w x = fst w y.

We can define the Hoare triple $\{P\}c\{Q\}$, using the continuation-passing idea introduced in Chapter 4. But be careful:

Wrong Definition semax (P: pred world) (c: command) (Q: pred world) :=
   ∀ κ, guards Q κ → guards P (c::κ).

This Wrong model does not support the frame rule of separation logic. To accommodate the frame rule, we need a more intricate model. First, we give a syntactic characterization of "variables modified by the command c." Then we use a semantic characterization of "variables not free in (irrelevant to) a predicate P".

Inductive modvars : command → var → Prop :=
| mod_assign: ∀ x y, modvars (Assign x y) x
| mod_load: ∀ x y, modvars (Load x y) x
| mod_seq1: ∀ x c1 c2, modvars c1 x → modvars (Seq c1 c2) x
| mod_seq2: ∀ x c1 c2, modvars c2 x → modvars (Seq c1 c2) x.

Definition nonfreevars (P: pred world) (x: var) : Prop :=
         ∀ stk hp v, P (stk,hp) → P (fun_set stk x v, hp).

Definition subset (S1 S2: var → Prop) := ∀ x, S1 x → S2 x.

Using these definitions, it is straightforward to define the separation-logic Hoare triple, $\{P\}\, c\, \{Q\}$. It means: for any frame assertion F, as long as c does not modify any variables free in F, then $P * F$ is a precondition for the safe execution of c, and the after-state will satisfy $Q * F$.

Definition semax (P: pred world) (c: command) (Q: pred world) : Prop :=
   ∀ F s, subset (modvars c) (nonfreevars F) →
   ∀ κ, guards (Q * F) κ → guards (P * F) c::κ.

This is a *denotational* definition of the axiomatic semantics:[6] instead

---

[6]Hoare logics are often called *axiomatic semantics* because one reasons about the program using axioms, instead of interpreting it operationally or denotationally. semax stands for *axiomatic semantics*, or *sémantique axiomatique* en français.

of presenting an inductive set of axioms and justifying their soundness using proof theory, we just give the model. We can prove the "axioms" of the Hoare logic as derived lemmas, proved by unfolding the definition of semax. See examples/sep/seplogic.v for the actual proof scripts.

Lemma semax_assign: $\forall$ P x y,
      semax (defined y && subst x y P) (Assign x y) P.

Lemma semax_load: $\forall$ x y z, x $\neq$ y $\rightarrow$ x $\neq$ z $\rightarrow$
      semax (mapsto y z) (Load x y) (mapsto y z && equal x z).

Lemma semax_store: $\forall$ x y z,
      semax (defined y && mapsto x z) (Store x y) (mapsto x y).

Lemma semax_seq: $\forall$ P c1 Q c2 R,
      semax P c1 Q $\rightarrow$ semax Q c2 R $\rightarrow$ semax P (Seq c1 c2) R.

Lemma frame: $\forall$ F P c Q, subset (modvars c) (nonfreevars F) $\rightarrow$
      semax P c Q $\rightarrow$ semax (P $*$ F) c (Q $*$ F).

Lemma semax_pre_post: $\forall$ P P' c Q' Q,
      P $\vdash$ P' $\rightarrow$ Q' $\vdash$ Q $\rightarrow$ semax P' c Q' $\rightarrow$ semax P c Q.

One could make a more general Floyd-style **Load** rule that permits reasoning about the command **Load** x x, but here we just require that x and y are different variables.

THE FUNDAMENTAL PROJECT OF THE VERIFIED SOFTWARE TOOLCHAIN is to design a program logic, prove the program logic sound with respect to the operational semantics of the programming language, and apply the program logic to real programs. In this case study we have achieved the first two of these three steps, for a toy example.

Chapter 10

Covariant recursive predicates

Recursive data types are used in programs and programming languages, so recursive predicates occur naturally in program logics for reasoning about these programs. In almost any programming language one can make recursive pointer-and-structure declarations to describe lists and trees—with pointers and struct in C, with datatype in ML, or with classes in object-oriented languages.

In logic, we generally define each predicate in terms of previously defined predicates; a predicate that refers to itself is not necessarily meaningful. A sound way to make such self-referential definitions is to define some sort of fixed-point function μ such that given F of type $A \to A$, μF is a fixed point of F. That is, $F(\mu F) = \mu F$. Then, to get the effect of $P(x) = \ldots x \ldots P \ldots$ we define

$$F(p) = \lambda x.(\ldots x \ldots p \ldots) \qquad P = \mu F$$

Then indeed, $P(x) = (\mu F)(x) = F(\mu F)(x) = (\ldots x \ldots (\mu F) \ldots)$. But depending on what μ we are clever enough to construct, there may be restrictions on what kinds of F will satisfy $F(\mu F) = \mu F$. In particular, consider these two datatype declarations in the programming language ML:

datatype list = nil | cons of int * list
datatype funopt = none | some of funopt → int

We may write $F_{\mathsf{list}} = \lambda x.1 + (\mathsf{int} \times x)$, and list $= \mu F_{\mathsf{list}}$, provided that we can find μ that works. Similarly, $F_{\mathsf{funopt}} = \lambda x.1 + (x \to \mathsf{int})$. (The type 1, called "unit," contains just one value, that we could write as (). The type $\tau_1 + \tau_2$ contains the values of τ_1 and τ_2.)

But building a μ that can find fixed points of F_{list} is easier than for F_{funopt}, because F_{list} is *covariant*. A function is *covariant* when bigger arguments lead to bigger results; that is, forall x, y, if $x \subset y$ then $F(x) \subset F(y)$. In the world of types (or predicates), we can say that $x \subset y$ whenever every value belonging to the type x also belongs to y. (Considering types as just sets of values is a bit naive, but it will suffice for this discussion.)

To see that F_{list} is covariant, suppose we have two sets $x = \{()\}$ and $y = \{(), 4, 7\}$. Then $F_{\text{list}}(x) = \{(), \langle i, () \rangle \,|\, i \in \text{int}\}$ and $F_{\text{list}}(y) = \{(), \langle i, () \rangle, \langle i, 4 \rangle, \langle i, 7 \rangle \,|\, i \in \text{int}\}$ so indeed $F_{\text{list}}(x) \subset F_{\text{list}}(y)$.

On the other hand, F_{funopt} is *contravariant*, that is, bigger arguments lead to smaller results. Let us say that the type $x \to \text{int}$ is the set of all function values that, when given an argument of type x, will successfuly return an int without crashing. Now suppose $x \subset y$. We have $(y \to \text{int}) \subset (x \to \text{int})$, because every function of type $y \to \text{int}$ can successfully accept an argument of type x.

THEOREM. If $x \subset y$, then $y \to \text{int} \subset x \to \text{int}$.
Proof. Let f be a function of type $y \to \text{int}$, that is, on any argument of type y it successfully returns an integer. Then suppose we apply f to an argument a of type x. Since $x \subset y$, then $a : y$, and thus f succeeds on a.

But the converse does not necessarily hold. Let x be the type of positive integers, and y the type of all integers. The square-root function sqrt has type $x \to \text{int}$, but crashes on -1. Therefore $x \subset y$, and sqrt belongs to $x \to \text{int}$ but not to $y \to \text{int}$.

Finding fixed points of contravariant functors is a hard problem; the first real solution was Scott's domain theory [84]. The trick is to consider a data type as a sequence of approximations. Subsequent formulations of recursive types use metric spaces [65] or step indexing [10] or indirection theory [52], but the trick is still the same: a sequence of approximations.

LET US MOVE FROM *recursive types* to *recursive predicates in separation logic*. As an example, consider the separation-logic definition of a linked list of tail pointers (single-word cells): →□→□→◻0◻

$$L(x) = x = 0 \wedge \mathsf{emp} \ \vee \ x \neq 0 \wedge \exists y. \ x \mapsto y * L(y)$$

We write $L(x)$ to mean that x is a pointer to one of these lists; but this is a pseudodefinition, as it refers to itself. To make a real definition, we define the function F,

$$F(g)(x) = x = 0 \wedge \mathsf{emp} \ \vee \ x \neq 0 \wedge \exists y. \ x \mapsto y * g(y)$$

and then write μF to derive a fixed point of F.

The list predicate L is not simply a predicate on heaps; it relates a pointer value x to a heap. That is, L has type address → pred heap. Therefore in a generic separation logic, we will be looking for fixed points of functions F of the form,

$$F : (B \rightarrow \mathsf{pred}\,A) \rightarrow (B \rightarrow \mathsf{pred}\,A).$$

To make the example really concrete, we will choose a heap type of finite partial maps from nat to nat, with the usual kind of mapsto operator:

Definition heap : Type := fpm nat nat.
Instance Join_heap: Join heap := Join_fpm (@Join_discrete _).
Instance Perm_heap: Perm_alg heap := Perm_fpm _ (Perm_discrete nat).

Definition mapsto (x y: nat) : pred heap :=
fun h ⇒ ∀ z, if eq_dec z x **then** lookup_fpm h z = Some y
            else lookup_fpm h z = None.

For linked lists the function F can be written as,

Definition lisfun (Q: nat → pred heap) (p: nat) : pred heap:=
!!(p=0) && emp || !!(p<>0) && EX r:nat, mapsto p r * Q r.

Now, how can we demonstrate that the fixed point of lisfun is the lis type?

Many applications use only covariant recursion, and do not require contravariant recursive predicates. List and tree data structures are covariant; it is only when function parameters or predicate bindings are "in the loop" that contravariance occurs.

One can do covariant recursion directly in Coq using inductive predicates.[1] Our list example could be written,

Inductive lis : nat → pred heap :=
| lis_nil : ∀ p w, (!!(p=0) && emp)%pred w → lis p w
| lis_cons: ∀ p w, (!!(p<>0) && EX r:nat, mapsto p r * lis r)%pred w
$$→ lis p w.$$

For interactive program proofs, or for automatic proofs where the set of data types is fixed in advance, this works very well. But to synthesize or transmit new predicates about data structures, one often wants to express predicates as Coq expressions—combinations of existing operators—so one does not want to create new inductive definitions. In those cases, a recursion operator μ is needed. We use the Knaster-Tarski fixed-point theorem:

Definition covariant {B A: Type}(F: (B→ pred A)→(B→ pred A)): Prop :=
  ∀ (P Q: B → pred A), (∀ x, P x ⊢ Q x) → (∀ x, F P x ⊢ F Q x).

Definition corec {B A} (F: (B→ pred A)→(B→ pred A)): B → pred A :=
  fun x w ⇒ ∀ P: B → pred A, (∀ x, F P x ⊢ P x) → P x w.

Lemma corec_fold_unfold {B A}: ∀ {F: (B → pred A) →(B → pred A)},
    covariant F →   corec F = F (corec F).

Clearly the definition covariant is just as described at the beginning of the chapter: bigger sets are transformed into bigger sets. The fixed point is the intersection of all sets P such that $F(P) \subset P$. To see the proof that corec(F) is a fixed point of F, step through the proof script for corec_fold_unfold in msl/corec.v. For the proof that it is the *least fixed point* of the function F (corec(F) is a subtype of any fixed point of F), see corec_least_fixedpoint.

To make use of corec, one must be able to prove the covariance of functors such as lisfun. We start by proving covariance of the individual

---

[1]examples/sep/corec_example.v

operators (and, or, separating conjunction, etc.) and then compose these proofs together.

$$\text{covariant\_sepcon} \frac{\text{covariant } P \qquad \text{covariant } Q}{\text{covariant (fun } (x : B \rightarrow \text{pred} A)\, (b : B) \Rightarrow P\, x\, b \, * \, Q\, x\, b)}$$

$$\text{covariant\_andp} \frac{\text{covariant } P \qquad \text{covariant } Q}{\text{covariant (fun } (x : B \rightarrow \text{pred} A)\, (b : B) \Rightarrow P\, x\, b \, \wedge \, Q\, x\, b)}$$

$$\text{covariant\_orp} \frac{\text{covariant } P \qquad \text{covariant } Q}{\text{covariant (fun } (x : B \rightarrow \text{pred} A)\, (b : B) \Rightarrow P\, x\, b \, \vee \, Q\, x\, b)}$$

$$\text{covariant\_const} \frac{}{\text{covariant (fun } \_ \Rightarrow P)}$$

$$\text{covariant\_const'} \frac{}{\text{covariant (fun } (P : B \rightarrow \text{pred} A)\, (\_ : B) \Rightarrow P\, c)}$$

$$\text{covariant\_id} \frac{}{\text{covariant (fun } (P : B \rightarrow \text{pred} A) \Rightarrow P)}$$

$$\text{covariant\_exp} \frac{\forall c : C.\ \text{covariant}(F\, c)}{\text{covariant (fun } (P : B \rightarrow \text{pred} A)\, (b : B) \Rightarrow \exists c : C.\ F\, c\, P\, b)}$$

Our simple list predicate[2] is easily defined using corec.

Definition lisfun (Q: nat $\rightarrow$ pred heap) (p: nat) : pred heap:=
  !!(p=0) && emp || !!(p<>0) && EX r:nat, mapsto p r * Q r.

Definition lis : nat $\rightarrow$ pred heap := corec lisfun.

Now to fold and unfold lists, all we need is the lemma,

Lemma lis_fold_unfold:
  $\forall$ p, lis p = !!(p=0) && emp
              || !!(p<>0) && EX r:nat, mapsto p r * lis r.

---

[2]examples/sep/corec_example.v

The proof of this is easy, using corec_fold_unfold, but we will need this supporting lemma:

Lemma covariant_lisfun: covariant lisfun.
Proof.
  apply covariant_orp.
    apply covariant_const. *(* !!(p=0) && emp *)*
    apply covariant_andp.
      apply covariant_const. *(* !!(p<>0) *)*
      apply covariant_exp; intro.
        apply covariant_sepcon.
          apply covariant_const. *(* mapsto p r *)*
          apply covariant_const'. *(* Q r *)*
Qed.

As you can see from the proof, we just traverse the expression
!!(p=0) && emp || !!(p<>0) && Ex r:nat, mapsto p r * Q r, applying
the appropriate covariant-operator lemma at each point. One could easily
automate this using **Hint** Resolve.

Chapter 11

Share accounting

Concurrent separation logic is used to reason about shared-memory concurrent programs.[1]

Thread A	Thread B
while (1) {	while (1) {
acquire mutex;	acquire mutex;
[p] := f();	[p] := g();
release mutex;	release mutex;
for (i=0; i<N; i++) {	for (i=0; i<N; i++) {
think();	think();
acquire mutex;	acquire mutex;
x := [p];	x := [p];
release mutex;	release mutex;
}	}
}	}

These two programs use standard Dijkstra-Hoare synchronization to avoid race conditions on access to shared-memory resource $[p]$. Chapter 30 will show how the acquire and release operators transfer resources (expressed in separation logic as $p \mapsto a$) from one thread to another.

---

[1]Readers interested only in sequential programs can skip this chapter, and just use full shares (Share.top or Tsh) where shares are called for.

If the threads read $[p]$ much more often than they write it, they could avoid some synchronization overhead by a *concurrent-read, exclusive-write* protocol. The basic idea is that all the threads have simultaneous read-only access to the resource. When one thread wants to write, it (somehow) acquires exclusive access (the other threads must stop reading), and then it can safely write the resource without danger of racing with other reads and writes. Then the writer can release the resource back to the mode where all threads have read-only access.

One way to model this is to say that the mapsto $\mapsto$ operator is labeled with a *permission share*. The full share, written •, grants write permission, and any nonempty share π grants read permission.

When a thread wants to acquire write permission, it must do synchronization operations that acquire all the fractional shares (at that location) from all the other threads. When the thread has obtained the full share, it knows that no other thread can have a nonempty share: *Whenever there are k threads of execution, at all times their resources must be disjoint (and joinable together), in the sense of separation algebras.*

In this chapter we will not show the synchronization operators (see Chapter 30); here we will focus on the calculus of share permissions. The appropriate inference rules include:

$$\frac{\pi_1 \oplus \pi_2 = \pi}{p \overset{\pi_1}{\mapsto} x \, * \, p \overset{\pi_2}{\mapsto} x \;\; \longleftrightarrow \;\; p \overset{\pi}{\mapsto} x} \qquad \{p \overset{\pi}{\mapsto} x\} \; y := [p] \; \{p \overset{\pi}{\mapsto} x \; \&\& \; y = x\}$$

$$\{p \overset{\bullet}{\mapsto} x\} \; [p] := y \; \{p \overset{\bullet}{\mapsto} y\}$$

The rule at left means that if shares π_1 and π_2 join to make π, then the separating assertion $p \overset{\pi_1}{\mapsto} x \, * \, p \overset{\pi_2}{\mapsto} x$ is equivalent to $p \overset{\pi}{\mapsto} x$. The rules at right mean that any nonempty share is sufficient to apply the separation logic Hoare triple for load, but a full share is required for store.

When one thread has some nonempty share π_1 of a resource $p \mapsto \_$, no other share can have a full share, but other threads may have complementary shares $\pi_2, \ldots \pi_k$ such that $\pi_1 \oplus \pi_2 \oplus \ldots \oplus \pi_k = \bullet$. This means that during this time, no thread has enough permission to *write* to address p, but any of these k threads may be simultaneously reading address p.

The threads may then use the synchronization operations of concurrent separation logic to transfer all of their resources (for address p) into a single thread. Then this thread (e.g., thread j) will have the resource

$$p \xmapsto{\pi_1} x * p \xmapsto{\pi_2} x * \ldots * p \xmapsto{\pi_k} x$$

which is equal to $p \xmapsto{\bullet} x$ by the inference rule shown above. At that time, thread j can write to address p, but no other thread can possibly have a nonempty share of address p—no other thread can read simultaneously with the write—there is no *race condition*.

THERE ARE TWO BASIC MODES OF USE where permission shares are helpful. The first is in divide-and-conquer algorithms where many threads share read access to some input data. This sort of read-sharing frequently occurs in algorithms that exhibit strong data parallelism; for example, a parallel matrix multiply is naturally organized in this way.

The other primary mode of use is the reader-writer lock. In this mode a lock is used to protect access to some resource — typically a datastructure — where read-only access to the resource is common but writing is rare. These sorts of locks are frequently used in operating systems to protect system-wide datastructures like the process list. A read-write lock can be in one of three states: unlocked, locked for writing, or locked for reading with n concurrent readers. A writer wishing to take the lock must wait until all readers unlock before the lock may be taken in the exclusive writing state.

These two use modes require different properties of a share model. As discussed by Bornat et. al [27], the divide-and-conquor mode requires a model of *splittable* shares, whereas the read-write lock mode requires the ability to do *token counting*. For splittable shares, the most important operation we need is the ability to split shares in half. When a thread forks a new child, it can split its share of all read-only resoures and pass half of the share on to its child and keep half for itself. When the threads later join, the parent thread regains the other half. For token counting, the idea is that there is a token factory representing the read-write lock. The token factory produces read tokens when a reader takes the lock and absorbs the read tokens again when a reader unlocks. To do the share accounting, we therefore need a share model that can represent both the token factory and the read tokens.

Bornat *et al.* presented two different, incompatible share models to deal this these two modes. The model for splittable shares is based on the rational numbers between 0 and 1. Two shares join by addition, and shares are disjoint if their sum is no greater than 1. A share may be split into two shares by the simple operation of division by 2. The model for token counting is quite different; it takes the integers as shares. Two token shares combine by addition, and they are disjoint if their signs are different. The integer 0 is the top share, and one must add a new distinguished element to get the empty share. Token factories are represented by nonnegative integers and tokens by negative integers. The main idea is that the positive integer n represents a read-write lock with n readers and the share -1 represents a read token used by a reader to access the resource.

Neither of Bornat *et al.*'s share models was sufficiently general for many kinds of real programs. The reason lies in this observation: when we divide a permission π into two halves, it's useful to be able to distinguish between the left half and the right half. This *disjointness* property, expressed in separation algebras by Disj_alg, allows one to distinguish trees from DAGs, and to reason about other patterns of use. Rationals do not give us disjointness, for in that model when we split the full share 1 into left-hand $\frac{1}{2}$ and right-hand $\frac{1}{2}$, obviously we have $\frac{1}{2} = \frac{1}{2}$. The token-counting integer model suffers a similar problem.

Therefore we build a more sophisticated permission-share system. Chapter 41 develops the model for *tree shares*; here we show their axioms and patterns of use. The relevant Coq files are msl/boolean_alg.v, with the module type SHARE_MODEL that axiomatizes permission shares; and msl/shares.v, that instantiates this axiomatization with a model and provides additional lemmas and definitions.

The type share has at least a full share and an empty share:

Definition share : Type := Share.t.
Definition emptyshare : share := Share.bot.   *notated as* ∘
Definition fullshare : share := Share.top.   *notated as* •

Shares form a boolean algebra with greatest-lower-bound, least-upper-bound and complement operators.

$$\text{lub\_upper1}\frac{}{x \sqsubseteq x \sqcup y} \qquad\qquad \text{lub\_upper2}\frac{}{y \sqsubseteq x \sqcup y}$$

$$\text{lub\_least}\frac{x \sqsubseteq z \qquad y \sqsubseteq z}{x \sqcup y \sqsubseteq z} \qquad\qquad \text{glb\_lower1}\frac{}{x \sqcap y \sqsubseteq x}$$

$$\text{glb\_lower2}\frac{}{x \sqcap y \sqsubseteq y} \qquad\qquad \text{glb\_greatest}\frac{z \sqsubseteq x \qquad z \sqsubseteq y}{z \sqsubseteq x \sqcap y}$$

$$\text{top\_correct}\frac{}{x \sqsubseteq \bullet} \qquad\qquad \text{bot\_correct}\frac{}{\circ \sqsubseteq x}$$

$$\text{distrib1}\frac{}{x \sqcap (y \sqcup z) = (x \sqcap y) \sqcup (x \sqcap z)}$$

$$\text{comp1}\frac{}{x \sqcup (\neg x) = \bullet} \qquad \text{comp2}\frac{}{x \sqcap (\neg x) = \circ} \qquad \text{nontrivial}\frac{}{\bullet \neq \circ}$$

Figure 11.1: Axioms for boolean algebras

Share.Ord: share → share → Prop   *notated in this chapter as* $\sqsubseteq$
Share.glb: share → share → share   *notated in this chapter as* $\sqcap$
Share.lub: share → share → share   *notated in this chapter as* $\sqcup$
Share.comp: share → share   *notated in this chapter as* $\neg$

Axioms for these operators are shown in Figure 11.1.

SHARES ALSO FORM a cancellative separation algebra:

Instance Share.Join_ba: Join share :=
   fun x y z : t $\Rightarrow$ x $\sqcap$ y = $\circ$ $\wedge$ x $\sqcup$ y = z.
Instance Share.pa: Perm_alg share.
Instance Share.sa: Sep_alg share.
Instance Share.ca: Canc_alg share.
Instance Share.da: Disj_alg share.
Instance Share.singa: Sing_alg share.

The single unit in this separation algebra is $\circ$, as expected:

$$\text{bot\_identity} \frac{}{\text{identity}(\circ)} \qquad\qquad \text{bot\_unit} \frac{}{\circ \oplus \pi = \pi}$$

ANY SHARE MAY BE SPLIT into left and right halves:

Share.split : share $\to$ (share $*$ share)

with the following axioms:

$$\text{split\_join} \frac{\text{split}\, x = (x_1, x_2)}{x_1 \oplus x_2 = x} \qquad\qquad \text{split\_injective} \frac{\text{split}\, x = \text{split}\, y}{x = y}$$

$$\text{split\_nontrivial} \frac{\text{split}\, x = (x_1, x_2) \quad x_1 = \circ \lor x_2 = \circ}{x = \circ}$$

$$\text{split\_disjoint} \frac{\text{split}\, x = (x_1, x_2)}{x_1 \sqcap x_2 = \circ} \qquad\qquad \text{split\_together} \frac{\text{split}\, x = (x_1, x_2)}{x_1 \sqcup x_2 = x}$$

$$\text{nonemp\_split\_neq1} \frac{x \neq \circ \quad \text{split}\, x = (x_1, x_2)}{x_1 \neq x}$$

$$\text{nonemp\_split\_neq2} \frac{x \neq \circ \quad \text{split}\, x = (x_1, x_2)}{x_2 \neq x}$$

WITH THESE OPERATORS one can split permissions into pieces and rejoin them, in reasoning about concurrent programs. For most applications one does not need the full power of boolean algebras—just the split and *join* $\oplus$ operators, the full share $\bullet$, and their simple axioms are enough.

A program verification that splits permissions for concurrent-read exclusive-write data structures may benefit from automated reasoning about shares, using the decision procedure by Bach *et al.* [13].

SHARE RELATIVIZATION AND PROJECTION. Chapter 41 describes "advanced" sharing protocols that make use of the greatest-lower-bound $\sqcap$ and least-upper-bound $\sqcup$ operators, as well as the *relativization* operator $\bowtie$. That chapter also describes constructions for synthesizing token factories from tree-shares.

Part II

Higher order separation logic

SYNOPSIS: *Instead of reasoning directly on the* model *(that is, separation algebras), we can treat separation logic as a syntactic formal system, that is, a logic. We can implement proof automation to assist in deriving separation-logic proofs.*

Reasoning about recursive functions, recursive types, and recursive predicates can lead to paradox if not done carefully. Step-indexing avoids paradoxes by inducting over the number of remaining program-steps that we care about. Indirection theory is a kind of step-indexing that can serve as models of higher-order Hoare logics. Using indirection theory we can define general (not just covariant) recursive predicates.

Recursive data structures such as lists and trees are easily modeled in indirection theory, but the model is not the same one conventionally used, as it inducts over "age"—the approximation level, the amount of information left in the model—rather than list-length or tree-depth. A tiny pointer/continuation language serves as a case study for separation logic with first-class function-pointers, modeled in indirection theory. The proof of a little program in the case-study language illustrates the application of separation logic with function pointers.

Chapter 12

Separation logic as a logic

A FORMAL SYSTEM (or, a *logic*) is a syntax of formulas together with a deductive apparatus by which some formulas can be derived from others. We can use the apparatus even if we don't know what the formulas mean.

Of course, a formal system is more satisfying if we can give meanings to the formulas—a semantic model— and use this model to prove soundness of the deductive apparatus. So far in this book we have taken a semantic approach: we introduce separation logic via its models. Separation algebras give simple and general models of separation logics.

Models for higher-order separation logics in actual applications (see Chapter 39) can be rather intricate. Therefore we want to seal the model under an abstraction layer, so that reasoning about actual programs can proceed using a given set of rules without descending into the details of the model. Such a rule-set is a formal system, a separation logic.

We formulate separation logics axiomatically as a set of layered type-classes in Coq, in the files msl/seplog.v and msl/alg_seplog.v:

Class NatDed (A: Type) ... *natural deduction*
Class SepLog (A: Type) {NA: NatDed A} ... *separation logic*
Class ClassicalSep (A: Type) {NA: NatDed A}{SA: SepLog A}
Class IntuitionisticSep (A: Type) {NA: NatDed A}{SA: SepLog A}

The type-class NatDed axiomatizes natural deduction as a formal system in Coq (see Figure 12.1). We use the same names that we did in Chapter 8, but these are different definitions, with different types. In the "semantic" chapters, when we wrote andp P Q, the types of P and Q were $A \to$ Prop or pred(A) for some type A; that is, P and Q were *semantic* predicates. Now, when we write andp P Q the types of P and Q are some abstract type T with no commitment about the structure of T.

Name :	andp	orp	imp	exp	allp	prop	derives
Coq notation :	&&	||	– – >	EX	ALL	!!	| – –

Figure 12.1 presents the inference rules in Coq; Figure 12.2 shows the same rules in a more conventional mathematical notation. Figure 12.3 shows a proof of a theorem in natural deduction; it relies on the axioms, plus a lemma modus_ponens: $\forall$ P Q, P && (P $\longrightarrow$ Q) $\vdash$ Q.

We introduce a notation scope %logic for the operators of natural deduction (and soon, separation logic), with definitions such as,

Delimit Scope logic **with** logic.
Infix "&&" := andp (at level 40, left associativity) : logic.
Notation "P '-->' Q" := (imp P Q) (at level 55, right associativity) : logic.

This **Notation** looks practically identical to the notation scope %pred introduced in Chapters 8 and 38, but it is not the same: it refers to these *abstract* operators derives, orp, andp, et cetera, instead of the *semantic* operators derives, orp, andp, defined in those chapters.

Henceforth, when we write %logic we mean implicitly,

Import msl.seplog msl.alg_seplog.
Open Scope logic.

and thus, the syntactic (axiomatic) view of separation logic.

Henceforth when write %pred we mean implicitly,

Import msl.msl_standard.
Open Scope pred.

and the semantic (separation-algebra) view of separation logic.

Separation logic is an extension of natural deduction, as shown in Figures 12.4 and 12.5.

```
Class NatDed (A: Type) := mkNatDed {
  andp: A → A → A;
  orp: A → A → A;
  exp: ∀{T:Type}, (T → A) → A;
  allp: ∀{T:Type}, (T → A) → A;
  imp: A → A → A;
  prop: Prop → A;
  derives: A → A → Prop;
  pred_ext: ∀ P Q, derives P Q → derives Q P → P=Q;
  derives_refl: ∀ P, derives P P;
  derives_trans: ∀ {P Q R}, derives P Q → derives Q R → derives P R;
  TT := prop True;
  FF := prop False;
  andp_right: ∀ X P Q:A, derives X P → derives X Q → derives X (andp P Q);
  andp_left1: ∀ P Q R:A, derives P R → derives (andp P Q) R;
  andp_left2: ∀ P Q R:A, derives Q R → derives (andp P Q) R;
  orp_left: ∀ P Q R, derives P R → derives Q R → derives (orp P Q) R;
  orp_right1: ∀ P Q R, derives P Q → derives P (orp Q R);
  orp_right2: ∀ P Q R, derives P R → derives P (orp Q R);
  exp_right: ∀ {B: Type} (x:B) (P: A) (Q: B → A),
                           derives P (Q x) → derives P (exp Q);
  exp_left: ∀ {B: Type} (P: B → A) (Q: A),
                  (∀ x, derives (P x) Q) → derives (exp P) Q;
  allp_left: ∀ {B}(P: B → A) x Q, derives (P x) Q → derives (allp P) Q;
  allp_right: ∀ {B}(P: A) (Q: B → A),
                  (∀ v, derives P (Q v)) → derives P (allp Q);
  imp_andp_adjoint: ∀ P Q R, derives (andp P Q) R ↔ derives P (imp Q R);
  prop_left: ∀ (P: Prop) Q, (P → derives TT Q) → derives (prop P) Q;
  prop_right: ∀ (P: Prop) Q, P → derives Q (prop P);
  not_prop_right: ∀ (P:A)(Q:Prop), (Q → derives P FF)→ derives P (prop(~Q))
}.
```

Figure 12.1: Natural deduction as a formal system

$$\text{derives\_refl} \frac{}{P \vdash P} \qquad \text{derives\_trans} \frac{P \vdash Q \quad Q \vdash R}{P \vdash R}$$

$$\text{andp\_left1} \frac{P \vdash R}{P \,\&\&\, Q \vdash R} \qquad \text{andp\_left2} \frac{Q \vdash R}{P \,\&\&\, Q \vdash R}$$

$$\text{andp\_right} \frac{X \vdash P \quad X \vdash Q}{X \vdash P \,\&\&\, Q} \qquad \text{orp\_left} \frac{P \vdash R \quad Q \vdash R}{P \,\|\, Q \vdash R}$$

$$\text{orp\_right1} \frac{P \vdash Q}{P \vdash Q \,\|\, R} \qquad \text{orp\_right2} \frac{P \vdash R}{P \vdash Q \,\|\, R}$$

$$\text{exp\_right} \frac{P \vdash Q(x)}{P \vdash \exists x.\, Q(x)} \qquad \text{exp\_left} \frac{\text{for all } x,\ (P(x) \vdash Q)}{\exists x.\, P(x) \vdash Q}$$

$$\text{allp\_left} \frac{P(x) \vdash Q}{\forall x.\, P(x) \vdash Q} \qquad \text{allp\_right} \frac{\text{for all } x, (P \vdash Q(x))}{P \vdash \forall x.\, Q(x)}$$

$$\text{imp\_andp\_adjoint} \frac{}{P \,\&\&\, Q \vdash R \ = \ P \vdash Q \longrightarrow R}$$

$$\text{pred\_ext} \frac{P \vdash Q \quad Q \vdash P}{P = Q} \qquad \text{prop\_left} \frac{P \,\&\&\, \top \vdash Q}{!!P \vdash Q}$$

$$\text{prop\_right} \frac{P}{Q \vdash !!P} \qquad \text{not\_prop\_right} \frac{Q \rightarrow (P \vdash \bot)}{P \vdash !!(\neg Q)}$$

Figure 12.2: Natural deduction in mathematical notation. This chart can serve as a reference guide to the names of commonly used axioms.

Lemma example {A}{NA: NatDed A}:
 ∀P Q R : A, (TT ⟶ P) && (Q ⟶ R) ⊢ Q ⟶ P && R.
Proof.
 intros. apply ⟶ imp_andp_adjoint.
 ((TT ⟶ P) && (Q ⟶ R) && Q ⊢ P && R *)*
 apply andp_right.
        ((TT ⟶ P) && (Q ⟶ R) && Q ⊢ P *)*
        apply andp_left1.
        ((TT ⟶ P) && (Q ⟶ R) && Q ⊢ R *)*
        apply andp_left1. *(* TT ⟶ P ⊢ P *)*
        apply derives_trans **with** (TT && (TT ⟶ P)).
                (TT ⟶ P ⊢ TT && (TT ⟶ P) *)*
                apply andp_right.
                        (TT ⟶ P ⊢ TT *)*
                        apply prop_right; auto.
                        (TT ⟶ P ⊢ TT ⟶ P *)*
                        apply derives_refl.
                (TT && (TT ⟶ P) ⊢ P *)*
                apply modus_ponens.
 ((TT ⟶ P) && (Q ⟶ R) && Q ⊢ R *)*
 apply derives_trans **with** (Q && (Q ⟶ R)).
        ((TT ⟶ P) && (Q ⟶ R) && Q ⊢ Q && (Q ⟶ R) *)*
        apply andp_right.
                ((TT ⟶ P) && (Q ⟶ R) && Q ⊢ Q *)*
                apply andp_left2. apply derives_refl.
                ((TT ⟶ P) && (Q ⟶ R) && Q ⊢ Q ⟶ R *)*
                apply andp_left1. apply andp_left2. apply derives_refl.
        (Q && (Q ⟶ R) ⊢ R *)*
        apply modus_ponens.
Qed.

Figure 12.3: A proof in natural deduction

```
Class SepLog (A: Type) {ND: NatDed A} := mkSepLog {
   emp: A;
   sepcon: A →A →A;
   wand: A →A →A;
   ewand: A →A →A;
   sepcon_assoc: ∀P Q R, sepcon (sepcon P Q) R = sepcon P (sepcon Q R);
   sepcon_comm: ∀P Q, sepcon P Q = sepcon Q P;
   wand_sepcon_adjoint: ∀(P Q R: A), (sepcon P Q ⊢R) ↔(P ⊢wand Q R);
   sepcon_andp_prop: ∀P Q R, sepcon P (!!Q && R) = !!Q && (sepcon P R);
   sepcon_derives: ∀P P' Q Q' : A,
            P ⊢P' →Q ⊢Q' →sepcon P Q ⊢sepcon P' Q';
   ewand_sepcon: ∀(P Q R : A), ewand (sepcon P Q) R = ewand P (ewand Q R);
   ewand_TT_sepcon: ∀(P Q R: A),
            andp (sepcon P Q) (ewand R TT) ⊢
               sepcon (andp P (ewand R TT)) (andp Q (ewand R TT));
   exclude_elsewhere: ∀P Q: A, sepcon P Q ⊢sepcon (andp P (ewand Q TT)) Q;
   ewand_conflict: ∀P Q R, sepcon P Q ⊢FF →andp P (ewand Q R) ⊢FF
}.
```

Notation "P '∗' Q" := (sepcon P Q) : logic.
Notation "P '-∗' Q" := (wand P Q) (at level 60, right associativity) : logic.

Figure 12.4: Axiomatic presentation of separation logic

The maps-to operator $p \mapsto v$ is not present in this axiomatization, because each type A will need its own syntax and style of maps-to operator. Some maps-tos have permission-shares, or types, or sizes; in any case we would need to specify a domain type and range type. So we leave it out, and instantiate later in each different instantiation of SepLog.

$$\text{sepcon\_assoc} \frac{}{(P * Q) * R = P * (Q * R)} \qquad \text{sepcon\_comm} \frac{}{P * Q = Q * P}$$

$$\text{wand\_sepcon\_adjoint} \frac{}{(P * Q \vdash R) \leftrightarrow (P \vdash Q \mathbin{-\!\!*} R)}$$

$$\text{sepcon\_andp\_prop} \frac{}{P * (!!Q \,\&\&\, R) = !!Q \,\&\&\, (P * R)}$$

$$\text{sepcon\_derives} \frac{P \vdash P' \qquad Q \vdash Q'}{P * Q \vdash P' * Q'}$$

Figure 12.5: Axiomatic presentation of Separation Logic, in math notation

A *classical* SEPARATION LOGIC is one in which we can reason about dealloca-tion of memory. We may have Hoare-triple rules such as,

$$\{p \mapsto x\} \ \text{free}(p) \ \{\text{emp}\}$$

With such rules, one can prove (for example) that a certain function deallocates an entire binary tree, by giving the postcondition emp. In classical separation logic, we would *not* like the input heap (that satisfies $p \mapsto x$) to also satisfy emp; otherwise our dealloc-binary-tree specification is vacuous.

For classical separation logic, add the axiom $P * \text{emp} = P$.

Class ClassicalSep (A: Type) {ND: NatDed A}{SL: SepLog A} := mkCS {
    sepcon_emp: $\forall$ P, P $*$ emp = P
}.

ON THE OTHER HAND, AN *intuitionistic* SEPARATION LOGIC is one in which every predicate P that holds on a heap h also holds on any extension of h. Such a logic is useful for reasoning about programming languages with garbage collection (no explicit deallocation). The characteristic axiom is $P * \top \vdash P$.

Class IntuitionisticSep (A: Type) {ND: NatDed A}{SL: SepLog A} :=
mkIS { all_extensible: ∀ P, sepcon P TT ⊢ P }.

THIS AXIOMATIZATION IS INCOMPLETE! That is, there are some theorems provable in the *model* (that is, the %pred theory of separation algebras) that are not provable from the %logic *axioms* we present.

In fact, complete axiomatizations of separation logic are rather unwieldy; they do not use simple sequent judgments such as the ones presented here. [29, 73] At the end of the next chapter, we explain a simple solution for tolerating incompleteness.

Chapter 13

From separation algebras to separation logic

Predicates (of type $A \to$ Prop) in type theory give a model for Natural Deduction. A separation algebra gives a model for separation logic. We formalize these statements in Coq.

For a more expressive logic that permits general recursive types and quasi-self-reference, we use step-indexed models built with indirection theory. We will explain this in Part V; for now it suffices to say that indirection theory requires that the type T be *ageable*—elements of T must contain an approximation index. A given element of the model contains only a finite approximation to some ideal predicate; these approximations become weaker as we "age" them—which we do as the some operational semantics takes its steps.

To enforce that T is ageable we have a typeclass, ageable(T). Furthermore, when Separation is involved, the ageable mechanism must be compatible with the separating conjunction; this requirement is also expressed by a typeclass, Age_alg(T).

THEOREM: SEPARATION ALGEBRAS SERVE AS A MODEL OF SEPARATION LOGIC.
Proof. We express this theorem in Coq by saying that given type T, the function algNatDed models an instance of NatDed(pred T). Given a SepAlg over T, the function algSepLog models an instance of SepLog(pred T). The

definability of algNatDed and algSepLog serve as a proof of the theorem.

What we show in this chapter is the indirection theory version (in the Coq file msl/alg_seplog.v), so ageable and Age_alg are mentioned from time to time. Readers interested in a similar development *without* indirection theory should consult the Coq file msl/alg_seplog_direct.v.

The proof obligations of the constructor mkSepLog are spelled out in Figure 12.4. The first obligation is labeled sepcon_assoc. To prove this, we turn to a theorem about the underlying model in separation algebras. That is, in the file msl/predicates_sl.v we have the lemma,

Lemma sepcon_assoc {A}{JA: Join A}{PA: Perm_alg A}
$\qquad\qquad$ {AG: ageable A}{XA: Age_alg A}:
$\forall$ (P Q R:pred A), ((P * Q) * R = P * (Q * R))%pred.
Proof.
$\quad$ intros; apply pred_ext; hnf; intros.
$\quad$ *(* Forward Direction *)*
$\quad$ destruct H as [x [y [H [[z [w [H0 [? ?]]]] ?]]]].
$\quad$ destruct (join_assoc H0 H) as [q [? ?]].
$\quad$ $\exists$ z; $\exists$ q; intuition. $\exists$ w; $\exists$ y; intuition.
$\quad$ *(* Backward Direction *)*
$\quad$ ... similar ...
Qed.

That is a proof about P, Q, R of type pred A, assuming that A is an ageable permission algebra. The notation-scope marker %pred is a hint that $P * Q$ is using the sepcon operator defined in predicates_sl.v as,

Program Definition sepcon {A}{JA: Join A}{PA: Perm_alg A}
$\qquad\qquad$ {AG: ageable A}{XA: Age_alg A}
$\qquad\qquad$ (p q:pred A) : pred A :=
fun x:A $\Rightarrow$ $\exists$ y:A, $\exists$ z:A, join y z x $\wedge$ p y $\wedge$ q z.

For every axiom required for NatDed and SepLog, we have already proved the corresponding lemma about separation algebras. We use these in the proofs of our theorems:

Instance algNatDed (T: Type){agT: ageable T} : NatDed (pred T).
  apply (mkNatDed _
        predicates_hered.andp predicates_hered.orp
        (@predicates_hered.exp _ _) (@predicates_hered.allp _ _)
        predicates_hered.imp predicates_hered.prop
        (@predicates_hered.derives _ _)).
  apply predicates_hered.pred_ext.
  apply predicates_hered.derives_refl.
  apply predicates_hered.derives_trans.
  apply predicates_hered.andp_right.
  apply predicates_hered.andp_left1.
  ... (* and so on *)
Defined.

Instance algSepLog (T: Type) {agT: ageable T}{JoinT: Join T}
        {PermT: Perm_alg T}{SepT: Sep_alg T}{AgeT: Age_alg T} :
    @SepLog (pred T) (algNatDed T).
  apply (mkSepLog _ (algNatDed T)
        predicates_sl.emp predicates_sl.sepcon predicates_sl.wand).
  apply predicates_sl.seplog_assoc.
  ... (* and so on *)
Defined.

One can see the place (just before (*and so on *) where the previously proved lemma seplog_assoc (at the semantic level) is slotted into the axiomatization (at the formal-system level). Thus, these definitions of algNatDed and algSepLog *are* a proof of soundness.

A cancellative separation algebra induces a classical separation logic:

Instance algClassicalSep (T: Type) {agT: ageable T}{JoinT: Join T}
    {PermT: Perm_alg T}{SepT: Sep_alg T}{CancT: Canc_alg T}
    {AgeT: Age_alg T}:
    @ClassicalSep (pred T) (algNatDed T)(algSepLog T).
  constructor; intros. simpl. apply predicates_sl.sepcon_emp.
Qed.

BY NOW WE HAVE PRESENTED two different proof theories for natural deduction / separation logic. The separation-algebra-based proof theory has *lemmas* such as

Lemma sepcon_assoc {A}{JA: Join A}{PA: Perm_alg A}
                   {AG: ageable A}{XA: Age_alg A}:
$\forall$ (P Q R:pred A), ((P $*$ Q) $*$ R = P $*$ (Q $*$ R))%pred.

The formal-system-based proof theory has *axioms* such as

Axiom sepcon_assoc {A}{NA: NatDed A}{SA: SepLog A}:
$\forall$ (P Q R:pred A), ((P $*$ Q) $*$ R = P $*$ (Q $*$ R))%logic.

Now consider these two proofs:

```
Import seplog.                      Import msl_standard.
Lemma andp_com1                     Lemma andp_com2
  {T}{NT: NatDed T}:                  {A}{agA: ageable A}:
  ∀ P Q: T,                           ∀ P Q: pred A,
  ( P && Q ⊢ Q && P )%logic.          ( P && Q ⊢ Q && P )%pred.
Proof.                              Proof.
 intros.                             intros.
 apply andp_right.                   apply andp_right.
  apply andp_left2.                   apply andp_left2.
  apply derives_refl.                 apply derives_refl.
  apply andp_left1.                   apply andp_left1.
  apply derives_refl.                 apply derives_refl.
Qed.                                Qed.
```

The left-hand proof is is done in **%logic** (separation logic) and the right-hand proof is done in **%pred** (separation algebras, the underlying semantic theory). Because we have taken care to state the corresponding axioms and lemmas just right, it is not surprising that they look the same. But it would be surprising if the underlying *Coq proof objects* were the same. So this next proof is perhaps surprising:

Lemma andp_com3 {A}{agA: ageable A}:
  ∀ P Q: pred A, (P && Q ⊢ Q && P)%logic.
Proof.
  simpl.
  (∗ ∀ P Q: pred A, (P && Q ⊢ Q && P)%pred. ∗)
  apply andp_com2.
Qed.

This shows that andp_com2 serves as a proof of the same statement as andp_com1! The reason is that the **Instance** algNatDed ended with the word **Defined** instead of **Qed**: it is *transparent*. The underlying proof objects are not the same, but they are equal (using proof irrelevance). Simplifying of the statement in logic gives exactly the corresponding statement in the model: the comment after simpl shows the proof goal at that point.

What this means is that one can build a complete proof theory for a complex separation logic, and prove its soundness with full access to the underlying model; then the same exact lemmas serve as proofs of an opaque, *logical* view of the same theory.

Because our proof theory of separation logic is incomplete, occasionally we will want to prove a theorem by recourse to the *model*—our separation algebras and join relation. This is easy to do: Our implementation of **Instance** algSepLog concludes with **Defined**, not with **Qed**. We mark this instance as **Opaque**, which is a *suggestion* that the user should treat it abstractly. The **Opaque** marking can be unsealed when needed by using Coq's **Transparent** command. This allows the client of **Instance** algSepLog to evade the abstraction when absolutely necessary.

Chapter 14

Simplification by rewriting

Proofs in separation logic often require many applications of simple lemmas to rearrange formulas. These would be tedious to write out by hand, so we employ proof automation—either programmed in Coq's tactic language, or by computational reflection.

In separation systems built semantically (Chapter 8), where $P * Q$ is equal to $\lambda h.\exists h_1, h_2.h_1 \oplus h_2 = h \wedge P(h_1) \wedge P(h_2)$, proof algorithms should not unfold $x \models p * q$ into its semantic meaning. Although it would be sound and correct to unfold sepcon into $\oplus$, this would expose y and z and a multiplicity of $\oplus$ facts. The point of separation logic is to hide these behind the $*$ abstraction. And of course, in separation systems built abstractly as a logic (Chapter 12), one cannot descend into $\oplus$.

Several authors have built tactic libraries for separation logic, including Appel [6], McCreight [66], Tuerk [88], Chlipala [33], and Bengtson [16]. Here we present one component of a proof automation system: normalization. This is a system of tactics for simplification by rewriting in separation logic. It demonstrates some principles and is useful in many proofs, such as the case study of Chapters 18–20. In Chapter 26 we describe other parts of our Floyd proof automation system for Verifiable C.

THE NORMALIZER IS A COLLECTION OF LEMMAS AND REWRITE RULES in msl/log_normalize.v. We start with a collection of equations used as rewrite rules to simplify formulas:

$$P * \text{emp} = P \qquad \text{emp} * P = P \qquad \top \wedge P = P \qquad P \wedge \top = P \qquad \bot \wedge P = \bot$$

$$P \wedge \bot = \bot \qquad P -> ((!!P) = \top) \qquad \neg P -> ((!!P) = \bot) \qquad P \wedge P = P$$

Recall that $!!Q$ means that the pure logic proposition Q (of type Prop) holds, regardless of whatever world or subheap is our current context. Here we write $->$ for Coq's native (meta-level) implication, distinct from the predicate-implication operator of our separation logic. Thus, $P -> ((!!P) = \top)$ means, "if the proposition P is true, rewrite $!!P$ to $\top$."

These tactical systems are meant to help in proving entailments of the form $P \vdash Q$ (pronounced "P |-- Q" or "derives P Q" in Coq). Consider how we prove an entailment in ordinary logic:

Goal $\forall (P\ Q\ R: \text{nat} \rightarrow \text{Prop})$,
   $(\forall\ z, P\ z \rightarrow Q\ (S\ z)) \quad \rightarrow \quad (\exists\ z, P\ z) \wedge R\ 0 \rightarrow (\exists\ y, Q\ y)$.
Proof. intros P Q R H.

At this point our proof goal is,

P : nat $\rightarrow$ Prop
Q : nat $\rightarrow$ Prop
R : nat $\rightarrow$ Prop
H : $\forall z$: nat, $P\ z \rightarrow Q\ (S\ z)$
$$\overline{(\exists z, P\ z) \wedge R\ 0 \quad \rightarrow \quad \exists y, Q\ y}(1/1)$$

and it is natural to intro H0 to move $(\exists z.Pz) \wedge R\,0$ above the line, followed by destruct H0 and so on.

In separation logic, one should not prove entailments this way, by simply "moving the left part above the line" using intro. Consider this proof with separating conjunction instead of ordinary conjunction:

Section Example.
Context {A}{NA: NatDed A}{SA: SepLog A}{CA: ClassicalSep A}.

Goal $\forall P\ Q\ R$: nat $\rightarrow A$, $(\forall\ z, P\ z \vdash Q\ (S\ z)) \rightarrow$
   $(\text{EX } z:\text{nat}, P\ z) * R\ 0 \vdash (\text{EX } y:\text{nat}, Q\ y) * \text{TT}$.
Proof. intros.

This gives us proof goal "*G*":

P : nat → A
Q : nat → A $\boxed{\text{Proof goal } G}$
R : nat → A
H : ∀z : nat, P z ⊢ Q (S z)
———————————————————————————————————————(1/1)
(EX z : nat, P z) * R 0   ⊢   (EX y : nat, Q y) * TT

If we were in %pred—the semantic, separation-algebra view, where ⊢ and
* are just abbreviations—we could intro and destruct to expose subheaps:

P,Q,R: nat → A
H : ∀z : nat, P z ⊢ Q (S z)
a,a1,a2 : A
H0 : join a1 a2 a
z : nat
H1 : (P z) a1
H2 : (R 0) a2
———————————————————————————————(1/1)
((EX y : nat, Q y) * TT) a

But it would be wrong. These subheaps and joins are best kept hidden
under the abstraction of separation logic. And if we are in %logic—the
formal-system view where ⊢ and * are abstract—then we cannot do intro
and destruct to expose subheaps. So our tactical system will be designed
operate abstractly on entailments, as in proof goal *G*.

We use these rewrite rules to pull existentials to the outside of formulas
(assuming x not free in *Q*):

$$(\exists x.Px) * Q = \exists x.(Px * Q) \qquad Q * (\exists x.Px) = \exists x.(Q * Px)$$

$$(\exists x.Px) \wedge Q = \exists x.(Px \wedge Q) \qquad Q \wedge (\exists x.Px) = \exists x.(Q \wedge Px)$$

If we apply these rewrites to goal *G*, we obtain G_2:

EX x : nat, (P x * R 0)   ⊢   EX y : nat, Q y * TT

The next two lemmas are operate on existentials underneath entailments:

$$\text{exp\_left} \frac{\forall x. \ (Px \vdash Q)}{(\exists x.P) \vdash Q} \qquad \text{exp\_right} \frac{P \vdash Qx}{P \vdash \exists x.Qx}$$

From goal G_2, we can write (apply exp_left; intro x) to move x "above the line," obtaining G_3:

P,Q,R: nat $\rightarrow$ A
H : $\forall z$: nat, P z $\vdash$ Q (S z)
x : nat
$$\rule{8cm}{0.4pt}(1/1)$$
P x $*$ R 0 $\vdash$ EX x0 : nat, Q x0 $*$ TT

The reason we want to move hypotheses and variables above the line is that Coq has a powerful system for naming, substituting, and applying variables and hypotheses. We want to take advantage of this where possible. Since the variable x is a natural number, an inhabitant of "pure logic" that is not affected by separation, we move it above the line. On the other hand, $P x$ is a separation-logic predicate, "impure," and we avoid moving it above the line so as not to expose "raw" join relations.

From G_3 we can finish the proof by

apply (exp_right (S x)); apply sepcon_derives; auto.

We make a **Hint Rewrite** database called norm containing all these rewrite rules (and more besides). We make a tactic called normalize that applies (autorewrite **with** norm) and applies lemmas such as exp_left where appropriate. Then the proof goal G can be solved with,

normalize. intro x. apply (exp_right (S x)). apply sepcon_derives; auto.
Qed.

Separation logic formulas often contain pure propositions, and these can also be moved "above the line" in Coq. An example lemma is this one:

$$\text{prop\_andp\_left} \frac{P \;\rightarrow\; (Q \vdash R)}{!!P \wedge Q \vdash R}$$

This converts the proof goal,

$$\rule{8cm}{0.4pt}(1/1)$$
!!P && Q $\vdash$ R

into the goal

$$
\frac{\text{H: } P}{Q \quad \vdash \quad R}\text{---}(1/1)
$$

where we can use the full power of Coq to manipulate P.

But to use this lemma, it's helpful to bring the proposition P all the way to the outside of any separating conjunctions in which it may be nested. For this we have rewrite rules:

$$(!!Q \wedge R) * P \; = \; !!Q \wedge (R * P) \qquad\qquad (!!Q \wedge P) * R \; = \; !!Q \wedge (R * P)$$

Now consider this proof goal G_5:

$$
\frac{\begin{array}{l}
Q : \text{nat} \rightarrow \text{Prop} \\
P : \text{nat} \rightarrow A \\
R : \text{nat} \rightarrow A \\
H : \forall z : \text{nat}, \; Q \; z \rightarrow Q \; (S \; z) \\
H0 : \forall z : \text{nat}, \; !!Q \; (S \; z) \; \&\& \; P \; z \vdash R \; z \\
z : \text{nat}
\end{array}}{P \; z \; \&\& \; !!Q \; z \quad \vdash \quad !!Q \; (S \; z) \; \&\& \; R \; z}\text{---}(1/1)
$$

Our normalize tactic does not *only* do rewriting, it applies lemmas such as prop_andp_left (shown above) to move propositions above the line. One application of normalize brings Qz above the line:

$$
\frac{\begin{array}{l}
H : \forall z : \text{nat}, \; Q \; z \rightarrow Q \; (S \; z) \\
H0 : \forall z : \text{nat}, \; !!Q \; (S \; z) \; \&\& \; P \; z \vdash R \; z \\
z : \text{nat} \\
H1 : Q \; z
\end{array}}{P \; z \vdash R \; z}\text{---}(1/1)
$$

Then we use the transitivity of entailment with hypothesis $H0$, that is, eapply derives_trans; [| apply H0]; to obtain the goal,

$$P \; z \vdash !!Q \; (S \; z) \; \&\& \; P \; z$$

which solves easily by apply andp_right; [apply prop_right; auto | auto].

Chapter 15

Introduction to step-indexing

Many kinds of recursive definitions and recursive predicates appear in the descriptions of programs and programming languages. Some recursive definitions, such as list and tree data structures, are naturally *covariant*; these are straightforward to handle using a simple least-fixed-point method as described in Chapter 10. But some useful kinds of self-referencing definitions are not covariant. When the recursion goes through function arguments, it may be *contravariant* (see F_{funopt} on page 64) or some mixture that is neither covariant nor contravariant. This kind of recursion requires more difficult mathematics, yet it is essential in reasoning about certain kinds of programs:

- Object-oriented programs in which class C has methods with a "this" or "self" parameter of type C;

- Functional programming languages with mutable references at higher types—such as ML;

- Concurrent languages with dynamically creatable locks whose resource invariants can describe other locks—a typical idiom in Pthreads concurrency;

- Functional languages (such as ML) where datatype recursion can go through function-parameters.

DOES THE C PROGRAMMING LANGUAGE HAVE THESE FEATURES? Well, yes. C's type system is rather loose (with casts to void∗ and back). C programs that use void∗ in design patterns similar to *objects* or *function closures* can be perfectly correct, but proving their correctness in a program logic may need noncovariant recursion.

This chapter, and the next two chapters (predicate implication and subtyping; general recursive predicates) present the logical machinery to reason about such recursions in the VST program logics.

For simplicity, we will illustrate using the linked-list data type—even though it is entirely covariant and does not require such heavy machinery. Here again are two (roughly) equivalent definitions:

$$F_{list} = \lambda Q. 1 + (int \times Q)$$

Definition lisfun (Q: nat → pred heap) (p: nat) : pred heap:=
  !!(p=0) && emp || !!(p<>0) && EX r:nat, mapsto p r ∗ Q r.

Consider what kinds of values properly belong to the list type, and what values *almost* belong or *approximately* belong. Here's a linked list x of length 4, terminated by the null-pointer 0:

On the other hand, the data structure y has a wild pointer in the third cell, that would be unsafe to dereference:

We say that x is a list, and y is approximately a list. To make this more precise, we consider the safety of functions that operate on linked lists, such as this function f:

int f (list p) { **while** (p≠0) p=p→ next; }

If we run the program $f(x)$, it will be safe; if we run $f(y)$, it will eventually dereference the wild pointer, and crash. This is because y is *not a list:* it is malformed.

But suppose we run $f(y)$ for only two or three steps—then it will not have a chance to crash. We say that $f(y)$ is *safe for 3 steps*. Any function on lists will be safe for 3 steps on argument y. Even if the function wastes no time on any operation other than p→next, three executions of p=p→next leaves p containing the wild pointer, not yet dereferenced.

To approximation 3, y is a linked list: any program that expects a linked list will be safe for at least 3 steps. The pointer z→☐↘↝ is a list to approximation 1, and any value is a list to approximation 0.

We want to prove that a program is safe (or correct). Usually we define that to mean that no matter how many steps it executes, the next step will not crash (or violate its partial-correctness specification). But suppose we have a limited attention span: we have time to run the program for only k steps before our coffee break, and we don't care if it crashes after that. We just want to prove it is *safe for k steps*. (We will prove this for an arbitrary k, and when the proof is done we will quantify over all k.)

Now, suppose we have a pointer p that is a list to approximation 3. That is, perhaps p $= x$ or p $= y$. *Later,* after we take one step q=p→next, we will know that q is a list to approximation 2.

It is critical that whenever we have a value p that belongs to type τ at approximation $k+1$, and we do an operation on p to get another value q of approximate type τ', it must be that q belongs to τ' to approximation at least k. (In our example of p→next, $\tau = \tau' =$ list.)

We can express this in the specification of the data structure by using the ▷ operator, pronounced "later." The predicate ▷P means that P holds *later*, or P holds *approximately*. If our goal is to ensure that some computation is safe for k steps, then $v \models {\triangleright}P$ means that value v is a member of P to at least approximation $k-1$. It would be unsafe to run k steps on v, but by the time we fetch v out of the data structure, we will have used up one step, so we have only $k-1$ steps remaining.

We use the ▷ later operator in the definition of recursive types and recursive predicates:

$$F'_{\text{list}} = \lambda Q.\, 1 + (\text{int} \times {\triangleright}Q)$$

Definition lisfun' (Q: nat → pred heap) (p: nat) : pred heap:=
  !!(p=0) && emp || !!(p<>0) && EX r:nat, mapsto p r * ▷ Q r.

Suppose $F'_{\text{list}}(Q)$ is testing whether some value x or y is a list to approximation k; that is, $F'_{\text{list}}(Q)$ is considering only whether executions of $\leq k$ steps
can go wrong. In such a test, the natural definition of a list will fetch the
tail-pointer out of the first list-cell—this pointer is called r in the definition
of listfun'—and test whether r is satisfies Q. But the ▷later operator in front
of Q ensures that $F'_{\text{list}}(Q)$ or listfun' can only test this to approximation
$k - 1$, that is, considering executions of strictly $< k$ execution steps.

Given two predicates P and Q, we say that $P = Q$ *to approximation k*
if, considering only executions of $\leq k$ steps, there is no value x such that
$P(x) \neq Q(x)$. We will make all of this more formal in Part V of the book.
Now we define a *step-indexing recursion operator* such that $\mu F = F(\mu F)$.
This μ operator is more powerful than the least-fixed-point μ used for
covariant recursion, but it requires F to be *contractive*—that is, whenever
$P = Q$ at approximation k then $F(P) = F(Q)$ at $k + 1$. Informally, if every
use of x within $F(x)$ is prefixed by ▷, then F will be contractive, provided
that all the other operators used in the definition of F are *nonexpansive*.

We say F is *nonexpansive* to mean, whenever $P = Q$ at approximation k
then $F(P) = F(Q)$ at k. The operators that we normally use in type systems
and separation logics are all naturally nonexpansive.

Theorem. lisfun' is contractive. **Proof.** ▷ is contractive, thus $\lambda Q.\lambda r.(\triangleright Q)r$
is contractive (by η-equivalence). Constant functions are contractive, thus
$\lambda Qr.p \mapsto r$ (which doesn't mention Q) is contractive. Separating conjunction
is nonexpansive, and the composition of a nonexpansive with a contractive
function is contractive, so $\lambda Qr.\, p \mapsto r * \triangleright Qr$ is contractive. The constant
function $\lambda Qr.\, !!(p = 0) \wedge$ emp is contractive. The operators EX, &&, || are
nonexpansive. Qed.

Corollary. $\mu(\text{lisfun}')$ is a fixed point of lisfun', and thus describes linked-list
data structures.

The idea of taking successively accurate approximations goes back to
Dana Scott [84]. The formulation as step-indexing is due to Appel and
McAllester [10], influenced by MacQueen, Plotkin, and Sethi [65]. Ahmed
[4] developed a more expressive step-indexed model to handle ML-style

mutable references; Appel *et al.* [11] reformulated this using the ▷ later
operator, influenced by Nakano [68]. Hobor, Dockins, and Appel [52]
generalized Ahmed's model to handle "predicates in the heap" and many
other patterns of recursive predicates and recursive types—the resulting
general formulation is called *indirection theory.*

Just as we represent natural deduction and separation logic as type-
classes (NatDed and SepLog) in Coq, we can define indirection theory as a
type-class. Class Indir adds the later ▷ operator to natural deduction, with
axioms that show how ▷ commutes over disjunction, conjunction, and so
on. SepIndir adds axioms for ▷ commuting with separating-conjuction *
and the magic wands —*, —∘. (See Figure 15.1.)

Class Indir (A: Type) {ND: NatDed A} := mkIndir {
  later: A → A;
  now_later: ∀ P: A, P ⊢ ▷P;
  later_K: ∀ P Q, ▷(P⟶Q) ⊢ ▷P ⟶ ▷Q;
  later_allp: ∀ T (F: T→A), ▷(ALL x:T, F x) = ALL x:T, ▷(F x);
  later_exp: ∀ T (F: T→A), EX x:T, ▷(F x) ⊢ ▷(EX x: F x);
  later_exp': ∀ T (any:T) F, ▷(EX x: F x) = EX x:T, ▷(F x);
  later_imp: ∀ P Q, ▷(P⟶Q) = ▷P ⟶ ▷Q;
  loeb: ∀ P, ▷P ⊢ P → TT ⊢ P
}.

Class SepIndir (A: Type) {NA: NatDed A}{SA: SepLog A}{IA: Indir A} :=
mkSepIndir {
  later_sepcon: ∀ P Q, ▷(P * Q) = ▷P * ▷Q;
  later_wand: ∀ P Q, ▷(P —* Q) = ▷P —* ▷Q;
  later_ewand: ∀ P Q, ▷(P —∘ Q) = (▷P) —∘ (▷Q)
}.

Figure 15.1: Indirection theory as a formal system (part 1).
Part 2, the rules for subtyping and recursion, are in Figure 16.1

Chapter 16

Predicate implication and subtyping

Let us continue the construction of the logical mechanism for describing recursive types.[1] Readers who merely want to *use* theories of recursive types, who do not need to *construct* these theories as this chapter and the next will explain how to do, might reasonably skip to Chapter 18.

When we describe a particular object in separation logic, we will use mapsto $\mapsto$ and separating conjunction $*$. But when we describe entire classes of objects, for example, datatypes such as lists and trees, we need a notion of *implication*.

Let P and Q be predicates on worlds of type A, that is, P : pred A. Then $P \rightarrow Q$ is a pred A; world w satisfies $w \models P \rightarrow Q$ iff, provided that $w \models P$ then $w \models Q$. Actually, it means more than that: because predicates (including $P \rightarrow Q$) must be preserved under the later $\triangleright$ operator: for any world w' in the future of w, if $w' \models P$ then $w' \models Q$.

So, $w \models P \rightarrow Q$ is a claim about w and its approximations. In contrast, the statement $P \vdash Q$ is a statement about *all* worlds: for all w, if $w \models P$ then $w \models Q$. This is a proposition (Prop), not a predicate about a specific world.

But sometimes we want a *formula* that in world w makes a claim about *all* worlds, not just about w—that is, we want to reflect the $\vdash$ operator into the logic. The naive reflection does not work, because of a technical restriction of indirection theory. Any predicate R must be preserved under

---

[1]The operators described in this chapter are defined in msl/subtypes.v.

the ▷ later operator, that is, $R \vdash \triangleright R$. But if $P\,[\vdash]\,Q$ were a predicate in the logic meaning "for all w, $w \models P$ implies $w \models Q$", then it would quantify over w in the *past*; unfortunately we cannot prove $(P\,[\vdash]\,Q) \vdash \triangleright(P\,[\vdash]\,Q)$.

That is, within an operator of our logic we cannot quantify over *all* worlds; in particular, we cannot quantify over worlds that occur in the *past*. But we *can* quantify over all present and future worlds, using the operator # (pronounced *fashionably*). The predicate $\#P$ means that P is "fashionable," it holds in all worlds of the current age and in all later worlds.

When we write $\#P$, it hardly matters what world we say it in, except for the age-level of the world. Even if P is a predicate on operational-semantic heaps, $\#P$ is a predicate that does not care anything about the internal structure of its particular world except the age. We emphasize this by saying that $\#P$ is *not* a predicate on heaps, it belongs to a special Natural Deduction system called Triv.

Definition Triv := predicates_hered.pred nat.
Instance TrivNatDed: NatDed Triv := algNatDed nat.
Instance TrivSeplog: SepLog Triv := algSepLog nat.

Triv really is trivial: At any particular age, it contains the predicates true $\top$ and false $\bot$. In contrast, a *nontrivial* natural deduction system can have predicates such as $3 \mapsto 5$ which are true in some worlds (heaps) but not others.

We say $n \models \#(P \longrightarrow Q)$ to mean, "for any heap w at age n or later, $w \models P \longrightarrow Q$." Even though P and Q are (nontrivial) predicates on heaps, the predicate $\#(P \longrightarrow Q)$ belongs to Triv: in deciding whether it is true or false, there's no extra information to be gained from the trivial semantic world in which $\#(P \longrightarrow Q)$ is interpreted.

Now we can formally introduce (Figure 16.1) the RecIndir class, that axiomatizes the parts of indirection theory that handle fashionability, subtyping, and recursive types.

Class RecIndir (A: Type) {NA: NatDed A}{IA: Indir A} := mkRecIndir {
  fash : A → Triv;
  unfash : Triv → A;
  HORec : ∀ {X} (f: (X → A) → (X → A)), X → A;
  unfash_fash: ∀ P: A, unfash (fash P) ⊢ P;
  fash_K: ∀ P Q, fash (P ⟶ Q) ⊢ fash P ⟶ fash Q;
  fash_derives: ∀ P Q, P ⊢ Q → fash P ⊢ fash Q;
  unfash_derives: ∀ P Q, P ⊢ Q → unfash P ⊢ unfash Q;
  later_fash: ∀ P, later (fash P) = fash (later P);
  later_unfash: ∀ P, later (unfash P) = unfash (later P);
  fash_andp: ∀ P Q, fash (P && Q) = fash P && fash Q;
  unfash_allp: ∀ {B} (P: B → Triv),
      unfash (allp P) = ALL x:B, unfash (P x);
  subp_allp: ∀ G B (X Y:B → A),
      (∀ x:B, G ⊢ fash (imp (X x) (Y x))) →
      G ⊢ fash (imp (allp X) (allp Y));
  subp_exp: ∀ G B (X Y:B → A),
      (∀ x:B, G ⊢ fash (imp (X x) (Y x))) →
      G ⊢ fash (imp (exp X) (exp Y));
  subp_e: ∀ (P Q : A), TT ⊢ fash (P ⟶ Q) → P ⊢ Q;
  subp_i1: ∀ P (Q R: A), unfash P && Q ⊢ R → P ⊢ fash (Q ⟶ R);
  fash_TT: ∀ G, G ⊢ fash TT;
  HOcontractive: ... (Chapter 17)
  HORec_fold_unfold : ∀ X (f: (X → A) → (X → A)),
      HOcontractive f   →   HORec f = f (HORec f)
}.

Figure 16.1: Logical operators for subtyping and recursion

$$\text{fash\_K} \frac{}{\#(P \to Q) \vdash \#P \to \#Q} \qquad \text{fash\_fash} \frac{}{\#\#P \;=\; \#P}$$

$$\text{fash\_derives} \frac{P \vdash Q}{\#P \vdash \#Q} \qquad \text{fash\_and} \frac{}{\#(P \wedge Q) \;=\; \#P \wedge \#Q}$$

$$\text{later\_fash} \frac{}{\triangleright\#P \;=\; \#\triangleright P} \qquad \text{fash\_allp} \frac{}{\#(\forall x.P) \;=\; \forall x.\#P}$$

We use # to define a predicate inclusion operator, $\#(P \to Q)$, written as $P \rightarrowtail Q$ and pronounced "P is a subtype of Q." That is, $n \models P \rightarrowtail Q$ means that for all worlds w whose level is $\le n$, if $w \models P$ then $w \models Q$.

Notation "P '>=>' Q" := (#(P --> Q))
         (at level 55, right associativity):pred.
Notation "P '<=>' Q" := (#(P <--> Q))
         (at level 57, no associativity):pred.

Subtyping is reflexive and transitive. Equityping ($P \Leftrightarrow Q$) is reflexive, symmetric, and transitive, and is equivalent (but not equal) to $P \rightarrowtail Q \wedge Q \rightarrowtail P$.

$$\text{subp\_top} \frac{}{\Gamma \vdash P \rightarrowtail \top} \qquad \text{subp\_andp} \frac{\Gamma \vdash P \rightarrowtail P' \qquad \Gamma \vdash Q \rightarrowtail Q'}{\Gamma \vdash (P \wedge Q) \rightarrowtail (P' \wedge Q')}$$

$$\text{subp\_bot} \frac{}{\Gamma \vdash \bot \rightarrowtail P} \qquad \text{subp\_impl} \frac{\Gamma \vdash P' \rightarrowtail P \qquad \Gamma \vdash Q \rightarrowtail Q'}{\Gamma \vdash (P \to Q) \rightarrowtail (P' \to Q')}$$

$$\text{subp\_later} \frac{}{\triangleright(P \rightarrowtail Q) = (\triangleright P) \rightarrowtail (\triangleright Q)}$$

Any subtyping or equityping formula $P \rightarrowtail Q$ or $P \Leftrightarrow Q$ is a formula in Triv, but sometimes we want to inject it into a NatDed system on some other type. We do this with the operator !, for example $!(P \rightarrowtail Q)$.

unfash {A}{NA: NatDed A}{IA: Indir A}{RA: RecIndir A} : Triv→A.

Notation "'!' e" := (unfash e) (at level 30, right associativity): pred.

Finally, we have one more typeclass SepRec to explain how unfash distributes over separation:

Class SepRec (A: Type) {NA: NatDed A}{SA: SepLog A}
$\qquad\qquad$ {IA: Indir A}{RA: RecIndir A} := mkSepRec {
$\quad$ unfash_sepcon_distrib: $\forall$ (P: Triv) (Q R: A),
$\qquad$!P && (Q*R) = (!P && Q) * (!P && R)
}.

EXAMPLE. Consider this use of subtyping. We'd like to say "P implies Q, and $P * R$, therefore $Q * R$." But it won't suffice to say $(P \longrightarrow Q)$ && $(P * R)$, because $P \longrightarrow Q$ is talking about the same world as $P * R$ is, and P probably doesn't hold in that world unless $R = $ emp. We say instead,

$$!\#(P \longrightarrow Q) \,\&\&\, (P*R) \vdash Q*R \qquad \text{or equivalently} \qquad !(P \rightarrowtail Q)\,\&\&\,(P*R) \vdash Q*R$$

We can prove this lemma as follows:

Lemma subtype_example {A}{NA: NatDed A}{SL: SepLog A}{IA: Indir A}
$\qquad\qquad$ {RA: RecIndir A}{SRA: SepRec A}:
$\quad \forall P \; Q \; R : A, \qquad !(P \rightarrowtail Q) \,\&\&\, (P * R) \vdash Q * R.$

Proof. First, rewrite by unfash_sepcon_distrib to get $(!(P \rightarrowtail Q) \,\&\&\, P) *$ $(!(P \rightarrowtail Q) \,\&\&\, R)$. Use sepcon_derives to get two subgoals, $!(P \rightarrowtail Q) \,\&\&\, P \vdash Q$ and $!(P \rightarrowtail Q) \,\&\&\, R \vdash R$; the latter is trivial by andp_left2. Then $!(P \rightarrowtail Q)$ is identical to $!(\#(P \longrightarrow Q))$ which by unfash_fash implies $P \longrightarrow Q$, and we finish by modus_ponens.

THE MOST IMPORTANT APPLICATION OF SUBTYPING $\rightarrowtail$ is in the specification of the recursion operator μ and the related notion of *contractiveness*; these are explained in the next chapter.

Chapter 17

General recursive predicates

Let mpred be our type of predicates on heaps, such as $x \mapsto y$. Another kind of mpred is the function-pointer specification $p : \{Q\} \to \{R\}$, which means that p is the address of a function with precondition Q and postcondition R.

To specify data types such as lists and trees we use recursive predicates:

lis(p: nat) : mpred :=
  !!(p=0) && emp || !!(p≠0) && EX r:nat, p↦r ∗ lis(r).

tree (p:nat) : mpred :=
  !!(p=0) && emp
  || !!(p≠0) && EX r1:nat, EX r2:nat, p↦r1 ∗ (p+1)↦r2 ∗ tree(r).

Because these definitions are self-referential, they are only informal. To avoid self-reference we take fixed points of the following functions:

F_{lis} (Q: nat → mpred) (p: nat) : mpred :=
  !!(p=0) && emp || !!(p≠0) && EX r:nat, p↦r ∗ Q(r).

F_{tree} (Q: nat → mpred) (p:nat) : mpred :=
  !!(p=0) && emp
  || !!(p≠0) && EX r1:nat, EX r2:nat, p↦r1 ∗ (p+1)↦r2 ∗ Q(r).

F_{funny} (Q: nat → mpred) (p:nat) : mpred :=
  !!(p=0) && emp || !!(p≠0) && p:{Q}→{Q}

An element of type funny is either a nullpointer or a nonzero pointer to a function from funny to funny.

These three functions on predicates—F_{lis}, F_{tree}, and F_{funny}—(can be adjusted to) have useful fixed points. The basic reason is they cannot get to their argument Q without traversing some sort of predicate that implies at least one step of computation, and that is the basis on which we can do an induction. For lis and tree the "step-related" predicate is $\mapsto$, hinting that given $p \mapsto x$ one cannot do anything with x without executing a **load** instruction. For funny it is the function arrow; given $p : \{Q\} \to \{Q\}$ one cannot notice whether an actual parameter fails to obey Q without doing a **call** instruction to address p.

But each of the next four functions does not have a useful fixed point, and the basic reason is that the use of Q is not tied to an execution step:

$F_{strange}$ (Q: nat $\to$ mpred) (p:nat) := Q(p+1).

Ω (Q: nat $\to$ mpred) (p:nat) := Q(p).

G (Q: nat $\to$ mpred) (p:nat) := Q(p) $\|$!!(p=0).

H (Q: B $\to$ mpred) (p:B) : mpred := fun w $\Rightarrow$ $\forall$ w', Q p w'.

In the case of Ω, given p one already has the value to which Q is applied—without any steps of computation. In the case of G, a disjunctive type does not use an actual machine-instruction to choose between Q or $(p = 0)$. The case of strange is a bit less obvious, but consider that n unfoldings of $F_{strange}$ can be accounted for by just one instruction that computes $p + n$. The H function "cheats" by applying Q at a world w' that may be at a *higher* level of accuracy than its argument w; this defeats our strategy of counting the remaining steps of computation.

Let us $\triangleright$ mark the place within the well-behaved functions where a computation step must be used before testing Q:

F'_{lis} (Q: nat $\to$ mpred) (p: nat) : mpred :=
  !!(p=0) && emp $\|$!!(p$\neq$0) && EX r:nat, p$\mapsto$r $*$ $\triangleright$ Q(r).

F'_{tree} (Q: nat $\rightarrow$ mpred) (p:nat) : mpred :=
 !!(p=0) && emp
 || !!(p$\neq$0) && EX r1:nat, EX r2:nat, p$\mapsto$r1 $*$ (p+1)$\mapsto$r2 $* \triangleright$ Q(r).

F'_{funny} (Q: nat $\rightarrow$ mpred) (p:nat) : mpred :=
 !!(p=0) && emp
 || !!(p$\neq$0) && p:{$\triangleright$Q}$\rightarrow${$\triangleright$Q}

This $\triangleright$ marking is not just a syntactic notation; it is our *later* operator. We say that instead of Q we have a slightly weaker approximation to it, $\triangleright Q$.

What is the connection between "executing at least one instruction before unfolding F" and "a weaker approximation to Q?" Suppose we had planned to run the program for just $k+1$ steps "before our coffee break," before we no longer care whether it crashes. Then Q in a Hoare assertion means that predicate Q holds to accuracy $k+1$, and $\triangleright Q$ means Q holds only to accuracy k. But we know that one instruction-step will be executed in executing the load or call instruction, so after that step, only k steps will remain "before the coffee break," so $\triangleright Q$ is a strong enough predicate.

Contractive predicate-functions $F(Q)$ apply their argument Q only at weaker approximations. To find a fixed point of a function F : pred$A \rightarrow$ pred$A$ in indirection theory, we need F to be contractive.

Definition contractive {A}{NA: NatDed A}{IA: Indir A}
                     {RA: RecIndir A} (F: A$\rightarrow$A) :=
 $\forall$ P Q, $\triangleright$(P $\Leftrightarrow$ Q) $\vdash$ F P $\Leftrightarrow$ F Q.

Definition nonexpansive {A}{NA: NatDed A}{IA: Indir A}
                     {RA: RecIndir A} (F: A$\rightarrow$A) :=
 $\forall$ P Q, (P $\Leftrightarrow$ Q) $\vdash$ F P $\Leftrightarrow$ F Q.

But in fact the F' are not just predicates in A, they are functions from nat to A. So we need a higher-order notion of contractiveness:

Definition HOcontractive {A}{NA: NatDed A}{IA: Indir A}
     {RA: RecIndir A} (X: Type) (F: (X$\rightarrow$A)$\rightarrow$(X$\rightarrow$A)) : Prop :=
 $\forall$ P Q, (All x:X, $\triangleright$(P x $\Leftrightarrow$ Q x)) $\vdash$ (ALL x:X, F P x $\Leftrightarrow$ F Q x).

Definition HOnonexpansive {A}{NA: NatDed A}{IA: Indir A}
    {RA: RecIndir A} (X: Type) (F: (X→A)→(X→A)) : Prop :=
    ∀ P Q, (ALL x:X, P x ⟺ Q x) ⊢ (ALL x:X, F P x ⟺ F Q x).

The ▷ later operator is itself contractive: ▷$(P \Leftrightarrow Q) \vdash \;$▷$P \Leftrightarrow$ ▷Q.
Proof: by derives_trans, later_fash1, fash_derives, later_and, later_impl.

A nonexpansive operator composed with a contractive operator is contractive. Any useful contractive operator is likely to be the composition of ▷ with nonexpansive operators. The operators andp (&&), imp (⟶), allp (ALL), exp (EX), sepcon (∗) are nonexpansive.

Figure 17.1 shows the rules for proving contractiveness. Each of these rules is proved as a lemma from the definition of contractiveness and the axioms about the various operators. To use the rules, first apply prove_HOcontractive, then the others follow in a goal-directed way.

THEOREM. F'_{lis} is contractive.
Proof. First apply prove_HOcontractive, yielding this proof goal:

P,Q : adr → mpred
x : adr
---(1/1)
ALL x0 : adr , ▷P x0 ⟺ ▷Q x0
⊢ !!(x = nil) && emp || !!(x <> nil) && (EX r : adr, next x r ∗ ▷P r) ⟹
    !!(x = nil) && emp || !!(x <> nil) && (EX r : adr, next x r ∗ ▷Q r)

Then the rest of the proof is deduced structurally from the form of the term:

Proof. unfold Flis'; apply prove_HOcontractive; intros.
    apply subp_orp.
        apply subp_refl.
        apply subp_andp.
        apply subp_refl.
            apply subp_exp; intro.
            apply subp_sepcon.
                apply subp_refl.
                apply allp_imp2_later_e1.
    Qed.

$$\text{prove\_HOcontractive} \frac{\forall P, Q.(\forall x. \ \triangleright Px \Leftrightarrow \triangleright Qx) \vdash FPy \Rrightarrow FQy}{\text{HOcontractive } F}$$

$$\text{subp\_refl} \frac{}{\Gamma \vdash P \Rrightarrow P} \qquad \text{subp\_imp} \frac{\Gamma \vdash P \Rrightarrow P' \qquad \Gamma \vdash Q \Rrightarrow Q'}{\Gamma \vdash (P \longrightarrow Q) \Rrightarrow (P' \longrightarrow Q')}$$

$$\text{subp\_top} \frac{}{\Gamma \vdash P \Rrightarrow \top} \qquad \text{subp\_andp} \frac{\Gamma \vdash P \Rrightarrow P' \qquad \Gamma \vdash Q \Rrightarrow Q'}{\Gamma \vdash (P \,\&\&\, Q) \Rrightarrow (P' \,\&\&\, Q')}$$

$$\text{subp\_bot} \frac{}{\Gamma \vdash P \Rrightarrow \bot} \qquad \text{subp\_orp} \frac{\Gamma \vdash P \Rrightarrow P' \qquad \Gamma \vdash Q \Rrightarrow Q'}{\Gamma \vdash (P \,\|\, Q) \Rrightarrow (P' \,\|\, Q')}$$

$$\text{subp\_subp} \frac{\Gamma \vdash P \Rrightarrow P' \qquad \Gamma \vdash Q \Rrightarrow Q'}{\Gamma \vdash (P \Rrightarrow Q) \Rrightarrow (P' \Rrightarrow Q')}$$

$$\text{subp\_sepcon} \frac{\Gamma \vdash P \Rrightarrow P' \qquad \Gamma \vdash Q \Rrightarrow Q'}{\Gamma \vdash (P * Q) \Rrightarrow (P' * Q')}$$

$$\text{subp\_allp} \frac{\forall x : B. \ \Gamma \vdash Px \Rrightarrow Qx}{\Gamma \vdash (\forall x.Px) \Rrightarrow (\forall x.Qx)} \qquad \text{subp\_allp} \frac{\forall x : B. \ \Gamma \vdash Px \Rrightarrow Qx}{\Gamma \vdash (\exists x.Px) \Rrightarrow (\exists x.Qx)}$$

$$\text{allp\_imp2\_later\_e1} \frac{}{(\forall x : B. \ \triangleright Px \Leftrightarrow \triangleright Qx) \vdash \ \triangleright Py \Rrightarrow \ \triangleright Qy}$$

$$\text{allp\_imp2\_later\_e2} \frac{}{(\forall x : B. \ \triangleright Px \Leftrightarrow \triangleright Qx) \vdash \ \triangleright Qy \Rrightarrow \ \triangleright Py}$$

Figure 17.1: Rules for proving contractiveness

In fact, it's so automatic that we put all the rules of Figure 17.1 into a **Hint** Resolve database "contractive," and solve such goals by auto 50 **with** contractive.

THE RECURSION OPERATOR HORec is our μ operator on higher-order predicates. In **??** we will describe its semantic definition, leading to the proof of the HORec_fold_unfold theorem.

Definition HORec {A}{NA: NatDed A}{IA: Indir A}{RA: RecIndir A}
{X: Type} (F: (X→A)→(X→A)) (x: X) : A := ...

Lemma HORec_fold_unfold{A}{NA: NatDed A}{IA: Indir A}{RA: RecIndir A} :
∀X F,   HOcontractive (X:=X) F   →   HORec F = F (HORec F).

THEOREM.

$$\text{HORec } (F'_{\text{lis}}) = F'_{\text{lis}} (\text{HORec } (F'_{\text{lis}}))$$
$$\text{HORec } (F'_{\text{tree}}) = F'_{\text{tree}} (\text{HORec } (F'_{\text{tree}}))$$
$$\text{HORec } (F'_{\text{funny}}) = F'_{\text{funny}} (\text{HORec } (F'_{\text{funny}}))$$

Proof. By HORec_fold_unfold, solving contractiveness by auto.

TO MAKE USE OF these equations, one must be able to accommodate the loss of accuracy implied by the ▷ operator. Define lis = HORec(F'_{lis}), and consider a typical situation such as this:

assert{p≠0 && lis(p)}
q := p→ next;
assert{p↦_ * lis(q)}

To prove this Hoare triple, we can unfold lis, then eliminate the disjunct that is inconsistent with $p \neq 0$:

assert{p≠0 && lis(p)}
assert{EX r:nat, p↦r * ▷ lis(r)}
assert{p↦r * ▷ lis(r)}

Next, using the frame rule and the load rule, we can fetch from p→ next. If the rule for load were simply

$$\{((p.next) \mapsto v * P)[v/q]\} \; q := p.next \; \{(p.next) \mapsto v * P\}$$

then we could prove

assert$\{p \mapsto r * \triangleright \, lis(r)\}$
q := p→ next;
assert$\{p \mapsto r * \triangleright \, lis(q)\}$

But this is not good enough: we have $\triangleright lis(q)$ (that is, $lis(q)$ holds to a weaker approximation) but we need the stronger fact $lis(q)$ demanded by the postcondition.

In fact, in a step-indexed separation logic, the Hoare triple for load is stronger:

$$\{((p.next) \mapsto v * \triangleright P)[v/q]\} \; q := p.next \; \{(p.next) \mapsto v * P\}$$

The difference is the $\triangleright$ operator: the precondition does not require that P hold *now*, it will suffice that it holds *soon*. If before executing the instruction we planned to execute no more than $k+1$ instructions, then $P[v/q]$ in the precondition means that $P[v/q]$ holds to accuracy $k+1$, while P in the postcondition means that P must hold to accuracy k. But accuracy $k+1$ is more than we need; after the instruction completes its step, only k steps remain for which we care about safety. Therefore it suffices that $P[v/q]$ holds with accuracy k, which we obtain by writing $\triangleright P[v/q]$. This Hoare triple is stronger because its precondition is slighly weaker, and it is typical of the style used in indirection theory.

For those many steps in a separation-logic proof that do not involve the unfolding of recursive types,v one can use the usual rule for load, with precondition $((p.f) \mapsto v * P)[v/q]$. This can be derived as a corollary, since $P \vdash \triangleright P$.

HERE WE HAVE PRESENTED magical rules involving the $\triangleright$ *later* operator, and justified them with just-so stories about coffee breaks. Somehow the Hoare triple $\{P\} \, c \, \{Q\}$ must apply P to a world at approximation-level $k+1$ but apply Q to a world at level k. Later, Part V will illustrate how this can be done.

Chapter 18

Case study: Separation logic with first-class functions

In a conventional separation logic we have a "maps-to" operator $a \mapsto b$ saying that the heap contains (exactly) one cell at address a containing value b. This operator in the separation logic corresponds to the load and store operators of the operational semantics.

Now consider two more operators of an operational semantics: function call and function definition. When function names are static and global, we can simply have a global table relating functions to their specifications—where a specification gives the function's precondition and postcondition. But when the address of a function can be kept in a variable, we want *local* specifications of function-pointer variables, and ideally these local specifications should be as modular as the rest of our separation logic. For example, they should satisfy the frame rule. That is, we might like to write assertions such as $(a \mapsto b) * (f : \{P\}\{Q\})$ meaning that a is a memory location containing value b, and a different address f is a function with precondition P and postcondition Q. Furthermore, the separation $*$ guarantees that storing to a will not overwrite the body of f.

To illustrate these ideas in practice, we will consider a tiny programming language called *Cont*.[1] The functions in this language take parameters

---

[1]This chapter describes the Coq development in examples/cont. The file

$f(x, y, z)$ but they do not return; thus, they are *continuations*.

adr	$v ::= 0, 1, 2, \ldots$
offset	$\delta ::= 0, 1, 2, \ldots$
var	$x, y, z, \ldots$

expr	$e ::= v$
	$\mid\ x$
	$\mid\ e + \delta$
	$\mid\ [e]$

control	$c ::= e_1 := e_2;\ c$
	$\mid$ If e Then c_1 Else c_2
	$\mid$ Go $e\ (e_0, \ldots, e_{n-1})$

Definition adr := nat.
Definition var := nat.

Inductive expr :=
 | Const: adr $\rightarrow$ expr
 | Var: var $\rightarrow$ expr
 | Offset: expr $\rightarrow$ nat $\rightarrow$ expr
 | Mem: expr $\rightarrow$ expr.

Inductive control :=
 | Assign:expr$\rightarrow$ expr$\rightarrow$ control
     $\rightarrow$ control
 | If: expr $\rightarrow$ control $\rightarrow$ control
     $\rightarrow$ control
 | Go: expr $\rightarrow$ list expr $\rightarrow$ control.

OPERATIONAL SEMANTICS. The small-step semantics operates on states comprised of (locals $\times$ heap $\times$ control), where:

locals is the local-variable environment mapping variables to addresses; we use tables exactly as in Chapter 9.

heap is a function from adr to option adr. We do not use tables because we do not want any restriction to a finite domain.

control is the "program counter," the command type shown above.

We will use big-step evaluation for expressions and small-step evaluation for commands. Expression evaluation is written $s, h \vdash_E e \Downarrow v$ in mathematical notation, expr_get $s\ h\ e$ = Some v in Coq. It evaluates expression e with locals s and heap h according to these rules:

examples/cont/language.v gives the syntax and operational semantics shown here.

$$\frac{}{s,h \vdash_E n \Downarrow n} \qquad \frac{s(x) = \text{Some}\, v}{s,h \vdash_E x \Downarrow s(v)} \qquad \frac{s,h \vdash_E e \Downarrow v}{s,h \vdash_E e + \delta \Downarrow v + \delta}$$

$$\frac{s,h \vdash_E e \Downarrow v \qquad h(v) = \text{Some}\, v'}{s,h \vdash_E [e] \Downarrow v'}$$

The function $\text{step}\, p\, \sigma = \text{Some}\, \sigma'$ implements the small-step relation $\sigma \xrightarrow{p} \sigma'$ for a program p, according to these rules:

$$\frac{s,h \vdash_E e \Downarrow v}{\langle s,h,(x := e;c)\rangle \xrightarrow{p} \langle s[x := v],h,c\rangle}$$

$$\frac{s,h \vdash_E e \Downarrow v \qquad s,h \vdash_E e' \Downarrow v'}{\langle s,h,([e] := e';c)\rangle \xrightarrow{p} \langle s,h[v := v'],c\rangle}$$

$$\frac{s,h \vdash_E e \Downarrow v \qquad v \neq 0}{\langle s,h, \text{If}\, e\, \text{Then}\, c_1\, \text{Else}\, c_2\rangle \xrightarrow{p} \langle s,h,c_1\rangle}$$

$$\frac{s,h \vdash_E e \Downarrow v \qquad v = 0}{\langle s,h, \text{If}\, e\, \text{Then}\, c_1\, \text{Else}\, c_2\rangle \xrightarrow{p} \langle s,h,c_2\rangle}$$

$$\frac{s,h \vdash_E e \Downarrow v \qquad p(v) = \text{Some}\, (\vec{x},c) \qquad s,h \vdash_E e_i \Downarrow v_i}{\langle s,h, \text{Go}\, e\, (e_0,\ldots,e_{n-1})\rangle \xrightarrow{p} \langle [(x_0,v_0),\ldots,(x_{n-1},v_{n-1})],h,c\rangle}$$

We will define multi-step execution as a **Fixpoint** rather than by **Inductive** so that Coq can evaluate programs by Compute. The function stepN runs program p for n steps: $\sigma \xrightarrow{p}^n \sigma'$.

Fixpoint stepN (p: program) (σ: state) (n: nat) : option state :=
  match n **with** O $\Rightarrow$ Some σ
  | S n' $\Rightarrow$ **match** step p σ **with** Some σ' $\Rightarrow$ stepN p σ' n'
  | _$\Rightarrow$ None **end**
  end.

OUR GOAL IS TO USE SEPARATION LOGIC TO PROVE SAFETY.[2] The small-step relation $\xrightarrow{p}$ gets *stuck* if it dereferences an unallocated memory location, if it assigns to an expression (e.g., Const 2) that is not an *l*-value, or if it jumps to an address that is not a function. A program is *safe* if it never gets stuck. To keep this case study simple, we say the only safe programs are those that infinite-loop.

A PROGRAM p IS A TABLE MAPPING ADDRESSES TO COMMANDS, for example,

Let a : var := 0. Let s : var := 1. Let p : var := 2. Let r : var := 3.
Let START : adr := 0. Let LOOP : adr := 1. Let DONE : adr := 2.

Definition myprog : program :=
  (START, ([a],
          Do Mem a := a .+ 1;
          Do Mem (a .+ 1) := a .+ 2;
          Do Mem (a .+ 2) := Const 0;
          Go LOOP ((a.+3)::(Var a)::(Var a)::(Const DONE)::nil)))
:: (LOOP, ([a,s,p,r],
          If p
          Then (Do p := Mem p;
                Go LOOP (Var a::Var s::Var p::Var r::nil))
          Else Go r (Var a::Var s::nil)))
:: (DONE, ([a,s],
          Go DONE (Var a::Var s::nil)))
:: nil.

This program can be written informally as,

START(a): [a]:= a+1; [a+1]:=a+2; [a+2]:=0; LOOP(a+3,a,a,DONE)
LOOP(a,s,p,r): if p≠0 then (p:=[p]; LOOP(a,s,p,r)) else r(a,s)
DONE(a,s): DONE(a,s)

Programs are executed from START (address 0) with an (infinite) initial heap starting at address a, and a variable environment (locals) containing

---

[2]And thereby correctness; see the discussion on page 30.

just the variable a. That is, a points to the beginning of a pool of heap cells from which the program can allocate memory; we write the assertion allocpool(a). Therefore, at entry to the START function, the assertion at left describes the initial heap at right:

allocpool(a)

The hatched region /////////// covers the range of addresses where the program resides; that is, the addresses START, LOOP, DONE are between 0 and a. After the first three store instructions of the START function, we have,

$a \rightsquigarrow 0 * \text{allocpool}(a + 3)$

where $a \rightsquigarrow 0$ means a list segment starting at address a and terminated by a null-pointer 0. At the first entry to LOOP we have

$s \rightsquigarrow p * p \rightsquigarrow 0 * \text{allocpool}(a) \ \wedge$
$r : \{[a,s]. \ s \rightsquigarrow 0 * \text{allocpool}(a)\}$

where there is an (empty) list segment $s \rightsquigarrow p$, a length-3 list $p \rightsquigarrow 0$, and an allocpool. The predicate $r : \{\ldots\}$ means that r is a function-pointer with the given specification.

On the second entry to LOOP we have

(same invariant)

but here $s \rightsquigarrow p$ is a nonempty list segment, the list $p \rightsquigarrow 0$ has length 2.

THIS IS A LANGUAGE OF *continuations,* not functions: the Go command is a kind of *jump-with-arguments* that passes actual parameters to the function's formal parameters. Therefore, Go LOOP [a.+3, Var a, Var a, Const DONE] enters the function LOOP with $a = a' + 3$, $s = a'$, $p = a'$, $r = \text{DONE}$, where a' means the value of a in the caller.

We use continuations in this case study to simplify the presentation, but of course many real languages (such as C) are direct-style languages, meaning that their functions actually return to the caller. The techniques we describe here do scale up to full-featured languages with not only function-call but function-return.[3]

Notice that the LOOP function "returns" by calling its parameter r, which is a function-pointer passed to it by START. We want to reason about function-pointers in our higher-order separation logic.

SEPARATION LOGIC FOR THE CONTINUATION LANGUAGE. We write $x \mapsto y$ as usual for a storage cell. We write allocpool(x) to mean that x is the beginning of an infinite region of cells all containing 0. When a program wants to allocate a cell of memory, it can use the equation

Lemma alloc: $\text{allocpool}(a) = a \mapsto 0 * \text{allocpool}(a + 1)$

We write lseg $x\, y$ (or notation $x \leadsto y$) to mean the list segment starting at address x and whose last tail-pointer is y (with $y \neq x$); if $x = y$ then the segment is empty.

We will write $f : \{S\}$ to mean that f is a (pointer to a) function with function-specification (funspec) S. In general, a funspec takes the form $\vec{x}.P$ where $\vec{x}$ are formal-parameter names and P is a precondition that may refer to the x_i. For example, $f : \{[a, s, p].\ \text{allocpool}(a) * s \leadsto p * p \leadsto 0\}$ means that we can call f safely, provided that we pass parameters (a, s, p) that satisfy the given memory layout. In Coq notation we write $\text{cont}\, S\, f$ for $f : \{S\}$.

The assertion call $S\, (\vec{e})$ means that if the arguments $\vec{e}$ were substituted for the formal parameters of S, then the predicate of S would be satisfied.

In this language there are no postconditions (because functions do not return), so instead of a Hoare triple we have a Hoare double: $\{P\}c$ means that P is an appropriate precondition for the safety of command c.

Our little START/LOOP/DONE program can be specified as follows

---

[3]Chlipala [33] argues that the Hoare logic of continuations can be better than direct-style functions not only for simplicity of presentation in a toy example, but for real software engineering.

(examples/cont/seplogic.v):

$$\begin{array}{rll}
\text{START}: & [a]. & \text{allocpool}(a)\\
\text{LOOP}: & [a,s,p,r]. & s{\rightsquigarrow}p * p{\rightsquigarrow}0 * \text{allocpool}(a) \;\wedge\\
& & r:\{[a,s].\ s{\rightsquigarrow}0 * \text{allocpool}(a)\}\\
\text{DONE}: & [a,s]. & s{\rightsquigarrow}0 * \text{allocpool}(a)\}
\end{array}$$

That is, a *program specification* (funspecs) is a table mapping addresses to funspec, so we can write the specification of this program in Coq as,

Definition assert := env $\rightarrow$ mpred.
Definition funspec := list var $\times$ assert.
Definition funspecs := table adr funspec.

Definition STARTspec : funspec := (a::nil,
　　fun ρ $\Rightarrow$ allocpool (eval (Var a) ρ)).
Definition DONEspec: funspec := (a::s::nil,
　　fun ρ $\Rightarrow$ lseg (eval (Var s) ρ) (eval (Const 0) ρ)
　　　　* allocpool (eval (Var a) ρ)).
Definition LOOPspec: funspec := (a::s::p::r::nil,
　　fun ρ $\Rightarrow$ lseg (eval (Var s) ρ) (eval (Var p) ρ)
　　　　* lseg (eval (Var p) ρ) (eval (Const 0) ρ)
　　　　* allocpool (eval (Var a) ρ)
　　&& cont DONEspec (eval (Var r) ρ)).
Definition myspec :=
　(START,STARTspec)::((LOOP,LOOPspec)::(DONE,DONEspec)::nil).

Here we see that assertions are really functions from variable-environments (env) to predicates on abstract heaps (mpred). Thus, in recent pages where we write assertions such as $s{\rightsquigarrow}0 * \text{allocpool}(a)$ we are cheating: we should write $\lambda\rho.\ \rho s{\rightsquigarrow}0 * \text{allocpool}(\rho a)$. In general, when an assertion contains an open expression e (that is, e has free program variables), we should write $[\![e]\!]_\rho$ (or in Coq, eval e ρ).

TYPE SYSTEM. Separation logic is most convenient when applied to well-typed programs, otherwise there are many trivial but annoying proof obligations to make sure that each variable has a defined value. In an informal Hoare logic we write rules such as the assignment rule: $\{P[e/x]\}\, x := e\, \{P\}$ but this implicitly assumes that e actually has a value, actually evaluates without getting stuck. How do we know that?

In real programming languages e might fail to evaluate for a variety of reasons: expression ill-typed, uninitialized variable, divide by zero, and so on. In some languages a *type system* can rule out many of these failures, for well-typed programs.

In the Cont language, the only expression failures come from the use of uninitialized variables, that is, variables that are not in the formal-parameter list. We will use something resembling a type system for the simple task of keeping track of initialized variables. A *type environment* Δ is just a set of variable-names. The judgment $\Delta \vdash_{exp} e$, written expcheck Δ e in Coq, means that every variable in expression e is in Δ.

The judgment $\Delta \vdash_{type} c$, written typecheck Δ c, means that every expression in c is well-typed, given that assignments within c can add more variables to Δ.

$$\frac{}{\Delta \vdash_{exp} \text{Const } v} \qquad \frac{x \in \Delta}{\Delta \vdash_{exp} x} \qquad \frac{\Delta \vdash_{exp} e}{\Delta \vdash_{exp} e + \delta}$$

$$\frac{\Delta \vdash_{exp} e \qquad x, \Delta \vdash_{type} c}{\Delta \vdash_{type} x := e;\ c}$$

$$\frac{\Delta \vdash_{exp} e \qquad x, \Delta \vdash_{type} c}{\Delta \vdash_{type} x := [e];\ c} \qquad \frac{\Delta \vdash_{exp} e_1 \qquad \Delta \vdash_{exp} e_2 \qquad \Delta \vdash_{type} c}{\Delta \vdash_{type} [e_1] := e_2;\ c}$$

$$\frac{\Delta \vdash_{exp} e \qquad \Delta \vdash_{type} c_1 \qquad \Delta \vdash_{type} c_2}{\Delta \vdash_{type} \text{If } e \text{ Then } c_1 \text{ Else } c_2} \qquad \frac{\Delta \vdash_{exp} e \qquad \forall i.\ \Delta \vdash_{exp} e_i}{\Delta \vdash_{type} \text{Go } e\ (e_0, \ldots, e_{n-1})}$$

There is no $\vdash_{exp}$ rule for memory-load expressions $[e]$ because these should not occur in general contexts; *only* as the entire right-hand side of an assignment, which is really a special case (in separation logic) for a *load* instruction, not an ordinary *assign*.

These rules are implemented as **Fixpoint**s in Coq, so that typechecking can be done efficiently by Compute.

AXIOMATIC SEMANTICS. Figure 18.1 shows the separation logic proof rules for the commands of our language. With these rules, along with auxiliary lemmas about separation logic, one can prove things about the bodies of functions. But we also need rules for function definitions, i.e. to prove that a function's body matches its specification.

$$\text{semax\_go} \frac{\Delta \vdash_{\text{type}} \text{Go } e \ (e_0, \dots, e_{n-1})}{\Delta; \Gamma \vdash \{e : \{S\} \wedge \text{call } S \ (e_0, \dots, e_{n-1})\} \text{ Go } e \ (e_0, \dots, e_{n-1})}$$

$$\text{semax\_assign} \frac{\Delta \vdash_{\text{type}} y \qquad x, \Delta; \Gamma \vdash \{P\} c}{\Delta; \Gamma \vdash \{\triangleright P[y/x]\} \ x := y; c}$$

$$\text{semax\_if} \frac{\Delta \vdash_{\text{type}} e \qquad \Delta; \Gamma \vdash \{e \neq 0 \wedge P\} c_1 \qquad \Delta; \Gamma \vdash \{e = 0 \wedge P\} c_2}{\Delta; \Gamma \vdash \{P\} \text{If } e \text{ Then } c_1 \text{ Else } c_2}$$

$$\text{semax\_load} \frac{\Delta \vdash_{\text{type}} e_1 \qquad x, \Delta; \Gamma \vdash \{P\} c}{\Delta; \Gamma \vdash \{(e_1 \mapsto e_2 * \text{T}) \wedge \triangleright P[e_2/x]\} \ x := [e_1]; c}$$

$$\text{semax\_store} \frac{\Delta \vdash_{\text{type}} e_1 \qquad \Delta \vdash_{\text{type}} e_2 \qquad \Delta; \Gamma \vdash \{e_1 \mapsto e_2 * P\} c}{\Delta; \Gamma \vdash \{e_1 \mapsto e_3 * P\} [e_1] := e_2; c}$$

$$\text{semax\_pre} \frac{\forall \rho. \ P \rho \vdash P' \rho \qquad \Delta; \Gamma \vdash \{P'\} c}{\Delta; \Gamma \vdash \{P\} c}$$

$$\text{semax\_G} \frac{\Delta; \Gamma \vdash \{P \wedge \text{funassert}(\Gamma)\} c}{\Delta; \Gamma \vdash \{P\} c}$$

Figure 18.1: Separation logic rules for the continuation language.

Recall that a function specification is an ordered pair $\langle f, S \rangle$ where f

is an address and $S = \vec{x}.P$ is a precondition for executing the code at address f. A program specification, funspecs, is a list of these pairs. Since a program is also a list of ordered pairs (address, function-body), then we can match a program to its specification using the judgment,

semax_func: funspecs $\rightarrow$ program $\rightarrow$ funspecs $\rightarrow$ Prop

The meaning of semax_func Γ p Γ', written $\Gamma \vdash_{\text{func}} p : \Gamma'$, is that each function-body in the list p satisfies the corresponding specification in the list Γ'. In proving each such function-body, we may find calls to other functions. To prove things about such calls, we may assume Γ.

Suppose the program p contains recursive or mutually recursive functions f and g. During the proof of $\Gamma' = f : \{S_f\}, g : \{S_g\}$ (that is, while proving the function body of f or g), we will need to assume $\Gamma = f : \{S_f\}, g : \{S_g\}$ (so that we can reason about calls to f or g). It seems that we are assuming Γ in order to prove Γ, which appears circular. But in fact it is sound; as Chapter 39 explains, there is a $\triangleright$ later operator applied to Γ in the semantic definition of semax_func Γ p Γ'. Therefore, in proving Γ' at approximation level $k + 1$, we assume Γ only at level k. In the semantic soundness proof of the higher-order separation logic, we use the *Löb rule* to tie the knot:

$$\text{loeb} \frac{\triangleright \Gamma \vdash \Gamma}{\vdash \Gamma}$$

If this is only approximately clear now, it will become more clear $\triangleright$ later.

BORROWING FROM Γ. The rule semax_G allows any function-specification in Γ to be copied into the precondition of c. The operator funassert converts $\Gamma = (f_1, S_1) :: (f_2, S_2) :: \ldots (f_n, S_n) :: \text{nil}$ to the assertion $f_1 : \{S_1\} \wedge f_2 : \{S_2\} \wedge \ldots \wedge f_n : \{S_n\}$. That is,

$$\text{funassert\_e} \frac{\Gamma(f) = S}{\text{funassert}\,\Gamma \vdash f : \{S\}} \qquad \text{semax\_G} \frac{\Delta; \Gamma \vdash \{P \wedge \text{funassert}\,\Gamma\}c}{\Delta; \Gamma \vdash \{P\}c}$$

These rules can be used in two ways: for a direct call to a global function f, with $\Gamma(f) = S$, we use semax_G immediately before semax_go to establish the precondition conjunct $e : \{S\}$. Or, if we wish to move a function-address into a function-pointer variable, we can write the assignment $x := $ Const f and use semax_G with semax_assign.

Predicates in the heap. What does it mean for a heap to "contain" a function-assertion? Clearly, if we can write $h \models x_0 : \{P_0\} * y \mapsto z$ that means $h = h_1 \oplus h_2$ where $h_1 \models x_0 : \{P_0\}$ and $h_2 \models y \mapsto z$. Therefore h_2 "contains" functions. But suppose the integer z encodes a machine-instruction that (safely) infinite-loops. Then y is a function too; it would be safe to jump to address y. In a sense, perhaps h_2 contains functions. But it does not contain function-assertions, of the form $x : \{P\}$.

The picture has a hatched region

in which there are no storable cells. In fact, we will employ the fiction that in the hatched region, at certain addresses, there are function-assertions:

In effect, the fiction $\circledP\!/\!/$ stands for the memory occupied by the machine-code for some function whose precondition is P_0. But our fictional heap does not actually contain the function-body, just the function-assertion about the *specification* of the function-body. We call this "predicates in the heap," and it is useful not only for function-pointers but also for the resource invariants of lock-pointers in concurrent separation logic.

Pure assertions. In separation logic, some assertions such as $x = y$ are *pure*, in that they don't claim a heap footprint. Pure assertions separate from themselves: $(x = y) * (x = y) \leftrightarrow (x = y)$. Heap assertions such as $x \mapsto y$ do claim a heap footprint, and do not self-separate: $x \mapsto y * x \mapsto y \vdash \bot$.

In this separation logic case study, we will treat function-assertions $f : \{S\}$ as pure. It is as if the function-specifications $\circledP\!/\!/$ are immutable, and cannot (must not) be modified by *store* commands to those addresses.

The opposite design choice—in which $f : \{S\}$ has the footprint f—can also be modeled easily in our framework, and may have application with systems that do run-time code generation of new functions. But the resulting separation logic is more cumbersome in reasoning about function pointers.

The rules for the $\vdash_{\text{func}}$ judgment are,

$$\text{semax\_func\_nil} \frac{}{\Gamma \vdash_{\text{func}} \text{nil} : \text{nil}}$$

$$\text{semax\_func\_cons} \frac{x \notin \text{map fst } \vec{F} \qquad \text{no\_dups}(\vec{y}) \qquad |\vec{y}| = |\text{formals}(S)| \\ \vec{y}; \Gamma \vdash \{\text{call } S \ \vec{y}\} c \qquad \Gamma \vdash_{\text{func}} \vec{F} : \Gamma'}{\Gamma \vdash_{\text{func}} \langle x, \vec{y}.c \rangle :: \vec{F} \ : \ \langle x, S \rangle :: \Gamma'}$$

The point of semax_func_cons is that if the *first* function-body meets its specification ($\vec{y}; \Gamma \vdash \{\text{call } S \ \vec{y}\} c$), and all the *rest* of the function bodies satisfy their specifications ($\Gamma \vdash_{\text{func}} \vec{F} : \Gamma'$), then $\vdash_{\text{func}}$ is satisfied; in addition there are three little items of syntactic bookkeeping (e.g., the list $\vec{y}$ of formal parameters should have no duplicates, the list of function-names should have no duplicates).

We consider a whole program p is *proved* when

$$\exists \Gamma. \ \ \Gamma \vdash_{\text{func}} p : \Gamma \ \wedge \ \Gamma(0) = ([a]. \ \text{allocpool}(a))$$

That is, there is some Γ such that all of the functions in p meet their specifications in Γ, and the specification of the function at address 0 matches the actual initial conditions for running programs in this language.

We have presented the Cont language, a program start/loop/done in the language, and a separation logic for the language. Chapters 19–20 show how to specify the list-segment data structures used in this program, then how to apply the separation-logic rules to prove the program correct. Later, in Chapter 39 we show *soundness*—that if program p is proved in the separation logic, then it is safe in the operational semantics.

Chapter 19

Data structures in indirection theory

Separation logic's *raison d'être* is to allow Hoare-logic proofs of programs with pointer and array data structures. Lists, list segments, trees, and arrays are the bread and butter of separation logic. In Chapter 3 we showed the proof of a program using lists and list-segments.

The list-segment operator $x \rightsquigarrow y$ is intended to satisfy an equation like,

$$x \rightsquigarrow y \quad \sim \quad x = y \land \mathsf{emp} \lor x \neq y \land \exists t.\ \mathsf{next}\, x\, t * t \rightsquigarrow y$$

That is, a list segment is either empty, or it is a list cell $\mathsf{next}\, x\, t$ separated from another list segment $t \rightsquigarrow y$.

In Chapter 10 we showed how to use the covariant fixpoint operator to define such recursive data-type predicates; then in Chapter 17 we showed a more powerful recursion operator that can "tie the knot" of mutually recursive function definitions and (as we will see in Chapters 36 and 18) specify function-pointers.

When working in an indirection-theory separation logic, for ordinary first-order data structures such as lists and trees we can use either of these recursion operators, the covariant corec or the higher-order HOrec. Which one *should* we use?

The answer is, it depends. For purely first-order structures, corec is entirely adequate and has simple induction principles. When contravariance appears (recursion through function parameters or mutex-lock resource invariants), one must use HOrec. If there will be a mix of first-order and contravariant data structures, it may be convenient to use the same HOrec recursion operator everywhere.

In this chapter we illustrate the use of HOrec to define simple list-segment shape predicates.[1] The same techniques generalize to list-segment *representation* predicates (such as listrep, page 20), trees, tree segments, and so on.

Although the *definition* of $\rightsquigarrow$ is recursive, Berdine and Calcagno designed a complete and terminating proof theory for list segments that avoids recursion or induction in proofs about programs [72, §4.4][17]. This theory was later reformulated in the as a *resolution* system by Navarro Perez and Rybalchenko [69], as we will discuss in Chapters 46 and especially 47. To model one of these proof theories, one needs the following identities (names given by Navarro Perez):

$$
\begin{array}{ll}
\text{N2}: & x \rightsquigarrow x \ \vdash \ \text{emp} \\
\text{N4}: & \text{emp} \ \vdash \ x \rightsquigarrow x
\end{array}
$$

$$
\begin{array}{ll}
\text{W1}: & \text{next}\,0\,y \ \vdash \ \bot \\
\text{W2}: & 0 \rightsquigarrow y \ \vdash \ y = 0 \\
\text{W3}: & \text{next}\,x\,y * \text{next}\,x\,z \ \vdash \ \bot \\
\text{W4}: & \text{next}\,x\,y * x \rightsquigarrow z \ \vdash \ x = z \\
\text{W5}: & x \rightsquigarrow y * x \rightsquigarrow z \ \vdash \ x = y \lor x = z
\end{array}
$$

$$
\begin{array}{ll}
\text{U1}: & \text{next}\,x\,z \ \longleftrightarrow \ x = z \lor x \rightsquigarrow z \\
\text{U2}: & \exists y.\text{next}\,x\,y * y \rightsquigarrow z \ \longleftrightarrow \ x = z \lor x \rightsquigarrow z \\
\text{U3}: & \exists y.x \rightsquigarrow y * y \rightsquigarrow 0 \ \longleftrightarrow \ x \rightsquigarrow 0 \\
\text{U4}: & \exists y.x \rightsquigarrow y * y \rightsquigarrow z * \text{next}\,z\,w \ \longleftrightarrow \ x \rightsquigarrow z * \text{next}\,z\,w \\
\text{U5}: & \exists y.x \rightsquigarrow y * y \rightsquigarrow z * z \rightsquigarrow w \ \longleftrightarrow \ z = w \lor x \rightsquigarrow z * z \rightsquigarrow w
\end{array}
$$

The significance of this is that the *only* proofs that require unfolding the recursive definition—whether it is covariant recursion as explained in Chapter 17 or indirection theory as we will explain here—are the proofs of these identities.

---

[1] See the file examples/cont/lseg.v for everything discussed in this chapter.

RECURSIVE DEFINITIONS IN INDIRECTION THEORY. Unlike corec(F) which requires that F be covariant, the step-indexed HOrec(F) requires that F be *contractive*. That is, $F(R)$ must be a predicate that applies only $\triangleright R$, a weaker predicate than R. We can define $\rightsquigarrow$ with a contractive functional as follows:

$$\mathsf{lseg} \;=\; \mathsf{HOrec}(\lambda R.\, \lambda(x, y).\; x = y \land \mathsf{emp} \;\lor\; x \neq y \land \exists t.\; x \mapsto t * \triangleright R(t, y))$$

From this definition we can prove the appropriate unfolding lemma:

Lemma lseg_unfold: $\forall x\ y,$
$$x \rightsquigarrow y \;\;=\;\; x = y \land \mathsf{emp} \;\lor\; x \neq y \land \exists t.\; x * \triangleright t \rightsquigarrow y.$$
Proof.
  intros. unfold lseg at 1. rewrite HORec_fold_unfold. reflexivity.
  auto 50 **with** contractive.
Qed.

The proof just uses HORec_fold_unfold, which requires proving contractiveness of $(\lambda R.\lambda(x, y)\ldots)$. But the MSL library provides lemmas for proving contractiveness that work using **Hint** Resolve to do this automatically, by auto 50 **with** contractive.

IN A REAL PROGRAM WITH TWO-WORD *cons* CELLS, we might expect that next $x\, t = x \mapsto \_ * x + 1 \mapsto t$. But in this chapter we will use one-word list cells comprising only a tail-pointer, i.e., $p{\rightarrow}\boxed{}{\rightarrow}\boxed{}{\rightarrow}\boxed{s}$ is a list segment $p \rightsquigarrow s$. Thus, next $x\, t = x \mapsto t$.

From lseg_unfold we can prove standard facts about list segments, including all the Berdine/Calcagno rules, and a rewriting rule that generalizes N2/N4:

$$\mathsf{lseg\_eq} :\; x \rightsquigarrow x = \mathsf{emp}$$

Let us examine the U4 identity. Why is it so complex, and in particular why does it require next $z\, w$ on both sides? Surely it would be nicer to have simpler rules such as, $x \rightsquigarrow y * y \mapsto z \vdash x \rightsquigarrow z$. But unfortunately this simpler rule is unsound. *Precise* list segments (such as ours here) must be acyclic. The unsound rule would allow a proof of $p \rightsquigarrow s$ in this case where $p = s$: $p \rightarrow \boxed{} \rightarrow \boxed{} \rightarrow \boxed{s}$. We cannot fix the problem by writing $x \neq z \wedge x \rightsquigarrow y * y \mapsto z \vdash x \rightsquigarrow z$, as this is unsound as well; consider this example: $x \rightarrow \boxed{} \rightarrow \boxed{y} \rightarrow \boxed{z}$.

We must ensure that z points nowhere within the segment $x \rightsquigarrow y$. One way to do that is to ensure that z conflicts with every cell within the segment. By writing $z \mapsto v$ we ensure this; but note that $z \mapsto v$ is part of the *frame*, not part of the segment $x \rightsquigarrow z$ that we are constructing. To make a sound cons-at-end rule we write $x \rightsquigarrow y * y \mapsto z * z \mapsto v \vdash x \rightsquigarrow z * z \mapsto v$.

IN A CONVENTIONAL COVARIANT-RECURSION SYSTEM our cons-at-end rule is proved by induction on the *structure* of the list segment $x \rightsquigarrow y$. But in an indirection-theory system we cannot assume that the entire list structure is traversable at a given age. That is, if a world at level n can represent the first n cells of a list segment, and beyond that the successive ▷ later operators mean that the lseg predicate makes no claim about the contents of the world.

Thus, the induction must be over the *age* of the world. The induction principle is the Löb rule:

$$\text{loeb} \frac{\triangleright P \vdash P}{\vdash P}$$

In this case, the magic induction hypothesis P is,

$$\forall x.\ (x \rightsquigarrow y * y \mapsto z) \wedge ((z \mapsto v) \multimap \top) \ \Rrightarrow\ x \rightsquigarrow z$$

where $\Rrightarrow$ is the subtype operator defined in Chapter 16. Recall that $Q \Rrightarrow R$ means, "in all worlds of the current age (and later), if Q holds on that world then so does R."

As we do the induction, we will be considering shorter segments each time, with every segment terminating in $y \mapsto z$. Thus, x varies but y and z do not, so we quantify over $\forall x$ but we may leave y and z fixed.

One might think that the hypothesis

$$\forall x.\ (x \rightsquigarrow y * y \mapsto z * z \mapsto v) \ \Rrightarrow\ x \rightsquigarrow z * z \mapsto v$$

could be used, but this runs into technical difficulties with the ⊳ later operator on $z \mapsto v$. The induction works best when the footprint is confined to $x \leadsto z$. The purpose of the conjunct $(z \mapsto v) \multimap \top$ is to guarantee that z is not anywhere in the footprint of $x \leadsto y * y \mapsto z$. The *existential magic wand* $\multimap$ is defined by,

$$ w \models P \multimap Q \;=\; \exists w_1, w_2.\; w_1 \oplus w = w_2 \land w_1 \models P \land w_2 \models Q $$

so therefore $(z \mapsto v) \multimap \top$ means "the current heap w separates from some heap w_1 in which $(z \mapsto v)$.

Applying the Löb rule, we have two proof obligations,

$$ (1) \quad \begin{array}{l} \triangleright \forall x.\; (x \leadsto y * y \mapsto z) \land ((z \mapsto v) \multimap \top) \Rrightarrow x \leadsto z \\ \vdash \quad \forall x.\; (x \leadsto y * y \mapsto z) \land ((z \mapsto v) \multimap \top) \Rrightarrow x \leadsto z \end{array} $$

which is the premise of loeb, and

$$ (2) \quad \frac{\forall x.\; (x \leadsto y * y \mapsto z) \land ((z \mapsto v) \multimap \top) \Rrightarrow x \leadsto z}{x \leadsto y * y \mapsto z * z \mapsto v \vdash x \leadsto z * z \mapsto v} $$

which takes the conclusion of loeb and proves the main result. Lemma (2) is straightforward—it is just an instantiation of the existential and the subtype (with a little bit of magic-wand hacking). Lemma (1) is not very difficult, but the current proof is rather ugly and it would be helpful to have a better set of separation-logic lemmas for manipulating and instantiating subtypes and (existential) magic wands. See Lemma lseg_cons_in_next_context in examples/cont/lseg.v.

In indirection theory, the identities U1–U5 must be written with ⊳later operators in appropriate places:

$$
\begin{array}{ll}
\text{U1}_{\triangleright}: & \text{next}\, x\, z \;\leftrightarrow\; x = z \lor x \leadsto z \\
\text{U2}_{\triangleright}: & \exists y.\text{next}\, x\, y * \triangleright y \leadsto z \;\leftrightarrow\; x = z \lor x \leadsto z \\
\text{U3}_{\triangleright}: & \exists y. x \leadsto y * \triangleright y \leadsto 0 \;\leftrightarrow\; x \leadsto 0 \\
\text{U4}_{\triangleright}: & \exists y. x \leadsto y * \triangleright y \leadsto z * \text{next}\, z\, w \;\leftrightarrow\; x \leadsto z * \text{next}\, z\, w \\
\text{U5}_{\triangleright}: & \exists y. x \leadsto y * \triangleright y \leadsto z * z \leadsto w \;\leftrightarrow\; z = w \lor x \leadsto z * z \leadsto w
\end{array}
$$

It should still be possible to use these identities as the basis of a decidable proof theory, but the experiment has not been tried. But we have these identities quite successfully in correctness proofs of C programs that manipulate lists.

When reasoning about functional correctness, not just shape, we want a list-segment relation of the form $x \overset{\sigma}{\rightsquigarrow} y$, meaning that the list segment from x to y represents the sequence of values σ. That is, we want a *representation relation*, not just a *shape predicate*. It is easy to define representation relations for recursive data types such as list segments and trees, either using covariant fixpoints or in indirection theory, using the same basic methods that we use for shape predicates. One can then prove identities analogous to N2, N4, W1–W5, U1–U5 for the representation relation.

However, these will not lead to a decidable proof theory (as they do for shape predicates). What makes the proof theory of list-segment shape predicates decidable is that, in a rule such as U2, the truth of a formula is quite indifferent to the length of the segment $y \rightsquigarrow z$. [17] But when we write a representation relation $y \overset{\sigma}{\rightsquigarrow} z$, of course the length of $y \rightsquigarrow z$ must match the length of σ. Thus, when proving the functional correctness of programs, we cannot entirely rely on decidable proof systems. This should come as no surprise to anyone since Turing.

Tree shapes and tree representations are easily definable, either using covariant fixpoints or in indirection theory. A *tree shape predicate* would satisfy the identity

$$\mathsf{tree}(p) = (p = 0 \wedge \mathsf{emp}) \vee \exists l, r. \ p \mapsto \_ * p + 1 \mapsto l * p + 2 \mapsto r * \mathsf{tree}(l) * \mathsf{tree}(r)$$

and a *tree representation relation* would take an extra argument τ saying what mathematical tree is represented. The tree shape shown here represents an entire tree, not a "tree segment."

We use list segments to reason about programs that cut and splice fragments of linked lists. For programs that cut and splice trees, obviously we should use tree segments. We can view a list segment as a "list with a hole," where the hole is the place (at the end of the segment) where the pointer to the next list is to be plugged in. A list segment has exactly one hole; a full list is just a list segment with the hole filled by nil; so the theory is quite simple. But a tree segment can have many holes where subtrees can be plugged in—so the theory of tree segments is not so simple. Gardner and Wheelhouse [41] give a theory of list segments with applications to manipulating XML documents.

THE EXISTENTIAL MAGIC WAND $\multimap$, SUBTYPE $\rightarrowtail$, AND LÖB RULE take nontrivial expertise to use. Some of the proofs of lemmas N2, N4, W1–W5, and U1–U5 in indirection theory use magic wand and Löb, and these proofs are lengthy, contrived, and difficult to automate.

Fortunately, once these identities have been proved, they are a complete proof theory for reasoning about lists. The statements of all these identities do not mention any of the "magic" parts of separation logic: $\multimap$, $\rightarrowtail$, or Löb. Reasoning using these identities is fairly straightforward; we can say these magic-free identities form a *Muggle theory of data structures*. Wizardry is used only internally, in the proof of the Muggle identities.

For more advanced theories of data structures, when we move from shape predicates to representation relations, when we move from lists to trees and other structures, it will usually be possible to contain the wizardry within the soundness proof of a magic-free interface.

Chapter 20

Applying higher-order separation logic

Now[1] let us apply the separation logic rules (page 119) to the loop-traversal program (pages 114–117). The program is a list of pairs (*address,body*), where *body* is a pair of formal-parameter list and command. The specification (funspecs) of the program is a list of pairs (*address,funspec*). The definitions myprog, myspec were given in Chapter 18.

Definition myprog : program :=
  (START,STARTbody)::(LOOP,LOOPbody)::(DONE,DONEbody)::nil.
Definition myspec :=
  (START,STARTspec)::(LOOP,LOOPspec)::(DONE,DONEspec)::nil.

We want to prove that a function-body satisfies its specification:

Definition semax_body (Γ: funspecs) (spec: funspec)
              (f: list var * control) :=
  semax (fst spec) Γ (fun s ⇒ call spec (map s (fst f))) (snd f).

The predicate call$(\vec{x}, P)\,\vec{v}$ says that the actual parameters $\vec{v}$ satisfy the precondition for calling a function with specification $[\vec{x}].P$:

Definition call (xP: list var * assert) (vl: list adr) : mpred :=
      (!! (length vl = length (fst xP)) && snd xP (arguments (fst xP) vl)).

---

[1] This chapter describes proofs contained in examples/cont/sample_prog.v

So, if spec is $[\vec{x}].P$, and function-body f is $[\vec{y}].c$, then semax_body Γ spec f is equivalent to

$$|\vec{x}| \models |\vec{y}| \;\; \wedge \;\; \vec{x}; \Gamma \vdash \{P[\vec{y}/\vec{x}]\}c$$

or in other words, "if you enter the function having satisfied the precondition, then the function body is safe to execute."

We do a semax_body proof for each function, then we use semax_func_cons (page 122) to tie the knot:

Lemma prove_START: semax_body myspec STARTspec STARTbody.
Lemma prove_LOOP: semax_body myspec LOOPspec LOOPbody.
Lemma prove_DONE: semax_body myspec DONEspec DONEbody.

Ltac func_tac :=
  apply semax_func_cons;
  [compute; reflexivity | compute; reflexivity | compute; reflexivity | |].

Lemma prove_myspec: semax_func myspec myprog myspec.
Proof.
  func_tac; [apply prove_START |].
  func_tac; [apply prove_LOOP |].
  func_tac; [apply prove_DONE |].
  apply semax_func_nil.
Qed.

The first three hypotheses of semax_func_cons are syntactic typechecking that are solved by (compute; reflexivity). The fourth is the proof of the function body, proved by the appropriate semax_body lemma. The fifth hypothesis is left for the next func_tac.

Inside the proofs of prove_START, prove_LOOP, etc. we illustrate *forward proof*, starting with the precondition and moving forward through the commands of the function body. This is in contrast to the *backwards proof* that is often used in Hoare logic (especially with verification-condition generators). VC-generators do not work especially well with separation logic, as they introduce magic-wand $\rightarrow\!\!*$ operators which are difficult to eliminate.

```
1   Lemma prove_START: semax_body myspec STARTspec STARTbody.
2   Proof.
3     eapply semax_pre; [intro ; call_tac; apply derives_refl | simpl ].
4     rewrite' alloc. apply semax_prop; auto; intros _.
5     forward. (* [a] := a + 1 *)
6     rewrite' alloc. rewrite' @sepcon_comm. rewrite' @sepcon_assoc.
7     forward. (* [a + 1] := a + 2 *)
8     rewrite' alloc. rewrite' @sepcon_comm. do 2 rewrite' @sepcon_assoc.
9     forward. (* [a + 2] := 0 *)
10    forward. (* Go loop(a + 3, a, a, done) *)
11    rewrite lseg_eq. normalize.
12    apply andp_derives; [ | apply funassert_e; reflexivity].
13    rewrite (sepcon_comm (allocpool _)). repeat rewrite <- sepcon_assoc.
14    rewrite (sepcon_comm (next (S (S (s0 a))) _)).
15    apply sepcon_derives; auto.
16    repeat rewrite sepcon_assoc. rewrite (next_gt_0 (s0 a)).
17    normalize.
18    eapply derives_trans; [ | eapply lseg_cons; try omega].
19    eapply sepcon_derives; [ apply derives_refl |].
20    rewrite sepcon_comm.
21    eapply derives_trans; [ | eapply lseg_cons; try omega].
22    eapply sepcon_derives; [ apply derives_refl |].
23    apply next_lseg; omega.
24  Qed.
```
Figure 20.1: A slightly automated function-body proof.

Figure 20.1 shows the program verification of the START function, recapitulating the pictorial explanation on page 115. Line 3 is the standard boilerplate for entering a function. At line 4, the proof obligation is,

semax (a :: nil) myspec (fun ρ : env $\Rightarrow$!!(1 = 1) && allocpool (ρ a))
    (Do (Mem a) := a .+ 1;
        Do (Mem (a .+ 1)) := a .+ 2;
        Do (Mem (a .+ 2)) := 0; Go LOOP ((a .+ 3) :: a :: a :: DONE :: nil))

The forward tactic solves a proof obligation of the form $\{P\}(c; c')$ when P happens to take the form convenient for subcommand c, and leaves a proof goal of the form $\{Q\}c'$. Most of the lines of proof-script are for the purpose of rearranging preconditions to fit the form needed by forward.

Line 4 uses the alloc rule to rewrite

$$\text{allocpool}(\rho a) \qquad \text{to} \qquad \rho a \mapsto 0 * \text{allocpool}(S(\rho a)),$$

then minor rearrangements to achieve the precondition,

fun ρ : env $\Rightarrow$!!(ρ a > 0) && mapsto (ρ a) 0 $*$ allocpool (S (ρ a)).

Line 5 uses the forward tactic to move past the first command. This same pattern repeats in lines 6–7 and again in 8–9. Line 10 uses forward through the Go command.

This leaves the proof goal,

next (S (S (ρ a))) 0 $*$
(allocpool (S (S (S (ρ a)))) $*$
 (next (ρ a) (S (ρ a)) $*$ next (S (ρ a)) (S (S (ρ a)))))) &&
funassert myspec
$\vdash$!!(4 = 4) &&
    (lseg (ρ a) (ρ a) $*$ lseg (ρ a) 0 $*$ allocpool (S (S (S (ρ a)))) &&
    cont DONEspec DONE)

which is proved by lines 11–23.

Tactics for separation logic

At present in sample_prog.v the the use of proof automation is modest, and therefore the proofs are rather long. The boilerplate at line 3, the rearrangements done at lines 4,6,8, and the entire entailment proof at lines 11–23 can be fully automated. Chapter 14 and Chapter 26 describe proof-automation systems for separation logic.

Chapter 21

Lifted Separation Logics
based on ideas by Jesper Bengtson, Jonas Jensen, and Lars Birkedal [16]

The separation logic presented in Chapters 18–20 has assertions that are predicates on local variable environments (sometimes called *stacks*) and memories (called *heaps*). This is very typical of separation logics. In "stack and heap" languages where one cannot take the address of (or make a pointer to) a local variable, there is no aliasing of local variables. Therefore, there is no need to apply a separation logic to the local variables; we need separation only to reason about aliasing in the heap.

The assertions are presented as env → mpred, that is, functions from environment to memory-predicate, using our natural deduction system NatDed(mpred) and separation logic SepLog(mpred). We can see this in the formulation of the Hoare axioms of separation logic, for example the rule for the Go statement. Figure 18.1 presents it in semi-formal mathematical notation,

$$\text{semax\_go} \frac{\Delta \vdash_{\text{type}} \text{Go } e \ (e_0, \dots, e_{n-1})}{\Delta; \Gamma \vdash \{e : \{S\} \ \wedge \ \text{call } S \ (e_0, \dots, e_{n-1})\} \ \text{Go } e \ (e_0, \dots, e_{n-1})}$$

To see how this looks presented in Coq, we examine the same rule in examples/cont/seplogic.v:

Axiom semax_go: $\forall$ vars G (P: funspec) x ys,
typecheck vars (Go x ys) = true $\rightarrow$
semax vars G
  (fun ρ $\Rightarrow$ cont P (eval x ρ) && call P (eval_list ys ρ))
  (Go x ys).

This says that the precondition for the command $Go\, x\, \vec{y}$ is that x is a function-pointer with specification P, and that P's entry precondition holds on the environment created by binding $\vec{y}$ to the parameters of P. More precisely, given an environment ρ, evaluate variable x in ρ and verify that P is indeed the function-specification at the resulting address (cont P (eval x ρ)); and evaluate the variables $\vec{y}$ in ρ and check the entry precondition on that argument list (call P (eval_list ys ρ)). This works all right; but Coq's inability to rewrite under a fun and its lack of higher-order matching (to open terms such as (eval x ρ) with its free variable ρ) can make it difficult to automate proofs.

ONE SOLUTION IS TO LIFT the assertion operators over the environment parameter. We use the operators lift0, lift1, lift2 to lift nullary, unary, and binary functions, respectively:

Definition lift0 {B} (P: B) : env$\rightarrow$B := fun ρ $\Rightarrow$ P.
Definition lift1 {A1 B} (P: A1$\rightarrow$B)(f1: env$\rightarrow$A1) : env$\rightarrow$B
  := fun ρ $\Rightarrow$ P (f1 ρ).
Definition lift2 {A1 A2 B}(P: A1$\rightarrow$A2$\rightarrow$B)
                (f1: env$\rightarrow$A1)(f2: env$\rightarrow$A2): env$\rightarrow$B
  := fun ρ $\Rightarrow$ P (f1 ρ) (f2 ρ).

Now the following two expressions are equal ($\beta\eta$-convertible):

(fun ρ $\Rightarrow$ andp (cont P (eval x ρ)) (call P (eval_list ys ρ)))
(lift2 andp (lift1 (cont P) (eval x)) (lift1 (call P) (eval_list ys)))

The second line is clumsier in certain ways (certainly to those who believe that Church's 1930 invention of the λ operator improved on Schönfinkel's 1924 combinators). But it better suits certain kinds of proof automation in Coq. And we do not even need to write lift2 andp, as the next development will show.

Given a separation logic over a type B of formulas, and an arbitrary type A, we can define a *lifted* separation logic over functions $A \to B$. The operations are simply lifted pointwise over the elements of A. Let $P, Q : A \to B$, let $R : T \to A \to B$ then define,

$$
\begin{aligned}
(P \,\&\&\, Q) : \ & A \to B \ := \ \text{fun } a \Rightarrow P a \,\&\&\, Q a \\
(P \,\|\, Q) : \ & A \to B \ := \ \text{fun } a \Rightarrow P a \,\|\, Q a \\
(\exists x. R(x)) : \ & A \to B \ := \ \text{fun } a \Rightarrow \exists x.\, R x a \\
(\forall x. R(x)) : \ & A \to B \ := \ \text{fun } a \Rightarrow \forall x.\, R x a \\
(P \longrightarrow Q) : \ & A \to B \ := \ \text{fun } a \Rightarrow P a \longrightarrow Q a \\
(P \vdash Q) : \ & A \to B \ := \ \forall a.\, P a \vdash Q a \\
(P * Q) : \ & A \to B \ := \ \text{fun } a \Rightarrow P a * Q a \\
(P \ast\!\!-\!\ast Q) : \ & A \to B \ := \ \text{fun } a \Rightarrow P a \ast\!\!-\!\ast Q a
\end{aligned}
$$

In Coq we formalize the typeclass instances LiftNatDed, LiftSepLog, LiftClassicalSep, etc., as shown in Figure 21.1. For a type B, whenever NatDed B and SepLog B (and so on) have been defined, the lifted instances NatDed $(A \to B)$ and SepLog $(A \to B)$ (and so on) are automagically provided by the typeclass system.

Now we have yet another $\beta\eta$-equivalent way to write the precondition for the Go rule:

Axiom semax_go: $\forall$ vars G (P: funspec) x ys,
    typecheck vars (Go x ys) = true $\to$
    semax vars G
            (lift1 (cont P) (eval x) && lift1 (call P) (eval_list ys))
            (Go x ys).

where the && operator is implicitly and automatically lifted, by the LiftNatDed instance. See the presentation of the continuation-language using Lifted logics is shown in examples/cont/lifted_seplogic.v; compare it to the presentation using (fun $\rho \Rightarrow$ ...) in examples/cont/seplogic.v.

The lifting operators lift2, lift1, lift0 can seem verbose, threading the environment ρ through an assertion. We might ask Coq itself to calculate the right lifting operator based on the *type* of the lifted expression.

Instance LiftNatDed(A B: Type){ND: NatDed B}: NatDed (A→B):=
mkNatDed (A →B)
    (∗andp∗) (fun P Q x ⇒ andp (P x) (Q x))
    (∗orp∗) (fun P Q x ⇒ orp (P x) (Q x))
    (∗exp∗) (fun {T} (F: T →A →B) (a: A) ⇒ exp (fun x ⇒ F x a))
    (∗allp∗) (fun {T} (F: T →A →B) (a: A) ⇒ allp (fun x ⇒ F x a))
    (∗imp∗) (fun P Q x ⇒ imp (P x) (Q x))
    (∗prop∗) (fun P x ⇒ prop P)
    (∗derives∗) (fun P Q ⇒ ∀x, derives (P x) (Q x))
- - - - - - - - - - - - - - - - - -
(∗ fill in proofs here ∗)
Defined.

Instance LiftSepLog (A B: Type) {NB: NatDed B}{SB: SepLog B}
    : SepLog (A →B).
apply (mkSepLog (A →B) _(fun ρ ⇒ emp)
        (fun P Q ρ ⇒ P ρ ∗ Q ρ) (fun P Q ρ ⇒ P ρ -∗ Q ρ)).
(∗ fill in proofs here ∗)
Defined.

Instance LiftClassicalSep (A B: Type) {NB: NatDed B}{SB: SepLog B}
    {CB: ClassicalSep B} :
    ClassicalSep (A →B).
apply mkCS.
(∗ fill in proofs here ∗)
Qed.

Figure 21.1: Lifted instances of natural deduction and separation logic

For example, to lift a term of type adr→ adr→_ (such as the mapsto function), we use lift2. For a term of type adr→_ (such as (cont P)) we use lift1. For a term of type _ (such as 0) we use lift0.

We define a generic type-directed lifting operator, and give it the notation ` (backquote), so that we can write

  `mapsto   to mean   lift2 mapsto
  `(cont P)   to mean   lift1 (cont P)   Using this notation, all three of
  `0   to mean   lift0 0

these assertions mean the same thing:

1.   (fun ρ ⇒ mapsto (eval x ρ) 0 && cont P (eval f ρ))
2.   lift2 mapsto (eval x) (lift0 0) && lift1 (cont P) (eval f)
3.   `mapsto (eval x) (`0) && `(cont P) (eval f)

The backquote is implemented in Coq using a calculus of Canonical Structures, in the file veric/lift.v.

Our separation logic for the C language (and its tactical proof-automation system) uses the backquote form. However, users of the system can write assertions using either the backquote notation, the explicitly lifted notation (with lift2,lift1,lift0) or the lambda-notation (with fun ρ ⇒ ...), and the rules and tactics will work equally well. All three forms are $\beta\eta$ equivalent, so one can change one to the other.

UNLIFTING THE RULE OF CONSEQUENCE. Separation logic has a *rule of consequence* which in our little continuation language is written:

$$\frac{P' \to P \qquad \Delta; \Gamma \vdash \{P\}c}{\Delta; \Gamma \vdash \{P'\}c}$$

Although we use a lifted separation logic for the Hoare judgments $\Delta; \Gamma \vdash \{P\}c$, when actually proving the subgoal $P' \to P$ we can work in an ordinary *unlifted* separation logic.

Suppose we are proving the premise $P' \to P$. As P is a lifted predicate in SepLog(env→ mpred), this is equivalent to $\forall \rho, P'\rho \to P\rho$. In a typical case, the predicates P' and P might look like this:

e1,e2: expr
i : ident
Frame: stack → mpred
───(1/1)
(fun ρ ⇒ !!(eval e1 ρ = ρ(i)))
         && (fun ρ ⇒ eval e1 ρ ↦ eval e2 ρ) ∗ Frame
⊢ (fun ρ ⇒ ρ(i) ↦ eval e2 ρ) ∗ Frame

After intro and simpl, the proof goal is now

e1,e2: expr
i : ident
Frame: stack → mpred
ρ: stack
───(1/1)
!!(eval e1 ρ = ρ(i))) && (eval e1 ρ ↦ eval e2 ρ) ∗ Frame ρ
⊢ (ρ(i) ↦ eval e2 ρ) ∗ Frame ρ

This goal is purely in the unlifted separation logic of heaps. All notational
distinctions between the backquote, the lift operators, and the (fun ρ ⇒ _)
notation have been unfolded.

There's a good reason to unlift. The environment (stack) ρ is the same
on both sides of the entailment ⊢. Now we can replace ρ(i) and eval e1 ρ
with abstract values, using Coq's set tactic—set (a:=eval e1 ρ)—to obtain,

e1,e2: expr
i : ident
Frame: stack → mpred
ρ: stack
a := eval e1 ρ
b := ρ(i)
c := eval e2 ρ
F := Frame ρ
───(1/1)
!!(a = b) && (a ↦ c) ∗ F ⊢ (b ↦ c) ∗ F

Then we can clearbody a b c F; clear ρ Frame e1 e2 i to obtain,

a,b,c : adr
F : mpred

$$\frac{\text{a,b,c : adr} \quad \text{F : mpred}}{!!(a = b) \,\&\&\, (a \mapsto c) * F \vdash (b \mapsto c) * F}(1/1)$$

Indeed, our proof-automation tactics for applying our separation logic to the C language do this task automatically. Without the environment (stack) to worry about, without needing to worry about lifted formulas, we can perform entailment proofs in ordinary separation logic.

HISTORICAL NOTE. The lifting operators were invented in 1924—before even the λ-calculus—by Moses Schönfinkel [83], who used the notation:

$$C = \text{lift0} \qquad S = \text{lift2}.$$

Schönfinkel showed that any formula of logic could be represented by combinations of these "argument-threading" functions. Schönfinkel's C is now conventionally called K in combinatory logic.

Part III

Separation logic for CompCert

SYNOPSIS: Verifiable C *is a style of C programming suited to separation-logic verifications; it is similar to the C light intermediate language of the CompCert compiler. We show the assertion language of separation-logic predicates for specifying states of a C execution. The judgment form* semax *of the axiomatic semantics relates a C command to its precondition postconditions, and for each kind of command there is an inference rule for proving its* semax *judgments. We illustrate with the proof of a C program that manipulates linked lists, and we give examples of other programs and how they can be specified in the Verifiable C program logic. Shared-memory concurrent programs with Dijkstra-Hoare synchronization can be verified using the rules of concurrent separation logic.*

Chapter 22

Verifiable C

Hoare logics (and separation logics) work well on languages in which: variables do not alias, expressions have no side effects, subexpressions do not access memory, well-typed expressions can't go wrong, and concurrency synchronization operations are explicit commands (instead of implicit as memory access).

To see why, consider some common Hoare rules. The assignment rule $\{P[e/x]\}\, x := e\, \{P\}$ substitutes e for all the occurrences of x in postcondition P, yielding the precondition. This makes little sense, logically, if e can modify the state or if e does not even evaluate. The LOAD rule, $\{e_1 \mapsto e_2\}\, x := [e_1]\, \{x = e_1 \,\wedge\, e_1 \mapsto e_2\}$ (when x not free in e_1, e_2) assumes that the *only* memory access in this command is at the explicit square brackets, and e_1 and e_2 must not have internal memory accesses. These restrictions are useful not only for Hoare logics, but for other kinds of static analysis such as abstract interpretation.

We wish to build a program logic for the C programming language, and yet C does not have any of these restrictions! Variables can be aliased if (anywhere in the function) their address is taken via the & operator; the assignment operator = can appear at any subexpression; and memory dereferences can occur at any subexpression. There are many conditions that cause legal, well-typed expressions to fail at runtime: divide by zero, operating on an uninitialized value, and so on.

To apply Hoare logics (or separation logic) to C, we will program C in a style that suits static reasoning. In short, we will obey all the restrictions described at the beginning of the chapter. Any such *Verifiable C* program will be compilable by any C compiler.

THE COMPCERT VERIFIED C COMPILER compiles the C language through several intermediate languages. The front-end language is called CompCert C, and is almost the entire C standard. It is compiled to an intermediate language called *Csyntax*, which is compiled to *C light*, then to *C#minor*, then *C minor*, and then through five or six more intermediate languages to the target assembly language. All the compiler phases from *Csyntax* to assembly language are proved correct, with respect to small-step operational-semantic specifications of the languages.

Verifiable C is a subset of C light, which is a subset of CompCert C, which is a subset of C. Verifiable C is just as expressive as CompCert C, in that every CompCert C program can be expressed in Verifiable C with only a few simple local transformations.

To illustrate, consider this C program:

```
struct list {int head; struct list *tail;};

int f(struct list *p, int y) {
    int a; struct list b; int d;
    b.tail = (a = p→tail→head, p→tail);
    g(&d);
    b.head = d;
    g(&y);
    return y;
}
```

This is a CompCert C program; it fails to be a C light program because (1) the assignment to b.tail has an internal side effect and (2) the formal parameter y has its address taken. The translation to C light yields:

```
int f(struct list *p, int y) {
    int a; struct list b; int d;
    int y0=y;
    a = p→tail→head;
```

```
    b.tail = p→tail;
    g(&d);
    b.head = d;
    g(&y0);
    return y0;
}
```

In this program we have addressable local variables (y0,d,b) whose address is taken by the & operator; nonaddressable local variables (a) to which & is not applied; and nonaddressable parameters (p,y). The variable b is considered addressable, even though the ampersand & is never applied to it, because it is a structure or array variable.

This C light program is not a Verifiable C program because (1) the assignment to a contains a load that is not top-level in the expression, and (2) the assignment to b.tail contains both a store and a load. The translation to Verifiable C yields:

```
int f(struct list *p, int y) {
    int a; struct list b; int d;
    int y0=y; struct list *q, *u;
    u = p→tail;
    a = u→head;
    q = p→tail;
    b.tail = q;
    g(&d);
    b.head = d;
    g(&y0);
    return y0;
}
```

Introducing the auxiliary variables u and q is necessary to allow separation-logic reasoning, in particular application of judgment rules that can handle only one load or store at a time. Not every expression must be broken up into atomic parts: the rules are (1) no side effects or function calls in subexpressions, (2) no loads in subexpressions (only at top level, and only in an assignment whose target is a nonaddressable local variable).

Pointer comparisons are a tricky corner of the C semantics. Under what conditions are the tests p==q or p<q permitted?

p==q If the *values* p and q are both integers (not pointers); or if one is a pointer and the other is zero; or if both are pointers into allocated (not yet deallocated) objects.

p<q If p and q are both integers; or if one is a pointer and the other is zero; or if both are pointers into the *same* allocated object.

Comparisons between a pointer p and a nonzero integer q are illegal ("stuck" in the operational semantics), because otherwise one could write program whose observable behavior changes under perfectly legal compiler optimizations and link-loading decisions.

The reason that p==q is legal only when both p and q are (still) allocated is subtle. Consider this program:

```
int *f(void) {int x; return &x;}
```

```
int g(void); {return f()==f();}
```

The function f returns a dangling pointer, which in itself is not illegal. One might think that, because of the way that stack frames work, the location of f's stack frames will be the same in the two different calls, and thus g will always return 1 (true). But we do not wish to impose a requirement that a stack frame is always at a fixed offset from the caller; this prevents certain kinds of "trampoline" implementations and breaks abstraction in other ways. Thus, this function f must be "stuck." In the program logic we will enforce that in order to execute p==q (where both are pointer values) one must have at least *existence permission* for both p and q. In Verifiable C one must factor this kind of pointer comparison into a separate statement. That is, when e_1 and e_2 can both denote pointer values, the statement **if** $(e_1{==}e_2)$ {...} **else** {...}   must be written as, t=$(e_1{==}e_2)$; **if** (t) {...} **else** {...}.

C light Abstract Syntax

A user of the VST separation logic for CompCert will reason on the syntax of C light programs, and reason about C light values and types. Therefore the following files must be imported from the CompCert Coq development:

Axioms: Various extensionality axioms used by CompCert and VST.

Integers: 32-bit unsigned and signed integers.

Floats: Floating point numbers.

Values: Compcert values, specified as the union of integer values, floating-point values, abstract pointer values, and undefined values.

Maps: Efficient lookup tables.

AST: Generic constructors for Abstract Syntax Trees.

Globalenvs: Global environments (of functions and global variables).

Ctypes: C-language types, unary and binary operators, evaluation and casting of unary and binary operators applied to values.

Cop: Expression operators and overloading resolution.

Clight: The syntax of C light: expressions, commands, and function declarations.

The interface (or specification) of our program logic is based on these files, but the *soundness proof* of the logic is with respect to the operational semantics of C light. Therefore the soundness proof (but not the end user) also imports the following files from CompCert:

Coqlib: General-purpose lemmas and tactics.

Memdata: Representations of values as sequences of abstract bytes.

Memtype: Interface (type signature) of the memory model.

Memory: Representation of the memory model.

Clight: Operational semantics of C light.

This is the *interface* of CompCert; CompCert has dozens more files that implement the C compiler and prove its correctness with respect to different target assembly languages. However, the VST does not need to import any of these, since the source-language operational semantics (Memory and Clight) specifies everything that we need to know.

Chapter 23

Expressions, values, and assertions

The C language has expressions whose grammar includes:

$$e ::= 1 \mid 1.0 \mid x \mid *e \mid -e \mid e+e \mid (\tau)e \mid e.\text{fld}$$

where 1 stands for any integer literal, 1.0 for any floating-point literal, and so on. This grammar is encoded by CompCert's abstract-syntax-tree (AST) data type representing expressions:

Inductive expr : Type :=
  | Econst_int: int → type → expr
  | Econst_float: float → type → expr
  | Evar: ident → type → expr
  | Etempvar: ident → type → expr
  | Ederef: expr → type → expr
  | Eaddrof: expr → type → expr
  | Eunop: unary_operation → expr → type → expr
  | Ebinop: binary_operation → expr → expr → type → expr
  | Ecast: expr → type → expr
  | Efield: expr → ident → type → expr.

Every expression is annotated with its type; this disambiguates overloaded operators and field-selection without needing a type environment to look up names. Furthermore, addressable variables Evar are distinguished from nonaddressable locals Etempvar (see page 144).

The user of Verifiable C does not build these AST data structures directly: CompCert's front end produces them from the C source code. To prove a program correct, one applies the program logic to the ASTs in Coq.

EXPRESSIONS AND VARIABLES IN C PROGRAMS evaluate to values at runtime. That is, expressions and variables are part of the *static* program, while values are in the *dynamic* execution.

C has *integer values, pointer values,* and *floating-point values.* An integer variable can contain an integer value or (by casting) a pointer value. A pointer variable can contain a pointer value or the NULL value, which is the integer 0. A floating-point variable can contain a floating-point value. Finally, we use the *undefined value* to reason about uninitialized variables and about error conditions such as divide-by-zero.[1]

The inductive type of values is defined by,

Inductive val: Type :=
| Vundef: val *(* undefined values *)*
| Vint: int → val *(* 32-bit signed or unsigned integers *)*
| Vfloat: float → val *(* 64-bit floating point *)*
| Vptr: block → int → val. *(* pointer *)*

The type int carried by the Vint constructor is not the native integer type of Coq (called Z). It is Int.int, CompCert's theory of 32-bit modular arithmetic. Similarly, float is not the real numbers, it is the Flocq [25] theory of IEEE floating point.

The pointer value Vptr b i denotes offset i within the symbolic block-number b. C permits address arithmetic within an allocated object (such as a *malloc*'ed block or a struct or array variable). C does not permit address arithmetic or inequality comparisons between pointers to distinct objects. All the addresses within an object will be at different offsets i from the same base pointer b; different objects will have different base pointers.

---

[1] CompCert C's operational semantics distinguishes between *undefined values,* which can exist (for example in uninitialized variables) without crashing the program, and *illegal operations,* which crash the program (by making the operational semantics "get stuck"). For Verifiable C we use Vundef for both undefined values and the results of illegal operations; but then we prove that any proved-correct program cannot perform any illegal operations.

WE EVALUATE EXPRESSIONS in an *environment* that provides values for the variables; call this ρ. That is, if a is the name of a local variable, then (eval_id a ρ) looks up the identifier a in environment ρ. If e is a C-language expression, (eval_expr e ρ) evaluates e in environment ρ.

We can mention values and expressions in the assertions of our . For example, !!(Vint(Int.repr 0) = eval_id _a ρ) means that program variable a has value 0 in the environment ρ. To parse this apart: !! is notation for the prop constructor defined in Chapter 12, that injects logical propositions (Prop) into a separation logic. Int.repr injects from Coq's Z type into the int type of 32-bit modular arithmetic. Vint injects from int to val. The identifer a from a C source program will be typically be denoted _a in the program logic. The Coq type of _a is just ident, a definition that unfolds to positive; this is what CompCert uses for identifiers.

The function eval_expr is a computable **Fixpoint** (defined in veric/expr.v). The function eval_id, for looking up the value of a variable in an environment, is also a computable definition. That is, operational aspects of expression evaluation are transparent in the program logic.

SPATIAL PREDICATES in a separation logic are constructed from application-specific primitives, combined using standard operators such as the separating conjunction $*$. For the Verifiable C application, there are two primitives, func_ptr and address_mapsto.

func_ptr (*fs*: funspec) (*v*: val): mpred.
means that value v is a pointer to a function with specification ϕ.

address_mapsto (*ch*) (*v*: val) (π_r: share) (π: share) (*l*:address): mpred expresses what is typically written $l \mapsto v$ in separation logic, that is, a singleton heap containing just value v at address l. The "memory_chunk" *ch* specifies the size and sign-extension of v, and π gives the ownership share.

WE RARELY USE address_mapsto DIRECTLY; instead we use these derived forms:

mapsto (π:share) (*t*:type) (v w: val) : mpred
describes a singleton heap with just one value w of (C-language) type t at

address v, with permission-share π.

mapsto_ (π:share) (t:type) (v:val) : mpred
describes an *uninitialized* singleton heap with space to hold a value of type t at address v, with permission-share π.

field_mapsto (π: share) (t: type) (fld: ident) (v w: val) : mpred
describes a heap that holds just field fld of struct-value v, belonging to struct-type t, containing value w.

field_mapsto_ (π: share) (t: type) (fld: ident) (v: val) : mpred
is the corresponding uninitialized structure-field.

typed_mapsto (π: share) (t: type) (v: val) (w : reptype t) : mpred
says that at address v there is an l-value of type t. If t is a structured type, *all* the fields of t have contents corresponding to components of w. In mathematical notations for separation logic, this is often written as $v \mapsto (w_1, w_2, \ldots, w_n)$ or $v \hookrightarrow (w_1, w_2, \ldots, w_n)$. The function reptype calculates a Coq type corresponding to the C type t, for example if t is struct {int x,y;} then reptype(t) is (int$*$int).

ADDRESSABLE LOCAL VARIABLES are described by these derived spatial assertions:

memory_block (π: share) (n: int) (v: val): mpred.
There is a (perhaps uninitialized) block of memory, n bytes long at address v with permission-share π.

var_block (π: share) (x: ident, t: type) (ρ: environ): mpred.
The addressable local variable x of type t is accessible (but perhaps uninitialized) with share π, at address (eval_var x ρ). This is equivalent to typed_mapsto_ π t (eval_var x ρ).

stackframe_of (f: function) (ρ: environ): mpred.
The entire stack frame of f (comprised of one var_block for each addressable local variable) is accessible with total ownership share Tsh.

GLOBAL VARIABLES AND THEIR INITIALIZATION are described by the following predicates:

init_data_list2pred (d: list init_data) (π: share) (v: val) (ρ: environ) : mpred.
Memory at v contains global external initialized data, with d as constructed by CompCert from the syntax of a global initializer; with ownership share π. Initializers can contain constant literals *and* the addresses of global variables; the environment ρ is used for looking up any such addresses.

main_pre (*prog*: program) (_: unit) (ρ: environ): mpred.
The standard precondition for the main function, which is that all the global variables have their initial values. This is calculated from CompCert's description of the initialized global variables, using init_data_list2pred.

Chapter 24

The VST separation logic for C light

The Verified Software Toolchain's separation logic for C light has Hoare-logic inference rules for C that are more complex than the simple Hoare rules of an idealized programming language. The form of the Hoare judgment is $\Delta \vdash \{P\} \, c \, \{R\}$,

semax (Δ: tycontext) (P: environ→ mpred) (c: statement) (R: ret_assert)

Δ : tycontext is a *type context*, giving

- the (C-language) types of function parameters,

- the types of addressable local variables,

- the types *and initialization status* of nonaddressable local variables *(temporaries)*,

- the types of global variables, and

- the type-signatures *and specifications (pre/postconditions)* of global functions.

P : environ $\rightarrow$ mpred is a *precondition,* a function from *variable environment* to *memory predicate.* Variable environments map identifiers to addresses of addressable local variables (including functions), addresses of global variables, and values of temporaries (nonaddressable local variables). In our program logic, the type mpred is the abstract type of predicates on memories, and environ → mpred means that an assertion P takes an environ ρ and returns an mpred.

c : statement is a statement in the C language.

R : ret_assert is a *return assertion*, giving postconditions for each of the ways that c can exit: by *fall-through*, by *continue*, by *break*, and by *return*.[1]

The very first argument of semax—before the Δ argument—is an implicit parameter {Espec: OracleKind} that is typically supplied by Coq's type-class system. It specifies properties of the external world, the *oracle* with which the C program interacts. Proofs of ordinary function bodies are quantified over all oracle-kinds, so usually this parameter can be ignored (or hidden).

$$\text{semax\_ifthenelse} \frac{\Delta \vdash \{P \wedge e\}\, c\, \{R\} \qquad \Delta \vdash \{P \wedge \neg e\}\, d\, \{R\}}{\Delta \vdash \{P\}\ \text{if}(e)\ c\ \text{else}\ d\ \{R\}}$$

Axiom semax_ifthenelse : forall (Δ:tycontext)
       (P:environ→ mpred) (e: expr) (c d: statement) (R: ret_assert),
  bool_type (typeof e) = true →
  semax Δ (P && local (`(typed_true (typeof e)) (eval_expr e))) c R →
  semax Δ (P && local (`(typed_false (typeof e)) (eval_expr e))) d R →
  semax Δ (local (tc_expr Δ e) && P) (Sifthenelse e c d) R.

The if-then-else rule illustrates several issues. The first line—**Axiom**—emphasizes that Hoare logic is an axiomatic semantics (*sémantique axiomatique* in French, hence semax). Really, though, **Axiom** is just Coq-ese for

---

[1] The program logic does not permit goto statements. These would not be particularly difficult to add to the logic. A table of goto-conditions (one precondition for each label in the function) could be made a part of Δ or R.

"lemma mentioned in a Module Type, whose proof is in another module." Indeed, this rule is in the module type CLIGHT_SEPARATION_LOGIC.

The second line, forall (Δ:tycontext) ... mentions the parameters Δ, c, P, R as explained above. Here e is a C-language expression.

The third line, bool_type (typeof e) = true, requires that the expression e have a *Boolean-compatible* type in the C language. C does not have a special-purpose Boolean type; instead, any nonzero value is considered true, and zero is false. The NULL pointer is really just 0 in C. A boolean-compatible type is one that contains a zero value:

Definition bool_type (t: type) : bool :=
  match t **with**
  | Tint _ _ _ | Tpointer _ _ | Tarray _ _ _ | Tfunction _ _ | Tfloat _ _ ⇒ true
  | _ ⇒ false
  end.

This term bool_type (typeof e) is *computable*, in the sense that when applied to any ground term (a concrete C expression from a real program) it will efficiently compute in Coq to true or false; and for any C expression found in a program that passes CompCert's (or gcc's) front-end typechecker, it will compute to true. When the rule is applied to actual programs, this premise is cheaply disposed of automatically.

The fourth line,

semax Δ (P && local (`(typed_true (typeof e)) (eval_expr e))) c R →

expresses the hypothesis $\Delta \vdash \{P \wedge e\} c \{R\}$, meaning that if we are executing the then-clause c, not only can we assume the precondition P but also that the expression e must be true.

"Expression e is true" is not such a simple claim. As an assertion, it must take environment ρ and return an mpred. But since expression-evaluation cannot depend on memory, in fact the mpred it returns must be of the form prop($f\,\rho$) for some function f : environ → Prop, where our operator prop : Prop → mpred injects Coq propositions into the separation logic.

We say that an assertion that depends only on the environment and not on the memory is *local*, in the sense that (for example in a shared-memory concurrent-threads execution) it depends only on thread-local information. The local operator makes an assertion out of an environ→ Prop function:

local (f: environ→ Prop) : mpred := lift1 prop   or, equivalently,

local (f: environ→ Prop) : mpred := fun ρ ⇒ prop (f ρ)

Thus the precondition $P \wedge e$ in the idealized presentation of semax_ifthenelse is really P && local f in our logic. But what is $f(\rho)$?

We evaluate expression e in ρ, yielding a value v : val; that is, v := eval_expr e ρ. Whether v is true depends on e's type, using the predicate typed_true:

Definition strict_bool_val (v: val) (t: type) : option bool :=
    match v, t **with**
    | Vint n, Tint ___⇒ Some (negb (Int.eq n Int.zero))
    | Vint n, (Tpointer __| Tarray ___| Tfunction __) ⇒
             if Int.eq n Int.zero **then** Some false **else** None
    | Vptr b ofs, (Tpointer __| Tarray ___| Tfunction __) ⇒ Some true
    | Vfloat f, Tfloat sz _⇒ Some (negb(Float.cmp Ceq f Float.zero))
    | _, _⇒ None
    end.

Definition typed_true (t: type) (v: val) : Prop :=
    strict_bool_val v t = Some true.

Definition typed_false (t: type)(v: val) : Prop :=
    strict_bool_val v t = Some false.

We use |typed_true| in the logic of lifted propositions (environ → Prop). That is, `(typed_true $\tau$) has type (environ → Prop) → (environ → Prop). (For a review of the `backquote notation for lifted propositions, see Chapter 21.) We apply `(typed_true $\tau$) to eval_expr e of type environ → Prop, and apply local to the whole thing. We apply our lifted conjunction && and get the precondition, P && local (`(typed_true (typeof e)) (eval_expr e)).

Line 5, the hypothesis corresponding to $\Delta \vdash \{P \wedge \neg e\} \, d \, \{R\}$, proceeds on similar principles.

Line 6 is the conclusion $\Delta \vdash \{P\}$ if(e)c else d $\{R\}$. The complication here is that perhaps e will not evaluate successfully to a boolean value. For example, x/y does not evaluate if $y = 0$. The typechecking clause tc_expr Δ e generates the appropriate precondition (of type environ $\rightarrow$ Prop) to ensure the evaluation of e does not get stuck. For example, if e is x/y then tc_expr Δ e will be (fun $\rho \Rightarrow (0 \neq$ eval_id y $\rho)$).

$$\text{semax\_seq} \frac{\Delta \vdash \{P\}\, c\, \{Q\} \qquad \Delta \vdash \{Q\}\, d\, \{R\}}{\Delta \vdash \{P\}\, (c; d)\, \{R\}}$$

Axiom semax_seq:
    $\forall \Delta$ (R:ret_assert) (P Q:environ$\rightarrow$ mpred) (c d: statement),
    semax Δ P c (overridePost Q R) $\rightarrow$
    semax (update_tycon Δ c) Q d R $\rightarrow$
    semax Δ P (Ssequence c d) R.

THE SEQUENCING RULE for a command $(c; d)$ is easy in idealized Hoare logic: execute c with precondition P to get postcondition Q, then execute d to get postcondition R.

In Verifiable C there are two more things to consider: initialization status of variables in Δ, and multi-exit postconditions.

First, the type-context Δ keeps track of which (nonaddressable) local variables are initialized. This allows the typechecker to avoid generating too many extra preconditions about initialized variables. The type-context update_tycon Δ c is like Δ but augments the set of initialized variables with all the ones that are unambiguously initialized in command c.

The statement **if** (1) {y=3; z=y;} **else** {z=2;} unambiguously initializes z but not y. The reader might notice that 1 is true, thus y really is initialized, but if the user of the separation logic wants to make use of that fact in the next command, she will have to write that explicitly in the postcondition of this statement, where it will not be difficult to prove.

Second, the postcondition of a semax is a |ret_assert|, not an ordinary environ$\rightarrow$ mpred. That is, it has assertions describing what postconditions c

must satisfy for ordinary fall-through, for a `continue` statement to the end
of the current loop body, for a `break` statement out of the current loop, or
for a `return` statement. The postcondition for command c must use Q as
its fall-through assertion, but any other kind of exit from c should use the
corresponding assertion from R. This is exactly what overridePost Q R does.

$$\Delta \vdash \{P\}(c_1;(c_2;c_3))\{Q\} \quad \longleftrightarrow \quad \Delta \vdash \{P\}((c_1;c_2);c_3)\{Q\}$$

Axiom seq_assoc: $\forall \Delta$ P (s1 s2 s3: statement) R,
    semax Δ P (Ssequence s1 (Ssequence s2 s3)) R $\longleftrightarrow$
    semax Δ P (Ssequence (Ssequence s1 s2) s3) R.

Command sequencing is associative, and the Hoare triple respects associativity. This axiom is inessential, in that any program provable with this
axiom is provable without it; but it's convenient and easy to understand.

$$\text{semax\_while} \frac{\Delta \vdash \{P \wedge e\} c \{R\} \qquad P \wedge \neg e \vdash R}{\Delta \vdash \{P\} \text{ while } e \text{ do } c \{R\}}$$

Axiom semax_while: $\forall \Delta$ P (e: expr) (c: statement) R,
  bool_type (typeof e) = true $\rightarrow$
  local (tc_environ Δ) && P $\vdash$ local (tc_expr Δ e) $\rightarrow$
  local (tc_environ Δ) &&
    local (`(typed_false (typeof e)) (eval_expr e)) && P
      $\vdash$ R EK_normal None) $\rightarrow$
  semax Δ (local (`(typed_true (typeof e)) (eval_expr e)) && P)
    c (loop1_ret_assert P R) $\rightarrow$
  semax Δ P (Swhile e c) R.

The while rule is similar in several aspects to the **if** rule:

- The test expression e must be boolean-compatible (bool_type).

- The precondition must ensure that e evaluates successfully (P --local (tc_expr Δ e)).

- The tests e and $\neg e$ are local, lifted (via lift1), and type-specific (typed_true (typeof e)).

Also, a the body of a while-loop may continue (skip to the loop test and next iteration) or break (skip to after the loop). Thus any postcondition is really four different assertions in one. The function loop1_ret_assert converts the while-loop postcondition R into a postcondition for the loop body:

Definition loop1_ret_assert (P: environ$\rightarrow$ mpred) (R:ret_assert): ret_assert :=
fun ek vl $\Rightarrow$ **match** ek **with**
        | EK_normal $\Rightarrow$ P
        | EK_break $\Rightarrow$ R EK_normal None
        | EK_continue $\Rightarrow$ P
        | EK_return $\Rightarrow$ R EK_return vl
     end.

That is, if the loop-body does a *normal* exit or a *continue* exit, it must satisfy the loop invariant P. If the body does a *break* exit, it must satisfy the postcondition of the loop. If the body *returns* from the function, it must satisfy the same function-return postcondition as R.

Axiom semax_loop :
$\forall \Delta$ (P Q: ASSERT) (e: expr) (c: statement) (R: ret_assert),
    semax Δ P c (loop1_ret_assert Q R) $\rightarrow$
    semax Δ Q e (loop2_ret_assert P R) $\rightarrow$
    semax Δ P (Sloop c e) R.

THE WHILE RULE IS NOT a primitive rule of our separation logic; it is a lemma *derived* from the more primitive loop, if, and break statements. The command Sloop c e can be written in C as {for (;;e) c}, where c is the loop body, and e is the increment performed between iterations.

In the semax_loop proof rule, as in the rule for while, the assertion P is the *loop invariant*, the one that must hold right before the loop body c. But here there also also a *continue* condition, Q, which must be satisfied whenever the body falls through or executes a continue. The command e must not break or continue (in the C language it must be a simple expression with no control flow), so loop2_ret_assert enforces break and continue postconditions of *false*.

The general form $\{for(e_{init};e_{test};e_{incr})c\}$ of the C-language for statement can be written in C light (and Verifiable C) as,

$$e_{init}; \text{ for } (;;e_{incr}) \ \{\text{if } e_{test} \text{ then } ; \text{ else break}; c\}$$

and one can derive a proof rule for the general three-expression for-loop with an *initialization* e_{init} and *test* e_{test} in addition to the *increment* e_{incr} and *body* c.

$$\text{semax\_set} \frac{}{\Delta \vdash \{\triangleright P[e/x]\} \ \{ \ x := e \ \}P}$$

Axiom semax_set: $\forall\,(\Delta{:}\text{tycontext})(P{:}\text{environ}\rightarrow\text{mpred})\ (x{:}\text{ident})\ (e{:}\text{expr})$,
  semax Δ ($\triangleright$ (local (tc_expr Δ e) &&
              local (tc_temp_id x (typeof e) Δ e) &&
              subst x (eval_expr e) P))
  (Sset x e) (normal_ret_assert P).

THE ASSIGNMENT RULE is like the idealized Hoare rule for assignment, except: The type of the variable must match the type of the expression: tc_temp_id x (typeof e) Δ e. The assertion tc_expr Δ e ensures that e evaluates. Since the assignment takes a step, the precondition can be weakened by the $\triangleright$ later operator. Since the assignment does not continue, break, or return, those three assertions of the postcondition are *false*:

Definition normal_ret_assert (Q: environ$\rightarrow$ mpred) : ret_assert :=
  fun ek vl $\Rightarrow$!!(ek = EK_normal) && (!! (vl = None) && Q).

semax_set_forward
$$\Delta \vdash \{ \triangleright P \}\ x := e\ \{ \exists v.\, x = (e[v/x]) \land P[v/x] \}$$

Axiom semax_set_forward:
  $\forall$ (Δ: tycontext) (P: environ$\rightarrow$mpred) (x: ident) (e: expr),
  semax Δ ($\triangleright$ (local (tc_expr Δ e) &&
                              local (tc_temp_id id (typeof e) Δ e) && P))
    (Sset x e)
    (normal_ret_assert
      (EX old:val,
        local (`eq (eval_id x) (subst x (`old) (eval_expr e))) &&
        subst x (`old) P)).

THE FLOYD ASIGNMENT RULE is provided as a forward-proof alternative to the Hoare assignment rule.

semax_load
$$\Delta \vdash \{ \triangleright(e \overset{\pi}{\mapsto} v * P) \}\ x := [e]\ \{ \exists v_{\mathrm{old}}.\, x = v \land (e \overset{\pi}{\mapsto} v * P)[v_{\mathrm{old}}/x] \}$$

Axiom semax_load: $\forall$ (Δ: tycontext) π (x: ident) P (e: expr) (v: val),
tc_temp Δ x (typeof e) $\rightarrow$
semax Δ
  ($\triangleright$(local (tc_lvalue Δ e) &&
      local (tc_temp_id_load x (typeof e) Δ v) &&
      (`(mapsto π (typeof e)) (eval_lvalue e) v * P)))
  (Sset x e)
  (normal_ret_assert
    (EX old:val, local (`eq (eval_id x) (subst x (`old) v)) &&
    (subst x (`old) (`(mapsto π (typeof e)) (eval_lvalue e) v * P)))).

THE PRIMITIVE LOAD RULE handles memory-loads from any kind of l-value. Specialized rules for array slots, structure fields, and *-dereference are synthesized from this primitive rule, which (therefore) will rarely be directly applied by users of the logic.

The syntactic form of the rule appears similar to that of the assignment rule—they both match Sset x e—but in this case the expression *e* must type-check as an lvalue, not as an expr. The distinction between *l*-values (values that can appear on the *left* or right of an assignment) and *r*-values (values that can only appear on the *right* of an assignment) can be explained by the evaluation function:

Fixpoint eval_expr (e: expr) : environ → val :=
  match e **with**
  | Econst_int i ty ⇒ `(Vint i)
  | Econst_float f ty ⇒ `(Vfloat f)
  | Etempvar id ty ⇒ eval_id id
  | Eaddrof a ty ⇒ eval_lvalue a
  | Eunop op a ty ⇒ `(eval_unop op (typeof a)) (eval_expr a)
  | Ebinop op a1 a2 ty ⇒ `(eval_binop op (typeof a1) (typeof a2))
                                    (eval_expr a1) (eval_expr a2)

  with eval_lvalue (e: expr) : environ → val :=
  match e **with**
  | Evar id ty ⇒ eval_var id ty
  | Ederef a ty ⇒ `force_ptr (eval_expr a)
  | Efield a i ty ⇒ `(eval_field (typeof a) i) (eval_lvalue a)
  | _⇒ `Vundef
  end.

That is, *r*-values include numeric constants, nonaddressable local variables (temps), taking the address of an *l*-value using the & operator, and unary and binary operator expressions. The *l*-values include addressable (local and global) variables, dereferencing an *r*-value using the * operator, and fields of structures and unions. By default, ill-formed expressions are *l*-values that evaluate to Vundef, but these will never occur in well-typed expressions.

So, the expression *e* must type-check as an *l*-value (tc_lvalue Δ e), and the variable x must have the same type as *e*. Loading takes a step, so the precondition is relaxed by the ▷ later operator. The old value of the variable is saved in logical-variable old.

We can read the load rule as follows. In the precondition, a heap cell at address e has contents v and some set of other locations (disjoint from e) satisfy P. After the load, variable x has value v, and the assertion $e \overset{\pi}{\mapsto} v * P$ still holds but occurrences of x must be interpreted with the x's old value.

The mapsto operator ensures that the type of v (sitting in memory at the address given by l-value e) matches the type specified for e:

Definition mapsto π t v1 v2 := !! (tc_val t v2) && umapsto π t v1 v2.

where umapsto is an "untyped maps-to" that permits v2 to be anything, including Vundef. Th tc_temp_id_load condition ensures that the type of v is castable to the type of the variable x.

There is an extra *semiframe P*. One might think, surely P is not necessary, as it could be omitted from the specification of semax_load and be added later by the frame rule! But P may mention the variable x, and the forward load rule substitutes in P to refer instead the old value of x; this could not be accomplished using the frame rule.

---

semax_store————————————————————————————

$$\Delta \vdash \{ \triangleright (e_1 \overset{\pi}{\mapsto} v * P) \} \, [e_1] := e_2 \, \{\}(e_1 \overset{\pi}{\mapsto} e_2 * P)$$

Axiom semax_store: $\forall \Delta$ (e1 e2: expr) π (P: environ→mpred),
  writable_share π →
  semax Δ
    (▷(local (tc_lvalue Δ e1) && local (tc_expr Δ (Ecast e2 (typeof e1))))
      && (`(mapsto_ π (typeof e1)) (eval_lvalue e1) * P)))
  (Sassign e1 e2)
  (normal_ret_assert
    (`(mapsto π (typeof e1)) (eval_lvalue e1)
      (`(eval_cast (typeof e2) (typeof e1)) (eval_expr e2)) * P)).

STORING INTO AN l-VALUE in C differs from the idealized separation-logic rule in these ways: The share π or sh must contain enough permission for writing (writable_share sh). There is an implicit cast of e_2 to the type of e_1. The typechecker ensures (in the precondition) that e_1 and (the casted) e_2 both evaluate.

The mapsto_ operator in the precondition means "maps-to anything", just as we write $p \mapsto \_$ to mean $\exists v.\ p \mapsto v$.

Definition mapsto_ π t v1 := EX v2:val, umapsto π t v1 v2.

Axiom semax_ptr_compare : $\forall (\Delta$: tycontext) P id cmp e1 e2 ty $\pi_1\ \pi_2$,
  is_comparison cmp = true $\rightarrow$
  typecheck_tid_ptr_compare Δ id = true $\rightarrow$
  semax Δ
    ($\triangleright$(local (tc_expr Δ e1) &&
       local (tc_expr Δ e2) &&
       local (`(blocks_**match** cmp) (eval_expr e1) (eval_expr e2)) &&
       (`(mapsto_ π_1 (typeof e1)) (eval_expr e1) $*$ TT) &&
       (`(mapsto_ π_2 (typeof e2)) (eval_expr e2) $*$ TT) &&
       P))
    (Sset id (Ebinop cmp e1 e2 ty))
    (normal_ret_assert
      (EX old:val,
        local (`eq (eval_id id)
               (subst id `old (`(cmp_ptr_no_mem (op_to_cmp cmp))
                    (eval_expr e1) (eval_expr e2)))) &&
      subst id `old P)).

COMPARING POINTERS FOR EQUALITY OR INEQUALITY has a complex semantics in C. Testing $p{=}{=}q$ or $p < q$ is unpredictable (illegal) if p or q has been deallocated (see page 145). The requirement $e_1 \mapsto \_ * \top$ assures that e_1 is still allocated, and similarly for e_2. Testing $p < q$ is illegal if p and q point into different allocated blocks; blocks_**match** checks for this. Users of the program logic must therefore (unfortunately) factor commands such as **if** $(p{<}q)$ c; **else** d; into x=$(p{<}q)$; **if** (x) c; **else** d; when p is a pointer expression.

THE C LANGUAGE HAS FUNCTION POINTERS. For example, this little program assigns a global function constant &f to a function-pointer variable p, then calls it:

```
int f(int z)
  {return z+1;}
int main()
  {int (*p)(int); p = &f; return p(3);}
```

Even calling a global function directly is done in two stages: evaluate an expression &f that yields a function-pointer, then call that pointer. In C the ampersands can be elided, so instead of (&f)(5) one usually writes f(5).

We can handle these two stages by separate rules in the program logic: obtain a function pointer from a global definition, then call it.

$$
\text{semax\_fun\_id} \frac{\Delta(x) = \text{func}\{P'\}\{Q'\} \qquad \Delta \vdash \{P \,\&\&\, x : \{P'\}\{Q'\}\}\, c\, \{Q\}}{\Delta \vdash \{P\}\, c\, \{Q\}}
$$

Axiom semax_fun_id: $\forall x\ (\phi\colon \text{funspec})\ \Delta\ P\ Q\ c,$
    (var_types Δ) ! x = None $\rightarrow$
    (glob_types Δ) ! x = Some(Global_func ϕ) $\rightarrow$
    semax Δ
        (P && `(func_ptr ϕ) (eval_lvalue (Evar x (type_of_funsig fsig))))
        c
        Q $\rightarrow$
    semax Δ P c Q.

TO ACCESS A FUNCTION POINTER FROM A GLOBAL DEFINITION, one uses the semax_fun_id rule. This looks up the identifier x in the local context (var_types) to make sure the global name is not shadowed, then looks up x in the global context to find the function specification. The type-context Δ contains not only the types but their entire function-specifications with pre- and postconditions. Then a function assertion applied to address &x is conjoined with the precondition P.

The function-assertion (func_ptr ϕ v) states that at address v there is a function whose *specification* is ϕ (see also page 171). When ϕ=mk_funspec fsig A P' Q' it means that fsig gives the names and types of function parameters, P' is a precondition of type $A \rightarrow$ environ $\rightarrow$ mpred, Q' is a postcondition of type $A \rightarrow$ environ $\rightarrow$ mpred, and the type A is the type of a value that is to be shared between P' and Q'. For example,

func_ptr (mk_funspec ((z,Tint)::nil, Tint)
    int
    (fun i:int $\Rightarrow$ `(eq (Vint i)) (eval_id z))
    (fun i:int $\Rightarrow$ `(eq (Vint (Int.add i (Int.repr 1)))) (eval_id retval))

gives a function-assertion for the f function shown above. For this function, the type A is chosen to be int. There is some integer i such that (in the precondition) function-parameter contains Vint i, and (in the postcondition) the return value equals Vint $i + 1$.

Therefore, to prove correctness of the assignment p=&f, when the initial proof goal is $\Delta \vdash \{P\}\,c\,\{Q\}$, we can apply semax_fun_id to yield a proof goal with a precondition of P && `(fun_assert...) (eval_lvalue...), where eval_lvalue(Evar f ...) is the l-value &f. From this we can prove a postcondition saying that the contents of variable x is also a (func_ptr ...).

TO CALL A FUNCTION, the function-expression must typecheck (tc_expr Δ a), the argument expressions must typecheck (tc_exprlist Δ bl), and the function-expression a must evaluate to an actual function with specification $[A]\{P\}\{Q\}$: (func_ptr (mk_funspec fsig A P Q) (eval_expr a). There is some function-signature typechecking as well: the type of a must match the function parameter-signature argsig and return-type retsig (this is what classify_fun checks), and the return-variable assignment must be missing if and only if the return-type is void.

The call-statement's precondition must divide into one subheap that satisfies the function-precondition P, and the rest of the heap that satisfies the *frame condition* F. For example, when calling a function that reverses a linked list, the linked list satisfies P and everything that's not part of the linked list satisfies F.

semax_call——————————————————————————————————
$$\Delta \vdash \{a : \{\vec{y}P\}\{Q\} \wedge F * (Px)[\vec{b}/\vec{y}]\}\ r := a(\vec{b})\ \{\exists v_0.\ F[v_0/r] * Qxr\}$$

Axiom semax_call: $\forall \Delta$ A (P Q: A $\rightarrow$ environ$\rightarrow$ mpred) (x:A)
  (F: environ$\rightarrow$ mpred) (ret: option ident) (argsig: list (ident*type))
                                (retsig: type) (a: expr) (bl: list expr),
Cop.classify_fun (typeof a) =
    Cop.fun_case_f (type_of_params argsig) retsig $\rightarrow$
(retsig = Tvoid $\leftrightarrow$ret = None) $\rightarrow$
semax Δ
  (local(tc_expr Δ a) &&
    local(tc_exprlist Δ (snd(split argsig)) bl) &&
      && (`(func_ptr (mk_funspec (argsig,retsig) A P Q)) (eval_expr a) &&
    (F * `(P x) (make_args' (argsig,retsig)
                             (eval_exprlist (snd(split argsig)) bl)))))
  (Scall r a bl)
  (normal_ret_assert
    (EX old:val, substopt r (`old) F * `(Q x) (get_result r))).

But it's not exactly P that must be satisfied. First, the precondition and postcondition can share a value x in common (see the example that used the variable i on page 166, so P is applied to x. Second, the *variable environment* for P is not the current one (the caller's local variables). Instead, it's a fresh environment made by binding the actual parameters $\vec{b}$ to the formal parameters $\vec{y}$—which is what make_args' does. The parameter-names $\vec{y}$ come from the argsig.

After the function call, the frame F is unchanged. However, if the assertion F mentioned the return-variable r, then F must be interpreted with the old value of r substituted in. Since C call-statements may or may not assign to a variable, i.e. r=f(x) or just f(x), r is actually an option, and the substitution of v_0/r is actually an optional substitution, substopt.

Finally, the function postcondition Q is applied to the non-frame part of the heap. First it's applied to x, so that P and Q can talk about their value in common. Then the return-result is bound to the variable named retval, which is the name by which function-postconditions can refer to the return value; this is what get_result does.

Of course, the typical function-call is not to a function-pointer variable, but to a global (extern) function. For those it's simpler to use a synthetic rule semax_call_id, which is derived from semax_fun_id and semax_call. We won't show it here; it follows the same principles as the two rules from which it's constructed.

$$\text{semax\_return}\,\frac{}{\Delta \vdash \{R_{\text{return}}(e)\}\;\text{return}\;e\;\{R\}}$$

Axiom semax_return : $\forall \Delta$ (R: ret_assert) (e: expr),
    semax Δ (local (tc_expropt Δ e (ret_type Δ)) &&
                    `(R EK_return) (cast_expropt e (ret_type Δ)) id)
    (Sreturn e) R.

To return from a function, one must simply satisfy the return-assertion component of the postcondition. A C-language return may or may not return a value, so e is an option(expr). The ret_asset R is applied to EK_return (which selects the return-assertion). A return-assertion is a function from (option val)→ environ→ mpred; it is applied to the result of evaluating the expression-option e. There is an implicit cast from the type of e to the return-type of the enclosing function; this latter type is remembered inside the type-context Δ.

The EK_return component of R will have been established upon entry to the enclosing function body; see the semax_func rule (page 171).

$$\text{semax\_skip} \frac{}{\Delta \vdash \{P\} \; ; \; \{P\}}$$

Axiom semax_skip:
  $\forall \Delta$ P, semax Δ P Sskip (normal_ret_assert P).

The empty statement has the empty explanation.

$$\text{semax\_frame} \frac{\Delta \vdash \{P\} s \{R\} \qquad \text{modv}(c) \cap \text{fv}(F) = \emptyset}{\Delta \vdash \{P * F\} c \{R * F\}}$$

Axiom semax_frame: $\forall \Delta$ (P: environ$\rightarrow$ mpred) (c: statement)
              (R: ret_assert) (F: environ$\rightarrow$ mpred),
    closed_wrt_modvars c F $\rightarrow$
  semax Δ P c R $\rightarrow$
    semax Δ (P $*$ F) c (frame_ret_assert R F).

The frame rule. The postcondition frame_ret_assert R F is the separating conjuction of a return-assertion R with an ordinary mpred F. The premise closed_wrt_modvars c F says that the variables modified by command c are disjoint from the free variables of predicate F.

$$\text{semax\_extract\_prop} \frac{Q \rightarrow (\Delta \vdash \{P\} c \{R\})}{\Delta \vdash \{!!Q \wedge P\} c \{R\}}$$

Axiom semax_extract_prop: $\forall \Delta$ (Q: Prop) P c R,
        (Q $\rightarrow$ semax Δ P c R) $\rightarrow$
        semax Delta (!!Q && P) c R.

Propositions in the precondition can be extracted "above the line" as hypotheses in Coq.

$$\text{semax\_pre\_post} \frac{P \vdash P' \qquad \Delta \vdash \{P'\} c \{R'\} \qquad R' \vdash R}{\Delta \vdash \{P\} c \{R\}}$$

Axiom semax_pre_post: $\forall$ P' (R': ret_assert) Δ P c (R: ret_assert) ,
(local (tc_environ Δ) && P $\vdash$ P') $\rightarrow$
($\forall$ ek vl, local(tc_environ (exit_tycon c Δ ek)) && R' ek vl $\vdash$
R ek vl) $\rightarrow$
semax Δ P' c R' $\rightarrow$ semax Δ P c R.

The rule of consequence in its simplest form would be,

$\forall$ P' (R': ret_assert) Δ P c (R: ret_assert) ,
P $\vdash$ P' $\rightarrow$ R' $\vdash$ R $\rightarrow$ semax Δ P' c R' $\rightarrow$ semax Δ P c R.

However, the stronger version of the rule gives more information when proving P' and when proving R: the environment ρ is well-typed.

The claim that a function definition f meets its specification *spec* is called semax_body. We are in a global context (V, Γ) of global-variable declarations V and global-function specifications Γ. What the claim means is that the body of the function (fn_body f) satisfies a Hoare triple $\Delta \vdash \{P'\} (\text{fn\_body} f) \{Q'\}$ where:

- The type-context Δ is constructed from the function parameters and local variables, as well as the globals V, Γ.

- The precondition P' is constructed from the function-specification precondition Px and a stack frame comprising all the addressable local variables.

- The postcondition Q' is constructed from the function-specification postcondition Qx as well as the addressable-local-variable frame.

The stack frame is just the separating conjunction of all the fn_vars of f. A function_body_ret_assert is one that permits a *return* exit, but no other

Record function : Type := mkfunction {
  fn_return: type;
  fn_params: list (ident * type);
  fn_vars: list (ident * type);
  fn_temps: list (ident * type);
  fn_body: statement
}.

Inductive funspec :=
  mk_funspec: funsig → ∀ A: Type, (A→ environ→ mpred) →
  (A→ environ→ mpred) → funspec.

Definition varspecs := list (ident * type).
Definition funspecs := list (ident * funspec).

Definition stackframe_of (f: function) : environ→ mpred :=
  fold_right sepcon emp (map (var_block Share.top) (fn_vars f)).

Definition semax_body (V: varspecs)(Γ: funspecs)(f: function)
                             (spec: ident * funspec) :=
  match spec **with** (_, mk_funspec _A P Q) ⇒
    ∀ x, semax (func_tycontext f V Γ)
        (P x * stackframe_of f)
        (fn_body f)
        (frame_ret_assert (function_body_ret_assert (fn_return f) (Q x))
           (stackframe_of f))
  end.

kind (not fall-through, continue, or break). Upon exit, the function-body must "give the addressable variables back," satisfying $Qx * stackframe$, and thus ensuring that none of the footprint of the local variables is used in satisfying Qx. The frame_ret_assert is just separating conjunction lifted to the ret_assert type.

Parameter semax_func:
  ∀ (V:varspecs)(Γ:funspecs)(fdecs:list(ident∗fundef))(Γ$_1$:funspecs), Prop.

Axiom semax_func_cons: ∀ fs id f (A: Type) P Q (V: varspecs)
(Γ Γ′: funspecs),
        (id_in_list id (map fst Γ) &&
          (negb (id_in_list id (map fst fs)) &&
          semax_body_**params**_ok f)) = true →
        semax_body V Γ f (id, mk_funspec (fn_funsig f) A P Q) →
        semax_func V Γ fs Γ′ →
        semax_func V Γ ((id, Internal f)::fs)
          ((id, mk_funspec (fn_funsig f) A P Q) :: Γ′).

Axiom semax_func_nil: ∀ V Γ, semax_func V Γ nil nil.

THE PROOF OF A PROGRAM is the demonstration that all the functions in the program satisfy their specifications. That is, semax_body must be proved for every function.

The abstract predicate semax_func $V \Gamma \vec{f} \Gamma'$ means that the list $\vec{f}$ of function-definitions meets the specifications in the corresponding list Γ' of the list of funspecs. By "meet the specifications" we mean semax_body, with some additional bookkeeping about the uniqueness of function-names within $\vec{f}$, the uniqueness of local-variable names within each individual function, and so on.

The base case, for $\vec{f}$ the empty list (and thus Γ' empty) is handled by the semax_func_nil rule. The inductive case, for $f_1 \cdot \vec{f}$ and $spec_1 \cdot \Gamma'$, is to handled by semax_func_cons.

Chapter 25

Typechecking for Verifiable C
with Josiah Dodds

MOST PRESENTATIONS OF HOARE LOGICS assume that expressions (in a
current environment) are interchangeable with their values. Implicit
in this presentation is that every expression evaluates to a value in
the evaluation relation. This is convenient for users of these logics
in accomplishing program verification: connecting a program with a
mathematical specification.

Unfortunately, C expressions do not always evaluate to values (and
occasionally evaluate to unusable values). Although this occurs only in
limited and predictable cases, we do not want to lose the power to reason
about expressions and values interchangeably in the many cases where
expressions can be statically guaranteed to evaluate. We will avoid the
cases where expressions may not evaluate, because we will show that
they do not arise in verified programs. We integrate a typechecker with
our Hoare-logic rules to detect these cases, and (mostly) restore the link
between expressions and values.[1]

CompCert's inductive definition of eval_expr does not assume that expressions always evaluate. CompCert denotes *failure to evaluate* by omitting

---

[1]This chapter describes Coq developments in veric/expr.v, veric/binop_lemmas.v,
veric/environ_lemmas.v, and veric/expr_lemmas.v.

tuples from the inductive definition of the compcert.Clight.eval_expr relation, following standard principles of contemporary structural operational semantics. In program verification, however, the cost to using an inductive definition is that in order to relate an expression to a value you must say something like: $\exists v. e \Downarrow v \land P(v)$, "there exists some value such that e evaluates to v and P holds on v."

WE WOULD RATHER SAY, "P holds on the value of e." We can do this with a total function (a **Fixpoint** in Coq).

Fixpoint eval_expr (e: expr) : environ → val := ...

Whenever compcert.Clight.eval_expr would fail to relate, our eval_expr produces an arbitrary value such as Vundef. Expressions that typecheck (as we will explain this chapter) cannot evaluate to this undefined value. As the curried form of the definition hints, our eval_expr does case-discrimination on the syntax of expressions without waiting to see the environment argument. This means that eval_expr(e) can simplify statically (in program verifications, for example) using only Coq's simpl, not rewrite.

That is, we define the expression-evaluation relation for tractable and convenient reasoning in the program logic. We take advantage of the fact that we are only interested in evaluating programs that will (provably) never get stuck (though it will be up to the user to complete this proof).

We then prove the relationship between the two definitions of evaluation on expressions that typecheck:

THEOREM. For dynamic environments ρ that are well typed with respect to a type context Δ, if expression e typechecks with respect to Δ, then CompCert's relational eval_expr evaluates e in ρ to the same value as our computational eval_expr.

Theorem eval_expr_relate :
$\forall$ (Δ: tycontext) (ρ: environ) (e: expr) (m: mem),
  ρ = construct_rho (filter_genv ge) ve te → typecheck_environ Δ ρ →
  (denote_tc_assert (typecheck_expr Δ e) ρ →
  Clight.eval_expr ge ve te m e (eval_expr e ρ)).

Many things can go wrong in a C expression — some are a bit surprising. These are expression behaviors that are undefined in the C90 standard used as the basis for the operational semantics of Clight [63]. Programs containing these undefined behaviors cannot take advantage of the correctness guarantees of either CompCert or our program logic (even though, in practice, the machine-language program may have predictable behavior).

These expressions are stuck in the CompCert operational semantics: shifting an integer value by more than the word size, dividing the minimum int by -1 (which overflows), subtracting two pointers with different base addresses (e.g., from different malloc'ed blocks), casting an out-of-range float to an int, dereferencing a null pointer, arithmetic on an uninitialized variable, and casts between integers and pointer (results in values that get stuck when used). Our typechecker produces program-logic predicates that (if satisfied) ensure the absence of these conditions.

Our typechecker uses a technique very similar to proof by reflection. We give an example of standard proof by reflection, followed by our approach in order to highlight differences.

Proof by reflection is a three-step process. A program is *reified* (made real) by translation from Prop to a data structure that can be reasoned about computationally. Computation is then performed on that data structure and the result is *reflected* back into Prop where it can be used in a proof (see bottom of Fig. 25.2).

We could use reflection, for example, to remove True and False from propositions containing conjunctions and disjunctions. (See Chlipala [34, *Reflection* chapter] for a fuller explanation of this technique.) The first step is to define a syntax tc_assert (see Figure 25.1) that represents the propositions of interest. We will use the same syntax that describes typechecking assertions, these match each case where a C expression does *not* evaluate.

Next we need a function to *reflect* this syntax into the logic of propositions, that is, denotation function denote_tc_assert (Figure 25.1).

Inductive tc_assert :=
| tc_FF: tc_assert
| tc_noproof : tc_assert
| tc_TT : tc_assert
| tc_andp': tc_assert → tc_assert → tc_assert
| tc_orp' : tc_assert → tc_assert → tc_assert
| tc_nonzero: expr → tc_assert
| tc_iszero: expr → tc_assert
| tc_isptr: expr → tc_assert
| tc_ilt: expr → int → tc_assert
| tc_Zle: expr → Z → tc_assert
| tc_Zge: expr → Z → tc_assert
| tc_samebase: expr → expr → tc_assert
| tc_nodivover: expr → expr → tc_assert
| tc_initialized: PTree.elt → type → tc_assert.

Definition denote_tc_nonzero (v: val) :=
   match v **with**
   | Vint i ⇒ **if** negb (Int.eq i Int.zero) **then** True **else** False
              | _⇒ False
      ⋮
   end.

Fixpoint denote_tc_assert (a: tc_assert) : environ → Prop :=
  match a **with**
  | tc_FF ⇒ `False | tc_TT ⇒ `True
  | tc_andp' b c ⇒ `and (denote_tc_assert b) (denote_tc_assert c)
  | tc_nonzero e ⇒ `denote_tc_nonzero (eval_expr e)
  | ...
end.

Figure 25.1: Reified (syntactic) type-checking assertions

If we were doing standard reflection—which we are not—we would then write a *reification* tactic,

```
Ltac p_reify P :=
   match P with
   | True ⇒ tc_TT       | False ⇒ tc_FF
   | ?P1 ∧ ?P2 ⇒ let t1 := p_reify P1 in
                 let t2 := p_reify P2 in
                 constr:(tc_andp t1 t2) ...
```

Finally, we *do* (as does standard reflection) write a simplification function that operates by recursion on tc_assert. Comparing the steps, we see that the reflection step, as well as any transformations on our reified data, will be computational. Reification, on the other hand, operates by matching proof terms. The computational steps are efficient because they operate in the same way as any functional program.

To avoid the costly reification step, the typechecker generates *syntax* directly—so we can perform the computation on it immediately, without need for reification. This keeps interactive proofs fast. The typechecker keeps all of its components real, meaning there are no reification tactics associated with it.

We use this design throughout the typechecker. We keep data reified for as long as possible, reflecting it only when it is in a form that the user needs to solve directly:

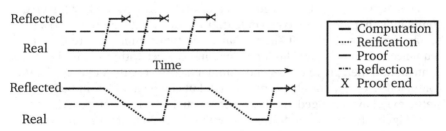

Figure 25.2: Our approach (top) vs. standard reflection (bottom)

The type context was briefly presented on page 153, along with the concept of initialization. We keep the type context *real* (reified) for fast proofs. The context is more than just an efficient way to store initialization—it is *predictable*. That is, some of the facts derivable from the context at some program points might also be derivable from the precondition (the user's assertions and invariants), but our proof automation can more easily digest the information from the type context than from user assertions. This is useful (for example) when our proof automation relates a variable name with its value (because we know it is initialized!). This is what allows go_lower (Chapter 27) to replace evaluated identifiers with values.

The type context is not always redundant with the precondition. A user who is proving only safety properties of a program—or functional correctness of a slice of the program with only shape properties of the rest of the code—may not care what an expression evaluates to, only that it doesn't crash the program. Keeping initialization information in the type context saves the user from needing to keep information about every single variable in each program, allowing them to focus only on the variables where one needs additional information about the value.

Although a typical typechecker makes recursive calls with a modified context Δ as it encounters variable declarations, typecheck_expr examines only (C light) expressions, which don't modify the state or contain internal variable bindings. Thus all recursive calls can use the same Δ.

The Hoare logic rules *do* keep track of updates to Δ, as they traverse commands that affect the type context. To understand how this works see semax_seq on page 157. It shows that when two commands are used in sequence, we must prove the first command correct with some initial type context, and then prove the second command correct with Δ updated by the command. No new variables are defined, but some variables' initialization status may have changed. updatetycon calculates which temporaries are unambiguously initialized during statement execution, and the Hoare rules for sequencing and if-then-else chain this information.

The Hoare logic is formulated to quantify only over dynamic environments that are well typed with respect to the type context. We can see how this is done in the definition of *guards* in Chapter 43. The Hoare rule that enters a function body uses the function:

func_tycontext (func: function) (V: varspecs) (G: funspecs): tycontext

to automatically build a type context given the program function, local, and global specifications. We have proved that the environment created by the operational semantics when entering a function body will always be well typed with respect to the context generated by this function.

The semax_seq rule for command sequencing (page 157) uses update_tycon to update Δ. There are two changes that can occur in Δ when a statement is executed, and they only affect initialization information. All other information about variables is available from the function header—C light does not permit variable declarations nested inside statements—so is described in Δ at the start of the function body.

For the sequence rule to be sound, we must prove that if an environment ρ is well typed with respect to a type context Δ, then ρ updated by command c (dynamically) is well typed with respect to Δ updated by c (statically). This is proved by induction over the form of commands.

Moving type context maintenance into the rules benefits the users of the rules: they don't need to worry about the contents of Δ, they never need to show that the environment typechecks, and they never need to mention Δ explicitly in preconditions. Our *rule of consequence* illustrates the automatic maintenance of Δ:

$$\frac{\text{typecheck\_environ}(\rho, \Delta) \wedge P \vdash P' \qquad \Delta \vdash \{P'\}\, c\, \{R\}}{\Delta \vdash \{P\}\, c\, \{R\}}$$

The conjunct (typecheck_environ(ρ, Δ) gives the user more information to work with in proving the goal. Without this, the user would need to explicitly strengthen assertions and loop invariants to keep track of the initialization status of variables and the types of values contained therein.

Although CompCert's operational semantics for statements and expressions are written as (noncomputational) inductive relations, these call upon some (computational) functions that can be used directly by our typechecker. For example, the typechecker calls upon CompCert's *classifi-cation* functions, that determine the behavior of overloaded operators by examining the types of their arguments.

Despite the reuse of CompCert code on operations, the typechecker still has many lines of code for checking binary operations. This is because of the operator overloading on almost every operator in C. There are eight operations the typechecker needs to be concerned with (shifts, boolean operators, and comparisons can each be grouped together as they have the exact same semantics with respect to the type returned). Each of these has around four behaviors in the semantics giving a total of around thirty cases that need to be handled individually for binary operations.

The typechecker matches on the syntax of the expression it is typecheck-ing. If the expression is an operation, we use CompCert's classify function to decide which overloaded behavior to use. From there, we generate the appropriate assertion. See Figure 25.3.

THEOREM (tc_expr_sound).   If the dynamic environment ρ is well-typed with respect to the static type context Δ, and the expression e typechecks in Δ producing an assertion that in turn is satisfied in ρ, then the value we get from evaluating e in ρ will match the type that e is labeled with.

typecheck_environ ρ Δ = true →
denote_tc_assert (typecheck_expr Δ e) ρ →
typecheck_val (eval_expr e ρ) (typeof e) = true

This theorem guarantees that an expression will evaluate to the right kind of value: integer, or float, or pointer. The undefined value belongs to no type, so as a corollary we guarantee the absence of Vundef.

COMPARISONS BETWEEN POINTERS present a unique challenge, as discussed on page 145. A comparison between two non-null pointers evaluates only if each points to an allocated object—if each has nonempty permission. Testing whether an object is allocated depends (dynamically) on the memory, or (statically, in a proof) on the spatial parts of the precondition. But our eval_expr does not see memory and our typechecker does not handle spatial assertions. Therefore our Hoare logic needs a special-case

```
Fixpoint typecheck_expr (Delta : tycontext) (e: expr) : tc_assert :=
  let tcr := typecheck_expr Delta in
  match e with
    | Econst_int _ (Tint _ _ _)
    | Econst_float _ (Tfloat _ _ _) ⇒ tc_TT
    | Etempvar id ty ⇒ (* nonaddressable local variable *)
      if negb (type_is_volatile ty) then
        match (temp_types Delta)!id with
          | Some ty' ⇒ if same_base_type ty (fst ty') then
                         if (snd ty') then tc_TT else (tc_initialized id ty)
                       else tc_FF (mismatch_context_type ty (fst ty'))
          | None ⇒ tc_FF (var_not_in_tycontext Delta id)
        end
      else tc_FF (volatile_load ty)
    | Eaddrof a ty ⇒ tc_andp (typecheck_lvalue Delta a)
                              (tc_bool (is_pointer_type ty) (op_result_type e))
    | Ebinop op a1 a2 ty ⇒ (* call typecheck_binop function *) ...
    | Evar id ty ⇒ (* global or addressable local, by-reference only *)
      match access_mode ty with
        | By_reference ⇒
          match get_var_type Delta id with
            | Some ty' ⇒
              tc_andp (tc_bool (eqb_type ty ty')
                               (mismatch_context_type ty ty'))
                      (tc_bool (negb (type_is_volatile ty))
                               (volatile_load ty))
            | None ⇒ tc_FF (var_not_in_tycontext Delta id)
          end
        | _ ⇒ tc_FF (deref_byvalue ty)
      end
    ⋮
  end.
```

Figure 25.3: Definition of the main typechecking function

rule, semax_ptr_compare (page 164), that can be applied only to the comparison of two pointers with nonempty permission.

The typechecker *can* guarantee that comparisons with the null pointer evaluate by generating an assertion that one of the two pointers is null. The comparison p==NULL returns a value even if p has empty permission. We can use the semax_set rule (page 161) for these comparisons because the typechecker can guarantee their evaluation.

To combine the two options for proving a pointer comparison, we create a new rule, derived from semax_set and semax_ptr_compare, that allows the user to decide which of the two cases to prove:

Lemma forward_ptr_compare': $\forall \Delta$ P Q R id cmp e1 e2 ty sh1 sh2 Post,
    is_comparison cmp = true $\rightarrow$
    typecheck_tid_ptr_compare Δ id = true $\rightarrow$

(PROPx P (LOCALx Q (SEPx R)) $\vdash$
        local (tc_expr Δ (Ebinop cmp e1 e2 ty)) &&
        local (tc_temp_id id ty Δ (Ebinop cmp e1 e2 ty))) $\lor$
(PROPx P (LOCALx (tc_environ Δ :: Q) (SEPx R))
        $\vdash$ local (tc_expr Δ e1) && local (tc_expr Δ e2) &&
        local (`(SeparationLogic.blocks_match cmp)
                    (eval_expr e1) (eval_expr e2)) &&
        (`(mapsto_ sh1 (typeof e1)) (eval_expr e1) * TT) &&
        (`(mapsto_ sh2 (typeof e2)) (eval_expr e2) * TT)) $\rightarrow$

(normal_ret_assert (EX old:val,
        PROPx P
        (LOCALx (`eq (eval_id id) (subst id `old
                        (eval_expr (Ebinop cmp e1 e2 ty))) ::
                    map (subst id `old) Q)
        (SEPx (map (subst id `old) R))))) $\vdash$ Post $\rightarrow$

    semax Δ (PROPx P (LOCALx Q (SEPx R)))
                (Sset id (Ebinop cmp e1 e2 ty))   Post.

The disjunction in the precondition allows the user to either prove the precondition for semax_ptr_compare or the precondition for semax_set. The postcondition is valid for either precondition because the typechecker allows eval_expr to return *whatever it wants* when the expression doesn't type check. We know that a comparison between two pointer values doesn't typecheck, so when eval_expr reaches that case we do exactly what the semantics specify in the case where both pointers point to allocated objects. The proof of this rule works in two cases:

1. We assume the left side of the disjunction, meaning that one of the expressions evaluates to the null pointer. In this case, we know the eval_expr in the post condition will give us a value that matches CompCert's semantics because we have the typechecking condition.

2. We assume the right side of the disjunction, meaning the correct mapstos appear in the precondition. This tells us that the pointers each point to allocated objects. Now eval_expr (which always assumes the pointers are at allocated objects) is exactly equivalent to the semantics.

To apply this rule, use the forward tactic when the first expression is a top-level pointer compare. Automation may be able to solve the disjunction, giving a result exactly like applying forward anywhere else. If the tactics can't solve the disjunction, it will be presented as a goal. The left (null pointer compare) or right (pointer pointer compare) tactic can be used to choose the solvable goal. Upon solving the goal, the rest of the proof will be the same as following any other use of forward.

Chapter 26

Derived rules and proof automation for C light

For convenient application of the VST program logic for C light, we have *synthetic* or *derived rules:* lemmas built from common combinations of the primitive inference rules for C light. We also have *proof automation:* programs that look at proof goals and choose which rules to apply.

For example, consider the C-language statements x:=e→f; and e1→f := e2; where x is a variable, f is the name of a structure field, and e,e1,e2 are expressions. The first command is a *load field* statement, and the second is a *store field*. Proofs about these statements could be done using the general semax_load and semax_store rules—along with the mapsto operator—but these require a lot of reasoning about field *l*-values. It's best to define a synthetic field_mapsto predicate that can be used as if it were a primitive:

Definition field_mapsto (sh:share)(t1:type)(fld:ident)(v1 v2: val): mpred.

We do not show the definition here (see floyd/field_mapsto.v) but basically field_mapsto π τ f v_1 v_2 is a predicate meaning: τ is a struct type whose field f of type τ_2 has address-offset δ from the base address of the struct; the size/signedness of f is ch, v_1 is a pointer to a struct of type τ, and the heaplet contains exactly $v_1 + \delta \overset{\pi}{\mapsto}_{ch} v_2$, (value v_2 at address $v_1 + \delta$ with permission-share π), where $v_2 : \tau_2$.

We can define a synthetic semax_load_field rule:

Lemma semax_load_field:
 $\forall$ (Δ: tycontext) sh id t1 fld P e1 v2 t2 i2 sid fields ,
 typeof e1 = Tstruct sid fields noattr $\rightarrow$
 (temp_types Δ) ! id = Some (t2,i2) $\rightarrow$
 t1 = typeof e1 $\rightarrow$
 t2 = type_of_field
        (unroll_composite_fields sid (Tstruct sid fields noattr) fields) fld) $\rightarrow$
 semax Δ
   ($\triangleright$ (local (tc_lvalue Δ e1) &&
       (`(field_mapsto sh t1 fld) (eval_lvalue e1) v2 * P)))
   (Sset id (Efield e1 fld t2))
   (normal_ret_assert
     (EX old:val, local (`eq (eval_id id) (subst id (`old) v2)) &&
       (subst id (`old)
         (`(field_mapsto sh t1 fld) (eval_lvalue e1) v2 * P)))).
Proof. (* in floyd/loadstore_lemmas.v *) **Qed**.

The typechecking premises (typeof, temp_types, type_of_field) are all purely computational; that is, in any particular program they are all proved by (compute; reflexivity). A synthetic semax_store_field rule is similar, for C statements of the form $e_1 \rightarrow f = e_2$.

IN STATEMENT PRECONDITIONS IT'S USEFUL TO SEGREGATE the assertion into three kinds of conjuncts:

PROP: Propositional conjucts, of the form !!P for some Coq P : Prop—these are independent of the program variables and the memory;

LOCAL: Local conjuncts, which depend on program variables but not on memory; and

SEP: Separation conjunctions, which may depend on both program variables and memory.

For easier processing and recognition of these conjunct classes,   we can write a *canonical form* of an assertion as,

$$\text{PROP}(P_0; P_1; \ldots, P_{l-1}) \text{ LOCAL}(Q_0; Q_1; \ldots, Q_{m-1}) \text{ SEP}(R_0; R_1; \ldots, R_{n-1})$$

defined formally as,

Definition PROPx (P: list Prop) (Q: assert) :=
        andp (prop (fold_right and True P)) Q.
Notation "'PROP' (x ; .. ; y) z" :=
    (PROPx (cons x%type .. (cons y%type nil) ..) z) (at level 10) : logic.
Notation "'PROP' ( ) z" := (PROPx nil z) (at level 10) : logic.

Definition LOCALx (Q: list (environ $\rightarrow$ Prop)) (R: assert) :=
        andp (local (fold_right (`and) (`True) Q)) R.
Notation " 'LOCAL' (x ; .. ; y) z" :=
    (LOCALx (cons x%type .. (cons y%type nil) ..) z) (at level 9) : logic.
Notation " 'LOCAL' ( ) z" := (LOCALx nil z) (at level 9) : logic.

Definition SEPx (R: list assert) : assert := fold_right sepcon emp R.

Notation " 'SEP' (x ; .. ; y)" :=
    (SEPx (cons x%logic .. (cons y%logic nil) ..)) (at level 8) : logic.
Notation " 'SEP' ( ) " := (SEPx nil) (at level 8) : logic.
Notation " 'SEP' () " := (SEPx nil) (at level 8) : logic.

Thus, $\text{PROP}(P_0; P_1) \text{ LOCAL}(Q_0; Q_1) \text{ SEP}(R_0; R_1)$ is equivalent to prop $P_0 \wedge$ prop P_1 && `prop $Q_0$ && `prop Q_1 && $(R_0 * R_1)$. No expressive power is gained by this—it just makes the components easier to match and process.

DERIVED RULES AND PROOF AUTOMATION go hand-in-hand: we formulate derived rules to suit the needs of proof automation. For example, we can write a corollary of the semax_load_field lemma in the PROP/LOCAL/SEP style:

```
1   Lemma semax_load_field'': ∀ π Δ (v: val) id fld P Q R e1 t2 i2 sid fields,
2       typeof e1 = Tstruct sid fields noattr →
3       (temp_types Delta) ! id = Some (t2,i2) →
4       t2 = type_of_field (unroll_composite_fields sid (typeof e1) fields) fld →
5       Cop.classify_cast t2 t2 = Cop.cast_case_neutral →
6       PROPx P (LOCALx(tc_environ Δ :: `isptr(eval_lvalue e1) ::Q) (SEPx R))
7                ⊢ local (tc_lvalue Δ e1) →
8       PROPx P (LOCALx(tc_environ Δ :: Q) (SEPx R))
9                ⊢ `(field_mapsto sh (typeof e1) fld) (eval_lvalue e1) `v * TT →
10      semax Δ (▷ PROPx P (LOCALx Q (SEPx R)))
11         (Sset id (Efield e1 fld t2))
12         (normal_ret_assert (
13           EX old:val, PROPx P
14                (LOCALx (`(eq v) (eval_id id) :: map (subst id (`old)) Q)
15                (SEPx (map (subst id (`old)) R)))))).
```

Not only do we characterize the pre-/postcondition in PROP/LOCAL/SEP form, but here we do not require the *first* spatial conjunct to be the field-mapsto in question. It suffices that the current precondition entail `(field_mapsto sh (typeof e1) fld) (eval_lvalue e1) `v * TT , and of course that entailment is modulo associativity/commutativity of the * operator, as well as any equality congruences implied by the local facts in $\vec{P}$ and $\vec{Q}$.

CONSIDER THE SITUATION DURING A PROGRAM VERIFICATION of a statement sequence $\{Pre_1\}\, c_1; c_2; c_3; c_4\, \{Post_4\}$ where c_2 is a *load* command such as h=p→head. Suppose we are partway through a forward proof, that is, we have just moved past c_1 by proving $\{Pre_1\}\, c_1\, \{Pre_2\}$. We keep our preconditions in canonical form for easy processing, that is, $Pre_2 = \mathrm{PROP}\,\vec{P}\,\mathrm{LOCAL}\,\vec{Q}\,\mathrm{SEP}\,\vec{R}$. Now our proof goal $\mathbf{G}_2$ is

```
semax Δ  (PROP P⃗ LOCAL Q⃗ SEP R⃗)
  (Ssequence (Sset _h (Efield (Ederef (Etempvar _p t_listptr) t_list)
                                _head t_int))
      (Ssequence c₃ c₄))
    Post₄
```

When preparing to verify the command c_2 in the sequence $c_2; c_3; c_4$ we apply the sequence rule (page 157) with a unification variable for the postcondition of c_2. That is, we eapply semax_seq, to obtain the two proof goals $\{Pre_2\}\, c_2\, \{?\}$ and $\{?\}\, c3; c4\, \{Post_4\}$.

We will use the rule semax_load_field'' to prove $\{Pre_2\}\, c_2\, \{?\}$. That lemma requires the later operator $\triangleright$ to be at the *outside* of the precondition, that is, $\triangleright$PROP(...) LOCAL(...) SEP(...). But in a typical situation, $Pre_2 = \vec{P}, \vec{Q}, \vec{R}$ looks like this:[1]

```
PROP()
LOCAL(`ptr_neq (eval_id _p) (`nullval);
         `(typed_true P.t_listptr) (eval_id _p);
         `(partial_sum contents (h :: r)) (eval_id P.i_s))
SEP( ▷ `(ilseg r) (`y) (`nullval);
         `(field_mapsto top t_list _head) (eval_id _p) (`(Vint n));
         `(field_mapsto top t_list _tail) (eval_id _p) (`y);
         TT))
```

Therefore the forward tactic calls upon our tactic hoist_later_in_pre to hoist and combine $\triangleright$ to the outside (or insert it *de novo*), using the rules $X \vdash \triangleright X$, $\triangleright X \wedge \triangleright Y = \triangleright(X \wedge Y)$, and $\triangleright X * \triangleright Y = \triangleright(X * Y)$. This works provided that any occurrence of $\triangleright$ is at top-level within a conjunct—this will be the case, when using typical indirection-theory recursive definitions for lists, trees, segments, objects, closures, and so on.

Then we can eapply semax_load_field'', which matches Δ, P, Q, R, id, e1, fld, t2 all from the current proof goal (the Hoare triple for c_2). This eapply creates unification variables for (the remaining quantified variables of the lemma) π, v, t2, i2, sid, fields, and produces six subgoals, for the premises of the lemma (listed on lines 2–8 on page 187). The first four premises (lines 2,3,4,5) are trivially proved by reflexivity, which at the same time instantiates sid,fields,t2,i2. The remaining two (lines 6,8) are entailments in separation logic; we prove these using an entailment solver described below. This process instantiates the remaining variables, π and v.

Thus, given the proof goal $\mathbf{G_2}$ it suffices that the field_mapsto conjunct appears anywhere within $\vec{R}$ with not more than one $\triangleright$ later operator applied

---

[1]This proof goal is from verifying the sumlist function shown in Chapter 27.

to it; the user applies forward, and the proof goal is then $\{Pre_3\}\, c_3;\, c_4\, \{Post_4\}$ for some Pre_3. If the field_mapsto conjunct is not manifest within $\vec{R}$, our entailer tactic may not find it—may be unable to solve the entailment premise of semax_load_field". In this case the user must do some proving work before applying the forward tactic. An example of this is at line 7 of Figure 3.1, where the precondition contains $\mathbf{v} \neq 0$ and $\mathbf{v} \overset{\sigma_2}{\leadsto} 0$ but *not* explicitly $\mathbf{v}.\text{next} \mapsto p$. The proofs from lines 7–10 unfold the list segment to expose $\mathbf{v}.\text{next} \mapsto p$, and then the automatic forward proof can continue (see the explanation on page 21).

THE TACTICAL SYSTEM for proving correctness properties of C light programs in the VST separation logic comprises:

normalize: General-purpose simplification by rewriting (see Chapter 14).

forward: Symbolic execution from the precondition of a statement to its postcondition.

go_lower: Reduces a proof goal from an entailment on environ$\rightarrow$mpred to one on mpred; unfolds PROP/LOCAL/SEP and all the lifting operators (back-ticks and lifted $*$ and &&, see Chapter 21) in an entailment; and changes C-language local variables into Coq variables. (go_lower is part of entailer, and not usually called directly.)

entailer: Partial solver for entailments in separation logic.

cancel: Proves entailments by rearrangement and cancellation, of the form $(P * Q) * (R * S) \vdash S * (P * R) * Q$, or $(P * Q) * (R * S) \vdash S * \mathsf{T} * Q$, or *frame inference* of the form $(P * Q) * (R * S) \vdash S * ? * Q$ where the $?$ will be instantiated with $P * R$.

There are also a few other tactics for symbolic execution and for entailment proving in separation logic.

THE forward TACTIC DOES SYMBOLIC EXECUTION. In practice, that means we apply Hoare logic rules. Suppose we want to prove a Hoare triple $\{P\}\text{x=y+1;y=p}\rightarrow\text{head};\{Q\}$. We can *almost* apply semax_set_forward (page 161); all we have to do is use the rule of consequence (semax_pre_post, page 170) to rearrange P into an assertion P_1 that has the form required by semax_set_forward. Starting on page 187 we illustrated that rearrangement for semax_load_field''. Then we apply the Hoare rule to $\{P_1\}$x=y+1;$\{?\}$—it is the nature of forward-style rules that an appropriate postcondition Q_1 can be calculated from the precondition P_1. Then if necessary we use the rule of consequence to rearrange Q_1 into an assertion P_2 that matches the semax_load_field'', as illustrated starting on page 187. Since semax_load_field'' is also a forward-style rule, we can apply it to $\{P_2\}$y=p$\rightarrow$head;$\{?\}$ yielding postcondition Q_2. Finally, we can use the rule of consequence to prove $Q_2 \vdash Q$.

In real execution, the program state has variables and memory locations containing actual integer and pointer values. In *symbolic execution* we describe the program state abstractly; in this case, we use assertions of separation logic to characterize the state as we "execute" the program by applying Hoare rules.

The forward tactic applies to a proof goal of the form $\Delta \vdash \{P\}\vec{c}\{Q\}$ where $\vec{c}$ is typically a sequence of commands. If forward can manage to rearrange P into a form required by a Hoare rule for the first command in $\vec{c}$, then it will do so (applying the rule of consequence), then it will apply the Hoare rule. This leaves a postcondition that will serve as the precondition for the *rest* of $\vec{c}$, and forward can be applied again.

On the other hand, if forward cannot see how to rearrange P into suitable form, the tactic will fail, and the user (of the interactive proof system) must apply proof rules, perhaps the rule of consequence, to massage P into a suitable form before going forward.

At the end of the line—in the case of $\{$x=y+1;y=p$\rightarrow$head;$\}$, after two applications of forward—there will remain an entailment (called $Q_2 \vdash Q$ above) that the user must prove.

How to prove entailments. The forward tactic sometimes leaves an entailment $P \vdash Q$ for the user to prove, or sometimes forward will fail unless the user first rearranges the precondition using the rule of consequence, again requiring the proof of an entailment. As explained in Chapter 21, proving entailments can be done in a simpler separation logic than the one we use for Hoare triples. When reasoning about $\{P\}c\{Q\}$, the program state (local-variable environment and memory) will be different before c (in P) than after (in Q). But for the entailment $P \vdash Q$, the program state is the same in both cases.

In our lifted separation logic, P and Q both have type env$\rightarrow$ mpred, function from local-variable environment ρ to a predicate on memory. By the definition of our lifted entailment, $P \vdash Q$ on the env$\rightarrow$ mpred separation logic means exactly $\forall \rho.\ P\rho \vdash Q\rho$. We can prove $P \vdash Q$ by first doing intro ρ in Coq, leaving the proof goal $P\rho \vdash Q\rho$.

Once ρ is fixed, there's no practical difference between a PROP term and a LOCAL term. Recall (from Chapter 21) that local$(Q)\rho$ is just $`(\text{prop})(Q)\rho$, which is just prop$(Q\rho)$. So we can unfold the PROPx,LOCALx,SEPx operators and all the lifting operators (backticks), then simplify.

This is what go_lower does. In addition, it recognizes C-language local variables and replaces them with Coq variables (see also page 139). Suppose an entailment contains eval_expr(Etempvar _a τ), for some program-identifier a. Coq sees _a as actually a constant of type ident, not as a logical variable of type τ. In any case, this expression simplifies to eval_id _a; then when go_lower has specialized to a particular environment ρ, this turns into eval_id _a ρ. In fact, if we are lucky, *all* the occurrences of ρ are exactly of this form (with various identifiers in place of _a).

We have designed our expression-evaluation semantics (eval_expr, eval_lvalue, eval_binop, etc.) and type-checking semantics (typecheck_expr, etc.) to be *curried in a type-directed fashion*. That is, these functions take their (C-language) type arguments first, then their value arguments. In the context of a program proof, all the type arguments in pre/postconditions will be instantiated by types from the program text. The go_lower tactic unfolds all these type-directed operators, and then (because the types are all instantiated) the semantics of expression-evaluation and type-checking simplifies away to primitive operations on values, with a few subterms of the form (eval_id _a ρ). These will be the only mentions of ρ, unless some subterms have user-defined predicates or quantifiers that prevent unfolding and simplification.

There are many implicit *casts* in C expressions, that the CompCert front-end makes explicit in the abstract syntax. The semantic casts (in the eval_expr of these abstract syntax expressions) will simplify, since the types are now concrete.

The Coq expression (eval_id _a ρ) has type val, the type of dynamic values in C expression evaluation. It would be more convenient to replace this with a : val, and eliminate the mention of ρ entirely. So the go_lower tactic does this for us: it introduces a new Coq variable a, and then "remembers" (eval_id _a ρ) as a. Then, if all the occurrences of ρ are eliminated this way, it can even clear ρ from the hypotheses.

This would not be very useful unless we could know that a$\neq$Vundef, that a is a defined value of appropriate (C-language) type. The typechecker allows us to accomplish this; see Chapter 25.

Entailment solving. The forward tactic generates entailments that need to be solved; and the user must sometimes explicitly use the rule of consequence, which also generates an entailment to be solved.

Our entailer tactic is a partial solver for entailments in the separation logic over mpred. If it cannot solve the goal entirely, it leaves a simplified subgoal for the user to prove. The algorithm is this:

1. Apply go_lower if the goal is in the lifted separation logic (over environ$\to$mpred).

2. Gather all the pure propositions to a single pure proposition on the left hand side (on each of the hypothesis and conclusion of the entailment). This is by rewriting using the gather_prop rules, such as !!P && (!!Q && R) = !!(P $\wedge$ Q) && R and P * (!!Q && R) = !!Q && (P * R).

3. Given the resulting goal !!($P_1 \wedge \ldots \wedge P_n$) && ($Q_1 * \ldots * Q_m$) $\vdash$!!($P'_1 \wedge \ldots \wedge P'_{n'}$) && ($Q'_1 \ldots * Q'_{m'}$), move each of the pure propositions P_i "above the line." Any P_i that's an easy consequence of other above-the-line hypotheses is deleted. Certain kinds of P_i are simplified in some ways, in the process.

4. For each of the Q_i, saturate_local extracts any pure propositions that are consequences of spatial facts, and inserts them above the line if they are not already present. For example, $p \mapsto_\tau q$ has two pure

consequences: isptr p (meaning that p is a pointer value, not an integer or float) and tc_val τ q (that the value q has type τ).

5. For any equations $(x = \ldots)$ or $(\ldots = x)$ above the line, substitute x.

6. Simplify C-language comparisons. In the then-clause of **if** $(i{<}j)$ or in the loop body of while $(i{<}j)$, the LOCAL part of the precondition will contain the semantics of $i < j$. But $i < j$ is actually rather complicated, depending on the integer or pointer types of i and j, on whether i and j type-check, on whether i is known to be the 32-bit representation of a mathematical integer represented in some Coq variable i', and so on. After typechecking and substitution, many of these complexities can be simplified away by the simpl_compare tactic.

7. Rewriting: the normalize tactic, as explained in Chapter 14.

8. Repeat from step 2, as long as progress is made.

9. Now the proof goal has the form $(Q_1 \ldots * Q_m) \vdash !!(P'_1 \wedge \ldots \wedge P'_{n'}) \,\&\&\, (Q'_1 \ldots * Q'_{m'})$. Any of the P'_i provable by auto are removed. If $Q_1 * \ldots * Q_m \vdash Q'_1 * \ldots * Q'_{m'}$ is trivially proved, then the entire $\&\& Q'_1 * \ldots * Q'_{m'}$ is removed.

AT THIS POINT the entailment may have been solved entirely. Or there may be some remaining P'_i and/or Q'_i proof goals on the right hand side. In that case the user actually has to do some thinking and some mathematics, to find the proof of the entailment. The idea is to prove each of the P'_i, and to massage the Q_i and Q'_i into a form where each Q_i cancels one Q'_i. The standard proof theory of Coq (with lemmas about separation logic), and standard tactical proving, may be used here.

CANCELLATION. Finally the proof goal might look like

$$Q_1 * Q_2 * \ldots * Q_n \vdash Q'_1 * Q'_2 \ldots * Q'_l.$$

In some cases one of the Q_i or Q'_i may be $\top$ or may even be an uninstantiated Coq logical variable (if *frame inference* needs to be performed). We say that $\top$ is *trivial*, as is an uninstantiated logical variable.

One simple proof strategy is to find a *nontrivial* Q_i that matches one of the nontrivial Q'_i, and cancel it from both sides of the entailment. This proof strategy is sound (i.e., if the subgoal can be proved, then so can the original goal), but it is not complete: it may turn a provable goal into an unprovable subgoal. Even though incomplete, it is still quite useful in practice; it is implemented by the cancel tactic. The **Hint** database called cancel contains primitive cancellation lemmas of the form $Q \vdash Q'$ that the cancel tactic uses for this purpose. Two examples of primitive cancellation rules are:

$$Q \vdash Q \qquad\qquad x \mapsto_\tau y \vdash x \mapsto \_$$

THIS WORKFLOW—forward/entailer/*think*/cancel—does most of the work in proving function-bodies correct. Somtimes entailer manages to dispose of the entire entailment, or leaves a goal that can directly be proved by cancel. The reason that entailer is distinct from cancel is that entailer (including go_lower, gather_prop, normalize, etc.) *does not lose information*—it never turns a provable goal into an unprovable goal—whereas cancel *is permitted to lose information*. For example, suppose we had already proved a lemma $A * B * C \vdash D * C$, and we have the goal, $A * B * C * E \vdash E * C * D$. Then the cancel tactic will leave the goal $A*B \vdash D$, which is not necessarily provable.[2] Therefore we leave the application of cancel to the user's discretion, unless it can solve the entire goal.

---

[2]It might seem strange that the presence of C is required to turn $A * B$ into D, but the theory of acyclic list segments has such lemmas. See the rule U4 on page 124.

Chapter 27

Proof of a program

We illustrate the use of tactical proof (semi)automation on the program shown in Figure 27.1. We compile this source program reverse.c into a C-light abstract-syntax data structure using the front end of CompCert, the clightgen utility. This produces a Coq file reverse.v with a sequence of definitions in the CompCert abstract-syntax tree structures (Figure 27.2).

Clightgen comprises CompCert's (unverified) parser into CompCert C, followed by CompCert's (verified) translation into C light. The fact that one or another of these front-end phases is unverified does not concern us, because we apply the program logic to the *output* of these translations. If we specify correctness properties of reverse.v and prove them, then the C light program will have those properties, regardless of whether it matches the source program reverse.c. Of course, it is very desirable for reverse.v to match reverse.c, so the programmer may reason informally about unverified properties of reverse.c such as timing, information flow, or resource consumption.

THIS PROGRAM USES LINKED LISTS of 32-bit integers. Before proceeding with the verification, we should develop the theory of list segments (a "theory" is just what we call a collection of definitions, lemmas, and tactics useful for reasoning about the subject matter). Chapter 19 explained the theory of list segments; in the file list.v we build an lseg theory parameterized by a C structure definition. Using this theory we can reason about any struct (such

```
#include <stddef.h>

struct list {int head; struct list *tail;};

struct list three[] = { {1, three+1}, {2, three+2}, {3, NULL} };

int sumlist (struct list *p) {
    int s = 0;
    struct list *t = p;
    int h;
    while (t) {h = t→head; t = t→tail; s = s + h;}
    return s;
}

struct list *reverse (struct list *p) {
    struct list *w, *t, *v;
    w = NULL;
    v = p;
    while (v) {t = v→tail; v→tail = w; w = v; v = t; }
    return w;
}

int main (void) {
    struct list *r; int s;
    r = reverse(three);
    s = sumlist(r);
    return s;
}
```

Figure 27.1: Program **reverse.c**

Definition _p : ident := 8%positive.
Definition _struct_list : ident := 5%positive.
...
Definition t_struct_list :=
  (Tstruct _struct_list
    (Fcons _head tint (Fcons _tail (Tcomp_ptr _struct_list noattr) Fnil))
    noattr).

Definition f_sumlist :=

  ...
  (Ssequence
   (Sset _t (Etempvar _p (tptr t_struct_list)))
   (Ssequence
    (Swhile
     (Etempvar _t (tptr t_struct_list))
     (Ssequence ...)))) ...

Figure 27.2: Coq definitions **reverse.v** (excerpt), produced from reverse.c
by the clightgen utility.

as t_struct_list in this program) with one link field (a pointer to the same
struct) and any number of data fields—regardless of the names of the fields
or the type of the data field. The user must simply build an Instance of the
listspec class that specifies the struct type and the name of the link field;
from this we can define the theory of list-segments over that C-language
struct type:

lseg: $\forall \{t_{struct}\}\{\iota_{link}\}(ls:$ listspec t_{struct} $\iota_{link})$
    $(\pi:$ share$)$ $(\sigma:$ list val$)$ $(p$ $q:$ val$)$, mpred.

An example of a listspec for our reverse.c program is,

Instance LS: listspec t_struct_list _tail.

which describes the list structure shown at the top of Figure 27.1.

We write lseg LS π σ p q for the list segment with ownership-share π, contents σ (a sequence of C-language values), starting at pointer p and ending at q; Coq learns the field-names from the LS.

It's provable (from the definition of lseg) that every element of σ must match the C-language type τ, the type of the struct's data field (as specified in LS). In our reverse.c program the τ of LS is tint; each of the list elements must typecheck as tint, so therefore must be a Vint value.

WE PROCEED WITH THE PROGRAM VERIFICATION (file progs/verif_reverse.v) by giving each function needs a specification. Consider the list-reverse program-fragment proved correct in Figure 3.1 (page 22). The precondition is $\{v \overset{\sigma}{\leadsto} 0\}$ and postcondition is $\{w \overset{\text{rev}\,\sigma}{\leadsto} 0\}$, and this must hold for whatever σ is the contents of the input list v. Supposing this program-fragment to be the function-body of the reverse function, we can specify the function as,

Definition reverse_spec : ident * funspec :=
  DECLARE _reverse
   WITH π : share, σ : list int
   PRE [_p OF (tptr t__struct_list)] !! writable_share π &&
       `(lseg LS $\pi$ $\sigma$) (eval_id _p) (`nullval)
   POST [(tptr t__struct_list)] `(lseg LS $\pi$ (rev $\sigma$)) retval (`nullval).

The DECLARE notation constructs an ident×funspec pair, where the ident is the name of the function (in this case, _reverse). The WITH clause gives the name(s) of Coq variable(s) that can be mentioned in both the precondition and the postcondition (so that we can say the result is the reverse of the *same* sequence σ, with the *same* permission-share π).

The PRE clause gives the function precondition, parametrized by the C-language names (_p) and C-language types (**struct** list *) of the formal parameters. Here, the precondition says that the fractional share π gives *at least* write-permission, and the local-variable-identifier _p is the head of a list-segment that terminates in nullval (= Vint 0).

The POST clause gives the function precondition, parametrized by the return value (always called retval) and the return type (in square brackets)).

The specification of main is special: The precondition of a program *prog* is always main_pre(*prog*) and the postcondition is main_post(*prog*). The main_pre operator constructs a separation-logic predicate describing the extern global initializers of the C program. Here the global initializers are

struct list three[] = { {1, three+1}, {2, three+2}, {3, NULL} };

and the corresponding predicate is, roughly speaking, the separating conjuction of six mapstos of the form,

$(three[0].head \mapsto 1) * (three[0].tail \mapsto \&three[1]) * (three[1].head \mapsto 2) * \dots$

Theorem. One can view the initializers of the extern global three as a linked list with contents (1::2::3::nil).

Lemma setup_globals:
    ∀ u rho, tc_environ (func_tycontext P.f_main Vprog Gtot) rho →
    main_pre P.prog u rho   '
    ⊢ lseg LS Ews (Int.repr 1 :: Int.repr 2 :: Int.repr 3 :: nil)
            (eval_var P._three (Tarray P.t_struct_list 3 noattr) rho)
            nullval.

Having specified all the individual functions, one builds a *program specification* Γ, which is just a list of the function specifications. This is exactly as shown in Chapter 18 (page 117), and for C it looks like this:

Definition Γ_{prog} : funspecs := sumlist_spec::reverse_spec::main_spec::nil.

To this we add the specifications of all the external functions callable in the runtime system.

Definition Γ := do_builtins (prog_defs P.prog) ++ Γ_{prog}.

When we prove each of the three function bodies in this program, we may assume Γ. The Γ hypothesis will be used if we want to call one of the functions specified in Γ (even recursively or mutually recursively).

Global variables are specified in a list of varspecs, that is, list(ident×type). For the reverse.c program we have,

Definition V_{prog} : varspecs := (P._three, Tarray P.t_struct_list 3 noattr)::nil.

One might wonder, "where is the initializer value?" but the varspec expresses only that which is invariant during the entire program execution— the initialized contents may be altered by the program, so we treat them as separation-logic precondition of main, not as an invariant.

Next, we prove that each function body meets its specification, that is,

semax_body V Γ f $spec_f$

meaning that in the context V, Γ (varspecs and funspecs), the function-definition f satisfies its specification $spec_f$. For example:

Lemma body_reverse: semax_body Vprog Gtot P.f_reverse reverse_spec.
Proof.
start_function.
name _p P._p.
name _v P._v.
name _w P._w.
name _t P._t.

A function-body proof always starts with the application of the start_function tactic, which unpacks the formal parameters. Then we name the local variables (formal parameters and nonaddressable locals).[1] The purpose of name _w P._w is to tell the go_lower tactic to use the name _w to hold the value in the program-variable whose identifier is P._w (henceforth we qualify with P. anything imported from reverse.v).

---

[1]This name tactic is needed because Coq's fresh tactic cannot handle a qualified name.

This is the proof goal at the completion of function entry:

```
sh : share
contents : list int
Δ := func_tycontext P.f_reverse Vprog Gtot : tycontext
H : writable_share sh
_p : name P._p
_v : name P._v
_w : name P._w
_t : name P._t
--------------------------------------(1/1)
semax Δ
  (PROP ()
   LOCAL()
   SEP(`(lseg LS sh contents) (eval_id P._p) (`nullval)))
  (Ssequence (Sset P._w (Ecast (Econst_int (Int.repr 0) tint) (tptr tvoid)))
     . . . rest of commands in function body
  )
  (function_body_ret_assert (tptr P.t_struct_list)
     (`(lseg LS sh (rev contents)) retval (`nullval)))
```

The first lines sh,contents come from the WITH clause of the funspec. The type-context Δ contains the types of all global variables, specifications of all functions in Γ, and types of all this function's local variables; it is computed automatically by func_tycontext (and *computed* is the right word; type contexts are entirely computational for efficient processing).

The hypothesis H was automatically extracted from the precondition of the function; this is done for the purely propositional components (in the PROP section) of the precondition.

FORWARD SYMBOLIC EXECUTION through assignment statements w=NULL; v=p; is easy, using two applications of the forward tactic. If the right-hand-side expression has nontrivial typechecking (which is rare) then forward might generate an entailment subgoal (to show that the current precondition entails the typechecking condition). Here (as usual) the

expressions NULL and p have typechecking conditions of True and are
handled automatically.

This leaves us at the while loop, with the proof goal,

```
sh : share
contents : list int
H : writable_share sh
_p : name P._p
_v : name P._v
_w : name P._w
_t : name P._t
Δ := initialized P._v (initialized P._w (func_tycontext ...))
-------------------------------------(1/1)
semax Δ
  (PROP ()
   LOCAL
   (`eq (eval_id P._v) (eval_expr(Etempvar P._p (tptr P.t_struct_list)));
    `eq (eval_id P._w)(eval_expr(Ecast(Econst_int Int.zero tint)(tptr tvoid)))
   SEP
   (`(lseg LS sh (map Vint contents)) (eval_id P._p) (`nullval)))
   (Ssequence
       (Swhile (Etempvar P._v (tptr P.t_struct_list))
           (... loop body ...)
       (Sreturn (Some (Etempvar P._w (tptr P.t_struct_list)))))
   (... function postcondition ...)
```

Each of the two assignment statements is now manifest in the precondition
of the following statement: the consequence of w=NULL appears as

```
`eq (eval_id P._w)(eval_expr(Ecast(Econst_int Int.zero tint)(tptr tvoid)))
```

and v=p appears similarly.

The general semax_set_forward rule has, in its postcondition, an existential binding of the "old" value of the assigned variable. But here the
assigned variable (such as _w) does not appear in the precondition, so
there's no need to mention its old value; a simpler (and weaker) version of

semax_set_forward has been used (automatically), that omits any mention of the old value.

Note that Δ now contains all its previous information derived from func_tycontext, *plus* the new information that v and w are initialized. The symbolic execution tactic has derived this information from the update_tycon clause in the Hoare rule for assignment.

SYMBOLIC EXECUTION OF A WHILE-LOOP requires the user to supply a loop invariant and a postcondition; this is done as arguments to the forward_while tactic:

```
forward_while
  (* loop invariant *)
  (EX cts1: list int, EX cts2 : list int,
    PROP(contents = rev cts1 ++ cts2)
    LOCAL()
    SEP(`(lseg LS sh (map Vint cts1)) (eval_id P._w) (`nullval);
        `(lseg LS sh (map Vint cts2)) (eval_id P._v) (`nullval)))
  (* loop postcondition *)
  (PROP() LOCAL()
    SEP(`(lseg LS sh (map Vint (rev contents)))
        (eval_id P._w) (`nullval))).
```

The loop invariant is just as in Figure 3.1 (page 22),

$$\exists \sigma_1, \sigma_2.\, \sigma = \text{rev}(\sigma_1) \cdot \sigma_2 \wedge w \overset{\sigma_1}{\rightsquigarrow} 0 \wedge v \overset{\sigma_2}{\rightsquigarrow} 0$$

expressed in clunky Coq notation. The postcondition is $w \overset{\text{rev}(\sigma)}{\rightsquigarrow} 0$.

Applying forward_while leaves five subgoals:

1. the loop precondition implies the loop invariant;

2. the invariant implies the typechecking condition of the loop-test expression;

3. the loop invariant and the negation of the loop-test together imply the loop postcondition;

4. the loop body (with the assumption the loop-test is true) preserves the loop invariant; and

5. symbolic execution of the rest of the function, after the loop.

Items 1,2,4 are entailments, proved by the general method described on page 194: entailer/*think*/cancel. Items 3,5 are symbolic execution, handled by forward (or forward_while if there are nested loops).

When a return statement is reached, forward leaves a proof obligation, to show that the value returned satisfies the postcondition of the function. For example, just before the return w at the end of reverse, we have the proof goal,

```
semax Δ
  (PROP () LOCAL()
   SEP(`(lseg LS sh (map Vint (rev contents))) (eval_id P._w)
      (`nullval)))
  (Sreturn (Some (Etempvar P._w (tptr P.t_struct_list))))
  (function_body_ret_assert (tptr P.t_struct_list)
      (`(lseg LS sh (rev (map Vint contents))) retval (`nullval)))
```

That is, the precondition is $w \overset{\mathrm{rev}(\sigma)}{\rightsquigarrow} 0$, and the postcondition for return is the *function body return assertion* for this function, which says that the return value must have type pointer-to-struct-list, and that *retval* $\overset{\mathrm{rev}(\sigma)}{\rightsquigarrow} 0$, where retval is the name always given to the return-value, the argument of return.

Forward symbolic execution through this statement produces a goal which after go_lower looks like,

```
lseg LS sh (map Vint (rev contents)) _w nullval
⊢ lseg LS sh (rev (map Vint contents)) _w nullval
```

which is easily proved by rewrite map_rev.

Function call and frame inference. Recall the specification of reverse on page 198. The precondition for calling reverse(p) is that (for some

π and σ), writable_share(π) $\wedge$ $p \overset{\sigma}{\rightsquigarrow}_\pi 0$. If the caller's current assertion
(precondition) is

$$(p \overset{a}{\rightsquigarrow}_{\pi'} p') * (s \mapsto 7) * (p' \overset{\beta}{\rightsquigarrow}_{\pi'} 0) * Q$$

then the precondition holds on a *portion* $(p \overset{a}{\rightsquigarrow}_{\pi'} p') * (p' \overset{a}{\rightsquigarrow}_\pi 0)$ of the
current heap, with *witness* $\pi = pi'$, $\sigma = \alpha \cdot \beta$. The remaining part $(s \mapsto 7) * Q$
is the *frame*.

In order to prove a function-call, both the witness and the frame must
be exhibited. The semiautomatic forward symbolic execution (through
a function-call) leaves an entailment subgoal with two uninstantiated
unification variables: the user must fill in the witness, and then the cancel
tactic automatically deduces the frame.

We illustrate (in the file progs/verif_reverse.v) in the main function that
has a call to reverse.[2] Going forward from the C statement r=reverse(three);
yields this proof goal:

semax Δ (PROP P LOCALQ SEPR)
   (Ssequence
     (Scall (Some x) (Evar P._reverse τ_{reverse}) (Evar P._three τ_{three}))
     (Sset P._r (Etempvar x (tptr P.t_struct_list))))
   (... postcondition ...)

Going forward yields a subgoal that looks like this:

witness := ?52 : share $*$ list int
Frame := ?53 : list assert
-----------------------------------(1/3)
PROP(P) LOCAL(Q) SEP(R)
$\vdash$ PROP() LOCAL(*typecheck arguments*) SEP(Pre_r(witness); Frame)

This means the user needs to find a witness such that the current precondition $(P/Q/R)$ implies the precondition of the function reverse, separated

---

[2]The Coq 1.12 clightgen front-end phases turn the command r=reverse(three); into
the commands x=reverse(three); r=x; where x is not used elsewhere in the function body.
Until this is fixed in some future version of CompCert, the symbolic-execution tactics will
match this pattern specially, to save work for the user, as if it were simply r=reverse(three).

from a Frame assertion. The first step in proving this is to exhibit a witness W by instantiating ?52, as follows:

instantiate (1:= (Ews, Int.repr 1 :: Int.repr 2 :: Int.repr 3 :: nil))
      in (Value of witness).

In this case, $W =$(Ews, Int.repr 1 :: ... :: nil).

The next step is to prove the entailment, typically by entailer followed by *think*. After doing so, a typical proof goal is something like this,

witness := (Ews, Int.repr 1 :: ... :: nil) : share * list int
Frame := ?53 : list assert
--(1/3)
$P * S * Q \vdash Q * P * \text{Frame}$

in which the Frame has still not been instantiated. The cancel tactic, which does rearrangement to cancel P and Q, then automatically takes care of instantiating (in this case) the term S as the Frame assertion.

Thus, to verify a function call, the pattern is,

forward. instantiate (1:=...) in (Value of witness).
enatailer. *think*. cancel.
auto with closed. *(* see note[3] *)*

NOW WE HAVE PROVED EACH FUNCTION INDIVIDUALLY, with these three lemmas:

Lemma body_sumlist: semax_body Vprog Gtot P.f_sumlist sumlist_spec.
Lemma body_reverse: semax_body Vprog Gtot P.f_reverse reverse_spec.
Lemma body_main: semax_body Vprog Gtot P.f_main main_spec.

We tie the function-body proofs together into a whole-program proof. We walk through the two parallel lists—the list of function definitions in the program (prog_funct P.prog) and the list of function specifications Gtot—and zip them together using semax_func_cons.

---

[3]At present, the system leaves one more proof obligation, to prove that the auxiliary variable x is not free in the Frame assertion. This will always be true, and provable using auto with closed.

Lemma all_funcs_correct:
  semax_func Vprog Gtot (prog_funct P.prog) Gtot.
Proof.
unfold Gtot, Gprog, P.prog, prog_funct; simpl.
repeat (apply semax_func_cons_ext; [reflexivity | apply semax_external_FF |]).
apply semax_func_cons; [reflexivity | apply body_sumlist |].
apply semax_func_cons; [reflexivity | apply body_reverse |].
apply semax_func_cons; [reflexivity | apply body_main |].
apply semax_func_nil.
Qed.

This proves that the whole program meets its specification. In the process it ensures that the specification of reverse *assumed* when proving the function-call from main to reverse, matches the specification actually *proved* about the implementation of reverse.

The reflexivity proofs all check the following *computational* premise of semax_func_cons:

(id_in_list id (map (@fst _ _) G)
  && negb (id_in_list id (map (@fst ident fundef) fs))
  && semax_body_**params**_ok f)   =   true

Respectively, the function-name appears in Γ, no two functions in the program have this name, and this function's parameters do not contain duplicates.

Chapter 28

More C programs

When we reason about programs that operate on structured data, it is useful to have a structured (type-directed) mapsto operator. In conventional presentations of separation logic it is common to write $p \mapsto (x, y)$ or $p \hookrightarrow (x, y)$ to mean $p.\text{fst} \mapsto x * p.\text{snd} \mapsto y$. In our Floyd system for reasoning about C programs, the operator is

typed_mapsto (π: share) (t: type) (v: val) (w: reptype t) : mpred.
typed_mapsto_ (π: share) (t: type) (v: val) : mpred.

This means, a heaplet containing just address v mapping to value w with ownership share π. To describe an uninitialized structure, or one with unknown contents, use typed_mapsto_ instead. The size of the footprint starting at v will be exactly sizeof(t).

For example, if t_{xy} is the C structure type **struct** {**int** x,y;}, then

typed_mapsto π t_{xy} v ((a,b): int*int) =
field_mapsto π t_{xy} _x v a * field_mapsto π t_{xy} _y v b.

We see that typed_mapsto is dependently typed. The type of w depends on the value t, using reptype(t), shown in Figure 28.1. This calculates a representation Type (in Coq) for any C-language type.

The internals of the typed_mapsto definition are rather complicated, because of the need for internal alignment-spacers in the layout of C-language structure types. However, Floyd provides some useful tactics for simplifying typed_mapsto and typed_mapsto_, in particular **Ltac** simpl_typed_mapsto.

```
Fixpoint reptype (ty: type) : Type :=
  match ty with
  | Tvoid ⇒ unit
  | Tint ___⇒ int
  | Tfloat __⇒ float
  | Tpointer t1 a ⇒ val
  | Tarray t1 sz a ⇒ list (reptype t1)
  | Tfunction t1 t2 ⇒ unit
  | Tstruct id fld a ⇒ reptype_structlist fld
  | Tunion id fld a ⇒ reptype_unionlist fld
  | Tcomp_ptr id a ⇒ val
  end

with reptype_structlist (fld: fieldlist) : Type :=
  match fld with
  | Fnil ⇒ unit
  | Fcons id ty fld' ⇒
          if is_Fnil fld'
                      then reptype ty
                      else prod (reptype ty) (reptype_structlist fld')
  end
with reptype_unionlist (fld: fieldlist) : Type :=
  match fld with
  | Fnil ⇒ unit
  | Fcons id ty fld' ⇒ sum (reptype ty) (reptype_unionlist fld')
  end.
```

Figure 28.1: reptype

We have already used a version of typed_mapsto—in particular a predicate structfieldsof—in constructing the theory of list segments that we use in specifying and proving reverse.c (Chapter 27).

IN THIS CHAPTER WE SHOW the specifications of three more C programs. The reader may view—and interact with—the proofs that these programs meet their specifications, in vst/progs.

In the sumarray.c program (Figure 28.2), the function sumarray adds up the elements of an array; the array four is a global extern initialized variable. To specify the contents of an array, we use the predicate array_at_range t π f lo hi v, which says that there is an array at address v whose elements from lo to $hi - 1$ all have C-language type t and ownership share π. Furthermore, the element at index i satisfies $f(i)$.

Definition rangespec (lo hi: Z) (P: Z → mpred) : mpred :=
$\forall i, lo \leq i < hi \rightarrow P(i)$.

Definition array_at (t:type) (π:share) (v:val) (i:Z) (e: reptype t): mpred :=
typed_mapsto π t (add_ptr_int t v i) e.

Definition array_at_range t π (f: Z → reptype t) (lo hi: Z) (v: val) :=
rangespec lo hi (fun i ⇒ array_at t sh v i (f i)).

These definitions can describe arrays of any element type, since array_at uses typed_mapsto.

The proof system for arrays in VST 1.0 is rather primitive. The logic is expressive enough to represent any reasonable assertion about arrays, using definitions such as array_at, but proofs tend to operate by unfolding of these definitions. It might be preferable to use higher-level proof theories that take advantage of the special structure of arrays and array indexing.

```
int sumarray(int a[], int n) {
  int i=0, s=0, x;
  while (i<n) {
    x=a[i]; s+=x; i++;
  }
  return s;
}
```

```
int four[4] = {1,2,3,4};

int main(void) {
  int s = sumarray(four,4);
  return s;
}
```

Definition add_elem (f: Z → int) (i: Z) := Int.add (f i).

Definition sumarray_spec :=
DECLARE _sumarray
WITH a0: val, sh : share, contents : Z → int, size: Z
PRE [_a OF (tptr tint), _n OF tint]
    PROP(0 <= size <= Int.max_signed)
    LOCAL(`(eq a0) (eval_id _a);
            `(eq (Vint (Int.repr size))) (eval_id _n);
            `isptr (eval_id _a))
    SEP(`(array_at_range tint sh contents 0 size) (eval_id _a))
POST [tint]
    local (`(eq (Vint (fold_range (add_elem contents) Int.zero 0 size)))
              retval)
          && `(array_at_range tint sh contents 0 size a0).

Definition four_contents (z: Z) : int := Int.repr (Zsucc z).

Lemma setup_globals:
    ∀ u rho, tc_environ (func_tycontext f_main Vprog Gtot) rho →
    main_pre prog u rho
      ⊢ array_at_range tint Ews four_contents 0 4
            (eval_var _four (tarray tint 4) rho).

Figure 28.2: sumarray.c and its specification

THE queue.c PROGRAM (FIGURE 28.3) DEMONSTRATES AN ABSTRACT DATA TYPE, as well as some interesting design issues for separation logic.

Consider a multithreaded application where a process control block (an *"element"*) is sometimes placed on a "ready queue," sometimes placed on the queue of threads contending for resource A, sometimes on the queue contending for resource B, and sometimes (when executing) not on any queue at all. The element is never on two queues at once.

The *queue* data type can be designed to avoid any memory allocation during ordinary queue operations. That is, we malloc to create a queue, we malloc to create an element, but the elements move into and out of various queues many times during their lifetimes without additional memory allocation/deallocation. This typical C programming idiom leads to an interface in which the queue elements are records with some non-queue-related fields, and one *next* field that is dedicated to the use of queues.

Our program's element type,

struct elem { int a, b; struct elem *next; };

has application-specific fields, a and b, and next is the *link* field.

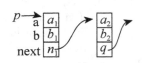

It's a bit clumsy to mix the application-specific data in the same record as the link field—but this is a typical C programming idiom, it *can* be done correctly, therefore our program logic *can* prove it.

THE WRONG SPECIFICATION. Given the two-element list shown above, we can write $p \overset{\sigma}{\rightsquigarrow} q$ where $\sigma = (a_1, b_1) :: (a_2, b_2) :: $ nil. Our lseg operator (in list_dt.v) calculates the Coq type (int*int) from the C type t_struct_elem by leaving out the next field, and relates p and q to σ.

This method is fine for situations where we care only about the *contents* of a list, but the process-descriptor is at a particular *location* that must be preserved as it enters and leaves different queues.

THE RIGHT SPECIFICATION is based on locations, just values. The thread that uses a process descriptor may want to load and store from its fields (other

```
extern void *mallocN (int n);
extern void freeN (
              void *p, int n);

struct elem {
  int a, b;
  struct elem *next;
};

struct fifo {
  struct elem *head;
  struct elem *tail;
};

struct fifo *fifo_new(void) {
  struct fifo *Q =
    (struct fifo *)
      mallocN(sizeof (*Q));
  Q→head = NULL;
  Q→tail = NULL;
  return Q;
}


struct elem *fifo_get (
              struct fifo *Q){
  struct elem *h, *n;
  h=Q→head;
  n=h→next;
  Q→head=n;
  return h;
}
```

```
int fifo_empty (struct fifo *Q) {
  struct elem *h;
  h = Q→head;
  return (h == NULL);
}

void fifo_put (struct fifo *Q,
              struct elem *p) {
  struct elem *h, *t;
  p→next=NULL;
  h = Q→head;
  if (h==NULL) {
    Q→head=p;
    Q→tail=p;
  }
  else {
    t = Q→tail;
    t→next=p;
    Q→tail=p;
  }
  return;
}


struct elem *make_elem (
              int a, int b){
  struct elem *p;
  p = mallocN(sizeof (*p));
  p→a=a;
  p→b=b;
  return p;
}
```

Figure 28.3: queue.c

than next) and rely on the fact that it is in the same place—before it is
enqueued, after it is dequeued, and even while it is on a queue.

Separation logic describes "ownership." The
location-based specification says that when a
record (a,b,next) is enqueued, ownership of
only the next field is transferred to the queue,
as shown at right; the dashed fields are re-
tained by the client.

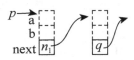

We describe this data structure as links QS π σ p q, where QS is the
structure-specification (just as in lseg), π is the ownership share of the next
fields, σ is the list of addresses $p :: n_1 :: $ nil, and p and q are the end pointers
of the segment. The predicates lseg and links are much alike, except that

- the σ for lseg is the list of contents of all but the link field, whereas
  the σ for links is the list of addresses of the records;

- the footprint of lseg includes all the fields, whereas the footprint of
  links includes only the link fields.

The struct fifo data type keeps track of the head and tail of the linked
list, with the head is at the "get" end and tail is at the "put" end. In the
empty queue, the head is NULL and the the tail points anywhere.

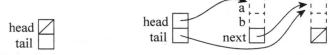

Definition fifo (contents: list val) (p: val) : mpred:=
  EX ht: (val∗val), **let** (hd,tl) := ht **in**
      field_mapsto Tsh t_struct_fifo _head p hd ∗
      field_mapsto Tsh t_struct_fifo _tail p tl ∗
      if isnil contents
      then (!!(hd=nullval) && emp)
      else (EX prefix: list val,
              !!(contents = prefix++tl::nil)
          && (links QS Tsh prefix hd tl ∗ link tl nullval)).

The representation relation for fifo queues is this: *p* is a fifo representing the sequence *contents* so long as there exists a head-pointer *hd* and a tail-pointer-pointer *tl* that are the contents of the header structure, and *either* the contents-list is empty head is NULL, *or* the contents-list is nonempty, there is a list of all-but-the-last elements (from *hd* to *tl*) and an ultimate element pointed to by *tl*.

We will define,

Definition link := field_mapsto Tsh t_struct_elem _next.
Definition link_ := field_mapsto_ Tsh t_struct_elem _next.

Once we have the representation relation, it's straightforward to specify each of the queue functions. fifo_new creates a new queue, representing the nil contents, out of emp.

Definition fifo_new_spec :=
DECLARE _fifo_new
  WITH u : unit
  PRE [ ] emp
  POST [(tptr t_struct_fifo)] `(fifo nil) retval.

Definition fifo_put_spec :=
DECLARE _fifo_put
  WITH q: val, contents: list val, p: val
  PRE [_Q OF (tptr t_struct_fifo) , _p OF (tptr t_struct_elem)]
        PROP() LOCAL(`(eq q) (eval_id _Q); `(eq p) (eval_id _p))
        SEP(`(fifo contents q); `(link_ p))
  POST [tvoid] `(fifo (contents++(p :: nil)) q).

To put *elem* into the queue at address *q*, start with a fifo at *q* representing the sequence *contents*, separated from the representation of *elem* at address _p; finish with the fifo at *q* enlarged by one element at the tail end.

To test a queue for empty, start with a fifo at *q*, finish with the same fifo at *q* but with the return-value =Vtrue if the *contents* was nil, otherwise Vfalse.

Definition fifo_empty_spec :=
 DECLARE _fifo_empty
  WITH q: val, contents: list val
  PRE [_Q OF (tptr t_struct_fifo)]
    PROP() LOCAL(`(eq q) (eval_id _Q)) SEP(`(fifo contents q))
  POST [tint]
    local (`(eq (**if** isnil contents **then** Vtrue **else** Vfalse)) retval)
    && `(fifo (contents) q).

Definition fifo_get_spec :=
 DECLARE _fifo_get
  WITH q: val, contents: list val, p: val
  PRE [_Q OF (tptr t_struct_fifo)]
      PROP() LOCAL(`(eq q) (eval_id _Q))
      SEP(`(fifo (p :: contents) q))
  POST [(tptr t_struct_elem)]
    local (`(eq p) retval) && `(fifo contents q) * `link_ retval.

To get the head element, the precondition requires the queue must not
be empty, it must contain at least a head element *elem* and a remaining
contents. Then fifo_get separates *elem* from the rest of the queue.

Finally, we have an (application-specific) initializer function for queue-
element records. The empty list of SEP() conjuncts is the same as emp.

Definition make_elem_spec :=
 DECLARE _make_elem
  WITH a: int, b: int
  PRE [_a OF tint, _b OF tint]
      PROP() LOCAL(`(eq (Vint a)) (eval_id _a);
                      `(eq (Vint b)) (eval_id _b)) SEP()
  POST [(tptr t_struct_elem)] `(elemrep (a,b)) retval.

Chapter 29

Dependently typed C programs

When C programmers wish to implement higher-order features such as objects or function pointers, they cast pointers to and from void∗. Statically, any pointer can be cast to/from void∗; dynamically, one hopes that when one actually dereferences a field, the appropriate data is present.

    We will illustrate using a little object-oriented program (progs/message.c). A *message* class describes a type that can be marshalled into a byte-string or unmarshalled from a byte-string. That is, *message* is a class with serialize and deserialize methods, as well as a constant bufsize that indicates the maximum possible message length that *this instance* of serialize will produce.

```
struct message {
    int bufsize;
    int (*serialize)(void *p, unsigned char *buf);
    void (*deserialize)(void *p, unsigned char *buf, int length);
};
```

What type is being serialized here, is not made explicit in the C-language typing of this program that uses void ∗p. Our specification in Coq will make it explicit. Meanwhile let us make an *instance* of this class, for a type of ordered pairs (x, y).

```
struct intpair {int x, y;};
```

We can write serialize and deserialize functions for intpair. Here we do something very simple: copy the integers verbatim, and force them into the array of characters. This is machine-dependent, but (for any target-machine instantiation of CompCert) it is well defined and our program logic *can* reason about it.

```
int intpair_serialize(               void intpair_deserialize(
     struct intpair *p,                   struct intpair *p,
     unsigned char *buf) {                unsigned char *buf, int length) {
   int x = p→x;                          int x = ((int *)buf)[0];
   int y = p→y;                          int y = ((int *)buf)[1];
   ((int *)buf)[0]=x;                    p→x = x;
   ((int *)buf)[1]=y;                    p→y = y;
   return 8;                             return;
}                                    }
```

Now we make the "instance" of the message class for intpair messages:

```
struct message intpair_message =
      {8, &intpair_serialize, &intpair_deserialize};
```

The maximum intpair message length is 8, the serialize function-pointer is intpair_serialize, and so on.

```
int main(void) {
   struct intpair p,q; unsigned char buf[8]; int len, x,y;
   int (*ser)(void *p, unsigned char *buf);
   void(*des)(void *p, unsigned char *buf, int length);

   p.x = 1; p.y = 2;
   ser = intpair_message.serialize;     len = ser(&p, buf);
   des = intpair_message.deserialize;   des(&q, buf, 8);
   x = q.x; y = q.y;
   return x+y;
}
```

Finally, we have a main function that creates an intpair p, serializes it into buf, then deserializes buf back into an intpair q. The pattern for calling a serialize "method" of a message "object" is to fetch the serialize function, and call it with two pointers, the value to be serialized and the buffer. Of course, this particular main function could have called intpair_serialize directly, but one can easily construct "object-oriented" functions that do not know what type they are handling.

This program is "lightweight object-oriented" (without *self* pointers), but the techniques described here can extend to full object orientation or to function-closures with code-pointers and bindings for free variables.

THE VERIFICATION OF OBJECT-ORIENTED MESSAGES begins with a specification of a message_format, which is not an object type but a *theory of serialization and deserialization*.

Record message_format (t: type) : Type :=
mf_build {
   mf_size: Z;
   mf_assert: $\forall$ (π: share) (buf: val) (len: Z) (data: reptype t), mpred;
   mf_size_range: 0 <= mf_size <= Int.max_signed;
   mf_bufprop: $\forall$ π buf len data,
         mf_assert π buf len data $\vdash$
         !!(0 <= len <= mf_size) && memory_block π (Int.repr len) buf;
   mf_restbuf := fun (π: share) (buf: val) (len: Z) $\Rightarrow$
      memory_block π (Int.repr (mf_size-len))
              (offset_val (Int.repr len) buf)
}.

A format $\phi(t)$ for a C type t has a *size* which is the maximum length of a serialized encoding of t. It has a representation assertion *assert π b l d*, meaning that the l bytes starting at address b represent a serialization of the Coq value d. (See page 208 for an explanation of reptype.) Format $\phi(t)$ has a *size_range* guarantee, that *size* is representable as a signed integer. The *buf_prop* is an axiom that whenver the representation assertion holds on a heaplet, that same heaplet can be viewed as a memory block of l bytes, where $0 \le l < size$. Finally, we make a *definition* for future use: the *rest of the buffer* is a memory block from $b + l$ to $b + size - l$.

We can instantiate this for intpair, that is, create ϕ(intpair),

Program Definition intpair_message: message_format t_struct_intpair :=
mf_build 8 (fun π buf len data $\Rightarrow$
        !!(len=8) && typed_mapsto π t_struct_intpair buf data)

_ _.

The underscores at the end represent the proofs of mf_size_range and mf_bufprop that we will omit here.

A *generic serialization specification* takes t and $\phi(t)$ as parameters, and gives the separation-logic specification for a serializer for t:

Definition serialize_spec {t: type} (format: message_format t) :=
    WITH data: reptype t, p: val, buf: val, sh: share, sh': share
    PRE [_p OF (tptr tvoid), _buf OF (tptr tuchar)]
            PROP(writable_share sh')
            LOCAL(`(eq p) (eval_id _p); `(eq buf) (eval_id _buf))
            SEP(`(typed_mapsto sh t p data);
                    `(memory_block sh' (Int.repr (mf_size format)) buf))
    POST [tint]
            EX len: Z,
            local (`(eq (Vint (Int.repr len))) retval) &&
            `(typed_mapsto sh t p data)
            * `(mf_assert format sh' buf len data)
            * `(mf_restbuf format sh' buf len).

The generic deserializer specification is similar. Then we can say that the intpair_serialize function is an instance of a generic serializer:

Definition intpair_serialize_spec :=
DECLARE _intpair_serialize (serialize_spec intpair_message).

Finally, after writing specifications for all the functions in a program, and combining them into Γ in the usual way (page 199), we can prove that the function-body of intpair_serialize matches this specification:

Lemma body_intpair_serialize:
    semax_body V Γ f_intpair_serialize intpair_serialize_spec.
Proof.
unfold intpair_serialize_spec.
unfold serialize_spec.
start_function.
name p0 _p.
name buf0 _buf.
name x _x.
name y _y.

   . . .

Qed.

We can also reason about object-oriented calls to this function, as in the proof of the main function in progs/verif_message.v.

What we have done is to make the static reasoning about void* sound, using dependent types in Coq.

Chapter 30

Concurrent separation logic

Concurrent threads operating on a shared state can be very difficult to reason about. On uniprocessors it has been half a century now that we have wanted such things as operating systems that support many independent threads of control operated on shared resoures. Parallel computers have existed also for about half a century, but it was about ten years ago that Moore's law (40% more transistors/chip every year) stopped being put into the service of faster uniprocessors, and started being used for multicore. Supporting concurrent and parallel computation is more important than ever.

Here we will focus on *shared-memory concurrency,* where multiple threads of control read and write to the same memory.[1] A typical problem is that one thread wants to do a *composite* operation on a data structure: wants to read and modify a data structure using a series of load and store operations.

For example, let r be a record whose n field contains an integer, and whose t field contains the nth triangular number $(n \cdot (n + 1)/2)$. We wish

---

[1] One might think that an alternate approach to concurrency, via message-passing, avoids some of the concerns that we will discuss here. But the threads of a message-passing program will still need to talk about named objects in an external world; simultaneous operations on an external named object can run into the same difficulties of atomicity that we have with pointers in a shared memory; and concurrent separation logic can help solve some of those same problems.

to increment n and maintain t:

$$\{i := r.n;\ r.n := i+1;\ j := r.t;\ r.t := j+i\}$$

This local sequence of operations must be *atomic*: during the sequence, other threads must not read or modify the same data structure because they would see or create an inconsistent state.

Dijkstra [37] identified this problem in 1965 and proposed that the solution is to treat the sequence of commands as a *critical section* in which the threads must maintain *mutual exclusion* (no two threads in the critical section at the same time) using *semaphores*. This is still the standard solution and the standard terminology. Hoare [48] developed and extended this idea (and ideas from Brinch-Hansen) into *monitors* with *condition variables*; the key concept (as we would now express it) is that an *abstract data type* has a set of interface functions that operate on a private representation; the interface functions use programming-language constructs for mutual exclusion to ensure that the private representation stays in a consistent state and maintains its *representation invariants*. We will call this the Dijkstra-Hoare paradigm for shared-memory programming, and it is now the standard method, as embodied in the Pthreads (Posix Threads) library for C, in the Java programming model, and in other languages.

Dijkstra and Hoare showed us how to *program* in this model and how to *reason informally* about it. In this century, O'Hearn showed how to reason *formally* about Dijkstra-Hoare concurrent programming, in *Concurrent Separation Logic* [71].

When we write concurrent programs (or some kinds of parallel programs) in a sequential programming language, we execute (mostly independent) sequential threads that occasionally interact. When we reason about a sequential thread using the separation logic Hoare triple $\{P\}\,c\,\{Q\}$, are saying (more or less) that command c reads only from the footprint of P, and neither modifies nor cares about the rest of memory. Thus, if we have two commands $\{P_1\}\,c_1\,\{Q_1\}$ and $\{P_2\}\,c_2\,\{Q_2\}$, we can say:

$$\text{parallel-composition} \frac{\{P_1\}\,c_1\,\{Q_1\} \quad \{P_2\}\,c_2\,\{Q_2\}}{\{P_1 * P_2\}\,c_1\|c_2\,\{Q_1 * Q_2\}}$$

which says that if P_1 and P_2 are invariants on *disjoint* footprints of memory, then commands c_1 and c_2 can run in parallel. (If they are not disjoint, then $P_1 * P_2$ is false, so the inference is still valid.) Separation Logic is a wonderful way of keeping track of this noninterference.

Concurrent threads must sometimes communicate, of course. In the Dijkstra-Hoare model a thread communicates as follows: acquire a lock (semaphore) controlling some resource (e.g., a data structure in memory); read and write the resource; release the lock. The lock enforces mutual exclusion (no two threads can hold the lock at the same time), so therefore the sequence of reads and writes is atomic.

Concurrent separation logic uses locks in this way. We associate with each lock a *resource invariant,* an assertion in separation logic. Let us write $l \boxdot\!\!\to R$ to say "l is a lock with resource invariant R." The assertion R must be *precise,* meaning if it is satisfied by any subheap of some heap m then it is satisfied by a unique subheap of m. Many common assertions are precise: maps-to $\mapsto$, list segment $\rightsquigarrow$, conjunctions $*$ of precise predicates, and so on. The assertion $\top$ is not precise.

Here are the rules for acquiring and releasing locks:

$$\text{acq} \frac{}{\{l \boxdot\!\!\to R\} \; \text{acquire} \, l \; \{R * l \boxdot\!\!\to R\}}$$

$$\text{rel} \frac{}{\{R * l \boxdot\!\!\to R\} \; \text{release} \, l \; \{l \boxdot\!\!\to R\}}$$

That is, if l is a lock, one can contend for the lock (do the $P(l)$ semaphore operation). Once it is acquired, this thread gains access to the resource, whose footprint and internal invariant are described by R.

The thread can load and store from the memory described by R; during which the resource might no longer satisfy R. Eventually, the thread may bring the resource into a state that once again satisfies R, at which point it may release the lock ($V(l)$ semaphore operation).

For example, let the lock l control access to the record r described earlier in the chapter. The resource invariant is

$$R \; = \; \exists x. \; r.n \mapsto x * r.t \mapsto x(x+1)/2$$

saying that the t field must contain the nth triangular number.

Let $C = (\mathsf{acquire}\,l;\ i := r.n;\ r.n := i+1;\ j := r.t;\ r.t := j+i;\ \mathsf{release}\,l)$. Then the triple $\{l \overset{\square}{\mapsto} R\}\,C\,\{l \overset{\square}{\mapsto} R\}$ is valid: Initially the thread has no access to the contents of r. After the acquire, the assertion $\{R * l \overset{\square}{\mapsto} R\}$ holds; once the existential x is extracted, the thread has access to $r.n$ (containing x) and $r.t$ (containing the nth triangular number). After the store to $r.n$, the resource invariant R does not hold, but no matter: by the time the release is executed, the resource invariant is established (with a different value of x).

In a simple CSL (concurrent separation logic), assertions $l \overset{\square}{\mapsto} R$ are static and nonspatial: that is, $l \overset{\square}{\mapsto} R = (l \overset{\square}{\mapsto} R) * (l \overset{\square}{\mapsto} R)$ and there is no way to create new locks at runtime. We can use the parallel composition rule to demonstrate that it is safe to run C in parallel with itself:

$$\frac{\dfrac{\{l \overset{\square}{\mapsto} R\}\,C\,\{l \overset{\square}{\mapsto} R\} \quad \{l \overset{\square}{\mapsto} R\}\,C\,\{l \overset{\square}{\mapsto} R\}}{\{l \overset{\square}{\mapsto} R * l \overset{\square}{\mapsto} R\}\,C \| C\,\{l \overset{\square}{\mapsto} R * l \overset{\square}{\mapsto} R\}}}{\{l \overset{\square}{\mapsto} R\}\,C \| C\,\{l \overset{\square}{\mapsto} R\}}$$

The parallel composition does not exactly mean that each instance of C runs in its own little disjoint world. The two instances do communicate, by "borrowing" the resource R and then returning it. So the parallel composition rule says something more subtle (and more useful) than complete isolation.

THE FOOTPRINT OF A RESOURCE INVARIANT NEED NOT BE STATIC. In the triangular-number example given above, the footprint is exactly two addresses, $r.n$ and $r.t$. But consider the assertion, $s \overset{\square}{\mapsto} (p \rightsquigarrow 0)$. The lock s controls access to a linked list of arbitrary nonzero length, starting at address p. The following commands increase the size of the resource, without changing the resource invariant:

```
acquire s;
t := p→next; r := alloc_list_cell();  r→next := t; p→next := r;
release s
```

NOT ONLY CRITICAL SECTIONS, BUT OTHER PATTERNS of synchronization can be expressed by semaphores, and by locks in CSL. The thread that acquires a lock need not be the one that releases it, as long as the resource is transferred. O'Hearn [71] describes many such patterns of use (invented since the 1960s) can be verified in CSL. For example,

$$
\begin{array}{ll}
\vdots & \vdots \\
\text{acquire}(\mathit{free}); & \text{acquire}(\mathit{busy}); \\
[10] := m; \quad \| & n := [10]; \\
\text{release}(\mathit{busy}); & \text{release}(\mathit{free}); \\
\vdots & \vdots
\end{array}
$$

in which the left process assigns a message m to address 10 and then signals the right process, which reads the message and then signals back that the buffer is now emptied.

Let us further assume that messages must be well formatted, for example that m must be an even number. Then the resource invariants are,

$$
\mathit{free} \boxdot\!\!\to (10 \mapsto \_) \qquad \mathit{busy} \boxdot\!\!\to (\exists i.\, \text{even}(i) \wedge 10 \mapsto i)
$$

and the assertion-annotated programs are,

$$
\begin{array}{ll}
\vdots & \vdots \\
\{\text{even}(m) \wedge \text{emp}\} & \{\text{emp}\} \\
\text{acquire}(\mathit{free}); & \text{acquire}(\mathit{busy}); \\
\{10 \mapsto \_\} & \{\exists i.\, \text{even}(i) \wedge 10 \mapsto i\} \\
[10] := m; \quad \| & n := [10]; \\
\{10 \mapsto m\} & \{\text{even}(n) \wedge 10 \mapsto \_\} \\
\text{release}(\mathit{busy}); & \text{release}(\mathit{free}); \\
\{\text{emp}\} & \{\text{even}(n) \wedge \text{emp}\} \\
\vdots & \vdots
\end{array}
$$

O'HEARN'S CSL IS AN INGENIOUS WAY to apply the local-reasoning strengths of separation logic to solve difficult modular-verification problems for concurrent programs. However, O'Hearn's idealized Algol differs in several ways from the way locks-and-threads libraries are used in languages such as C and Java. O'Hearn's locks and threads are static: all exist at the start of program execution, and none can be created dynamically. O'Hearn assumes a parallel-composition operator $c_1 \| c_2$ of the programming language, where C spawns a thread by passing a function-pointer to the create function. O'Hearn assumes that $c_1 \| c_2$ can share read-only local variables, whereas C threads cannot share local variables with each other. O'Hearn omits discussion of read-only sharing between threads in concurrent-read exclusive-write (CRXW) patterns of synchronization. In our CSL for the C language, we address all these issues.

DYNAMICALLY ALLOCATED LOCKS. A typical object-oriented pattern of use (even in the C language) is that one field of a structure is a lock that controls access to the other fields. The program mallocs a structure, then makes a Pthread call mutex_init() to turn (e.g.) the first field into a semaphore. Henceforth, the program must not use ordinary loads and stores to access that field, but must use synchronization operations such as compare-and-swap, which are encapsulated within the Pthreads library's lock() and unlock() functions. Finally, when the object is to be deallocated, the program first calls mutex_destroy to turn the lock field back into an ordinary data field.

A dynamically created lock at address l is not a pure fact that will be true forever, it is a resource subject to separation. We write $l \overset{\pi}{\boxdot\!\!\rightarrow} R$ to mean a lock at address l with (nonempty) visibility share π and resource invariant R. Any nonempty visibility share gives permission to contend for the lock, that is, to perform the acquire operation that blocks until the lock is available. The full visibility share $\bullet$ gives permission to convert the lock back into ordinary data.

Figure 30.1 gives the inference rules for lock creation and deallocation (makelock/freelock), lock acquire and release (acq/rel), and thread creation and exit (spawn/exit).

An integer memory-field can be turned into a lock via the makelock command. The lock starts out in the locked state, which means that the resource invariant is not necessarily satisfied at present but must be satisfied

$$\text{makelock} \frac{R \text{ positive} \qquad R \text{ precise}}{\Delta \vdash \{l \mapsto 0\} \text{ makelock } l \; \{l \overset{\bullet}{\boxdot\!\!\rightarrow} R\}}$$

$$\text{freelock} \frac{}{\Delta \vdash \{R * l \overset{\bullet}{\boxdot\!\!\rightarrow} R\} \text{ freelock } l \; \{R * l \mapsto 0\}}$$

$$\text{splitlock} \frac{\pi_1 \oplus \pi_2 = \pi}{l \overset{\pi_1}{\boxdot\!\!\rightarrow} R * l \overset{\pi_2}{\boxdot\!\!\rightarrow} R \;\;\leftrightarrow\;\; l \overset{\pi}{\boxdot\!\!\rightarrow} R}$$

$$\text{acq} \frac{}{\Delta \vdash \{l \overset{\pi}{\boxdot\!\!\rightarrow} R\} \text{ acquire } l \; \{R * l \overset{\pi}{\boxdot\!\!\rightarrow} R\}}$$

$$\text{rel} \frac{}{\Delta \vdash \{R * l \overset{\pi}{\boxdot\!\!\rightarrow} R\} \text{ release } l \; \{l \overset{\pi}{\boxdot\!\!\rightarrow} R\}}$$

$$\text{spawn} \frac{}{\Delta \vdash \{(a : \{\vec{y}P\}\{\text{emp}\}) \wedge (Px)[\vec{b}/\vec{y}] * F\} \text{ spawn } a(\vec{b}) \; \{F\}}$$

$$\text{exit} \frac{}{\Delta \vdash \{\text{emp}\} \text{ exit}() \; \{\bot\}}$$

Figure 30.1: CSL rules for threads and locks

before the lock can be released.

The lock can be turned back into an ordinary value location using freelock. The requirement to satisfy R in the precondition guarantees that the lock l is in the locked state, held by this thread. Freeing the lock does not unlock the lock, does not release the resource R.

When the lock is first created, one thread has a full visibility share in the predicate $l \boxdot\!\!\rightarrow R$) and no other thread has any access (the black circle • above the arrow represents the a full share). A lock is not very useful for synchronization between threads unless more than one thread can see it. Therefore, the next step (in a program, or in a proof) is to split the predicate

$l \boxdot^{\bullet}\!\!\rightarrow R$ into parts such as $l \mathbin{\overset{\frown}{\boxdot \rightarrow}} R * l \mathbin{\overset{\frown}{\boxdot \rightarrow}} R$, and distribute some of the parts to other threads. This can be done by releasing some *other* lock, already shared between the threads, whose resource invariant contains $l \mathbin{\overset{\frown}{\boxdot \rightarrow}} R$; or it can be done by passing the lock l (with accompanying lock-visibility resource) in the arguments to spawn $a(\vec{b})$ when creating a new thread.

CONSIDER THE EXAMPLE of a three-field structure type whose *lock* field controls access to n and t, and t is the nth triangular number.

struct triang {**int** lock; **int** n; **int** t;}

```
p = (struct triang *)malloc(sizeof(*p));
p→ lock = 0;
makelock(&p→ lock);
tell_another_thread_about(p);
p→ n=0; p→ t=0;
release(&p→ lock);
```

For any instance p of this type, the resource invariant of $p\rightarrow$ lock is,

$$(p\rightarrow lock)\boxdot^{\bullet}\!\!\rightarrow R \qquad \text{where} \qquad R = \exists i.\, p\rightarrow n \mapsto i * p\rightarrow t \mapsto i(i+1)/2$$

and indeed, the program assertion immediately after the makelock command is, $p\rightarrow\text{lock})\boxdot^{\bullet}\!\!\rightarrow R * p\rightarrow n \mapsto \_ * p\rightarrow t \mapsto \_.$

The program must now send the pointer p to another thread, otherwise there was no point in making a lock to synchronize access to n and t. It's safe to communicate p before initializing the n and t fields, because those are private to the creating thread until the release.

Suppose there is already a communications-buffer data structure already set up for this purpose, akin to the busy/free example on page 226. The buffer contents will be pointer values such as p, and the resource invariant for the *busy* lock will be,

$$\text{busy}\boxdot\!\!\rightarrow S \qquad \text{where} \qquad S = \exists q.\, 10 \mapsto q * (q\rightarrow\text{lock} \mathbin{\overset{\frown}{\boxdot \rightarrow}} R)$$

THE RESOURCE INVARIANT S DESCRIBES the binding of another resource invariant R to a location $q\rightarrow$lock. We call this phenomenon "predicates in the heap." Just as the assertion $10 \mapsto q$ describes a heap cell at address 10 containing value q, the assertion $q \rightarrow R$ describes a heap cell at address q "containing" the predicate R.

The resource-invariant R has an existential quantifier ($\exists i$) in it. In this case the variable i ranges over a base type, the integers. In object-oriented languages, in languages with ML-style polymorphism or C++ style templates, or in C programs that use object-oriented programming styles (Chapter 29) resource invariants may contain quantifiers over abstract data types. Those quantifiers may be instantiated with assertions that themselves contain quantifiers. This is known as *impredicative quantification*. It is remarkably tricky to make a semantic model (for a soundness proof) of that combines *predicates in the heap* with impredicative quantification. It is for that combination that we apply Indirection Theory, which can construct this powerful kind of semantic model (see Part V of this book).

In our example we create a new object with its lock. In order to communicate it to another thread we use an existing lock that is already shared with the other thread. But how did that lock become shared? Is it turtles all the way down? No: the other way to share a lock is to pass it in the initialization parameters of a newly spawned thread.

The thread-creation rule (Figure 30.1) describes the command spawn $a(\vec{b})$, which creates a new thread executing the function a with arguments $\vec{b}$, where the evaluation of expressions a and b_i are done in the caller's context. The function precondition $\vec{y}P$ means that separation logic assertion P has formal parameters $\vec{y}$, which are matched to the actual parameters $\vec{b}$. The memory footprint covered by $P[\vec{b}/\vec{y}]$ is transferred to the new thread.

The postcondition emp for a spawned function a implies that when the function a completes, it must have given away all its resources.[2] A thread can exit either by returning from its initial function a or by calling exit.

---

[2] The way to give away resources is to release a lock. To release a lock, one needs at least the resource $l \overset{\pi}{\boxdot} R$. In the rel rule (of Figure 30.1) the postcondition of release still contains $l \overset{\pi}{\boxdot} R$, which is bigger than emp. To be able to release *all* resources, Hobor [49,

Hobor's PhD thesis [49] describes a concurrent separation logic with dynamic locks and threads, an operational-semantic model as a variant of the CompCert operational semantics, and a CSL program logic with soundness proof in Coq with respect to the operational model. One significant limitation was that his CompCert variant had "predicates in the heap," whereas standard CompCert does not. Recent research since Hobor's thesis (by L. Beringer, G. Stewart, and A. W. Appel, summarized in Chapters 33 and 42) has shown how to adjust the CompCert semantics to permit shared-memory interaction (but without predicates in the heap), and then how to interface the predicates-in-the-heap semantics model to this adjusted CompCert semantics.

At the time of this writing the Verified Software Toolchain *at the user level* does not support concurrency or concurrent separation logic. We expect to support concurrency in the near future, as the difficult semantic issues are largely solved.

---

§4.8,4.9] shows a stronger release rule, which we can write,

$$\text{rel-rec} \frac{R = R' * l \xrightarrow{\pi}_{\boxdot} R}{\Delta \vdash \{R\} \text{ release } l \ \{\text{emp}\}}$$

The premise, that R somehow can contain a binding of l that refers to R itself, can be obtained using the recursion operator, as Hobor explains.

Part IV

Operational semantics of CompCert

SYNOPSIS: *Specification of the interface between CompCert and its clients such as the VST separation logic for C light, or clients such as proved-sound static analyses and abstract interpretations. This specification takes the form of an operational semantics with a nontrivial memory model. The need to preserve the compiler's freedom to optimize the placement of data (in memory, out of memory) requires the ability to rename addresses and adjust block sizes. Thus the specification of shared-memory interaction between subprograms (separately compiled functions, or concurrent threads) requires particular care, to keep these renamings consistent.*

Chapter 31

CompCert

PROGRAM LOGICS FOR CERTIFIED COMPILERS: We prove that the program logic is *sound* with respect to the operational semantics of a source language— meaning that if the program logic proves some claim about the observable behavior of a program, then the source program actually respects that claim when interpreted in the source-language semantics. But computers don't directly execute source-language semantics: we also need a proof about the correctness of an interpreter or a compiler.

COMPCERT (*compilateur certifié* in French) is a formally verified optimizing compiler for the C language , translating to assembly language for various machines (Intel x86, ARM, PowerPC) [62]. Like most optimizing compilers, it translates in several sequential phases through a sequence of intermediate languages. Unlike most compilers, each of these intermediate languages has a formal specification written down in Coq as an operational semantics. Each phase is proved correct: the form of the proof is a *simulation theorem* expressing that the observable behavior of the target program corresponds to the observable behavior of the source program. The composition of all these per-phase simulation theorems gives the compiler correctness theorem.

Although there had been formally verified compilers before [67, 36, 61, 60], CompCert is an important breakthrough for several reasons:

Language: One of Leroy's goals has been that CompCert should be able to compile *real* high-assurance embedded C programs, such as the avionics software for a commercial jetliner. Such software is not trivially modified: any tweak to the software—let alone rewriting it in another language— requires months or years of rebuilding an assurance case. Thus CompCert compiles the ANSI/ISO standard C language—or rather, a sufficiently large subset to compile industrial software.

Specification: Before proving that a translation is correct with respect to operational semantics, one must *have* a semantics. A formal specification of the C language semantics is an important contribution of the CompCert project.

Optimization: CompCert is an optimizing compiler. At present the performance is similar to the code generated by gcc -O1, and about 5% worse than gcc -O2. But it's significantely better than trusted C compilers now used in avionics—which deliberately do not optimize very much for fear of bugs. CompCert's code size is about 25% smaller and compiled-code execution time is about 18% faster than a compiler currently used for avionics.[1] [15].

Memory model: A big hurdle in verifying optimizing compilers is the need for a *symbolic* model of memory addressing. Each optimization phase may relocate memory blocks, or adjust the size of memory blocks by adding new fields, or merge (concatenate) memory blocks. Previous verified compilers that assumed a traditional flat, concrete model of memory addressing could not express the specification and proof of such optimizing compiler passes.

THE BIGGEST CHALLENGE IN SPECIFYING AND VERIFYING an optimizing C compiler is the treatment of access to memory. C permits address arithmetic within a malloc'ed or statically allocated object, so one might think that addresses must be treated as integers (perhaps modulo 2^k). On the other hand, in order to account for register allocation, spilling, and return addresses, each phase of an optimizing compiler *must* be free to

---

[1]Worst-case execution time, cited here, is of particular interest to developers of software with hard real-time constraints, such as fly-by-wire avionics.

adjust the size of stack frames and to choose whether some objects are in addressible memory or nonaddressible registers. Furthermore, a global flat address space of integers will overspecify too much—will improperly allow properties of programs to be proved that should be left unspecified. For example, the C standard [57] says that the subtraction of pointers to different allocated objects is undefined, but in a flat-address-space model they're both numbers and of course a numeric difference must exist.

So, the address space must permit arithmetic but must not permit *too much* arithmetic. Leroy and Blazy's approach [64] is that an *address* should be a pair of a symbolic base pointer with an integer offset. A *memory* is, informally, a mapping from addresses to *values*, where a value is either an integer, a floating-point number, an address, or undefined. At any stage of compilation, one must give the next compiler/linker phases the freedom to insert blocks, delete blocks (if they are dead, or to promote them to registers), to increase the size of blocks (when spilling register into stack frames), and in general to do transformations such as linking and relocation. *Within* each block, integer addressing is permitted.

A compiler phase can arbitrarily rename/permute the symbolic base pointers, delete some blocks, and change the integer offset of each block for internal numeric addressing: Leroy and Blazy call this a *memory injection*. The compiler can add extra words at the beginning or end of a block, useful for accreting register-spills or return-addresses onto stack frames: this is a *memory extension*. The observable behavior of every program must somehow be invariant under injections and extensions—otherwise an optimizing compiler would change the program's observable behavior.

The Leroy/Blazy memory model—with symbolic blocks, hybrid symbolic/numberic addresses, injections, and extensions—was very successful in permitting a semantics for C that is sufficiently abstract, but concrete enough for the address arithmetic programmers expect; while permitting the compiler freedom to optimize.

But the Leroy/Blazy model had some significant weaknesses as well. CompCert could not support reasoning about the optimizing compilation of shared-memory concurrent threads, because the permission model was not fine-grained enough. Chapter 32 describes our improvements in that direction.

CompCert's most significant limitation is that it does not permit shared memory interaction with an operating system, and does not permit separate compilation. The reason is exactly the symbolic nature of the memory model. Each module must have the freedom to independently renumber blocks for optimizing compilation, and yet all the separately compiled modules (or the client and its operating system) must jointly agree on the renumbering. It is a very difficult problem to specify how this should work.

The original CompCert could evade this problem by targeting the problem domain of whole-program single-threaded embedded systems, where there is no operating system. Without an operating system, the execution thread has no shared-memory interaction, just the output and input of atomic integer values to/from external devices. But we want the Verified Software Toolchain to work in more general applications. So the difficult problems with shared-memory interaction must be solved, and we explain the approach in Chapter 33.

Chapter 32

The CompCert memory model

by Xavier Leroy, Andrew W. Appel, Sandrine Blazy, and Gordon Stewart

The imperative programming paradigm views programs as sequences of commands that update a *memory state*. A *memory model* specifies memory states and operations such as reads and writes. Such a memory model is a prerequisite to giving formal semantics to imperative programming languages, verifying properties of programs, and proving the correctness of program transformations.

For high-level, type-safe languages such as ML or the sequential fragment of Java, the memory model is simple and amounts to a finite map from abstract memory locations to the values they contain. At the other end of the complexity spectrum, we find memory models for shared-memory concurrent programs with data races and relaxed (non sequentially consistent) memory, where much effort is needed to capture the relaxations (*e.g.* reorderings of reads and writes) that are allowed and those that are guaranteed never to happen [1].

For CompCert we focus on memory models for the C language and for compiler intermediate languages, in the sequential case and with extensions to data race-free concurrency. C and our intermediate languages feature both low-level aspects such as pointers, pointer arithmetic, and nested objects, and high-level aspects such as separation and freshness guarantees.

For instance, pointer arithmetic can result in aliasing or partial overlap between the memory areas referenced by two pointers; yet, it is guaranteed that the memory areas corresponding to two distinct variables or two successive calls to malloc are disjoint. A very abstract memory model, such as the popular Burstall-Bornat model [30, 26], can fail to account for desirable features of the languages we are interested in, such as casts between incompatible pointer types. A very concrete memory model, such as the hardware view of memory as an array of bytes indexed by addresses that are just machine integers [87], fails to enforce separation and freshness guarantees, and makes it impossible to prove the correctness of standard compiler passes and even of late, link-time or loading-time placement of code and data in memory.

Version 1 of the CompCert memory model is described in detail by Leroy and Blazy [64] and summarized in this chapter. In the years following that publication, several limitations of this "v1" memory model appeared, some related to low-level programming idioms used in embedded systems, others related to the extension of CompCert towards race-free concurrent programming as investigated in the Verified Software Toolchain project [7].

These limitations led us to refine the CompCert memory model in two directions. One is to expose the byte-level machine representation of integers and floating-point numbers, while keeping abstract the machine representation of pointers, as required to preserve crucial invariance properties of invariance by generalized renaming of block identifiers. The other direction is to add fine-grained *permissions*, also known as access rights, on every byte of the memory state, giving precise control of which memory operations are permitted on these bytes. For instance, the in-memory representation of a C string literal can be given read-only permissions, allowing reads but preventing writes and deallocation.

The CompCert memory model, version 1

We first review version 1 of the CompCert memory model, referring the reader to Leroy and Blazy [64] for full details. Underlined text describes aspects that *no longer apply* in version 2.

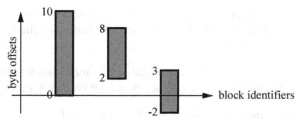

Memory states m are collections of *blocks*, each block being an array of abstract bytes. Pointers are represented by pairs (b, i) of a block identifier b and a byte offset i within this block. Each block b has two integer bounds, low_bound $m\ b$ and high_bound $m\ b$. Valid offsets within block b range between low_bound $m\ b$ inclusive and high_bound $m\ b$ exclusive.

The CompCert C and C light semantics [23] associate a different block to every global variable of the program, to every addressable local variable of every active invocation of a function of the program, and to every invocation of malloc. For local variables, fresh blocks are allocated at function entry and deallocated when the function returns. The memory model's alloc and free do not directly model the C library `malloc` and `free`; they model the creation of fresh blocks at function entry and their destruction at function return, and could also be used to model acquisition of address space via system calls.

Pointer arithmetic modifies the offset part of a pointer, keeping its block identifier unchanged: $(b, i) + n \stackrel{\text{def}}{=} (b, i + n)$. As a consequence, blocks are separated by construction: from a pointer to block b, no amount of pointer arithmetic can create a pointer to block $b' \neq b$; pointer arithmetic can only create other pointers within block b, or illegal pointers outside b's bounds.

As an abstract data type, memory states are presented as a type mem, a constant empty : mem, and the four operations,

$$
\begin{aligned}
\text{alloc} \quad &: \quad \text{mem} \rightarrow \text{Z} \rightarrow \text{Z} \rightarrow \text{mem} \times \text{block} \\
\text{free} \quad &: \quad \text{mem} \rightarrow \text{block} \rightarrow \underline{\text{mem}} \\
\text{load} \quad &: \quad \text{mem} \rightarrow \text{memory\_chunk} \rightarrow \text{block} \rightarrow \text{Z} \rightarrow \text{option val} \\
\text{store} \quad &: \quad \text{mem} \rightarrow \text{memory\_chunk} \rightarrow \text{block} \rightarrow \text{Z} \rightarrow \text{val} \rightarrow \text{option mem}
\end{aligned}
$$

alloc m l h allocates a fresh block of size $h - l$ bytes, with low bound l and high bound h. It returns the updated memory state and the block identifier for the fresh block.

free m b deallocates block b, returning the updated memory state in which b has bounds $(0, 0)$ and therefore can no longer be read or written.

store m τ b i v stores value v with type τ in block b at offset i.

load m τ b i reads a value of type τ from block b at starting offset i.

Values are the discriminated union of 32-bit machine integers, 64-bit floats, pointer values, and Vundef which denotes an unknown value:

$$v ::= \mathsf{Vint}(i) \mid \mathsf{Vfloat}(f) \mid \mathsf{Vptr}(b, i) \mid \mathsf{Vundef}$$

Memory types τ indicate the size, type and signedness of the value being stored:

τ	::=	Mint8signed | Mint8unsigned	8-bit integers
	|	Mint16signed | Mint16unsigned	16-bit integers
	|	Mint32	32-bit integers or pointers
	|	Mfloat32 | Mfloat64	32-bit and 64-bit floats

Each type τ comes with a size $|\tau|$ in bytes and a natural alignment $\langle \tau \rangle$.

As shown by the option mem return type, memory stores can fail because they perform bounds and alignment checking. The store succeeds and returns Some m' (where m' is the updated memory state) if and only if bounds and alignment constraints are respected:

$$\langle \tau \rangle \text{ divides } i \ \wedge \ \text{low\_bound } m\ b \leq i \ \wedge \ i + |\tau| \leq \text{high\_bound } m\ b$$

Otherwise, store returns None.

A load succeeds and returns Some v (where v is the value read) if and only if bounds and alignments constraints are respected, as in the case of store. Otherwise, None is returned.

The following "good variable" laws characterize most of the semantics of these four memory operations.

Load after alloc: if alloc m l $h = (m', b)$,

- load m' τ' b' $i' =$ load m τ' b' i' if $b' \neq b$
- If load m τ b $i =$ Some v, then $v =$ undef

Load after free: if free m $b = m'$,

- load m' τ' b' $i' =$ load m τ' b' i' if $b' \neq b$
- load m τ b $i =$ None.

Load after store: if store m τ b i $v =$ Some m',

- Disjoint case: load m' τ' b' $i' =$ load m τ' b' i' if $b' \neq b$ or $i' + |\tau'| \leq i$ or $i + |\tau| \leq i'$
- Compatible case: load m' τ' b $i =$ Some(convert τ' v) if $|\tau'| = |\tau|$
- Incompatible case: if load m' τ' b $i =$ Some v' and $|\tau'| \neq |\tau|$, then $v' =$ Vundef
- Overlapping case: if load m' τ' b $i' =$ Some v' and $i' \neq i$ and $i' + |\tau'| > i$ and $i + |\tau| > i'$, then $v =$ Vundef

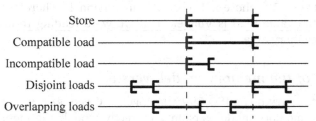

The four cases of the "load after store" laws are depicted above. The disjoint case corresponds to a load outside the memory area affected by the store. In the compatible case, we load exactly from the memory area affected by the store, in which case we obtain the value just stored, after conversion to the destination type τ':

$$\begin{aligned}
\text{convert } (\text{Vint}(n)) \text{ Mint8unsigned} &= \text{Vint(8-bit zero extension of } n) \\
\text{convert } (\text{Vint}(n)) \text{ Mint8signed} &= \text{Vint(8-bit sign extension of } n) \\
\text{convert } (\text{Vint}(n)) \text{ Mint16unsigned} &= \text{Vint(16-bit zero extension of } n) \\
\text{convert } (\text{Vint}(n)) \text{ Mint16signed} &= \text{Vint(16-bit sign extension of } n) \\
\text{convert } (\text{Vint}(n)) \text{ Mint32} &= \text{Vint}(n) \\
\text{convert } (\text{Vptr}(b,i)) \text{ Mint32} &= \text{Vptr}(b,i) \\
\text{convert } (\text{Vfloat}(f)) \text{ float32} &= \text{Vfloat}(f \text{ normalized to single precision}) \\
\text{convert } (\text{Vfloat}(f)) \text{ float64} &= \text{Vfloat}(f) \\
\text{convert } v\ \tau &= \text{Vundef} \quad \text{in all other cases}
\end{aligned}$$

In the two remaining cases, "incompatible" and "overlapping", the bytes being read by the load include some but not all of the bytes written by the store, possibly combined with other bytes that were not affected by the store. To specify the result of the load in these two cases, we would need to expose the byte-level representation of values in memory: Are integers stored in big-endian or little-endian representation? What is the byte-level encoding of floats? We chose not to do this in version 1. Therefore, we just say that the value read is Vundef, as if we were reading from an uninitialized memory area.

Assessment of the memory model, version 1

CAPABILITY: ACCOUNTING FOR ISO C99 AND POPULAR C PROGRAMMING IDIOMS. The CompCert memory model version 1 correctly models the memory behavior of C programs that conform to the ISO C99 standard [57]. As specified in section 6.5 of the C99 standard, a C "object" (memory-resident data) has an effective type, which is either its declared static type, if any, or the type of the latest assignment into this object, if it has no declared static type. A conformant program always accesses an object through an l-value whose type is compatible with that of the effective type of the object. Compatibility includes addition or removal of qualifiers, as well as changes in signedness. This corresponds to the "compatible" case of the load-after-store laws:

if store m τ b i v = Some m' and $|\tau'| = |\tau|$
then load m' τ' b i = Some(convert(τ', v))

Indeed, two C types t, t' that are compatible in the sense of the C99 standard encode into CompCert memory chunks τ, τ' that have the same size (and differ only in signedness). Moreover, the C semantics guarantee that the value v being stored with type t has been normalized (casted) to type t before storing. In this case, CompCert's conversion-at-load-time convert(τ', v) behaves like the C type cast (t') v.

Besides standard-conformant C programs, the CompCert memory model can give meaning to several popular C programming idioms that have undefined behavior according to the C standards. For example, in CompCert, the representation of pointer values is independent of their static pointer types. Therefore, casting from any pointer type to any other pointer type and then back to the original pointer type is well defined and behaves like the identity function:

```
int x = 3;
*((int *) (double *) &x) = 4; // equivalent to x = 4;
```

For another example, CompCert memory blocks are accessed at byte offsets within a block. The CompCert C and C light semantics compute the byte offsets corresponding to array elements or struct fields before performing memory accesses [23]. This makes it possible to give semantics to non-conformant programs that access elements of arrays or structs via nonstandard casts or pointer arithmetic. For example:

```
struct { int x, y, z; } s;
s.y = 42;
((int *) &s)[1] = 42;
*((int *) ((char *) &s + sizeof(int))) = 42;
```

All three assignments above are well defined in CompCert C and have the same semantics, namely storing the integer 42 at offset 4 in the block associated with variable s.

The same tolerance applies to non-discriminated unions. Consider:

```
union point3d {
    struct { double x, y, z; } s;
    double d[3];
};
```

For any object p of type union point3d, its three coordinates can be accessed indifferently as p.s.x, p.s.y, p.s.z or as p.d[0], p.d[1], p.d[2].

LIMITATION: NO ACCESS TO IN-MEMORY DATA REPRESENTATIONS. Systems or library C codes often cannot be written in standard-conformant C because they need to operate over the in-memory representation of data, at the level of individual bytes or bits. For example, changing the endianness of an integer (converting it from little-endian to big-endian representation, or conversely) is often written as follows:

```
unsigned int bswap(unsigned int x) {
    union { unsigned int i; char c[4]; } src, dst;
    int n;
    src.i = x;
    dst.c[3] = src.c[0]; dst.c[2] = src.c[1];
    dst.c[1] = src.c[2]; dst.c[0] = src.c[3];
    return dst.i;
}
```

In this example, the memory objects for src and dst are accessed simultaneously with types int and char. This is not supported by version 1 of the CompCert memory model: we fall in the "incompatible" and "overlapping" cases of the load-after-store laws, therefore src.c[0], ..., src.c[3] read as Vundef values, and likewise dst.i reads as Vundef instead of the byte-reversed value of x as expected.

The example above is not too serious because it can be rewritten into standard-conformant code:

```
unsigned int bswap(unsigned int x) {
    return (x & 0xFF) << 24 | (x & 0xFF00) << 8
         | (x & 0xFF0000) >> 8 | (x & 0xFF000000) >> 24; }
```

More delicate examples arise in floating-point libraries that need to exploit the IEEE 754 bit-level representation of floating-point numbers to implement basic float operations. For instance, taking the absolute value of a single-precision IEEE 754 float amounts to clearing the top bit of its representation:

```
float fabs_single(float x) {
    union { float f; unsigned int i; } u;
    u.f = x;
    u.i = u.i & 0x7FFFFFFF;
    return u.f;
}
```

Giving semantics to this function using the CompCert memory model version 1, we obtain that it always returns Vundef instead of the expected float result: the read u.i after the write u.f falls in the "incompatible" case of the load-after-store laws.

Sometimes, "bit surgery" over floating-point numbers must be performed by the compiler itself, to implement primitive C operations for which the microprocessor provides no dedicated instructions. For example, the PowerPC 32 bits architecture lacks an instruction to convert a 32-bit integer to a double-precision float. This conversion must be implemented by machine code equivalent to the following C code:

```
double double_of_signed_int(int x) {
    union { double d; unsigned int i[2]; } a, b;
    a.i[0] = 0x43300000; a.i[1] = 0x80000000;
    b.i[0] = 0x43300000; b.i[1] = 0x80000000 + x;
    return b.d -a.d;
}
```

This code exploits not only the fact that the PowerPC is a big-endian architecture, but also the bit-level IEEE 754 representation: the bit pattern of a, namely, 0x4330000080000000 represents the float $2^{52} + 2^{31}$, and the bit pattern of b represents the float $2^{52} + 2^{31} + $ (double)x; moreover, the floating-point subtraction between these two floats is exact, resulting in (double)x. Again, version 1 of the CompCert memory model fails to give the intended semantics to this code, predicting an Vundef result instead.

Finally, some library functions work over byte-level data representations in a highly portable (but not standard-conformant) manner. This is the case for the following naive implementation of the memcpy function from the C standard library:

```
void * memcpy(void * dest, const void * src, size_t n) {
    for (i = 0; i < n; i++)
        ((char *) dest)[i] = ((const char *) src)[i];
    return dest;
}
```

According to the CompCert memory model version 1, this memcpy works as intended if it is passed arrays of char (signed or unsigned), or other compound types consisting only of char fields. Otherwise, for example if src points to an array of int or double, the read ((const char *) src)[i] returns Vundef, and the destination block dest is filled with Vundef values.

CAPABILITY: INVARIANCE BY MEMORY TRANSFORMATIONS. In the implementation of the memory model, block identifiers are integers (in CompCert 2.0, positives) and are assigned consecutively at each alloc operation. However, the operations of the memory model and the CompCert C formal semantics are insensitive to this particular choice of block identifiers. For instance, the CompCert C semantics, following the C99 standard, enables programs to test whether two block identifiers are equal (using the == pointer comparison), but not whether one identifier was allocated before another one (the < comparison is undefined between pointers designating different blocks). Consider two programs that are identical except for the order of definition of some variables:

```
int x = 10;          int y = 20;
int y = 20;          int x = 10;
```

When executed according to the CompCert C semantics, the program on the left will bind x to (say) block identifier 1 and y to block 2, while the program on the right will bind x to block 2 and y to block 1. Nonetheless, the observable behaviors of the two programs are the same, because both the memory model and the CompCert C semantics are invariant by a *renaming* of block identifiers.

Invariance properties stronger than renamings are necessary to prove the correctness of CompCert's compiler passes. Here are two examples of compilation passes that modify the memory layout of the program:

1. Local scalar variables whose addresses are never taken (using the & operator) are "pulled out of memory" and put into a variable environment separate from the memory state. (This enables much more aggressive optimizations on uses of these variables.) Moreover, to simplify the semantics of Cminor and later intermediate languages, the remaining local variables are packed together as sub-blocks of a single memory block representing the stack frame of the function.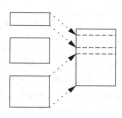

2. In the "stacking" pass performed after register allocation, local variables that could not be allocated to register are "spilled" to memory locations within the stack frame of the current function. This stack frame, therefore, needs to be extended to make room for spilled variables.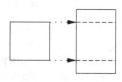

To reason about such transformations, CompCert introduces the notion of *memory injections*, which are a generalization of renamings of block identifiers; and *memory extensions*, to permit extra fields to be added to a block. A memory injection is a function F with type

$$F : \text{block} \rightarrow \text{option}(\text{block} \times \mathbb{Z})$$

Let b be a block identifier in the memory state of the original program. $F(b) = \text{None}$ means that this block was "pulled out of memory" by the program transformation. $F(b) = \text{Some}(b', \delta)$ means that this block is mapped to a sub-block of block b' in the memory state of the transformed program, said sub-block starting at offset δ.

A memory injection F induces a relation $F \vdash v_1 \hookrightarrow v_2$ between the values v_1 of the original program and the values v_2 of the transformed program. This relation corresponds to relocating pointer values as specified by F. It also enables Vundef values in the original program to be replaced by more defined values in the transformed program.

$$\frac{}{F \vdash \mathsf{Vundef} \hookrightarrow v_2} \qquad \frac{}{F \vdash \mathsf{Vint}(n) \hookrightarrow \mathsf{Vint}(n)}$$

$$\frac{}{F \vdash \mathsf{Vfloat}(n) \hookrightarrow \mathsf{Vfloat}(n)} \qquad \frac{F(b_1) = \mathsf{Some}(b_2, \delta) \quad i_2 = i_1 + \delta}{F \vdash \mathsf{Vptr}(b_1, i_1) \hookrightarrow \mathsf{Vptr}(b_2, i_2)}$$

Likewise, a memory injection F induces a relation $F \vdash m_1 \mapsto m_2$ between the memory states m_1 of the original program and m_2 of the transformed program. In version 1 of the CompCert memory model, this relation is defined as "every load in m_1 from a mapped block is simulated by a load in m_2 from the image of this block":

$$F(b_1) = \mathsf{Some}(b_2, \delta) \wedge \mathsf{load}\ \tau\ m_1\ b_1\ i = \mathsf{Some}(v_1)$$
$$\Rightarrow \exists v_2, \mathsf{load}\ \tau\ m_2\ b_2\ (i + \delta) = \mathsf{Some}(v_2) \wedge F \vdash v_1 \hookrightarrow v_2$$

As demonstrated by Leroy and Blazy [64, section 5], memory injections enjoy nice properties of commutation with the store, alloc and free operations of the memory model. These properties, in turn, support the proof of semantic preservation for the CompCert compiler passes that modify the memory behaviors of programs.

In conclusion, a crucial feature of the CompCert memory model version 1 is that block identifiers are kept relatively abstract and can be renamed, deleted or injected as sub-blocks of bigger blocks while preserving the observable behaviors of programs. Without this feature, several passes of the CompCert compiler could not be proved to preserve semantics.

LIMITATION: LIMITED COMPOSITIONALITY OF INJECTIONS AND EXTENSIONS. Different compiler passes do various injections and extensions, and the forward simulation proofs of all passes must be composed to make the CompCert correctness proof. Therefore it would be convenient to reason about the composition of injections and extensions, but the version 1 definitions do not fully permit this. The CompCert correctness proofs survived this awkwardness as long as there was no shared-memory interaction between compilation units (see Chapter 33).

Limitation: Pointer comparison. A standard-conformant C program can only compare pointers to (certain offsets from) *allocated* blocks. To see the danger, consider this program:

```
int *f(void) {int x; return &x;}
int g(void) {int *p = f(); int *q = f(); return (p==q);}
```

Most C implementations will have a consistent stack-frame size and interframe padding, leading to p==q evaluating true. But it is quite legal to have variable interframe padding, such as might occur when a C system inserts a *trampoline frame* between g's frame and f's frame. In such a case, p==q may be false. Thus the C standard makes comparisons to deallocated pointers undefined.

Early version 1 modeled this by requiring nonempty bounds on blocks p and q, but this would have prohibited certain legitimate patterns of use in shared-memory programs in which one thread wants to (temporarily) give away write permission while retaining the ability to compare pointers. *Late* version 1 modeled this in a different way that was in fact unsound.

Limitation: Coarse-grained access control. In version 1 of the memory model, a load or store operation succeeds as long as the accessed location is aligned and within the bounds of its enclosing block, and a free operation always succeeds, even if the given block was already freed. This behavior is too coarse in several situations that we now illustrate.

First, it should be the case that free fails if the given block has not been allocated before, or was already freed earlier. In this way, programs that perform double-free errors have undefined semantics, as they should. Attempts to free global variables should also fail, for similar reasons.

Second, memory blocks corresponding to const variables in C or to string literals should be marked read-only, so that a store into one of these blocks always fails. Besides making the semantics of CompCert C closer to the C standards, reflecting const-ness into the memory model in this way supports interesting optimizations such as constant propagation of const global variables:

```
const int cst = 4;            const int cst = 4;
int f(x) { return x * cst; }  →  int f(x) { return x << 2; }
```

Third, fine-grained access control over memory locations is also useful to extend CompCert towards data race-free concurrent programs, as proposed in the Verified Software Toolchain project [7, 9, 51]. In the VST approach, data races are avoided by a locking discipline enforced via a concurrent separation logic. Each area of shared memory is logically associated with a lock through concurrent separation logic formulas. When a thread releases an exclusive lock, the calling thread loses all access rights on the associated memory area. If, later, this lock is reacquired, the calling thread recovers these rights. Since our concurrent separation logic supports fractional permissions, it is also possible for a thread to temporarily abandon write rights, giving other threads the right to read (but not write) to this memory area, while retaining read rights for itself.

At the source language level, the access rights mentioned above are implied and enforced by the separation logic. The CompCert compiler must, then, guarantee that these access rights are respected during compilation. A typical violation would be for CompCert to move a load or store before a lock acquisition or after a lock release. One way to prove that this does not happen would be to apply the separation logic discipline to all intermediate languages and compilation passes of CompCert. A much simpler approach, which we follow in version 2 of the CompCert memory model, is to equip the memory model with a notion of fine-grained, per-byte permissions, governing for instance whether a byte can be written to. Concurrent operations such as lock and unlock are, then, modeled as changing the memory permissions as well as memory contents in an unpredictable manner, under control of an oracle external to the semantics. This suffices to prevent the compiler from moving memory accesses across lock and unlock operations.

The changes to memory permissions that occur at external function calls—in what appears to CompCert to be an "unpredictable" manner— can be reasoned about in a logic *external* to CompCert and its memory model. That logic might use fractional or token-based permission models (Chapter 41) to prove race freedom in a very predictable way. These complex permission-models do not need to be completely reified into the CompCert memory model; instead, a summary of their effects can be described by the abstract permissions that we will show at page 252.

The CompCert memory model, version 2

Version 2 of the CompCert memory model enhances version 1 to address the limitations described above without losing the *invariance* property or ISO-C99 compatibility. The main changes are:

- exposing the byte-level, in-memory representation of integers and floats, while keeping that of pointers abstract;

- introducing fine-grained, byte-level permissions in replacement for memory bounds; and

- adding new operations over memory states: loadbytes, storebytes, and drop_perm.

Operations

Version-2 memory states are presented as a type mem, a constant empty : mem denoting the empty memory state, and the seven operations

$$
\begin{array}{rcl}
\text{alloc} &:& \text{mem} \to Z \to Z \to \text{mem} \times \text{block} \\
\text{free} &:& \text{mem} \to \text{block} \to Z \to Z \to \text{option mem} \\
\text{load} &:& \text{mem} \to \text{memory\_chunk} \to \text{block} \to Z \to \text{option val} \\
\text{store} &:& \text{mem} \to \text{memory\_chunk} \to \text{block} \to Z \to \text{val} \to \text{option mem} \\
\text{loadbytes} &:& \text{mem} \to \text{block} \to Z \to Z \to \text{option(list memval)} \\
\text{storebytes} &:& \text{mem} \to \text{block} \to Z \to \text{list memval} \to \text{option mem} \\
\text{drop\_perm} &:& \text{mem} \to \text{block} \to Z \to Z \to \text{permission} \to \text{option mem}
\end{array}
$$

alloc, load and store are as in version 1 of the model. The free operation, free m b l h, no longer frees the whole block b, but rather the range of offsets $[l, h)$ within block b. This change simplifies the definition of a separation logic on top of the memory model. It also makes it possible to reduce the size of a block after allocation, and to "punch holes" within a block, two possibilities that CompCert does not exercise currently. Another change is that free can now fail, typically if the locations to be freed have been freed already, or if a (concurrent) thread does not have exclusive access to the block.

Three new operations were added. loadbytes and storebytes are similar to load and store, but instead of reading or writing a value, they read or write a list of byte contents (type memval, explained at page 256). loadbytes and storebytes are useful to give semantics to block copy operations such as memcpy, and also to reason over byte-level, in-memory representation of data.

Finally, drop_perm m b l h p lowers the permissions (access rights) over locations $(b, l), \ldots, (b, h - 1)$, setting them to p. A typical use of drop_perm is to set to read-only a memory block corresponding to a const C variable, after it has been initialized.

Permissions.

Memory states associate permissions, or access rights, to every byte location. The various permissions are:

Freeable	full permissions: can compare, read, write, and free
Writable	can compare, read and write but not free
Readable	can compare and read but not write nor free
Nonempty	can only compare

In the table above, "compare" refers to the ability of comparing a pointer to the given location with other pointers.[1]

---

[1] In CompCert C as in the C standards, pointer comparison involving invalid pointers (e.g. pointers to freed locations) have undefined semantics. For the purpose of giving semantics to pointer comparisons, we take that a pointer $\mathrm{Vptr}(b, i)$ is valid if the location (b, i) has at least Nonempty permission.

Permissions are cumulative: having permission p implies having all permissions $p' < p$, where the ordering on permissions is

$$\text{Nonempty} < \text{Readable} < \text{Writable} < \text{Freeable}$$

It is possible for a location to have no permission at all. In this case, we say that the location is *empty*. This is typically the case for locations that have not been allocated yet, or have been freed already. Every byte location is associated not to one, but to two permissions: the *current* permission and the *maximal* permission. At any time in the execution, the current permission is less than or equal to the maximal permission. The maximal permission evolves predictably throughout the lifetime of the location: when the location is allocated, it has maximal permission Freeable; this permission can later be lowered by a drop_perm operation; finally, freeing the location removes all its maximal permissions, making the location empty. The maximal permission can only decrease once the location has been allocated. In contrast, the current permission can decrease or increase (without ever exceeding the maximal permission) during the lifetime of the location. For example, in the extension to shared memory concurrency, an unlock operation temporarily drops current permissions, which can be recovered by a subsequent lock operation. Here is an illustration of the evolution of a location's permissions:

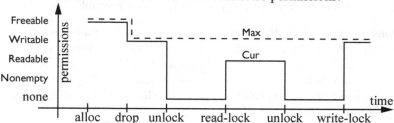

The association of permissions to locations is exposed as a Coq predicate:

$$\text{perm} : \text{mem} \rightarrow \text{block} \rightarrow Z \rightarrow \text{perm\_kind} \rightarrow \text{permission} \rightarrow \text{Prop}$$

where perm_kind is the enumerated inductive type Max | Cur. The proposition perm m b i k p holds if and only if in memory state m, location

(b, i) has k-permission at least p. The cumulativity of permissions, and the fact that current permissions are never above maximal permissions, are expressed by the following implications:

$$\text{perm } m \; b \; i \; k \; p \wedge p' \leq p \Rightarrow \text{perm } m \; b \; i \; k \; p'$$
$$\text{perm } m \; b \; i \; \text{Cur } p \Rightarrow \text{perm } m \; b \; i \; \text{Max } p$$

Instead of checking block offsets against block bounds, as in version 1 of the memory model, the load and store operations check that the accessed locations have current permissions at least Readable, resp. Writable. Likewise, the free and drop_perm operations check that the affected locations have current permissions at least Freeable. Defining

Definition range_perm (m: mem) (b: block) (lo hi: Z)
                       (k: perm_kind) (p: permission) : Prop :=
      $\forall$ ofs, lo $<=$ ofs $<$ hi $\rightarrow$ perm m b ofs k p.

we have the following properties:

Operation...	succeeds if and only if...
load $m \; \tau \; b \; i$	range_perm $m \; b \; i \; (i + |\tau|)$ Cur Readable
store $m \; \tau \; b \; i \; v$	range_perm $m \; b \; i \; (i + |\tau|)$ Cur Writable
free $m \; b \; l \; h$	range_perm $m \; b \; l \; h$ Cur Freeable
drop_perm $m \; b \; l \; h \; p$	range_perm $m \; b \; l \; h$ Cur Freeable

Owing to the availability of per-byte permissions, it is no longer useful to associate low and high bounds to memory blocks. Version 2 of the memory model therefore removes the low_bound and high_bound functions of version 1. The main use of these functions in CompCert's proofs was to state that a location (b, i) is valid, *i.e.* already allocated but not yet freed, using the following definition:

$$(b, i) \text{ is valid in } m \stackrel{\text{def}}{=} \text{low\_bound } m \; b \leq i < \text{high\_bound } m \; b$$

Using version 2 of the model, the following alternate definition works just as well:

$$(b, i) \text{ is valid in } m \stackrel{\text{def}}{=} \text{perm } m \; b \; i \; \text{Max Nonempty}$$

Permissions are preserved by operations over memory states, with the following exceptions.

Operation	Effect on permissions
alloc $m\ l\ h = (m', b)$	$(b, l) \ldots (b, h - 1)$ get Freeable perms (Max & Cur)
free $m\ b\ l\ h$	$(b, l) \ldots (b, h - 1)$ lose all permissions
drop_perm $m\ b\ l\ h\ p$	$(b, l) \ldots (b, h - 1)$ get Max and Cur permissions p

To strengthen intuitions about permissions, it is useful to consider their meaning in a shared-memory concurrent extension of CompCert. Different threads will have different permissions over a given memory location. Using a concurrent separation logic with fractional permissions (Chapter 41), and projecting these rich logical permissions on CompCert's simple permissions, we can ensure that the permissions of two threads A and B over a given memory location always fall within one of the following cases:

A's perm	B's perm	What A can do	What B can do
Freeable	none	compare, load, store, free	nothing
Writable	$\leq$ Nonempty	compare, load, store	compare
Readable	$\leq$ Readable	compare, load	compare, load
Nonempty	$\leq$ Writable	compare	compare, load, store
none	any	nothing	compare, load, store, free

Combined with the permission checks performed by the various operations, this interpretation of permissions causes programs containing data races to have undefined semantics ("getting stuck"). If two threads are in danger of approaching a data race, at least one of the threads will be "stuck" in its own sequential operational semantics because it will have insufficient permission. For example, if thread A stores at a location while thread B loads from the same location, one or both of the load and store operations will fail by lack of sufficient permissions. A similar failure occurs if A compares a pointer while B is freeing the location. However, concurrent loads are possible if the location has permission Readable in both threads.

In-memory data representations

Memory states include a contents map that associates a value of type memval to each byte, that is, each pair (block identifier, byte offset).

> Inductive memval: Type :=
> | Undef: memval
> | Byte: byte → memval
> | Pointer: block → int → nat → memval.

The contents of a given memory byte can be either

- Undef, standing for an unspecified bit pattern such as the contents of an uninitialized memory area;

- Byte n where n is a concrete 8-bit integer in the range $0 \ldots 255$;

- Pointer $b\ i\ n$, standing for the nth byte of the abstract pointer (b, i).

The intent of this representation is that integer and float values, when stored in memory, are decomposed into a sequence of bytes $n_1, \ldots, n_k$, taking endianness and IEEE encoding of floats into account, then stored in the contents map as the memvals Byte $n_1, \ldots,$ Byte n_k. (This is exactly what the hardware processor does.) In contrast, when storing a pointer value Vptr(b, i), we hide its hardware representation by storing the memvals Pointer $b\ i\ 0, \ldots,$ Pointer $b\ i\ 3$. Loading from memory performs the reverse operation, recovering a value from a sequence of memvals.

These conversions between values and lists of memvals are governed by a memory_chunk τ describing the encoding, and encapsulated in the following two functions (see Figures 32.1 and 32.2):

> encode_val: memory_chunk → val → list memval
> decode_val: memory_chunk → list memval → val

The decode_val function is carefully engineered to be the left inverse of encode_val: encoding a value, then decoding the resulting list of bytes, recovers the original value modulo normalization of the value to the memory_chunk used:

$$\text{decode\_val } \tau \ (\text{encode\_val } \tau \ v) = \text{convert } \tau \ v$$

$$\text{encode\_val Mint8unsigned } (\text{Vint}(n)) = [\text{Byte } x_1]$$
$$\text{encode\_val Mint8signed } (\text{Vint}(n)) = [\text{Byte } x_1]$$
$$\text{where } (x_1) = \text{encode\_int } 1 \; n$$
$$\text{encode\_val Mint16unsigned } (\text{Vint}(n)) = [\text{Byte } x_1; \text{Byte } x_2]$$
$$\text{encode\_val Mint16signed } (\text{Vint}(n)) = [\text{Byte } x_1; \text{Byte } x_2]$$
$$\text{where } (x_1, x_2) = \text{encode\_int } 2 \; n$$
$$\text{encode\_val Mint32 } (\text{Vint}(n)) = [\text{Byte } x_1; \text{Byte } x_2; \text{Byte } x_3; \text{Byte } x_4]$$
$$\text{where } (x_1, \ldots, x_4) = \text{encode\_int } 4 \; n$$
$$\text{encode\_val Mint32 } (\text{Vptr}(b, i)) = [\text{Pointer } b \; i \; 0; \ldots; \text{Pointer } b \; i \; 3]$$
$$\text{encode\_val Mfloat32 } (\text{Vfloat}(n)) = [\text{Byte } x_1; \text{Byte } x_2; \text{Byte } x_3; \text{Byte } x_4]$$
$$\text{where } (x_1, \ldots, x_4) = \text{encode\_int } 4 \; (\text{bits\_of\_single } n)$$
$$\text{encode\_val Mfloat64 } (\text{Vfloat}(n)) = [\text{Byte } x_1; \ldots; \text{Byte } x_8]$$
$$\text{where } (x_1, \ldots, x_8) = \text{encode\_int } 8 \; (\text{bits\_of\_double } n)$$
$$\text{encode\_val } \tau \; v = [\underbrace{\text{Undef}; \ldots; \text{Undef}}_{|\tau| \text{ times}}] \text{ otherwise}$$

encode_int l n returns the list of the low l bytes of integer n, either in big-endian or little-endian order depending on the target architecture. bits_of_single and bits_of_double return as an integer the IEEE 754 representation of a single-precision or double-precision float, respectively.

Figure 32.1: Definition of encode_val

This property still holds if the bytes are decoded with an integer memory_chunk τ' differing only in signedness from the τ used for encoding:

$$\text{decode\_val } \tau' \; (\text{encode\_val } \tau \; v) = \text{convert } \tau' \; v$$
$$\text{if } \{\tau, \tau'\} = \{\text{Mint8u}, \text{Mint8s}\}$$
$$\text{or } \{\tau, \tau'\} = \{\text{Mint16u}, \text{Mint16s}\}$$

$$\text{decode\_val Mint8u } [\text{Byte } x_1] = \text{Vint}(n)$$
$$\text{decode\_val Mint8s } [\text{Byte } x_1] = \text{Vint}(\text{sign}_\text{e}\text{xtends}(n))$$
$$\text{where } n = \text{decode\_int } [x_1]$$
$$\text{decode\_val Mint16u } [\text{Byte } x_1; \text{Byte } x_2] = \text{Vint}(n)$$
$$\text{decode\_val Mint16s } [\text{Byte } x_1; \text{Byte } x_2] = \text{Vint}(\text{sign}_\text{e}\text{xtends}(n))$$
$$\text{where } n = \text{decode\_int } [x_1; x_2]$$
$$\text{decode\_val Mint32 } [\text{Byte } x_1; \ldots; \text{Byte } x_4] = \text{Vint}(n)$$
$$\text{decode\_val Mfloat32 } [\text{Byte } x_1; \ldots; \text{Byte } x_4] = \text{Vfloat}(\text{single\_of\_bits}(n))$$
$$\text{where } n = \text{decode\_int } [x_1; \ldots; x_4]$$
$$\text{decode\_val Mfloat64 } [\text{Byte } x_1; \ldots; \text{Byte } x_8] = \text{Vfloat}(\text{double\_of\_bits}(n))$$
$$\text{where } n = \text{decode\_int } [x_1; \ldots; x_8]$$
$$\text{decode\_val Mint32 } [\text{Pointer } b\ i\ 0; \ldots; \text{Pointer } b\ i\ 3] = \text{Vptr}(b, i)$$
$$\text{decode\_val } \tau\ L = \text{Vundef in all other cases}$$

decode_int L combines the given list of bytes L into an integer, using either big-endian or little-endian convention depending on the target architecture.

Figure 32.2: Definition of decode_val

Moreover, encoding as a Mint32 and decoding as a Mfloat32, or conversely, gives access to the IEEE bit-level representation of single-precision floats:

$$\text{decode\_val Mfloat32}(\text{encode\_val Mint32 }(\text{Vint}(i))) = \text{single\_of\_bits}(i)$$
$$\text{decode\_val Mint32}(\text{encode\_val Mfloat32 }(\text{Vfloat}(f))) = \text{bits\_of\_single}(f)$$

Algebraic laws

LOAD AND LOADBYTES; STORE AND STOREBYTES. A load operation is equivalent to a loadbytes operation plus a decode_val and an alignment check:

$$\text{load } m\ \tau\ b\ i = \text{Some }(\text{decode\_val } \tau\ B) \iff$$
$$\text{loadbytes } m\ b\ i\ |\tau| = \text{Some } B \land \langle \tau \rangle \text{ divides } i$$

Similarly for a store operation and the corresponding storebytes operation:

$$\text{store } m \ \tau \ b \ i \ v = \text{Some } m' \iff$$
$$\text{storebytes } m \ b \ i \ (\text{encode\_val } \tau \ v) = \text{Some } m' \ \wedge \ \langle \tau \rangle \text{ divides } i$$

DECOMPOSING LOADBYTES AND STOREBYTES OPERATIONS. A loadbytes operation on a range of locations is equivalent to two loadbytes operations on two adjacent ranges:

$$\text{loadbytes } m \ b \ i \ (n_1 + n_2) = \text{Some } B \iff$$
$$\exists B_1, \exists B_2, \ B = B_1.B_2 \ \wedge \ \text{loadbytes } m \ b \ i \ n_1 = \text{Some } B_1$$
$$\wedge \ \text{loadbytes } m \ b \ (i + n_1) \ n_2 = \text{Some } B_2$$

Likewise, a storebytes operation decomposes into two storebytes:

$$\text{storebytes } m \ b \ i \ (B_1.B_2) = \text{Some } m' \iff$$
$$\exists m_1, \ \text{storebytes } m \ b \ i \ B_1 = \text{Some } m_1$$
$$\wedge \ \text{storebytes } m_1 \ b \ (i + |B_1|) \ B_2 = \text{Some } m'$$

LOAD AFTER ALLOC: Same properties as in version 1 of the model: if alloc $m \ l \ h = (m', b)$,

- load $m' \ \tau' \ b' \ i' = \text{load } m \ \tau' \ b' \ i'$ if $b' \neq b$

- If load $m \ \tau \ b \ i = \text{Some } v$, then $v = \text{Vundef}$

LOAD AFTER FREE: if free $m \ b \ l \ h = m'$,

- load $m' \ \tau' \ b' \ i' = \text{load } m \ \tau' \ b' \ i'$ if $b' \neq b$ or $i' + |\tau'| \leq l$ or $h \leq i'$

- load $m \ \tau \ b \ i = \text{None}$ if $l \leq i$ and $i + |\tau| \leq h$.

LOADBYTES AFTER STOREBYTES If storebytes $m \ b \ i \ B = \text{Some } m'$,

- Compatible case: loadbytes $m' \ b \ i \ |B| = \text{Some } B$

- Disjoint case: loadbytes $m' \ b' \ i' \ n' = \text{loadbytes } m \ b' \ i' \ n'$ if $b' \neq b$ or $i' + n' \leq i$ or $i + |B| \leq i'$

Cases of partial overlap can be reasoned upon by decomposing the storebytes or the loadbytes operation into multiple operations.

LOAD AFTER STORE. if store m τ b i v = Some m',

- Disjoint case: load m' τ' b' i' = load m τ' b' i' if $b' \neq b$ or $i' + |\tau'| \leq i$ or $i + |\tau| \leq i'$

- Compatible case: load m' τ' b i = decode_val τ' (encode_val τ v) if $|\tau'| = |\tau|$. In particular, if τ' and τ are identical or differ only in signedness, load m' τ' b i = convert τ' v.

Compared with version 1 of the memory model, it is no longer the case that the load must return an Vundef value in the "incompatible" and "overlapping" cases. For example, if we write a 64-bit float f at location (b, i), then read a 32-bit integer from this location, the result is not Vundef but an integer corresponding to one half of the IEEE bit-level representation of f. This is a strength of the new memory model, as it addresses the limitations described at page 244. However, we can still say something in the "incompatible" and "overlapping" cases if the value v just stored is a pointer value.

- Incompatible case for pointer values: if v is a pointer value and load m' τ' b i = Some v' and $\tau \neq$ Mint32 $\vee$ $\tau' \neq$ Mint32, then $v' =$ Vundef.

- Overlapping case for pointer values: if v is a pointer value and load m' τ' b i' = Some v' and $i' \neq i$ and $i' + |\tau'| > i$ and $i + |\tau| > i'$, then $v' =$ Vundef.

These special cases are related to a more general integrity property for stored pointer values, described next.

INTEGRITY OF POINTER VALUES. As discussed above, it is possible to load integer or float values that were never stored in memory, but arise from combinations of byte-level representations of other integer or float values previously stored in memory. However, the memory model guarantees that this cannot happen for pointer values:

If store m τ b i v = Some m' and load m' τ' b' i' = Some(Vptr(b'', i'')), then either

- the pointer value that is loaded is the value just stored: $\tau = \tau'$ = Mint32 and $b' = b$ and $i' = i$ and v = Vptr(b'', i'');

- or the load is disjoint from the store: $b' \neq b$ or $i' + |\tau'| \leq i$ or $i + |\tau| \leq i'$; therefore, the pointer value that is loaded was already present in the original memory state: load m τ' b' i' = Some(Vptr(b'', i''))

This integrity property is important: if pointer values could arise "out of thin air" by loading byte-level representations of other values, the properties of invariance by memory transformations (page 246) would be invalidated, and several passes of the CompCert compiler could no longer be proved semantics-preserving.

Implementation.

The CompCert Coq sources provide an implementation of the memory model in module Memory, which is proved to satisfy the algebraic laws listed above and all the other properties specified in module Memtype. Memory states are represented by the following record type:

```
Definition block : Type := positive.
```

```
Record mem : Type := mkmem {
  mem_contents: PMap.t (ZMap.t memval);
  mem_access: PMap.t (Z → perm_kind → option permission);
  nextblock: block;
  access_max: ∀ b ofs, perm_order'' (mem_access#b ofs Max)
                                     (mem_access#b ofs Cur);
  nextblock_noaccess:
    ∀ b ofs k, b ≥ nextblock → mem_access#b ofs k = None
}.
```

A memory state is composed of three pieces of data:

- A block identifier nextblock, which tracks the first nonallocated block. The next alloc operation will return this block identifier.

- A map mem_contents from (block, offset) pairs to memvals. This map is implemented using the Pmap and ZMap data structures from CompCert's Maps library. PMap (respectively, Zmap) provides an efficient implementation of P-indexed (resp., Z-indexed) finite maps with a default value. (Efficiency of the model makes no difference to the speed of CompCert itself, or to the quality of the generated assembly language. It makes a difference to *simulators* that execute the memory model.)

- A map mem_access from (block, offset, permission-kind) triples to the type option permission. This maps records, for every location, the greatest Cur permission and the greatest Max permission. None means no permissions at all.

Additionally, three invariants are packaged with this data: no location's Cur permission exceeds its Max permission; blocks that have not been allocated yet have empty permissions; and any byte not explicitly mapped defaults to Undef.

To give a flavor of the implementation, here is the definition of the store operation:

```
Definition store (chunk: memory_chunk) (m: mem)
                  (b: block) (ofs: Z) (v: val) : option mem :=
  if valid_access_dec m chunk b ofs Writable then
    Some (mkmem (PMap.set b (setN (encode_val chunk v) ofs
                            (m.(mem_contents)#b))
                       m.(mem_contents))
                m.(mem_access)
                m.(nextblock)
                m.(access_max)
                m.(nextblock_noaccess)
                (... contents_default ...))
  else
    None.
```

valid_access_dec decides whether the offset is aligned with respect to the memory chunk and whether all addressed bytes have Cur,Writable permissions. If not, store fails, returning None. If so, an updated memory state is returned, where the locations $(b, ofs), \ldots, (b, ofs + |chunk \vdash 1)$ are set (by the auxiliary function setN) to the list of memvals returned by encode_val chunk v, and all other locations are unchanged.

Some clients of the CompCert memory model, such as libraries of lemmas about program transformations and program logics, often find it convenient to reason about the constructive definitions (such as the one shown here for store) instead of their axiomatizations. Other clients, such as the correctness proofs for CompCert's compilation passes, only need the axiomatization in terms of algebraic laws outlined at page 258.

Assessment of the memory model, version 2

Version 2 of the memory model preserves the main features of version 1. It gives the expected semantics to ISO C99 conformant programs. It gives the expected semantics to those nonconformant C programs that perform wild casts between pointers and make assumptions about the memory layout of structs, unions and arrays. It enjoys useful properties of invariance by memory transformations. The notion of memory injections initially developed for version 1 extends easily to version 2 of the model and was shown to commute with memory operations. We now discuss how version 2 removes the limitations of version 1.

Capability: Low-level programming idioms on integers and floats. Version 2 of the model is able to give precise semantics to programs that make assumptions about the memory representations of base types (integers and floats). We now revisit the examples (see pages 244ff) to illustrate this new capability.

Endianness change. Using the store-storebytes equivalence, we see that at program point 1, the memory block associated with src contains the encoding [Byte x_1; Byte x_2; Byte x_3; Byte x_4] of the integer x, where $(x_1, \ldots, x_4) = $ encode_int 4 x.

```
unsigned int bswap(unsigned int x) {
    union { unsigned int i; char c[4]; } src, dst;
    int n;
    src.i = x;
    /* point 1 */
    dst.c[3] = src.c[0]; dst.c[2] = src.c[1];
    dst.c[1] = src.c[2]; dst.c[0] = src.c[3];
    /* point 2 */
    return dst.i;
}
```

Using the loadbytes-storebytes laws, we obtain that at program point 2, the memory block associated with dst contains the memvals [Byte x_4; Byte x_3; Byte x_2; Byte x_1]. The load-loadbytes equivalence, then, shows that the integer returned by the function is decode_int $[x_4, x_3, x_2, x_1]$, which is indeed the byte-swapping of integer x.

SINGLE-PRECISION ABSOLUTE VALUE. According to the load-store-compatible law, the value of u.i at program point 3 is

$$\text{decode\_valMint32(encode\_valMfloat32x)} = \text{bits\_of\_single(x)}$$

that is, the 32-bit integer corresponding to the IEEE 754 representation of the single-precision float x.

```
float fabs_single(float x) {
    union { float f; unsigned int i; } u;
    u.f = x;
    /* point 3 */
    u.i = u.i & 0x7FFFFFFF;
    /* point 4 */
    return u.f;
}
```

Using the same law again, the return value of the function is single_of_bits(n), where n is the value of u.i at point 4. Since $n = $ bits_of_single(x)&0x7FFFFFFF, it follows that fabs_single computes the function

$$x \mapsto \text{single\_of\_bits(bits\_of\_single}(x)\&\text{0x7FFFFFFF})$$

Using a formalization of IEEE 754 such as Flocq [25], it can be proved that this function is floating-point absolute value.

CONVERTING INTEGERS TO DOUBLE-PRECISION FLOATS, POWERPC-STYLE.
Using many of the memory model laws (store-storebytes and load-loadbytes equivalence; loadbytes-storebytes laws; and loadbytes and storebytes decomposition properties) and assuming a big-endian architecture,

```
double double_of_signed_int(int x) {
    union { double d; unsigned int i[2]; } a, b;
    a.i[0] = 0x43300000; a.i[1] = 0x80000000;
    b.i[0] = 0x43300000; b.i[1] = 0x80000000 + x;
    /* point 5 */
    return b.d − a.d;
}
```

we obtain that at point 5,

$$a.d = \text{double\_of\_bits(0x4330000080000000)}$$
$$b.d = \text{double\_of\_bits(0x4330000080000000} + x)$$

The return value of the function is, therefore, the double-precision floating-point difference between these two floats. Using Flocq, it remains to prove that this difference is indeed the float (double) x, taking advantage of the fact $-2^{31} \leq x < 2^{31}$. The point is that the correctness of this function was reduced to a pure floating-point arithmetic problem; the byte-level manipulations over floats are now precisely defined thanks to the new memory model.

LIMITATION: NO ACCESS TO BIT-LEVEL REPRESENTATIONS OF POINTERS.
Consider again the block copy example (page 244):

```
void * memcpy(void * dest, const void * src, size_t n) {
    for (i = 0; i < n; i++)
        ((char *) dest)[i] = ((const char *) src)[i];
    return dest;
}
```

Version 2 of the memory model is able to show that this function executes as expected, but only if the source array src contains no pointer values; more precisely, if the memvals at src...src + n − 1 are all of the Byte or Undef kind.

Indeed, when loaded with C type char, the memval Byte x reads as the integer x or x's sign extension (depending on whether the char type is signed). Storing this integer with C type char amounts to storing the memval Byte x. If the source memval is Undef, it reads as the value Vundef, and writes back as the memval Undef. Finally, if the source memval is a pointer fragment Pointer b i n, it reads as the value Vundef and writes as Undef.

Assuming no overlap between the src and dest memory areas, the net effect of memcpy's loop, is, therefore, to copy the memvals contained in src to the area pointed by dest, turning pointer fragments into Undef memvals and preserving Byte and Undef memvals. In other words, the expected behavior of memcpy, namely, making an exact copy of src into dest, is guaranteed by CompCert's semantics only if src contains integers and floats, but no pointers.

Similar limitations arise in examples other than memcpy. One is the memcmp function from the C standard library, which compares the contents of two memory areas as if they were arrays of characters. (Unlike memcpy, the informal semantics of memcmp is very unclear to begin with, because it observes the values of padding bytes introduced by compilers in compound data structures.) Another example is the occasional need to reverse the endianness of a pointer, for instance when a big-endian processor exchanges linked data structures with a little-endian USB controller.

Is this a serious limitation? More practical experience with embedded critical codes is needed to answer this question, but here are a few thoughts about this issue.

First, the C standards guarantee the existence of a correct memcpy function in the C standard library, but never say that it can be written in conformant C, as the simple byte-per-byte copy loop above or in any other ways. Our memory model version 2 is perfectly able to axiomatize the behavior of such a correct memcpy function, as a loadbytes operation over the whole range $src \ldots src + n - 1$ followed by a storebytes at dest.

Second, like many C compilers, CompCert provides a predefined block copy operation, __builtin_memcpy, whose semantics is precisely definedd as a loadbytes operation followed by a storebytes (plus checks for absence of overlap). A current limitation of this built-in operation is that the number n of bytes to copy must be a compile-time constant. In exchange, CompCert is able to produce very efficient assembly code for __builtin_memcpy, using multi-byte memory accesses and unrolling the copy loop when appropriate. The point is that CompCert-compiled systems code should never define its own memcpy function and call it as memcpy(dest, src, sizeof(src)): using __builtin_memcpy is not only better defined semantically speaking, but also much more efficient.

Third, if the need arises to copy arrays of pointers, we can define a version of memcpy specialized for this case:

```
void * memcpy_ptr(void ** dest, const void ** src, size_t n) {
    for (i = 0; i < n / sizeof(void *); i++)
            dest[i] = src[i];
    return dest;
}
```

Both version 1 and version 2 of the CompCert memory model show that this function correctly copies arrays of pointers. With version 2, it might be possible to show that structs containing a mixture of pointer fields and numerical fields, or arrays of such structs, are copied unchanged as well. This conjecture relies on the fact that pointer fields in structs are always 4-aligned, and force the alignment of the enclosing struct to be at least 4.

CAPABILITY: MORE PRECISE SEMANTICS. The permission mechanism introduced in version 2 of the model is effective to better control the memory operations that are allowed on global variables.

The initial memory state in which a program starts execution is built as follows by the CompCert operational semantics. For every global variable of the C program, a memory block is allocated, then filled with the initial value provided for this variable, if any, or by a default value of "all zeroes" otherwise; then, permissions over the whole block are dropped to

- Nonempty if the type of the global variable is volatile;

- Readable if this type is const but not volatile;

- Writable, otherwise.

(CompCert treats string literals as global, initialized arrays of characters with type const char [], hence string literals, too, get Readable permissions.)

Dropping permissions over global variables has several benefits. First, attempting to deallocate a global variable or string literal by calling free on its address now has undefined semantics, as it should. (This follows from the fact that memory blocks corresponding to global variables always lack the Freeable permission.) Second, it is now a semantic error for a program to try to assign into a const global variable, or to access a volatile global variable through normal load and store operations.

The latter point deserves more explanations on how CompCert handles the volatile modifier. Accesses to l-values having volatile static type are compiled and given semantics not via normal load and store operations, but via special built-in functions, __builtin_volatile_read and __builtin_volatile_write that check whether the location actually accessed is an object declared volatile or not. In the former case, the volatile access is treated as an input/output operation, communicating with the outside world through an event in the trace of observables for the program, and bypassing the memory model entirely. In the latter case, the volatile access is treated as a regular load/store operation. To summarize:

Static type	Semantics & compilation	Actual location accessed	
		not volatile	volatile
not volatile	regular load/store operation	load/store	error
volatile	__builtin_volatile operation	load/store	I/O event

The semantic error in the top right case is a consequence of the accessed location lacking Readable and Writable permissions. It agrees with the prescriptions of the C standards, which state that undefined behavior arises if a volatile object is accessed through a non-volatile *l*-value, as can arise if a pointer cast is used to remove the volatile modifier from the type of the pointed object.

The discussion above is framed in terms of global variables. For function-local variables, CompCert essentially ignores the const and volatile modifiers: volatile local variables make little sense, as they cannot correspond to a hardware memory device; const local variables cannot have their permissions dropped, because there would be no way to raise these permissions back to Freeable before deallocating them at function return time.

CAPABILITY: MORE AGGRESSIVE OPTIMIZATIONS. We improved the constant propagation pass of CompCert 1.11 to take advantage of the "const-ness" of global variables. Consider:

```
const int n = 1;
const double tbl[3] = { 1.11, 2.22, 3.33 };
double f(void) { return tbl[n]; }
```

Owing to the const modifiers, the value of n is always 1 throughout execution, and the value of tbl[1] is always 2.22. It is therefore legitimate to optimize function f into

```
double f(void) { return 2.22; }
```

This is what the improved constant propagation pass now does. Its correctness proof (semantic preservation) nicely exploits the new features of the CompCert v2 memory model. Namely, the proof shows that the contents of const global variables are identical in the initial memory state and in the memory state at any point of the program execution. Indeed, a successful store operation performed by the program cannot change the contents of a memory block attached to a const global variables, because (1) such a memory block has maximal permission Readable (at most) in the initial memory state; (2) maximal permissions over already-allocated blocks can only decrease during execution; and (3) a successful store requires Writable current permissions over the locations it modifies.

Constant propagation of const global variables noticeably improves the quality of the assembly code produced by CompCert in some cases. One example that we observed is C code automatically generated from Scade, where the C code generator puts many numerical constants in const global variables rather than naming them with macros.

CAPABILITY: IMPROVED COMPOSITIONALITY OF INJECTIONS AND EXTENSIONS. Following a suggestion by Tahina Ramananandro, we refined the definition of memory injections in such a way that the composition of two memory injections, or of a memory injection and a memory extension, is itself a memory injection:

Lemma extends_inject_compose:
  $\forall$ f m1 m2 m3, extends m1 m2 $\rightarrow$ inject f m2 m3 $\rightarrow$ inject f m1 m3.

However, for reasoning about shared-memory interaction (threads, separate compilation) we will also want all CompCert passes to satisfy a *self-injection* property: any memory must inject to itself (by the appropriate choice of f). This is the subject of current work, in connection with the research we describe in Chapter 33.

Conclusions and perspectives

Version 2 of the CompCert memory model enables the semantics of the source and intermediate languages of CompCert to describe the memory behavior of programs with increased precision, while preserving all the properties of memory operations that CompCert's correctness proof relies on. This increase in precision translates into two improvements: More of the popular, low-level, non-standard-conformant C programming idioms, such as bit-level manipulations of in-memory representations of integers and floats, can be given well-defined semantics and, proved correct with respect to their high-level specifications, but also guaranteed to be compiled by CompCert in a semantics-preserving manner. (2) More of the serious C undefined behaviors, such as modifying a string literal, can be captured as errors by the CompCert formal semantics, enabling the CompCert compiler to perform more aggressive optimizations. (Verification tools based on CompCert's semantics can guarantee the absence of such errors.)

The main limitation that remains CompCert's memory model is its inability to model byte-level access to pointer values, as can happen in block copy operations, for instance. We argued that this limitation seems to be of low practical importance. Nonetheless, we see two ways to lift this limitation:

- The first approach is fairly *ad-hoc* and consists in extending Comp-Cert's type of values with a fifth case, $\mathsf{Vptr\_fragment}(b, i, n)$, denoting the n-th byte of the in-memory representation of pointer $\mathsf{Vptr}(b, i)$. Byte-sized load and store operations would translate between the $\mathsf{Vptr\_fragment}(b, i, n)$ value and the $\mathsf{Pointer}(b, i, n)$ memval without loss of information. Most if not all arithmetic operations would be undefined over values of the Vptr_fragment kind. This is the minimal extension that would give semantics to the memcpy example.

- The second approach is much more radical: replace CompCert's current "value" type (a discriminated union of integer, float, pointer and undefined values) by the type list memval of lists of byte-level, in-memory representations of values. This is the approach followed by Norrish in his Cholera formal semantics for the C language [70]: r-value expressions evaluate (conceptually) to their byte-level, in-memory representations. In this approach, encoding and decoding integer/float/pointer values to and from lists of bytes is no longer performed at load/store time, but at arithmetic operations. This is a major departure from the approach followed in CompCert so far.

Finally, the introduction of fine-grained permissions in the memory model is a first step towards extending CompCert to shared-memory, data-race-free concurrency. Further steps in this direction include re-engineering the operational semantics of CompCert's languages as described in the next chapter.

Chapter 33

How to specify a compiler
by Lennart Beringer, Robert Dockins, and Gordon Stewart

In Part III we described program verification for C: tools and techniques to demonstrate that C programs satisfy correctness properties. What we ultimately want is the correctness of a compiled machine language binary image, running on some target hardware platform. We will use a *correct compiler* that turns source-level programs satisfying correctness properties into machine-level programs satisfying those same properties. But defining formally the interface between a compiler correctness proof and a program logic has proven to be fraught with difficulties. Resolving these difficulties is still the object of ongoing research. Here we will explore some of the issues that have arisen and report on the current state of the integration effort.

THE TWO ISSUES that have caused the most headaches revolve around understanding and specifying how compiled programs interact with their environment. First, how should we reason about the execution environment when it may behave in unpredictable ways at runtime? In other words, how do we reason about program nondeterminism? Second, how do we specify correctness for programs that exhibit shared memory interactions?

The first question regarding nondeterminism is treated in detail in Dockins's dissertation [38]. Dockins develops a general theory of refinements for nondeterministic programs based on bisimulation methods. This theory gracefully handles the case where the execution environment is nondeterministic, and it has the critical feature that it allows programs to become *more defined* as they are compiled. This is important for a compiler for C, which has a large number of situations where program behavior is undefined (e.g., indexing into an array out of bounds). The compiler cannot, in general, detect when undefined behavior will occur, so it must simply emit some compiled program under the assumption that the program is well defined. When it is not, the actual behavior at runtime will be unpredictable. Dockins's behavioral refinement allows us to reason precisely about this situation. Dockins also defines a notion of refinement that allows us to reason about *unspecified* behaviors in C, such as the evaluation order of expressions.[1]

One significant result of this work is that we validate, in a richer setting, Leroy's claim [62] that proving forward simulation passes is sufficient for correctness when the target language of compilation is deterministic. Leroy proved his claim under the assumption that the external environment is deterministic as well as the target compilation language. Dockins lifted this assumption on the environment and proved that, under the weaker assumption that the target language is *internally* deterministic and under a mild assumption on the source language (receptiveness to external events), forward simulation implies behavioral refinement.

By lifting the assumption that the external world is deterministic, we can now model realistic external interactions involving nondeterminism, such as: the nondeterminism introduced by thread scheduling in multithreaded programs; or that introduced by consulting a hardware source of entropy; or that introduced by modeling an unpredictable agent (i.e., a human) interacting with the program via hardware peripherals.

The proper way to reason about shared-memory interactions remains an area of active research. The CompCert 1.x model of external interaction did not allow shared-memory interactions with the environment. This means that we could not faithfully model common patterns of interaction

---

[1]However, refinement with respect to unspecified behavior is not relevant to the "verifiable C" subset examined in this book, because verifiable C does not have unspecified behaviors.

in systems programs, such as the POSIX read and write system calls, which communicate via in-memory buffers.

The rest of this chapter describes the reformulation of CompCert's correctness theorem that lifts this restriction, made over a period of years 2006-2013 and still ongoing. We describe as "CompCert 1.x" early versions of CompCert dating from 2006 in which Leroy *et al.* focused on whole-program single-threaded execution. CompCert 2.0 (2013) has adopted many of our suggestions for specification of the memory model, of small-step operational semantics, and of interaction with external functions. These adjustments to CompCert's specification were made piecemeal between 2006 and 2013 in discussion with Leroy. And, of course, Leroy *et al.* have made many other improvements to CompCert that are unrelated to our discussions with him of the specification interface for shared-memory concurrency and separate compilation. We call this version, and near-future versions in which other related adjustments to the specification may be made to improve compositionality of shared-memory interaction, "CompCert 2.x".

The main difficulty that arises is the fact that the compiler must be free to reorganize some aspects of memory layout during compilation. This means we cannot simply expose the state of memory at each interaction point and specify that the source language memory will be the same as the target language memory. Instead, the memories will be *related* in a sophisticated way that abstracts from the identities of pointer values and the way that memory is organized into blocks.

The net result is a view of compiler correctness that has a logical relations flavor: related programs, when run in related memories, yield related results. In our model of fine-grained interaction for shared-memory applications, we focus on the following four ingredients:

Core Semantics uniformly specify the interactions of running threads, hiding language-specific details such as how control and local state (*e.g.*, the local environment or registers) are represented, while exposing memory.

Compositional Simulation Relations evolve CompCert 1.x's notions of
   compiler correctness simulations to the setting of shared memory, exposing appropriate aspects of memory transformations such as block
   relocation, and are compatible with core semantics. Compositionality
   is obtained by showing that memory-aware compiler correctness
   proofs compose transitively along the phases of the compiler.

Extensibility of core semantics (with respect to operational models of
   external functions) enables flexible models of separate compilation
   and linking, multithreaded concurrency, the integration of OS func-
   tionality, and the gradual refinement of external functions to code.
   All of this is achieved independently of any given language semantics.

Rely-Guarantee Composition of core semantics and external function
   specifications ensures the compatibility of extensible core semantics
   with compilation.

A SMALL-STEP OPERATIONAL SEMANTICS $s \longmapsto s'$ specifies how one step of
computation evolves state s into s'. We denote multistep executions with
the Kleene star, $s \longmapsto^* s'$.

   When discussing compiler correctness, it is useful to distinguish between
core steps—the operational semantics of the programming language itself,
for which the compiler has responsibility—and *external* steps, calls to
external functions, system calls, and synchronization operations that permit
other threads to execute. Typically, the arguments to and return values from
such external calls include pointers to memory. Thus, compiler correctness
needs to be formulated *compositionally*, paving the way for shared-memory
cooperation with separately compiled and linked modules, multithreaded
execution, and interaction with the operating system. On the other hand,
not *all* aspects of a module's memory behavior should be globally visible:
compiling a module *should* be permitted to relocate any memory block that
is unreachable from the pointers communicated to other modules, and *must*
be permitted to extend the memory by spill locations or other compiler-
internal data, even if these are typically placed in regions accessible from
other modules, as is the case for return addresses held in the stack frame.

When discussing program correctness using indirection theory, we are particularly interested in the question, "is the execution safe for at least n steps?" That is, within n steps of the $\longrightarrow$ relation, can we reach a state that has no successor, that is *stuck*?

We discuss safety in the context of a *core semantics* and an *external specification*:

Section safety.
Context $\{G \ C \ M \ Z : \mathsf{Type}\}$.
Context (Hcore:CoreSemantics $G \ C \ M$).
Variable (Hspec:external_specification M external_function Z).

Here, Hcore is the small-step semantics of a programming language, for example C light. We say *core* semantics to emphasize that it covers small-steps only of the programming language itself, not of calls to external functions. A small-step semantics is a relation $(c, m) \longmapsto (c', m')$ over states comprising a memory $m : M$ and a core-state $c : C$ comprising a control stack and local variables. For C light, M is the type of CompCert memories and C is C light core states (corestate in veric/Clight_new.v). The type Z describes states of the external context.

An operational state is safeN(n) if it cannot get stuck within n small-steps. We write

$$\mathsf{safeN} \ \mathsf{Hcore} \ \mathsf{Hspec} \ (g : G) \ (n : \mathsf{nat}) \ (z : Z) \ (\sigma : C)(m : M) \ : \ \mathsf{Prop}$$

to mean that it is safe to execute n steps starting from the global environment g (giving the addresses of global variables), the oracle state z, the local state σ, and memory m. At each of these (up to) n steps, if the state is halted then safeN is True; if the state is at_external then the ext_spec precondition for the external call must be satisfied and we continue with any state that satisfies the ext_spec postcondition; otherwise we must be able to take a core step (a small-step of the C-light operational semantics).

The interface exposed by core semantics is organized according to the lifetime stages of a running thread. A core semantics' internal notion of states is opaque, but states are classified as being either, an

initial state of a single thread, *i.e.* a function applied to its arguments; a

running state of the programming language's operational semantics; an

at_external state denoting an execution point at which a running thread
relinquishes control to the environment; an

after_external state at which internal execution is resumed, if and when
the environment yields back control; or a

halted state signifying successful termination of a thread.

A core semantics is equipped with a small-step relation of the form
$c, m \longmapsto c', m'$ where c and c' represent the language-specific internal state
components (local environment, program representation), and m and m'
are externally visible CompCert memories. Additional constraints stipulate
(for example) that $c, m \longmapsto c', m'$ is only defined if c is a **running** state—
at_external states do not step *within* the core semantics. In general, core
semantics adhere to the following protocol.

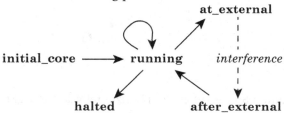

Interaction points (initial, at- & after-external, and halted states) do not
expose *core* components c, but do expose memories, arguments, and return
values. Thereby, pointers and integers are exchanged between threads that
employ different notions of cores.

The resulting model generalizes from the CompCert 1.x interaction
model, which exposed traces of observable events but coalesced call-
and return events to single external function call events, and limited
arguments and return values to be integers. (For example, CompCert 1.8
slightly generalized external-call arguments to permit pointers to statically

allocated global data, but still did not permit pointers to dynamically allocated objects and still did not permit shared memory external calls.)

THE SEMANTIC CORRECTNESS OF COMPILER PHASES in CompCert (1.x and 2.x) is formalized in terms of *simulation relations* between the appropriate source and target languages. Leroy's article [62] expertly lays out the design space and the relationship between different variants of simulations. In the context of the VST, the most crucial property is the preservation of safety along compilation, leading us to focus our effort on *forward* simulations when adapting the CompCert 1.x infrastructure to the setting of shared memory.

The core challenge of compiler correctness is to identify a precise sense in which computation interacts with (commutes with) compilation. For a compiler pass with source language Src and target language Tgt, this means that forward simulations are captured by diagrams of the shape

$$\sigma_{\text{Src}} = (c_1, m_1) \sim (c_2, m_2) = \sigma_{\text{Tgt}}$$
$$\downarrow \qquad\qquad \downarrow$$
$$\sigma'_{\text{Src}} = (c'_1, m'_1) \sim (c'_2, m'_2) = \sigma'_{\text{Tgt}}$$

where

- Compilation Src $\to$ Tgt evolves horizontally, left-to-right.

- Execution proceeds vertically, top-to-bottom.

- States σ_{Src} and σ_{Tgt} of the respective languages take the form $\sigma_{\text{Src}} = (c_1, m_1)$ and $\sigma_{\text{Tgt}} = (c_2, m_2)$, respectively. That is, language-dependent cores $c_1 : C_{\text{Src}}$ and $c_2 : C_{\text{Tgt}}$ are paired with language-independent memories.

- Progress $\to$ in execution direction may refer to an *internal* evolution according to the core's small-step relation $\sigma \longmapsto \sigma'$, its multistep variants $\sigma \longmapsto^n \sigma'$, $\sigma \longmapsto^+ \sigma'$, or $\sigma \longmapsto^* \sigma'$, or to an *environmental* evolution $\sigma \rightsquigarrow \sigma'$, in which case it represents the (terminating) execution of an external function call[2]. CompCert 1.x's model of observation events already includes a number of axioms that external calls are expected to safisfy. Our development imposes rephrasings of these axioms as appropriate for refactored core semantics. Additional aspects of external evolutions—in particular the concept of *compilability*, the refinement of environmental evolution into code—will be briefly discussed later in this section.

- Horizontal relationships take the form of a binary *matching* relation $\sim$ that associates source language states to target language states and is to be preserved by execution. Matching relations $\sim$ also exist for values and memories—in fact, the exposure of memory requires us to consider different kinds of simulation relations and to relax some of the preservation conditions, as we outline below.

We will also use

- Solid fonts and solid arrows to indicate data assumed by a diagram. Such data is typically universally quantified and is constrained by terms that appear in negative positions in the nonpictorial formulation of a diagram; and

- Dashed arrows to indicate conditions that are to be satisfied by the existentially quantified items in the diagram. Such conditions typically occur in positive positions in the nonpictorial formulation of a diagram.

The refinement of CompCert 1.x's memoryless forward simulations to simulations for shared memory interation takes loose inspiration from the theory of *logical relations* [77]. In the setting of higher-order typed languages, such relations are defined in a type-directed manner: $\sim$ is given by a type-indexed family of relations, so program execution is required to preserve type structure.

In our setting, the absence of an expressive type system is partially compensated for by the protocol stages we impose: we require that $\sim$

---

[2]To simplify the presentation we elide arguments and return values from diagrams.

respect the classification into initial, running, at-external, after-external, and halted cores.

Spelling out the conditions in more detail, and overloading $\sim$ to also refer to underlying match relations on values and memories, we require that initial cores be related by $\sim$ when paired with matching memories and function arguments, and that $(c_1, m_1) \sim (c_2, m_2)$ implies the following:

if $c_1, m_1 \longmapsto_{Src} c_1', m_1'$, **then** there exist $c_2' : C_2$ and m_2' such that $c_2, m_2 \longmapsto^*_{Tgt}$ c_2', m_2' and $(c_1', m_1') \sim (c_2', m_2')$;

$$
\begin{array}{ccc}
c_1, m_1 & \sim & c_2, m_2 \\
\Big\downarrow & & \Big\downarrow * \\
c_1', m_1' & \cdots & \exists c_2', m_2'
\end{array}
$$

if halted(c_1), **then halted**(c_2), with matching return values and memories;

if at_external$(c_1) = (f, \vec{a_1})$, **then at_external**$(c_2) = (f, \vec{a_2})$ for some $\vec{a_2}$ such that $\vec{a_1} \sim \vec{a_2}$, and $m_1 \sim m_2$: the functions invoked by c_1 and c_2 must coincide, and the lists of arguments must contain matching values, and the memories must match;

At function returns, it must be possible to reestablish the simulation relation $\sim$ for any pairs of related return-values and memories delivered by the environments. Given the data c_i and m_i from the at-external clause, and given return values $v_1 \sim v_2$ and return memories $m_1' \sim m_2'$ (which are external evolutions of the m_1 and m_2), we require that $\sim$ relates (c_1', m_1') with (c_2', m_2'), where the after-external cores c_i' arise from the at-external cores c_i by appropriately injecting the return values v_1 and v_2.

$$c_1, m_1 \quad \sim_F \quad c_2, m_2$$

$$\mathbf{at\_external}(c_i) = (f, \overrightarrow{a_i})$$
$$\overrightarrow{a_1} \sim \overrightarrow{a_2}$$
$$m_1 \sim m_2$$
$$m_i \rightsquigarrow m_i'$$
$$v_1 \sim v_2$$
$$m_1' \sim m_2'$$

$$c_1', m_1' \quad \dashrightarrow_{F'} \quad \exists c_2', m_2' \qquad \mathbf{after\_external}(c_i, v_i) = c_i'$$

Although we employ a formulation without contexts, the similarity to logical relations is arguably most pronounced in the clauses for function calls: indeed, type-indexed logical relations require a function $f : A \rightarrow B$ to return $\sim_B$-related results whenever provided with $\sim_A$-related arguments. Our condition on **after_external** states treats Src and Tgt in a symmetric fashion: it does not ask us to *prove the existence* of appropriate m_2' and v_2 but merely that the simulation relation be reestablished whenever *given* such data. That is, compilation steps of the module under consideration must preserve semantics independently of changes in the environmental behavior; even failure of the environment to yield back is not the module's fault. Indeed, as we are mostly interested in preservation of safety, a scenario in which parts of the environment are refined to code (see below) would allow an external call to be transformed into an infinite loop, a translation that is legal from the point of view of the present module and also (w.r.t. safety) from a whole-program perspective.

In contrast, the clauses for coresteps, halted executions, and at-external states propagate the protocol stage information from Src to Tgt. Indeed, these stages concern execution of the present execution thread rather than environmental behavior, so the preservation of behavior should be preserved under compilation of *this* core.

For realistic verified compilers such as CompCert, it is absolutely essential that compiler correctness proofs be transitively composable along the phases of the compiler. In this way, each phase (of which there are 20 in CompCert 2.0!) can be proved correct independently of all the others. Then the individual proofs of each phase can be strung together to recover correctness end-to-end. This is significantly more modular than proving the compiler correct monolithically.

Pictorially, transitive compositionality of simulations along the compilation axis can be depicted as follows: given diagrams

representing compiler correctness of adjacent compiler passes Src → Mid and Mid → Tgt, we wish to obtain

$$
\begin{array}{ccc}
\sigma_{\text{Src}} & \sim & \sigma_{\text{Tgt}} \\
\downarrow & & \downarrow \\
\sigma'_{\text{Src}} & \sim & \sigma'_{\text{Tgt}}
\end{array}
$$

For the memory-ignorant observation model of CompCert 1.x, simulations for adjacent compiler phases indeed compose rather easily.

In the presence of memory, the situation is significantly more complex. First, the memories in a simulation $(c_1, m_1) \sim (c_2, m_2)$ need not be equal. Instead, they may be related by a *memory injection* $F \vdash m_1 \mapsto m_2$ or a *memory extension* $m_1 \rightarrowtail m_2$. (see Chapter 32). Consequently, there are three kinds of forward-simulation stuctures $\sim$: simulations $\cong$ apply to memory equality passes, where matching states have equal memories; simulations $\simeq$ apply to passes that are memory extensions; and simulations $\approx_F$ apply to memory injection passes, where the index F denotes a concrete injection F.

Each kind of simulation structure imposes appropriately refined versions of the above compatibility conditions between execution and compilation. For example, the clause for coresteps for injection simulations is as follows[3]:

---

[3]We write $F\ _{m_1}\bowtie_{m_2} F'$ for the condition that $b_1 \notin \text{dom}(m_1)$ and $b_2 \notin \text{dom}(m_2)$ holds whenever $b_1 \mapsto (b_2, o)$ in $F' \setminus F$, where $\text{dom}(m)$ denotes the valid blocks in m.

$$c_1, m_1 \approx_F c_2, m_2 \qquad F \subseteq F'$$

$$\downarrow \qquad\qquad \downarrow^* \qquad F_{m_1} \bowtie_{m_2} F'$$

$$c'_1, m'_1 \approx_{F'} \exists c'_2, m'_2$$

For $(c_1, m_1) \approx_F (c_2, m_2)$ and $c_1, m_1 \longmapsto_{Src} c'_1, m'_1$ there exist c'_2, m'_2, and F' such that $c_2, m_2 \longmapsto^*_{Tgt} c'_2, m'_2$ and $(c'_1, m'_1) \approx_{F'} (c'_2, m'_2)$, where F' contains F, and $F_{m_1} \bowtie_{m_2} F'$.

At interaction points, memories that are *supplied* by the environment are *assumed* to be related by appropriate injections; this affects the clauses for *initial* and *after_external* cores. In exchange, the clauses for *halted* and *at_external* cores must guarantee relatedness of the memories they provide to the environment.

The evolution from $\approx_F$ to $\approx_{F'}$ in the above corestep-diagram—and a similar evolution in the clause for *after_external*—captures correspondencies between newly allocated blocks in the two executions, a pattern that is well known from treatments of information flow and from Kripke logical relations [59].

Second, the exposure of memories and memory transformations complicates the composition of simulations: the kind of $\sim^{Src \to Tgt}$ depends on the kinds of $\sim^{Src \to Mid}$ and $\sim^{Mid \to Tgt}$, like this:

Src → Mid	Mid → Tgt	Src → Tgt
$\cong$	$\sim$	$\sim$
$\sim$	$\cong$	$\sim$
$\simeq$	$\simeq$	$\simeq$
$\approx$	$\sim$	$\approx$
$\sim$	$\approx$	$\approx$

Each of the nine cases cases requires the definition of an appropriate simulation relation between states (c_1, m_1) and (c_3, m_3), with proofs that the compatibility conditions regarding the protocol stages of executions in *Src* and *Tgt* are satisfied, based inductively on the similar clauses for $\sim^{Src \to Mid}$ and $\sim^{Mid \to Tgt}$.

For example, the case in which both passes are memory injection phases admits $\sim^{\text{Src}\to\text{Tgt}}$ to be defined as the injection simulation $\approx_F$ that existentially quantifies over an intermediate state (c_2, m_2) and requires F to decompose into $F = F_2 \circ F_1$ with $(c_1, m_1) \approx^{\text{Src}\to\text{Mid}}_{F_1} (c_2, m_2) \approx^{\text{Mid}\to\text{Tgt}}_{F_2} (c_3, m_3)$.

The most interesting case in the verification of the compatibility clauses is the one for *after_external*. In order to apply the induction hypotheses (*i.e.*, the *after_external*-clauses of $\sim^{\text{Src}\to\text{Mid}}$ and $\sim^{\text{Mid}\to\text{Tgt}}$), it is necessary to construct an *interpolating memory* m'_2 that is applicable when the external call returns in execution Mid, together with appropriate injections F'_1 and F'_2:

More specifically, given

- an injection $F \vdash m_1 \mapsto m_3$ that splits via $F = F_2 \circ F_1$ into injections $F_1 \vdash m_1 \mapsto m_2$ and $F_2 \vdash m_2 \mapsto m_3$,

- outer vertical evolutions $m_1 \rightsquigarrow m'_1$ and $m_3 \rightsquigarrow m'_3$ representing the external calls as handled by the environments of Src and Tgt, and

- an injection $F' \vdash m'_1 \mapsto m'_3$ that represents the assumption that the environment returns appropriately related memories; in particular, F' contains F and satisfies $F_{\,m_1}\bowtie_{m_3} F'$,

we need to show that a memory m'_2 and injections F'_1 and F'_2 can be constructed such that

- $F'_1 \vdash m'_1 \mapsto m'_2$ and $F'_2 \vdash m'_2 \mapsto m'_3$,

- $m_2 \rightsquigarrow m'_2$,

- $F' = F'_2 \circ F'_1$, and

- for $i \in \{1, 2\}$, F_i' contains F_i, and $F_i \; {}_{m_i}\!\bowtie_{m_{i+1}} F_i'$.

The construction of m_2' proceeds block by block, and pointwise inside each block, as indicated in the following example[4].

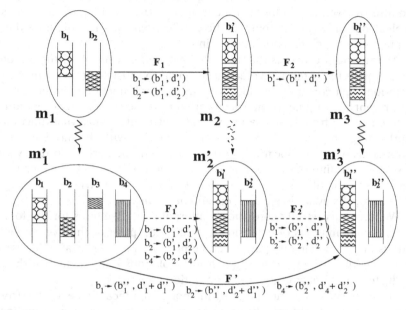

Blocks such as b_1 and b_2 that were already valid in m_1 are mapped by F_1' as prescribed by F_1. Thus, the external function's effect on the content at individual offsets in these blocks is propagated from $m_1 \rightsquigarrow m_1'$ to $m_2 \rightsquigarrow m_2'$. Additionally, we propagate content in b_1' from m_2 to m_2' that does not orginate in m_1; typically, these locations are used for compiler-internal purposes such as spilling and are unmodified by the external function. Blocks valid in m_1 but not mapped by F_1 are not mapped by F_1' either.

Blocks allocated by the external call, like b_3 and b_4, fall into two categories: blocks not mapped by F', like b_3, are not mapped by F_1' either.

---

[4] Note that the sets of nonprimed/primed/double-primed block numbers are not necessarily distinct.

Blocks mapped by F', like b_4, are mapped by F_1' to a fresh block b_2' that is distinct from all blocks in m_2. Finally, injection F_2' is obtained by extending F_2 so that $F' = F_2' \circ F_1'$ is satisfied.

In order to satisfy all conditions required by the dashed relationships—and also the well-definedness of memory m_2'—the mapping of each block involves not only the mapping of the data content but also defining the permissions of each individual offset in m_2'.

An important aspect is that the *after_external*-clauses of all simulation kinds require the external evolutions $m_i \rightsquigarrow m_i'$ to satisfy certain *confinement* conditions that constrain the locations an external function may modify. In our present development, the specification of these confinement relations is directly lifted from CompCert's original constraints on external functions, intertwining properties of the injections F_1 and F_2 with the modification permissions of certain locations in the *at_external* memories. Future work may seek to refine these conditions to a notion of *rely* that is easier to handle but can still be established to hold for $m_2 \rightsquigarrow m_2'$ whenever being satisfied for the evolutions $m_1 \rightsquigarrow m_1'$ and $m_3 \rightsquigarrow m_3'$.

We have successfully constructed interpolating memories for the four possible combinations of extension and injection passes—the five combinations involving equality passes can be proven in a more straightforward manner, without the need for explicit interpolations—and combined these results to a proof of transitivity of simulation structures.

The construction of interpolating memories significantly benefitted from a recent upgrade to the specification of CompCert's memory transformations (at CompCert 1.13, late in the 1.x→2.x transition) ensuring that injections compose, and additionally suggests a handful of additional tweaks to the memory model that may be included in a future version of CompCert.

Extension mechanism. In order to model composition of core semantics (as is required to model linking of separately compiled modules, multi-threaded concurrency etc.), we introduce a generic *extension mechanism*—an endofunctor on core semantics that allows a core to be combined with external code collections (individual functions, external libraries, or other code modules) to yield an enlarged core. Typically, the code extensions provide implementations for at least some of the original core's external functions. As the extended core again adheres to the generic interface, such combinations are transparent to external code modules.

We have defined a number of instantiations of the extension mechanism. We have proved generic *preservation of safety,* which guarantees semantic well-behavedness of extensions in compositional fashion.

We have identified the issues that make the specification of real-world compilation so difficult: It is the combination of shared-memory external interaction with an optimizing compiler that modifies and relocates memory access. We have designed solutions, with Coq-verified proofs (in the sepcomp directory). For (shared-memory) external calls to an operating system, our proofs are complete. For shared-memory external calls that implement synchronization operators for concurrent threads, our theorems should suffice, but we are still working on the *angelic erasure theorem*—see page 404. For separate compilation—external calls to functions that themselves will be compiled by an optimizing compiler—our framework will be directly applicable, but we will probably need one more modification of CompCert's operational semantics: each thread will need to identify its own set of private locations at external function calls—locations that are not to be touched by the oracle.

Although the transition from the CompCert 1.x interaction model to the 2.x model was nontrivial, it is certainly worth the trouble. We expect from a C compiler that it supports modular separate compilation, that it supports shared-memory concurrency, and that it supports optimizations such as register allocation and spilling.

Almost a decade ago, Hans Boehm pointed out the bugs in interactions between optimizing compilers and shared-memory concurrency libraries [24]. He wrote, "we point out the important issues, and argue that they lie almost exclusively with the compiler and the language specification itself, not with the thread library or its specification." Here, we have developed a language-independent framework for compiler and language specifications, that addresses the problems Boehm described.

Chapter 34

C light operational semantics

CompCert defines a formal small-step operational semantics for every intermediate language (including C light) between C and assembly language.

For Verifiable C, we use the C light syntax with an alternate (nonstandard) operational semantics of C light (file veric/Clight_new.v). Our nonstandard semantics is quite similar to the standard, but it makes fewer "administrative small-steps" and is (in this and other ways) more conducive to our program-logic soundness proof. We prove a simulation relation from our alternate semantics to the CompCert standard C light semantics. This ensures that the soundness we prove relative to the alternate semantics is also valid with respect to the standard semantics.

In our operational semantics, an operational state is either *internal*, when the compiled program is about to execute an ordinary instruction of a single C thread; or *external*, when the program is requesting a system call or other externally visible event.

An *internal* operational state contains:

genv Global environment, mapping identifiers to addresses of global (extern) variables and functions, and a separate mapping of function-addresses to function-bodies.

ve Variable environment, mapping identifiers to addresses of addressable local variables—those to which the C-language & (address-of) operator is somewhere applied.

te Temp environment, mapping identifiers to values of ordinary local variables—those to which & is never applied.

κ Continuation, representing the stack of control and data (including the program counter, return addresses for function calls, and local variables of suspended functions).

m Memory, representing the extern static variables, stack-allocated local variables, and heap-allocated data. Any of these memory addresses can be potentially shared with other threads. The CompCert operational semantics does not *explicitly* know about this sharing; instead, each address is marked in the CompCert memory model as Writable, Readable, No-access, and so on.

In addition, a CompCert memory contains the *abstract heap boundary* (called "nextblock"), showing what is the highest-allocated (abstract) block address (see page 261). This nextblock is primarily used for reasoning about the allocation of stack blocks at function calls.

$$\text{set}\frac{\langle ge, ve, te \rangle, m \vdash_{\text{expr}} e \Downarrow v}{ge \vdash (ve, te, (x := e) \cdot \kappa), m \longmapsto (ve, te[v/x], \kappa), m}$$

The step_set (assignment-to-local-variable) rule steps from the state with variable-environment ve, temp-environment te, control $\text{Kseq}(\text{Sset } x \ e)::\kappa$, and memory m to the state $(ve, te[v/x], \kappa), m$, provided that e evaluates (as an r-value) to v.

Unlike our program logic, which distinguishes between assignments that load from memory and those that do not, the operational-semantic rule permits the expression e to have zero, one, two, or more subexpressions that load from memory—but one cannot use our program logic to reason about multi-load commands.

$$\text{assign}\frac{\langle ge, ve, te \rangle, m \vdash_{\text{lvalue}} e_1 \Downarrow (b, z) \quad \langle ge, ve, te \rangle, m \vdash_{\text{expr}} e_2 \Downarrow v_2 \quad (v_2)^{\text{typeof } e_1}_{\text{typeof } e_2} = v}{ge \vdash (ve, te, (e_1 := e_2) \cdot \kappa), m \longmapsto (ve, te, \kappa), m[(b, z) :=_{\text{typeof } e_1} v]}$$

The step_assign rule, shown here, is for storing into memory. It steps from the state with variable-environment ve, temp-environment te, control Kseq(Sassign e_1 e_2)::κ, and memory m to the state $(ve, te, \kappa), m'$, provided that the type of e_1 is not volatile (hypothesis not shown here), e_1 evaluates as an l-value to the address (b, z), e_2 evaluates as an r-value to the value v_2, that v_2 when cast from the type of e_2 to the type of e_1 is value v, and that when typed store operation (assign_loc) is done in m at address (b, z) with value v, the resulting memory is m'. The expressions e_1 and e_2 may have subexpressions that load from memory.

$$\frac{\langle ge, ve, te \rangle, m \vdash_{\text{expr}} e \Downarrow v_f \quad ge(v_f) = \text{internal } f \quad f_{\text{type}} = \vec{\tau} \to \tau_r}{\langle ge, ve, te \rangle, m \vdash_{\text{exprlist}} (\vec{\tau}) \vec{e} \Downarrow \vec{v} \quad \text{alloc\_variables } ve_0 \; m \; f_{\text{fn\_vars}} = ve', m'}$$

$$\text{bind\_parameter\_temps } f_{\text{fn\_params}} \; \vec{v} \; (\text{create\_undef\_temps } f_{\text{fn\_temps}}) = te'$$

$$\overline{ge \vdash (ve, te, (x := e(\vec{e})) \cdot \kappa), m \longmapsto (ve', te', f_{\text{body}} \cdot \text{return} \cdot (\text{Kcall } x \; f \; ve \; te) \cdot \kappa), m'}$$

step_call_internal: To call a function e with arguments $\vec{e}$, first e is evaluated yielding the address v_f of the function; then the function-body f is looked up in the global environment; suppose f has formal-parameter-types $t\vec{a}u$ and return type τ_r. Suppose f satisfies some conditions (not shown) that it has no repeated formal-parameter names or local-variable names. Then the expression-list $\vec{e}$, each value is casted to the correspnding type in $t\vec{a}u$, yielding a list $\vec{v}$ of actual-parameter values. A new variable-environment ve is created by allocating locations starting at nextblock(m), and binding those locations to the addressable-local-variable names $f_{\text{fn\_vars}}$; the Vundef value is stored at those locations. A new temp-environment te' is created by binding the nonaddressable local variables $f_{\text{fn\_temps}}$ to Vundef values, and binding the formal parameters $f_{\text{fn\_params}}$ to the values $\vec{v}$. Then a new control-continuation is created, using the entire function-body followed by a return statement, followed by a function-call context Kcall that records the caller's context: what variable to assign the function's return value to, the caller's local-variable environments, and the caller's continuation κ. This rule is actually more general, permitting x to be absent for void-returning functions, but we do not show that here.

$$\frac{\kappa = \ldots \cdot \mathsf{Kcall}\ x\ f\ ve'\ te' \cdot \kappa' \quad \mathsf{free\_list}\ m\ (\mathsf{blocks\_of\_env}\ ve) = m' \quad \langle ge, ve, te \rangle, m \vdash_{\mathrm{expr}} e \Downarrow v_f \quad (v)^{\mathrm{fn\_return}\ f}_{\mathrm{typeof}\ e_2} = v'}{ge \vdash (ve, te, (\mathsf{return}\ e) \cdot \kappa), m \longmapsto (ve', te'[v'/x], \kappa), m'}$$

step_return: Find the first Kcall continuation in κ, and restore the local environment ve', te' from that. Evaluate the expression e, cast it to the function-return type, and update the value of x in te'. Free the memory blocks for all addressable local variables. The case for void functions (where $\mathsf{fn\_return}(f) = \mathsf{Tvoid}$ and e is not present) is similar, but simpler.

$$\frac{\langle ge, ve, te \rangle, m \vdash_{\mathrm{expr}} e \Downarrow v_f \quad ge(v_f) = \mathsf{external}\ f \quad f_{\mathrm{type}} = \vec{\tau} \to \tau_r \quad \langle ge, ve, te \rangle, m \vdash_{\mathrm{exprlist}} (\vec{\tau})\vec{e} \Downarrow \vec{v}}{ge \vdash (ve, te, (x := e(\vec{e})) \cdot \kappa), m \longmapsto \mathsf{ExtCall}(f, \vec{\tau} \to \tau_r, \vec{v}, x, ve, te, \kappa), m}$$

step_call_external: To call an external function, the function-expression e and arguments $\vec{e}$ are evaluated—in fact, only after e is looked up in ge is it known that the function is external. Then the small-step is to a special ExtCall state that signals to the context that the core semantics wishes to interact with its external environment.

$$\mathrm{seq}\frac{ge \vdash (ve, te, c_1 \cdot c_2 \cdot \kappa), m \longmapsto \sigma', m'}{ge \vdash (ve, te, (c_1; c_2) \cdot \kappa), m \longmapsto \sigma', m'}$$

$$\mathrm{skip}\frac{ge \vdash (ve, te, \kappa), m \longmapsto \sigma', m'}{ge \vdash (ve, te, \mathsf{skip} \cdot \kappa), m \longmapsto \sigma', m'}$$

The sequence-statement $c1; c2$ steps by making a control-continuation with c_1 followed by c_2 and seeing what that steps to. In Leroy's standard C light semantics, the rule looks like, $ge \vdash (ve, te, (c_1; c_2) \cdot \kappa), m \longmapsto (ve, te, c_1 \cdot c_2 \cdot \kappa), m$, which actually takes a step to unpack the semicolon. In our program logic based on indirection theory, if unpacking the semicolon takes a small-step, then we (unfortunately) cannot prove these associativity rules:

$$\{P\} (c_1; c_2); c_3 \{Q\} \longleftrightarrow \{P\} c_1; (c_2; c_3) \{Q\}.$$

$$\{P\} c; \text{skip} \{Q\} \longleftrightarrow \{P\} c \{Q\} \longleftrightarrow \{P\} \text{skip}; c \{Q\}.$$

The reason is related to the step-indexing, the counting of small-steps. When possible, of our control-rules (for sequencing and loop control) By avoiding these *administrative* steps—by using rules such as the seq and skip rules shown above—we enable transformation rules such as associativity of sequencing, even in our step-indexed logic.

$$\frac{\langle ge, ve, te \rangle, m \vdash_{\text{expr}} e \Downarrow v \quad \text{bool\_val}_{\text{typeof } e} v = \text{Some } true}{ge \vdash (ve, te, (\text{if}(e) c_1;\ \text{else } c_2) \cdot \kappa), m \longmapsto ge \vdash (ve, te, c_1 \cdot \kappa), m}$$

step_ifthenelse: The rule for *if* is straightforward; here we show only the $e \Downarrow true$ case.

C light handles all loops through the construct loop c_1 c_2 which means the same as the C for-loop, for$(\ ; ; c_2)\ c_1$. That is, execute the infinite loop $c_1; c_2; c_1; c_2; c_1 \ldots$ (unless c_1 exits the loop using a break or return command). Furthermore, if c_1 executes a continue command, then control should pass to c_2 (and then $c_1; \ldots$).

$$\text{loop} \frac{}{\begin{array}{l} ge \vdash (ve, te, (\text{loop } c_1\ c_2) \cdot \kappa), m \longmapsto \\ \qquad (ve, te, c_1 \cdot \text{continue} \cdot (\text{Kloop1 } c_1\ c_2) \cdot \kappa), m \end{array}}$$

$$\text{loop2} \frac{}{\begin{array}{l} ge \vdash (ve, te, (\text{Kloop2 } c_1\ c_2) \cdot \kappa), m \longmapsto \\ \qquad (ve, te, c_1 \cdot \text{continue} \cdot (\text{Kloop1 } c_1\ c_2) \cdot \kappa), m \end{array}}$$

$$\text{continue} \frac{}{ge \vdash (ve, te, \text{continue\_cont}(\kappa)), m \longmapsto (ve, te, \text{continue} \cdot \kappa), m}$$

$$\text{break} \frac{}{ge \vdash (ve, te, \text{break\_cont}(\kappa)), m \longmapsto (ve, te, \text{break} \cdot \kappa), m}$$

In our vocabulary of control-continuations κ, Kloop1 c_1 c_2 represents the *continue*-cont just before c_2, and Kloop2 c_1 c_2 represents the continuation following c_2, when c_1 is about to be re-executed. The function continue_cont(κ) searches in κ until it finds the first Kloop1 c_1 $c_2 \cdot \kappa'$, then returns $c_2 \cdot$ Kloop2 c_1 $c_2 \cdot \kappa'$. The function break_cont(κ) searches for Kloop1 c_1 $c_2 \cdot \kappa'$ or Kswitch c_1 $c_2 \cdot \kappa'$, then returns κ'.

CompCert translates the C-language {while (e) c} to the statement loop {if (e) skip **else** break} c. **Definition** Swhile is a derived statement form for this pattern. The translation of a standard for-loop is similar. The clightgen pretty-printer will recognize the while-loop pattern and output an Swhile command.

The C light operational semantics also has rules for switch statements and goto statements, which we do not show here. At present there are no rules in our program logic for reasoning about these, but in principle there is no obstacle to implementing such rules.

IN PART VI WE WILL show how to build a semantic model of our VST program logic with respect to this operational semantics. But first, in part Part V, we establish some semantic foundations for higher-order program logics.

Part V

Higher-order semantic models

SYNOPSIS: *Indirection theory gives a clean interface to higher-order step indexing. Many different semantic features of programming languages can be modeled in indirection theory. The models of indirection theory use dependent types to stratify quasirecursive predicates, thus avoiding paradoxes of self-reference. Lambda calculus with mutable references serves as a case study to illustrate the use of indirection theory models.*

When defining both Indirection and Separation one must take extra care to ensure that aging commutes over separation. We demonstrate how to build an axiomatic semantics with using higher-order separation logic, for the pointer/continuation language introduced in the case study of Part II.

Chapter 35

Indirection theory

by Aquinas Hobor with Andrew Appel and Robert Dockins

In Part II we explained an application of indirection theory to a higher-order separation logic. In this Part we explain what indirection theory really *is*.

In a naive set-theoretic model (in which pred A is simply $A \to$ Prop), we can define predicates characterizing recursive data structures such as,

$$\text{list}(p) = \ p = 0 * \text{emp} \lor p \neq 0 \land \exists h, t. \ p \mapsto h * p + 1 \mapsto t * \text{list}(t).$$

But certain kinds of higher-order reasoning are difficult or impossible in naive models. Consider contravariant recursive types such as

$$\text{object} = \{\text{data} : \text{ref } \mathbb{N}; \ \text{get} : \text{object} \to \mathbb{N}; \ \text{set} : (\text{object} \times \mathbb{N}) \to \text{unit}\}$$

in which an object is a record (named tuple) with field data (a memory cell containing a natural number) and two accessor methods get and set. Observe that the type of the accessor methods contains object itself[1] to the left of the arrow—that is, in a contravariant position. This form of recursion is used in many programming languages (Java, ML, even C) and naive semantic techniques cannot model such predicates/types. In C, of course,

---

[1]In many object-oriented languages, this formal parameter is elided in the concrete code. It is referred to explicitly via the "this" keyword, or implicitly simply by referring to the fields or methods of the "current object".

the type system *permits* but does not fully *support* such programs; it is up to our program logic to reason soundly about them, as in Chapter 29.

The recurring problem with such systems is to find semantic models with three features: First, contravariant recursion, as in the example above. Second, indirect reference: indirection via pointers gives us mutable references; indirection via locks can be used for shared storage; and indirection via code pointers gives us complex patterns of computation and recursion. Models of program logics for systems utilizing indirection need to associate invariants (or assertions, or types) with addresses in the store; and yet invariants are predicates on the store: tying this "knot" has been difficult. Third, clean abstraction—that is, impredicative quantification.

Consider adding general references to the polymorphic λ-calculus. The type of mutable references should be ref τ into which one can store values of type τ. By saying that references are *general* we mean that our choice for τ should be any valid type, including quantified types, function types, reference types, or arbitrary combinations thereof.

Ahmed [2] was the first to give a semantic model for general references; the problem she solved is illustrated by considering the following *flawed* semantic model of types for this calculus:

$$
\begin{aligned}
\text{value} &\equiv \text{loc of address} + \text{num of } \mathbb{N} + \ldots \\
\text{type} &\equiv (\text{memtype} \times \text{value}) \to \mathbb{T} \\
\text{memtype} &\approx \text{address} \rightharpoonup \text{type}
\end{aligned}
\tag{35.1}
$$

Values are a tagged disjoint union, with the tag loc indicating a memory address. $\mathbb{T}$ is some notion of truth values (*e.g.*, the propositions of the metalogic such as Prop in Coq) and a natural interpretation of the type $A \to \mathbb{T}$ is the characteristic function for a set of A. We write $\approx$ to mean "we wish we could define things this way" and $A \rightharpoonup B$ to indicate a finite partial function from A to B.

The typing judgment has the form $\psi \vdash v : \tau$, where ψ is a memory typing (memtype), v is a value, and τ is a type; the semantic model for the typing judgment is $\psi \vdash v : \tau \equiv \tau(\psi, v)$. Memory typings are partial functions from addresses to types. The motivation for this attempt is that the type "ref τ" can use the memory typing to show that the reference's location has type τ:

$$\text{ref } \tau \;\equiv\; \lambda(\psi, v).\, \exists a.\, v = \text{loc}(a) \;\wedge\; \psi(a) = \tau.$$

That is, a value v has type ref τ if it is an address a, and according to the memory typing ψ, the memory cell at location a has type τ.

Unfortunately, this series of definitions is not well-founded: type contains a contravariant occurrence of memtype, which in turn contains an occurrence of type. A standard diagonalization proves that no solution to these equations exists in set theory.

Ahmed's solution was to create a sequence of increasingly close approximations $\{\text{memtype}_0, \text{memtype}_1, \text{memtype}_2, \ldots\}$ that in the limit "converge" to the desired model. Each element memtype_n in this sequence is a well-defined model for a memory typing that can be "used" no more then n times to determine the type associated with a memory cell. In a very real sense the number of times a memory typing can be used is the amount of "information" it contains, and a crucial ingredient in step-indexed models is connecting the number of steps executed operationally with the amount of information contained within the model such that no more than one "information quantum" need be used per operational step. Given this connection, we can use this style of model, by simply choosing an element in the sequence that is "big enough" to prove the desired theorem—for example, if we decide that we want to prove that a program will not get stuck before we go on our coffee break in 100 instructions, we simply choose memtype_{100}.

In practical proofs, managing the bookkeeping of approximation indices n can be quite tedious. The "very modal model" [11] significantly improved the presentation of step-indexing, using a model logic to hide the indices. Even so, we want to apply the basic step-indexing idea to a much broader range of applications—without mixing up the complexities of step-indexing with the complexities of the application domains or having to rebuild the model from scratch each time. The solution is indirection theory, whose model is characterized by just two axioms, which are equational, orthogonal, complete, expressive, and modular.

A KEY OBSERVATION UNDERLYING INDIRECTION THEORY is that many domains can be described by the pseudoequation:

$$K \approx F((K \times O) \to \mathbb{T}), \tag{35.2}$$

where $F(X)$ is a covariant functor, O is some arbitrary set of "other" data and K is the object that we wish to construct. In the case of the polymorphic λ-calculus with references discussed above, we select memtype for K, value for O, and $F(X)$ as address $\to X$ to reach:

$$\text{memtype} \approx \text{address} \to ((\text{memtype} \times \text{value}) \to \mathbb{T}) \tag{35.3}$$

The cardinality argument shows why we cannot construct K in set theory. The motivation for indirection theory is that it can construct a clean, generic approximation to K. We will start by explaining the construction of basic indirection theory along the lines of our 2010 result [52]. Then we will present a refinement that gives better guarantees about "hereditary predicates"; it is this version we use to model higher-order separation logics.

F must be covariant: it's as if any value of type $F(X)$ is a data structure with "positive" instances of values of type X sprinkled throughout. If, on the other hand, $F(X)$ was the function type $X \to Y$ demanding inputs of type X, then F would be contravariant; and more complicated functors with both positive and negative occurences are "mixed-variant"; we cannot apply indirection theory to contravariant or mixed-variant functors.

To continue: given F and O, indirection theory constructs K such that:

$$K \preceq \mathbb{N} \times F((K \times O) \to \mathbb{T}) \tag{35.4}$$

Here $X \preceq Y$ means the "small" type X is related to the "big" type Y by two functions: squash : $Y \to X$ and unsquash : $X \to Y$. The squash function "packs" an element y of the big type Y into an element of the small type X, applying an approximation when the structure of y is too complex to fit into X. The unsquash function reverses the process, "unpacking" an element of X into an element of Y; since Y is bigger than X, unsquash is lossless.

The squash and unsquash functions form a section-retraction pair, meaning that squash $\circ$ unsquash : $X \to X$ is the identity function and unsquash ∘ squash : $Y \to Y$ is an approximation function. Thus $X \preceq Y$ is *almost* an isomorphism, and informally one can read $X \preceq Y$ as "X is approximately Y". Thus, with equation (35.4), indirection theory says that the left hand side of pseudoequation (35.2) is approximately equal to a pair of a natural number and the right hand side of pseudoequation (35.2).

APPLICATIONS FOR INDIRECTION THEORY.   In "A theory of indirection via approximation" [52] we show seven different previously published semantic models by several different authors, all of which can be cleanly modeled in indirection theory. These include,

1. general references in the λ-calculus,

2. general references on von Neumann machines,

3. object references,

4. substructural state,

5. embedding semantic assertions in program syntax,

6. concurrent separation logic with first-class locks, and

7. an industrial-strength CSL model for Concurrent C minor.

Indirection theory, as embodied in the VST's ageable class, can be used for each of these applications. We briefly gave the model for general references in the λ-calculus above, and Chapter 36 will explain this case study in full.

Axiomatic characterization.

Our primary goal here is to present the "user view" for indirection theory— that is, the axiomatization. Readers who do not even need this "user view," whose only need for indirection theory is the particular application to resources in the Verified Software Toolchain, may be able to get by entirely with the discussion of the ▷ *later* operator and its use in building recursive predicates and reasoning about recursive programs in Chapter 15, Chapter 17, and Chapter 18.

FUNCTORS. We use the concept of covariant functors from category theory to specify the kind of input required to utilize indirection theory. Let Type stand for the types of the metalogic and $F :$ Type $\to$ Type be a type function (such as "list", which is parameterized by the type of the list items). Equip F with a function fmap $: (A \to B) \to F(A) \to F(B)$ that satisfies the following two axioms, in which id_τ is the identity function on Type τ:

$$\text{fmap } id_A \; = \; id_{F(A)} \tag{35.5}$$
$$\text{fmap } f \circ \text{fmap } g \; = \; \text{fmap } (f \circ g) \tag{35.6}$$

The function fmap can be thought of as a generalization of map from functional languages, which applies a function to all the elements in a list. Thus, fmap(g) should apply g to every X within an $F(X)$. In Coq, this idea is captured by the functor typeclass given in figure 35.1. As with the other mathematical structures we utilize, we predefine a number of functor constructions—over constants, pairs, and so on—in msl/functors.v.

INPUT TO INDIRECTION THEORY. Start with a type O ("other data") and a functor F, as captured by the following Coq module type from msl/knot_hered:

Module Type TY_FUNCTOR_PROP.
   Parameter F : Type $\to$ Type.
   Parameter f_F : functor F.
   Existing **Instance** f_F.

   Parameter other : Type.
End TY_FUNCTOR_PROP.

For example, here is fmap for general references in the λ-calculus from page 296, utilizing functional composition $\circ$ for partial functions:

$$\text{fmap} \quad \equiv \quad \lambda g. \, \lambda \psi. \, g \circ \psi$$

Clearly equations (35.5) and (35.6) hold for this fmap. In Coq these definitions and the associated proofs for identity and composition are nearly trivial to define using the prebuilt functor constructors:

Record functorFacts (PS : Type → Type)
     (fmap : ∀ A B (f : A → B), PS A → PS B) : Type :=
FunctorFacts {
  ff_id : ∀ A, fmap _ _ (id A) = id (PS A);
  ff_comp : ∀ A B C (f : B → C) (g : A → B),
    fmap _ _ f oo fmap _ _ g = fmap _ _ (f oo g)
}.

Class functor (F : Type → Type) : Type := Functor {
  fmap : ∀ A B (f : A → B), F A → F B;
  functor_facts : functorFacts F fmap
}.

Lemma fmap_id {F} `{functor F} : ∀ A, fmap (id A) = id (F A).

Lemma fmap_comp {F} `{functor F} : ∀ A B C (f : B→C) (g : A→B),
  fmap f oo fmap g = fmap (f oo g).

Lemma fmap_app {F} `{functor F} : ∀ A B C (f : B→C) (g : A→B) x,
  fmap f (fmap g x) = fmap (f oo g) x.

Figure 35.1: Functor typeclass, from msl/functors.v

Module TFP <: TY_FUNCTOR_PROP.
  Definition F : Type → Type := fun K ⇒ addr → option K.
  Definition f_F := f_fun addr (f_option f_identity).

  Definition other : Type := value.
End TFP.

Here f_fun is the functor for function composition,[2] f_option is the functor
for options, and f_identity builds the identity functor for K. Note that these

---

   [2]Assuming the argument is a constant type, addr in this case.

constructors build both the fmap function *and* the required functor proofs for identity and composition. The functor is normally easy to define once F is known.

Output. Indirection theory then constructs the following:

$$\text{K} \quad : \quad \text{Type} \tag{35.7}$$
$$\text{pred} \quad \equiv \quad \text{K} \times O \to \mathbb{T} \tag{35.8}$$
$$\text{squash} \quad : \quad (\mathbb{N} \times F(\text{pred})) \to \text{K} \tag{35.9}$$
$$\text{unsquash} \quad : \quad \text{K} \to (\mathbb{N} \times F(\text{pred})) \tag{35.10}$$

The definitions of K (also called *knot*), squash, and unsquash are abstract (hidden from the user). A *predicate* (pred) is a function in the metalogic from a pair of a knot K and other data O to truth values $\mathbb{T}$. As explained previously, squash and unsquash are coercion functions between the "small" type knot (K) and the "big" type $\mathbb{N} \times F(\text{pred})$.

   To coerce an object from the small type to the big one is lossless, but to go from big to small requires approximation. Equations (35.11) and (35.12) define the approximation used in indirection theory:

$$|k| \quad \equiv \quad (\text{unsquash}(k)).1 \tag{35.11}$$

$$\text{approx}_n : \text{pred} \to \text{pred} \quad \equiv \quad \lambda P.\, \lambda(k,o). \begin{cases} P\,(k,o) & |k| < n \\ \bot & |k| \geq n. \end{cases} \tag{35.12}$$

The key idea is that knots have *levels*, which can be accessed using the level function $|k|$. A knot with a higher level is able to "store more information" than a knot with a lower level. The way to determine the level of a knot is to unsquash it and then take the first component (equation 35.11). The approx_n function (equation 35.12) does the actual approximation by "forgetting" how a predicate behaves on knots with levels greater than or equal to n. When an approximated predicate is passed a knot of too high a level it just returns the default value $\bot$; if the level is low enough then the underlying original predicate is used.

The behavior of squash and unsquash are specified by the following two axioms, which constitute all of indirection theory:

$$\text{squash (unsquash } k) \;=\; k \qquad\qquad (35.13)$$

$$\text{unsquash (squash}(n,x)) \;=\; (n, \text{fmap approx}_n\, x). \qquad (35.14)$$

Equation (35.13) guarantees that squash and unsquash form a section-retraction pair, and demonstrate that unsquash is lossless. In contrast, squash is lossy; equation (35.14) precisely specifies where the information is lost. *When an $F(\text{pred})$ is squashed to level n, all of the predicates inside it are approximated to level n.*

The simplicity of the axioms is a major strength of indirection theory. *The axioms are parametric over $F(X)$,* whereas previous models exposed numerous axioms specialized to their domains. For example, Hobor's earlier model for higher-order concurrent separation logic [51] had more than fifty axioms, all of which follow from equations (35.13) and (35.14) once $F(X)$ is chosen. We view this pleasing fact as evidence that the axiomatization is right. Later in this chapter we explain that the axiomatization is categorical, providing a more formal kind of evidence.

Corollaries. The file msl/knot_lemmas.v contains a number of easy corollaries to the axiomatization of squash and unsquash, such as the fact that unsquash is injective and squash is surjective. Most of these are useful but unsurprising; in contrast, the following fact is noteworthy:

Any predicate (pred) "pulled out" of an unsquashed knot has already been approximated to the level of the knot:

$$\text{unsquash } k = (n,F) \;\Rightarrow\; F = \text{fmap approx}_n\, F \qquad (35.15)$$

That is, whenever (n,F) is the result of an unsquash then F is unaffected by approximating it to level n. All the information "above" n has already been lost, so throwing it away again has no effect. This property is in fact fundamental. Notice that this implies that a predicate P which was "pulled out" of a knot k *is not able to judge k itself.* This is exactly how indirection theory "approximates the circularity" given by the unsound pseudoequation (35.2) to reach a sound construction.

THE CONSEQUENCES OF THIS APPROXIMATION are profound. Suppose we are in the λ-calculus with references and wish to model the type ref τ (where τ is any other type, including another ref τ'). Recall from the discussion surrounding pseudoequation 35.3 above that a memory typing k is a squashed map from addresses to types. The intuition is that a value v has type ref τ if the value is an address a and according to the memory typing, the memory cell at location a has type τ. That is[3]:

$$\psi \vdash v : \text{ref } \tau \quad \overset{?}{\equiv} \quad \text{let } (n, \psi) = \text{unsquash } k \text{ in} \qquad (35.16)$$
$$\exists a.\, v = \text{loc}(a) \wedge \psi(a) = \tau.$$

Actually, this is almost correct. The only problem is that since $\psi(a)$ has been extracted from a knot k of level n, by equation (35.15) we know that $\psi(a)$ has been approximated to level n—that is,

$$\psi(a) = \text{approx}_n \psi(a).$$

Comparing $\psi(a)$ to τ, which may not have been approximated, is too strong. Instead we introduce the idea of *approximate equality*:

$$P =_n Q \quad \equiv \quad \text{approx}_n P = \text{approx}_n Q. \qquad (35.17)$$

That is, two predicates (type in this model) are approximately equal at level n if they are equal on all knots of level less than n.

With approximate equality it is easy to fix equation 35.16:

$$\text{ref } \tau \quad \equiv \quad \lambda(k, v).\, \text{let } (n, \psi) = \text{unsquash } k \text{ in} \qquad (35.18)$$
$$\exists a.\, v = \text{loc}(a) \wedge \psi(a) =_n \tau$$

This definition for ref τ is correct and can type general references in the polymorphic λ-calculus.[4] Chapter 36 presents this semantic construction in full detail.

---

[3] We write $k \vdash v : \tau \equiv \dots$ as a more pleasant notation for $\tau \equiv \lambda(\psi, v).\ \dots$.

[4] A reader may worry that it would be easy to write the incorrect definition (35.16) by mistake. However, we will shortly define a restricted class of *hereditary* predicates (types) which reject (35.16) but allow (35.18).

The previous example shows that we must be mindful whenever comparing predicates extracted from (the unsquashing of) a knot. A second danger can be illustrated by considering the question of how a memory typing k ($\approx$ address $\rightarrow$ type) is related to a memory m (address $\rightarrow$ value). The intuition is that the memory typing k is a valid typing of the memory m, written $k \vdash m$ valid, if all the values in m have the type given by k:

$$k \vdash m \text{ valid} \stackrel{?}{\equiv} \text{let } (n, \psi) = \text{unsquash } k \text{ in} \atop \forall a. \ k \vdash m(a) : \psi(a). \tag{35.19}$$

Unfortunately, this definition is not quite right. The first problem is that as the λ-calculus with references steps it allows new memory cells to be allocated, such as during the execution of the expression new e. We will defer the solution to this aspect of the problem until Chapter 36.

The second problem with pseudoequation (35.19) is more fundamental. Notice that $\psi(a)$—that is, the predicate associated with address a in the memory typing ψ unsquashed from k—is being applied to k itself! By (35.15) and the definition of approx$_n$, this will always be the constant $\bot$. Again, this is exactly where we weaken the unsound pseudodefinition in equation (35.2) to achieve a sound definition: *predicates cannot say anything meaningful about the knot from whence they came.* Accordingly, we must weaken (35.19) so that k is valid if the types in it describe the memory *after k has been approximated:*

$$k \vdash m \text{ valid} \equiv \text{let } (n, \psi) = \text{unsquash } k \text{ in} \atop \forall a, n'. \ n > n' \Rightarrow \text{squash } (n', \psi) \vdash m(a) : \psi(a) \tag{35.20}$$

By equation (35.14), squash (n', ψ) is the same as k except the predicates inside it have been further approximated ("rounded down") to level $n' < n$.

We call the process of unsquashing a knot and then resquashing it to a lower level, causing it to become more approximate, *aging the knot*. Since we must do so whenever we wish to use (apply) a predicate that we pull out of a knot, we have developed some useful auxiliary definitions. The age1 partial function reduces the level of a knot by first unsquashing and then resquashing at one level lower, if possible:

$$\text{age1 } k \equiv \text{squash } (n, x), \text{ where unsquash } k = (n + 1, x) \tag{35.21}$$

Record ageable_facts (A:Type) (level: A → nat) (age1:A → option A) :=
{ af_unage : ∀x':A, ∃x, age1 x = Some x'
; af_level1 : ∀x, age1 x = None ↔ level x = 0
; af_level2 : ∀x y, age1 x = Some y → level x = S (level y)
}.

Class ageable (A:Type) := mkAgeable {
  level : A → nat
; age1 : A → option A
; age_facts : ageable_facts A level age1
}.

Definition age {A} `{ageable A} (x y:A) := age1 x = Some y.

Figure 35.2: The ageable class and the age relation from msl/ageable.v.

Note that age1 is undefined (None) when $|k| = 0$. Define the age(k, k') relation between knots exactly when age1$(k) = $ Some k'—that is, when the predicates in k' are slightly-more-approximate versions of the corresponding predicates in k. We write necR and laterR to denote the reflexive and irreflexive transitive closures of the age relation. All of these ideas are captured in Coq using the typeclass ageable from Figure 35.2. As usual for the mathematical structures we defined, the file msl/ageable.v also contains useful lemmas and constructors for building more complex ageable objects in a modular way.

A key observation: the age relation is noetherian (i.e., the world can only be aged a finite number of times) because the level of k' is always decreasing towards 0. In practice, we will age the knot once each time we might wish to pull a predicate out of it (e.g., once per step in the operational semantics). The particular (but arbitrary, i.e. universally quantified) level of our original knot will thus commit us to a proof about a finite-length execution (before our coffee break).

The repeated aging of our knots results in a third subtle problem. Aging is essentially a technicality forced by the approximation inherent in the underlying model; we do not want this technicality to cause any more proof burden than is absolutely required. In particular, if we know that some predicate P holds on a (k, o) pair, and we age k to k', then we really expect P to hold on (k', o). To be more concrete, consider the λ-calculus: if, given some memory typing k, a value v has type ref (ref int), then we expect v to still have type ref (ref int) in any "more aged" version of k.

In general, we say that a predicate is *hereditary* over an age relation when its truth is preserved under aging;[5] that is:

$$P(w) \quad \rightarrow \quad age(w, w') \quad \rightarrow \quad P(w')$$

Are all predicates hereditary? Sadly not! Consider the following:

$$P_{bad}(k, o) \quad \equiv \quad |k| > 5$$

This predicate changes from $\top$ to $\bot$ as k ages from level 6 to level 5.

The existence of nonhereditary predicates is a major hassle. Not only do they force us to have to prove that our predicates are stable under aging, but all the "useful" predicates seem to be actually hereditary. In other words, the nonhereditary predicates are all pain with no gain.

The solution is to explicitly restrict the predicates we use to only those function which are hereditary. That is, instead of predicate $\equiv (K \times O) \rightarrow \top$, we will use

$$\text{predicate} \quad \equiv \quad \{P \in (K \times O) \rightarrow \mathbb{T} \mid hereditary(P)\}. \tag{35.22}$$

In Coq we carry this hereditary side condition around via a dependent type as given in Figure 35.3. We then must prove that each predicate we use actually is hereditary. Chapter 37 shows how to build a large, expressive, and generic (independent of F) logic using these kinds of predicates: as elsewhere in our approach (separation algebras, functors, etc.), the key is to have suitable building blocks that allow one to construct large objects (predicates, in this case) in a modular way.

---

[5]Here we extend the age relation to pairs of (k, o) by aging the knot and leaving the other data constant; in Coq this is the ag_prod constructor from msl/ageable.v.

Definition hereditary {A} (R:A→A→Prop) (p:A→Prop) :=
    ∀ a a':A, R a a' → p a → p a'.

Definition pred(A:Type){AG: ageable A} :=
    {p:A→Prop| hereditary age p}.
Definition app_pred {A}{AG: ageable A}(p:pred A) : A→Prop :=
    proj1_sig p.
Coercion app_pred : pred >-> Funclass.

Delimit **Scope** pred **with** pred.   Bind **Scope** pred **with** pred.

Lemma pred_hereditary {A}`{ageable A} (p:pred A) :
                                  hereditary age (app_pred p).
Proof. ... **Qed**.
Global Opaque pred.

Figure 35.3: Hereditary predicates in Coq (msl/predicates_hered.v). The
Scope directives govern notation-scopes for operators over predicates. The
coercion app_pred allows us to write P(x) instead of (proj1_sig P)(x).

Now we have an annoying mismatch: predicates inside the knot (which
we obtain via unsquash) are not hereditary, whereas predicates outside
the knot (defined using the constructor of equation 35.22) are hereditary.
This will make proofs difficult: a user of indirection theory might fetch a
predicate from the heap (the precondition of a function or the resource
invariant of a lock) and need the assurance that it is preserved under aging.

The solution is to reformulate the model to satisfy an axiomatization
in which predicates obtained from unsquash are hereditary. We have
done this (msl/knot_hered.v), but axiomatization itself must be adjusted,
as shown in Figure 35.4. First, the predicate type is built from the
dependent-product constructor of equation 35.22. Second, the age1
function is now opaque. Recall that in equation 35.21 we *defined* age1 as
squash(level(k) − 1, unsquash k). In Figure 35.4, the Axiom knot_age1 is an

Module Type KNOT_HERED.
  Declare Module TF:TY_FUNCTOR_PROP.
  Import TF.

  Parameter knot:Type.
  Parameter ag_knot : ageable knot.
  Existing **Instance** ag_knot.
  Existing **Instance** ag_prod.

  Definition predicate := pred (knot * other).

  Parameter squash : (nat * F predicate) → knot.
  Parameter unsquash : knot → (nat * F predicate).
  Parameter approx : nat → predicate → predicate.

  Axiom squash_unsquash : ∀ k:knot, squash (unsquash k) = k.
  Axiom unsquash_squash : ∀ (n:nat) (f:F predicate),
    unsquash (squash (n,f)) = (n, fmap (approx n) f).

  Axiom approx_spec : ∀ n p k,
    proj1_sig (approx n p) k = (level k < n ∧ proj1_sig p k).

  Axiom knot_level : ∀ k:knot, level k = fst (unsquash k).

  Axiom knot_age1 : ∀ k,
    age1 k =
    match unsquash k **with**
    | (O,_) ⇒ None
    | (S n,x) ⇒ Some (squash (n,x))
    end.

End KNOT_HERED.

Figure 35.4: Hereditary knot axiomatization, from msl/knot_hered.v

equation, not a definition. This equality is proved as a theorem, inside the model.

The model for KNOT_HERED is rather more complex than the model for "simple" knots that can contain nonhereditary predicates. It follows all the same basic principles, but now there are quasicircularities in types as well as in values. See msl/knot_hered.v for details.

INDIRECTION THEORY CAN BE EXTENDED in other ways. First, we can consider an extension to an input expressed as a bifunctor rather than an ordinary covariant functor, which allows the circularity to appear in additional positions within F. Second, we can force the predicates inside the knot to be hereditary over more general relations than aging (both over the knot and over the other data). Finally, we can allow the right hand side of predicates to be more general than $\mathbb{T}$. Readers interested in any of these bells and whistles should examine msl/knot_full.v.

Soundness and (a form of) completeness

INDIRECTION THEORY IS SOUND. We prove this by constructing a model in CiC (the logic behind Coq). Here we will sketch the construction of the simpler, nonhereditary knot mechanized in msl/knot.v. Hobor *et al.* [52, §8] give the same construction in considerably more detail in a pen-and-paper style; with one exception (type coercions between equivalent dependent types), the mechanization follows that explanation quite closely. The construction of the hereditary knot, whose Coq axiomatization is given above in figure 35.4, is broadly similar but considerably more delicate; interested readers are referred to msl/knot_hered.v.

In the discussion the follows we elide the "other" data O, which adds no fundamental difficulties but clutters the explanation.

STRATIFIED PREDICATES AND KNOTS. We start by taking a covariant functor (F, fmap) as input. Now define an approximation to pred called pred_n, a finitely stratified type constructor indexed by the natural number n:

$$\text{pred}_n \equiv \begin{cases} \text{unit} & n = 0 \\ \text{pred}_{n-1} \times (F(\text{pred}_{n-1}) \to \mathbb{T}) & n > 0. \end{cases} \tag{35.23}$$

For $n > 0$, $P : \text{pred}_n$ is a pair whose second component $P.2$ is an approximation to the recursive pseudodefinition (35.2) and whose first component $P.1$ is a simpler approximation $P' : \text{pred}_{n-1}$. A pred_n is thus a specialized sort of list where the **type** of list members gets larger as the list gets longer. The type of stratified knots of level n, K_n, is $F(\text{pred}_n)$: a "data structure" whose skeleton is F and whose "leaves" are stratified predicates of level n.

KNOTS AND PREDICATES. A knot (K) hides the index with a dependent sum:
$$\mathsf{K} \equiv \Sigma(n : \mathbb{N}). \, \mathsf{K}_n. \tag{35.24}$$

That is, a knot is a dependent pair of a natural n and an F with elements of pred_n inside. Those who are less familiar with dependent types can consider the right hand side of the above definition to be the type-theoretic version of the infinite union $\bigcup_{n \in \mathbb{N}} \mathsf{K}_n$ definable in set theory.

Some care is required to understand the definition of K. While K might appear to be, in some sense, "infinitely stratified", each element $k : \mathsf{K}$ contains some particular K_n—in other words, every element of K only contains some finite amount of stratification. Define the *level* of a knot k as:

$$\text{level}(k) = k.1 \qquad \text{that is,} \qquad \text{level}(n, f) = n. \tag{35.25}$$

A knot's level gives how many layers of stratification it contains.

Now we can define the type of predicates (pred):

$$\text{pred} = \mathsf{K} \to \mathbb{T}. \tag{35.26}$$

A pred is an "infinitely stratified" pred_n. Notice that, unlike K itself, a $P : \text{pred}$ can nontrivially judge knots of arbitrary level, as illustrated in equation 35.18. That is, knots always contain some finite amount of stratification, but predicates are not limited in the same finite way, essentially because they are able to examine the (finite) amount of information provided to their argument before rendering their judgment: the power of contravariance.

This is the key to creating an "initial knot" corresponding to the beginning of a program execution. Indirection theory is typically used to prove safety of an operational semantics. We do this by saying, "for all k, the semantics is safe for k steps." Once some abstract k is selected by this universal quantification, we take some predicate of interest (such as ref in equation 35.18) and squash it to level k. See also Chapter 39.

STRATIFICATION AND UNSTRATIFICATION. The key question is: how is the "infinitely stratified" type $F(\text{pred})$ related to the finitely stratified type K?

Define a function $\text{strat}_n : \text{pred} \rightarrow \text{pred}_n$ that collapses an infinitely stratified pred into a finitely stratified pred_n:

$$\text{strat}_n(P) = \begin{cases} () & n = 0 \\ (\text{strat}_{n-1}(P),\ \lambda f.\ P(n-1, f)) & n > 0. \end{cases} \tag{35.27}$$

The strat_n function constructs the list structure of pred_n by recursively applying P to knots of decreasing level. The finitely stratified type pred_n is not big enough to store the behavior of P on knots of level $\geq n$, and so that information is thrown away.

To invert, first define a "floor" operator that given a $P : \text{pred}_{n+m}$, constructs a $P' : \text{pred}_n$ by stripping off the outer m approximations:

$$\lfloor P \rfloor_n^m \equiv \begin{cases} P & m = 0 \\ \lfloor P.1 \rfloor_n^{m-1} & m > 0. \end{cases} \tag{35.28}$$

Now define $\text{unstrat}_n : \text{pred}_n \rightarrow \text{pred}$, which takes a finitely stratified pred_n and constructs an infinitely stratified pred from it:[6]

$$\text{unstrat}_n(P) = \lambda k. \begin{cases} (\lfloor P \rfloor_{\text{level}(k)+1}^m.2)\ k.2 & n = \text{level}(k) + m + 1 \\ \bot & n \leq \text{level}(k). \end{cases} \tag{35.29}$$

[6]Note that the cases are exhaustive, though given in a slightly abnormal manner.

When given a knot of level $< n$, the $\mathsf{unstrat}_n$ function uses the floor operator to "look up" how to behave in the finite list of predicates inside a pred_n. When applied to a knot k of level $\geq n$, the $\mathsf{unstrat}_n$ function returns $\bot$ since the pred_n P does not contain any way to judge k.

What happens when we compose strat_n and $\mathsf{unstrat}_n$? The answer, the key to indirection theory, is given by the following lemma.

LEMMA ($\mathsf{unstrat}_n$ AND strat_n FORM A SECTION/RETRACTION PAIR):

$$(\mathsf{strat}_n \circ \mathsf{unstrat}_n)\, P_n \;=\; P_n \tag{35.30}$$

$$(\mathsf{unstrat}_n \circ \mathsf{strat}_n)\, P \;=\; \lambda k. \begin{cases} P(k) & \text{when } \mathsf{level}(k) < n \\ \bot & \text{when } \mathsf{level}(k) \geq n \end{cases} \tag{35.31}$$

SQUASHING AND UNSQUASHING. Finally, we define squash and unsquash by using fmap to lift strat_n and $\mathsf{unstrat}_n$ to covariant structures as follows:

$$\mathsf{squash}(n, f) \;\equiv\; (n, \mathsf{fmap}\ \mathsf{strat}_n\ f) \tag{35.32}$$

$$\mathsf{unsquash}(k) \;\equiv\; (\mathsf{level}(k), \mathsf{fmap}\ \mathsf{unstrat}_{\mathsf{level}(k)}\ k.2). \tag{35.33}$$

Notice that the "internal" $\mathsf{level}(k)$ (35.25) and the "external" $|k|$ (35.11) are extensionally equal, implying (by the key lemma above) that

$$\mathsf{approx}_n = \mathsf{unstrat}_n \circ \mathsf{strat}_n.$$

The axioms of indirection theory follow immediately. *That is, the axioms of indirection theory are sound, as they are derivable from a model.*

THE AXIOMATIZATION IS CATEGORICAL: that is, not only is indirection theory sound but there is a sense in which it is complete as well.

THEOREM. The axioms of indirection theory are categorical, that is, determine the model uniquely up to isomorphism. More formally:

Assume that we have a single input (F, fmap). Now consider two models A and B. To distinguish the operations defined on one construction from the other, we will write, *e.g.*, squash_A or squash_B.

A and B will be isomorphic if we can find $f : K_A \to K_B$ such that f is a bijection and preserves squash and unsquash as follows. Define $\Phi : F(\mathrm{pred}_A) \to F(\mathrm{pred}_B)$, which lifts the bijection f to objects of type $F(\mathrm{pred})$, as $\Phi \equiv \mathrm{fmap}\ (\lambda P_B.\ P_B \circ f^{-1})$. Since f is a bijection and fmap distributes over function composition, Φ is a bijection as well. Now prove:

1. $f(\mathrm{squash}_A(n, \psi_A)) = \mathrm{squash}_B(n, \Phi(\psi_A))$

2. $f^{-1}(\mathrm{squash}_B(n, \psi_B)) = \mathrm{squash}_A(n, \Phi^{-1}(\psi_B))$

3. $\mathrm{unsquash}_B(f(k_A)) = (n, \Phi(\psi_A))$, where $(n, \psi_A) = \mathrm{unsquash}_A(k_A)$, and

4. $\mathrm{unsquash}_A(f^{-1}(k_B)) = (n, \Phi^{-1}(\psi_B))$, where $(n, \psi_B) = \mathrm{unsquash}_B(k_B)$.

PROOF. At first, the construction of f seems quite easy:

$$f \overset{?}{\equiv} \mathrm{squash}_B \circ \mathrm{unsquash}_A. \qquad (35.34)$$

That is, take a $k_A : K_A$, unsquash it to get to a common form (of type $\mathbb{N} \times F(\mathrm{pred})$), and then squash it into an element of type K_B. Unfortunately, this approach does not work since $\mathrm{unsquash}_A$ produces an element of type $\mathbb{N} \times F(\mathrm{pred}_A)$, while squash_B requires an element of type $\mathbb{N} \times F(\mathrm{pred}_B)$. We cannot assume that pred_A is compatible with pred_B without begging the question, so (35.34) is invalid. The problem is tricky because the types are isomorphic but need not be equal. The real construction requires significant machinery to coerce the types from one construction to the other. Readers interested in an informal sketch should consult [52, §9]; the full details can find them in msl/knot_unique.v.

CATEGORICAL AXIOMATIZATIONS ARE SUFFICIENTLY UNCOMMON that it is worthwhile to ponder the implications. Most importantly, the axioms of indirection theory are in some sense complete: they define a particular class of models in a definitive way. Moreover, there seems to be little point in developing alternatives to the construction we presented above, at least in CiC. We view these facts as powerful evidence that these axioms are the correct way to characterize step-indexing models.

USING INDIRECTION THEORY—step indexing—we have proved the soundness of the lambda calculus with mutable references. A different way to manage the packing of step indexing is *ultrametric spaces* [21]; perhaps these could be used just as well in a verified toolchain.

Could we have avoided step-indexing altogether? One can use *syntactic indirection*, such as in Harper's semantics for general references [46] or Gotsman *et al.*'s semantics of storable locks [44]. But syntactic indirection works best on whole-program semantics; when trying to express the semantics of modular program components one runs into difficulties, because the syntactic indirection table cannot be complete.

Chapter 36

Case study: Lambda-calculus with references
by Robert Dockins

Here we present a simple λ-calculus with references to illustrate the use of indirection theory.[1] The λ-calculus is well understood and its type system presents no surprises, so it provides us as a nice vehicle for explaining how to apply indirection theory.

One reason this language is interesting, from our point of view, is that it was historically rather difficult to find a semantic theory for general references—that is, references that may contain data of any type, including quantified types. In contrast, the theory of references at base types (e.g., only containing integers) is much simpler. Tofte had an syntactic/operational theory of general references as early as 1990 [86], but it was not until the step-indexed model of Ahmed, Appel and Virga [4, 2] in 2003 that a *semantic* theory of general references was found.[2] The model of Ahmed et al. was refined and generalized in the following years by Appel et al. [11], and then further refined by Hobor et al. [52] into the indirection theory that appears in this book.

---

[1] The Coq development for this chapter is in examples/lam_ref/

[2] To be clear, we mean that the meanings of *types* are given semantically; they still used operational methods for the dynamic semantics of the language, as do we.

The λ-calculus with references is a bit of a detour from our main aim in this book, which is building program logics for C. However, it provides a relatively simple, self-contained example that illustrates the techniques we will be using later in more complicated settings. In particular, we will use indirection theory to build the Hoare tuple for program logics for C along similar lines to how we construct the expression typing predicate in this chapter.

The syntax of the language we investigate in this chapter is given below. The language has a single base type (the natural numbers), and ML-style references in addition to the usual functions of λ-calculus.

nat	$n ::= 0, 1, 2, \ldots$
loc	$\ell ::= 0, 1, 2, \ldots$
var	$v ::= 0, 1, 2, \ldots$

Definition var_t : Type := nat.
Definition addr : Type := nat.

Inductive expr : Type :=
| Nat : $\forall$ n : nat, expr

expr	$e ::=$ Nat n
	| Prim $f\ e$
	| Var v
	| Loc ℓ
	| λe
	| $e\ e$
	| New e
	| $!e$
	| $e_1 := e_2;\ e_3$

| Prim : $\forall$ (f:nat $\rightarrow$ expr)
        (e:expr), expr
| Var : $\forall$ n : var_t, expr
| Loc : $\forall$ l : addr, expr
| Lam : $\forall$ e : expr, expr
| App : $\forall$ e1 e2 : expr, expr
| New : $\forall$ e : expr, expr
| Deref : $\forall$ e : expr, expr
| Update : $\forall$ e1 e2 e3: expr, expr.

We use a presentation of the λ-calculus based on de Brujin indices, which means λ abstractions do not bind named variables. Instead, variables are natural numbers, refering to the ith enclosing lambda. For example λVar 0 is more usually written $\lambda x.\ x$, and $\lambda\lambda$(Var 1) (Var 0) is the same as $\lambda x.\ \lambda y.\ x\ y$.

The Nat syntactic form represents natural number values. The Prim form allows us to build all sorts of primitive functions over naturals. The intuitive meaning of Prim $f\ e$ is that we first evaluate the expression e to a value n (expected to be a natural number) and then compute the resulting expression by passing n to f (which is a function in Coq).

The Loc form represents *location* values. Locations are essentially the addresses of allocated reference cells. Locations are not allowed to appear in programs users write, but can only occur during evaluation. The New form allocates a new reference cell, returing the location where the cell was allocated, and !e dereferences the value of a cell. The form $[e_1] := e_2; e_3$ causes the value of e_2 to be written into the cell e_1 and then evaluates e_3.

Among the expressions, we select a subset of values: these consist of the natural numbers, the location constants, and the lambda abstractions. We will also be interested in the subset of closed expressions, i.e., those with no free variables.

Fixpoint closed' (n : nat) (e : expr) : Prop :=
  match e **with**   *(* No vars greater than n in e *)*
  | Var n' ⇒ n' < n
  | Prim f e ⇒ closed' n e
  | Lam e ⇒ closed' (n + 1) e
  | Nat _⇒ True
  | Loc _⇒ True
  | App e1 e2 ⇒ closed' n e1 ∧ closed' n e2
  | New e ⇒ closed' n e
  | Deref e ⇒ closed' n e
  | Update e1 e2 e3 ⇒ closed' n e1 ∧ closed' n e2 ∧ closed' n e3
  end.
Definition closed (e : expr) : Prop := closed' 0 e.

Definition openValue (e:expr) : Prop :=
  match e **with** Nat _⇒ True | Loc _⇒ True | Lam _⇒ True | _⇒ False
  end.

Definition isValue (e : expr) : Prop := closed e ∧ openValue e.

Definition value : Type := {v : expr | isValue v}.

In order to defined the notion of closed expressions, we need the auxiliary closed' definition, which says that an expression contains no free variables above a cutoff. The cutoff value is incremented every time we pass under a λ. Values are then defined as expressions that are both closed and of one of the three value forms.

The semantics of this language is an unsurprising call-by-value small-step operational semantics. The states of the operational semantics consist of a memory and an expression. Evaluation proceeds by reducing the expression, using the memory to store the values of reference cells.

We define memories very directly, as a pair of a "break" value and a function from locations to values. The break value is the lowest location number not yet allocated. Allocating a new reference cell is done by simply incrementing this break value.

Definition mem : Type := (nat $*$ (addr $\rightarrow$ value))%type.

Definition new (m : mem) (v : value) : (mem $*$ addr) :=
   match m **with** (n, m') $\Rightarrow$
   ((S n, fun a $\Rightarrow$ **if** beq_nat a n **then** v **else** m' a), n)
   end.

Definition deref (m : mem) (a : addr) : value := (snd m) a.

Definition update (m : mem) (a : addr) (v : value) : mem :=
   match m **with** (n, m') $\Rightarrow$
   (n, fun a' $\Rightarrow$ **if** beq_nat a a' **then** v **else** m' a')
   end.

Definition state : Type := (mem $*$ expr)%type.

Because we are presenting a call-by-value operational semantics we expect only to substitute values, not general expressions. Values have no free variables, and we can therefore simplify the definition of substitution for de Brujin terms as compared to a fully general definition, which must shift and unshift the free variables.

Fixpoint subst (var : var_t) (v : value) (e : expr) : expr :=
  match e **with**
    | Nat n ⇒ Nat n
    | Prim f e ⇒ Prim f (subst var v e)
    | Loc l ⇒ Loc l
    | Var var' ⇒ **if** (beq_nat var var') **then** val_to_exp v **else** Var var'
    | Lam e ⇒ Lam (subst (var + 1) v e)
    | App e1 e2 ⇒ App (subst var v e1) (subst var v e2)
    | New e ⇒ New (subst var v e)
    | Deref e ⇒ Deref (subst var v e)
    | Update e1 e2 e3 ⇒
        Update (subst var v e1) (subst var v e2) (subst var v e3)
  end.

Finally we are ready to present the operational semantics and the safety policy. The relation step *st st'* is defined by the rules in figure 36.1. The safety policy is totally standard—a state *st* is safe if every reachable *st'* is either a value or can take an additional step.

(∗ Reflexive, transitive closure of stepping ∗)
Inductive stepstar : state → state → Prop :=
    | step_refl : ∀ st, stepstar st st
    | step_trans: ∀ st1 st2 st3,
        stepstar st1 st2 → stepstar st2 st3 → stepstar st1 st3
    | step1 : ∀ st st', step st st' → stepstar st st'.

(∗ Statement of safety policy ∗)
Definition can_step (st : state) : Prop := ∃st', step st st'.

Definition at_value (st : state) : Prop := isValue (snd st).

Definition safe (st : state) : Prop :=
  ∀ st', stepstar st st' → can_step st' ∨ at_value st'.

Definition safe_prog (e:expr) : Prop := ∀ m, safe (m, e).

$$\text{app1}\frac{\text{step }(m, e_1)\,(m', e_1')}{\text{step }(m, e_1\,e_2)\,(m', e_1'\,e_2)} \qquad \text{app2}\frac{\text{step }(m, e_2)\,(m', e_2')}{\text{step }(m, (\lambda e_1)\,e_2)\,(m', (\lambda e_1)\,e_2')}$$

$$\text{app3}\frac{\text{isValue }e_2}{\text{step }(m, (\lambda e_1)\,e_2)\,(m, \text{subst }0\,e_2\,e_1)}$$

$$\text{new1}\frac{\text{step }(m, e)\,(m', e')}{\text{step }(m, \text{New }e)\,(m', \text{New }e')} \qquad \text{new2}\frac{\text{isValue }e \qquad \text{new }m\,e = (m', \ell)}{\text{step }(m, \text{New }e)\,(m', \text{Loc }\ell)}$$

$$\text{deref1}\frac{\text{step }(m, e)\,(m', e')}{\text{step }(m, !e)\,(m', !e')} \qquad \text{deref2}\frac{\text{deref }m\,\ell = v}{\text{step }(m, !(\text{Loc }\ell))\,(m, v)}$$

$$\text{update1}\frac{\text{step }(m, e_1)\,(m', e_1')}{\text{step }(m, [e_1] := e_2; e_3)\,(m', [e_1'] := e_2; e_3)}$$

$$\text{update2}\frac{\text{step }(m, e_2)\,(m', e_2')}{\text{step }(m, [\text{Loc }\ell] := e_2; e_3)\,(m', [\text{Loc }\ell] := e_2'; e_3)}$$

$$\text{update3}\frac{\text{isValue}(e_2) \qquad \text{update }m\,\ell\,e_2 = m'}{\text{step }(m, [\text{Loc }\ell] := e_2; e_3)\,(m', e_3)}$$

$$\text{prim1}\frac{\text{step }(m, e)\,(m', e')}{\text{step }(m, \text{Prim }f\,e)\,(m', \text{New }f\,e')}$$

$$\text{prim2}\frac{\text{isValue}(f(n))}{\text{step }(m, \text{Prim }f\,(\text{Nat }n))\,(m, f(n))}$$

Figure 36.1: Operational semantics of λ-calculus with references

OUR GOAL IS TO BUILD A TYPE SYSTEM for this λ-calculus and prove it sound. For us, soundness will mean that well-typed programs are safe in the sense defined above. Our approach is to assign mathematical meanings to the usual constructs of the type system so that our desired theorem (safety) follows as a simple corollary. Note that in this development we will not address other concerns that are sometimes of interest for type systems: decidability of type checking or type inference. Such questions only make sense for a particular *syntactic presentation* of a type system—that is, an explicit collection of inductively-closed typing rules. We will not be giving such a presentation.

Instead, we will be concentrating on building a semantic model of types. Roughly, the meaning of a type is a set of values. The meaning of types can then be extended to general expressions—the intuition is that an expression has type τ if it evaluates to a value of type τ (or fails to terminate). Some types are quite easy to define. For example, the type nat simply denotes all the values of the form Nat n for some $n \in \mathbb{N}$. Function types are somewhat more involved, but are handled by well known techniques. The type $A \to B$ contains λ-abstractions such that substituting in a value of type A results in an expression of type B.

However, reference types require some additional work. Suppose we want to define the meaning of ref τ—the idea is that reference types denote location values, where the referenced location contains a value of type τ. However, given just a location, we do not have enough information to determine if the cell referenced by ℓ contains a value of type τ.

One option is to change the meaning of types, so that they denote sets of *states*, that is pairs of memories and values. Then the meaning of ref τ can refer to the current memory, so it can simply look up the value at ℓ to evalutate τ. However, this simple plan also does not work, because ML-style references are so-called *weak* references that are guaranteed to keep the same type throughout their lifetime. Simply examining the current memory works fine for *strong* references (whose type can change over time) but is unworkable here because strong references cause subject reduction to fail. The essential difference is that the type of strong references refers only to the *current* state of the machine, whereas the type of weak references also gives a guarantee about future behavior. In other words, the type of a weak reference is an *invariant* of a program.

Instead, we want to keep track of the type at which each reference was initially created in a *memory type*. A memory type is simply a partial map from locations to types. Then, the denotation of types examines both a value and a memory type. We call a pair of a memory type and a value a *world*—the purpose of the value component is to keep track of the first unallocated location. We say that the meaning of a type is a set of worlds. To evaluate the meaning of ref τ, we require the value to be a location ℓ and that the memory type tells us that location ℓ has type τ.

If all this seems confusing now, don't worry—it will be explained later in more detail. For now, the main point is that we want to define the denotation of types as sets of memory types and values, and that memory types are partial functions from locations to types.

In other words we would like to build a semantic domain satisfying the following equations:

$$\text{type} = (\text{mtype} \times \text{value}) \rightarrow \text{Prop}$$
$$\text{mtype} = \text{loc} \rightharpoonup \text{type}$$

Unfortunately, there are no solutions to this series of equations in set theory (or in type theory). Basically, this is because type occurs in contravariant recursive position in its own definition. A simple diagionalization argument shows that there can be no sets satisfying these equations. For the rest of this section, we will set aside this issue—in the following section we will see how to use indirection theory to build an *approximation* to these equations that will suffice for our purposes.

Before getting into the technical details, however, we will first lay out a roadmap that should help orient the reader when we start getting into the formal definitions. Our main task is to build the three basic type constructors that correspond to the computational aspects of the system: the base type of natural numbers, the ref type constructor, and the arrow type of functions. Given the appropriate definitions of these main type formers, it will be fairly straighforward to define the main typing judgment, prove that typing implies program safety, and to prove the usual typing rules of the call-by-value λ-calculus with references as derived lemmas.

The base type nat is by far the simplest of the three; the type nat accepts any world where the value component is Nat n for some $n \in \mathbb{N}$.

The type ref τ is somewhat more complicated, and is the reason we introduced memory typings. The type ref τ accepts a world (ψ, v) when $v = \text{Loc } \ell$, for some location value ℓ, and when $\psi(\ell) = \tau$. In other words, the reference type accepts location values that have type τ claimed in the memory type. As we shall see, the actual definitions will be a bit more complicated, but this is the basic idea.

Finally, we consider the function type $\tau_1 \to \tau_2$. The intuition here is that a value of type $\tau_1 \to \tau_2$ is a lambda abstraction whose body has the property that whenever a value of type τ_1 is substituted into it, an expression of type τ_2 results. Note carefully that until now we have only talked about types applying to values—however, to discuss the type of functions, we need a notion of types applying to general *expressions* as well. The main difficulty in defining the function type involves finding the correct way to lift the notion of types from values to expressions.

Finally, we can define the meaing of the typing judgment. $\Gamma \vdash e : \tau$ holds when substituting values of the types listed in Γ for the free variables of e results in an expression of type τ. This allows us to prove the main type safety theorem without too much difficulty. A term e which is typeable in the empty context is simply a closed expression of type τ, and the semantic definition of expression typing implies the safety theorem we desire by a simple induction.

Once these definitions are made, it is a straightforward proof exercise to prove that the usual typing rules hold. The proof for these rules typically breaks down into two distinct parts: one part closely resembles the proof one would do in a standard subject reduction proof, whereas the other part closely resembles a case in a progress proof.

Unfortunately, the simple picture painted above is complicated somewhat by the need to account for some tricky details. The first of these is the fact that the defining equations above for type and mtype are inconsistent. The second detail is the need to build into our type system the invariant that all type judgments are stable under the allocation of new reference cells. In other words, allocating a new cell cannot cause values to change their types or to become untypeable. In a syntactic presentation of a type system, such a fact would be a derived lemma, but here we must build it into the semantic definitions of types. In the next several sections, we show how these details are handled in the formal proof before moving on to the main type definitions.

It is not possible to build a simple set-theoretic model, because contravariance between types and memory types leads to a Cantor paradox. Fortunately, we have a way to handle this problem—we developed indirection theory expressly to build approximate solutions to such systems of equations. Recall from Chapter 35 that indirection theory applies to covariant functors F and an arbitrary set O of other data and constructs a type knot where:

$$\text{knot} \preceq \mathbb{N} \times F((\text{knot} \times O) \to \text{Prop})$$

We can instantiate this pattern to our current situation by setting:

$$F(X) = \text{loc} \rightharpoonup X$$
$$O = \text{value}$$

Indirection theory then constructs the approximation, and we can proceed by setting:

$$\text{mtype} = \text{knot} \preceq \mathbb{N} \times (\text{loc} \rightharpoonup \text{type})$$
$$\text{world} = \text{mtype} \times \text{value}$$
$$\text{type} = \text{pred world}$$

We call a pair of a memtype and a value a *world*, which means that a type is a predicate on worlds (recall that the second component is just to keep track of the boundary between allocated and unallocated locations). Furthermore, a memtype is approximately a partial map from locations to types. As usual when working with step-indexed models built using indirection theory, we are only interested in predicates on worlds that are closed with respect to approximation. This is built into the definition of pred. For a type A equipped with an ageable structure, pred A represents the predicates on A that are hereditary: that is, closed under approximation.

The Coq code that sets up the indirection theory structure needed for this example is given below.

```
Module TFP <: TY_FUNCTOR_PROP.
  Definition F : Type → Type := fun K ⇒ addr → option K.
  Definition f_F := f_fun addr (f_option f_identity).

  Definition other : Type := value.
End TFP.

Export TFP.

Module K := KnotHered(TFP). (* Wow, that was easy... *)
Module KL := KnotHered_Lemmas(K).

Export K KL.

(* Let's define our typing system on values *)
Definition mtype : Type := knot.
Definition world : Type := (mtype * value)%type.

Definition world_ag : ageable world :=
  ag_prod mtype value ag_knot.
Existing Instance world_ag.
```

For someone new to doing proofs in this style, it may not be obvious what is going on with the appoximations built by indirection theory, so here we will explain how the pieces fit together in more detail. The main idea to keep in mind is that the level of an mtype is a step-index. This means that an mtype of level n will correctly describe a program that runs for *no more than n steps*. An mtype of level n contains predicates that are only accurate for worlds of level $n - 1$. However, this turns out to be sufficent because dereferencing a cell takes a step of computation. In other words, every time we make essential use of a type stored in an mtype, the program must use a step of computation. Thus, if the mtype is good for n steps, then its stored types are good for $n - 1$ steps—and by the time it matters, we will have used a step of computation so $n - 1$ steps is enough.

The preceeding paragraph puts a design constraint on the operational semantics of programs if one wishes to use indirection theory. Basically, this constraint is that every memory access must take at least one operational step. One should not, for example, write an operational rule that follows an entire chain of pointers in one step, otherwise the step-indexing proof will break down.

With this in mind, let us review the constructions of indirection theory, specalized to the current λ-calculus example. When we invoke indirection theory, it builds two functions squash and unsquash:

$$\text{squash} : \mathbb{N} \times (\text{loc} \rightharpoonup \text{type}) \to \text{memtype} \tag{36.1}$$

$$\text{unsquash} : \text{memtype} \to \mathbb{N} \times (\text{loc} \rightharpoonup \text{type}) \tag{36.2}$$

squash takes a pair of a *level* and an element of the intially desired object (in this case partial functions from locations to types) and constructs an mtype. The function unsquash reverses this process, returning the level and the mapping. However, for the same cardinality reasons as before, these two functions cannot be inverses. Instead, they form a section-retraction pair, which means that the composed function squash ∘ unsquash is the identity function, but composition in the other direction results in an approximation function.

$$\text{squash}(\text{unsquash}(k)) = k \tag{36.3}$$

$$\text{unsquash}(\text{squash}(n, \psi)) = (n, \text{fmap approx}_n \ \psi) \tag{36.4}$$

The function fmap, when applied to a partial map, simply applies the given function to every element in the map. In this case, it applies the function approx_n to every type in the map. The function approx_n takes a pred world and returns a new pred world that accepts the same worlds as the original, provided their level is strictly less than n. Thus, fmap $\text{approx}_n \ \psi$ is a new map from locations to types where every type in the map is approximated to only accept worlds of level (strictly) less than n.

The reader may be confused as to why we would want to approximate predicates—why throw away information? The answer is that this approximation is necessary to get a well-founded construction. By making the predicates contained within an mtype only accept worlds of strictly smaller level, we can stratify the entire construction according to level, which allows us to complete the construction. Dealing with the approximation is the price we must pay for a sound construction.

In addition to the notion of approximating predicates, there is also an important notion of approximating knots. Approximating knots involves decreasing their level and approximating all their enclosed predicates down to the new, lower, level. This is accomplished by first unsquashing the knot at level $n + 1$ and then squashing the enclosed map at level n. This process is called "aging" the knot. Aging knots is how we implement the step-indexing strategy; roughly, the knot (mtype in this instance) gets aged every time we take a step in the operational semantics.[3]

Because we are constantly aging knots as we execute programs, we are usually only interested in predicates on worlds that are stable under approximation. In other words, if a predicate P holds on a world w, then we also want P to hold on all worlds w' that are approximations of w. In our current setting, this means that when a type holds on a value, it continues to hold as the mtype becomes more approximate over time. This is critical to ensure that subject reduction holds in the system.

We call predicates with this property *hereditary* predicates. Hereditary predicates are so critical that we require *all* predicates to be hereditary. Recall from Chapter 37 that pred world refers only to sets of worlds that are closed under approximation, i.e., that are hereditary. In the formal proofs, whenever a new primitive predicate is introduced, it must be proved hereditary at the time of definition. Ususally, this is straightforward; however, it occasionally requires some thought to build an appropriately hereditary predicate. As we shall see later, the definition of ref τ requires some care in order to get a hereditary predicate.

Associated with the action of aging knots there is a modality $\triangleright$, which can be read "approximately," or "later." The predicate $\triangleright P$ means that P holds on all strictly more approximate worlds. Because of the tight tie between the levels of worlds and steps of the operational semantics $\triangleright P$ can

---

[3]This restriction to age every step can be relaxed in some instances, but aging every operational step is a good rule of thumb.

also reasonably be read "*P* will hold after taking one more step."
Recall that the formal definition of ▷ is:

$$(\psi, v) \models \triangleright P \equiv \forall \psi'. \; \mathsf{age}^+(\psi, \psi') \rightarrow (\psi', v) \models P$$

Here age is a relation on knots (here, mtypes) built by indirection theory that corresponds to the "unsquash and then squash again at a lower level" process discussed above.

IN ADDITION TO BECOMING MORE APPROXIMATE, there is another way that mtypes change as program execution proceeds. Every time a new reference cell is allocated, the mtype needs to be *extended* with the type of that new cell. Because we are modeling ML-style references, once a reference comes into existence, it persists forever (in principle) and retains the same type throughout its lifetime.

It is convenient to set up a modality to represent extension of the mtype, much as ▷ represents approximation. To do this we follow the general recipe for setting up a new modality (cf. Chapter 37), which involves defining a relation on worlds and proving that it commutes with the age relation. Informally, we say a memory type ψ is extended by ψ' when, for every location ℓ in the domain of ψ it is the case that the $\psi(\ell) = \psi'(\ell)$.

The formal definition is more complicated because of the need to deal with unsquashing the knots.

Definition knot_extends (k1 k2 : knot) : Prop :=
  match (unsquash k1, unsquash k2) **with**
    ((n, psi), (n', psi')) ⇒ n = n' ∧
     ∀ a, (psi a = None) ∨ (psi' a = psi a)
  end.

Definition R_extends (w1 w2 : world) : Prop :=
  match (w1, w2) **with**
    ((k1, v1), (k2, v2)) ⇒ knot_extends k1 k2 ∧ v1 = v2
  end.

Definition R_contracts := transp _R_extends.

R_extends holds between two worlds when their values are the same and both knots have the same level, but the second knot may have more locations defined. The relation R_contracts is simply the transpose (inverse) of R_extends. To make these relations into modalities, we must prove that they commute with aging. This done, we defined the corresponding modalities and define % as notation for the box modality of extension.

Definition extendM: modality := exist _ R_extends R_extends_valid_rel.
Definition contractsM: modality := exist _ R_contracts R_contracts_valid_rel.
Notation "'%' e" := (box extendM e)
            (at level 30, right associativity): pred.

Thus, when we write the predicate %P, this means that P holds on the current world and also on all extended worlds. In order to achieve the desired invariant that all types are closed under extension, we will make frequent use of the % mode in the definitions that follow. In one important case, we will also use the complementary mode diamond contractsM, which expresses that a predicate holds on *some* extended world.

WE ARE NOW READY TO DEFINE the operators of our type system. First, we define two auxiliary predicates. The just v predicate claims that the value in the world is equal to v, whereas the with_val v p predicate *replaces* the current value in the world with v before evaluating predidate p.

Program Definition just (v:value) : pred world :=
    fun w ⇒ snd w = v.
Next Obligation. ... **Qed**.

Program Definition with_val (v:value) (p:pred world) : pred world :=
    fun w ⇒ p (fst w,v).
Next Obligation. ... **Qed**.

Note here we are using Coq's "Program Definition" facility. This allows us to state the definition of these predicates directly and relegate the proof that they are hereditary to a proof oblibation we can discharge later using tactics. Both of these predicates are easy to show hereditary.

With these in hand, it is straightforward to define the type of naturals.

Definition ty_nat := EX n:nat, just (v_Nat n).

The meaning of ty_nat is quite simple—it simply ignores the memory type and examines the value to see if it is a natural number value.

Next, we are going to start working toward the definition of reference types, which we will take in several steps. First, we need a notion of "approximate equality," which says that two predicates are equal up to a certain level of approximation.

Definition approx_eq (n : nat) (τ_1 τ_2 : predicate) : Prop :=
approx n τ_1 = approx n τ_2.

This simply states that two predicates are equal when they are approximated to level n. We use approximate equality to define the predicate type_at, which claims that cell l in the memory type contains type τ.

Program Definition type_at (l:addr) (τ:pred world) : pred world :=
fun w:world $\Rightarrow$ **let** (n,ψ) := unsquash (fst w) **in**
            match ψ l **with**
            | None $\Rightarrow$ False
            | Some p $\Rightarrow$ approx_eq n p τ
            end.
Next Obligation. ... **Qed**.

This predicate first unsquashes the memory type to get the underlying map and looks up the type a cell l, which must exist and be approxmately equal to the given type. In order to get a hereditary predicate, we must use approximate equality to compare the types. Now we can complete the definition of reference types.

Definition ty_ref (τ: pred world) : pred world :=
EX a:addr, just (v_Loc a) && type_at a τ.

Much like the type of natural numbers, we say that a world satisfies the reference type if its value is a location; however, we *also* require that the type at that location be τ.

The final major type constructor we need for our type system is $\tau_1 \Rightarrow \tau_2$, the constructor for the function space. The main idea here is that a value is of type $\tau_1 \Rightarrow \tau_2$ if it is a lambda term such that substituting a value of type τ_1 into the body of the term results in a term of type τ_2. Note that this refers to the type of both *values* and of *terms*.

Types, by definition, apply only to values. To understand the typing of function bodies (and to have a useful type system), we will need to define what it means to apply types to general expressions. We lift the notion of typing to expressions by codifying the commonsense idea that an expression has type τ if it reduces to a value of type τ.

Formally, we define expression typing as a predicate in our logic so that the predicate expr_type e τ holds if expression e has type τ according to the memory typing in the current world. The definition, rougly, means that expr_type e τ holds if either e is a value of type τ OR if e can take additional steps and every expression e' that e may step to is an expression of type τ. Therefore, expression typing captures the familiar "progress and preservation" properties common to syntactic type soundness proofs.

expr_type is a recursive definition, characterized by the equation:

```
expr_type e τ =
%ALL m:mem, mtype_valid m ⟶
   (ALL m':mem, ALL e':expr, !!(step (m,e) (m',e')) ⟶
      ▷(diamond contractsM (mtype_valid m' && expr_type e' τ)))
   &&
   (!!(stopped m e) ⟶ EX H:isValue e, with_val (exp_to_val e H) (%τ)).
```

Let us postpone briefly a discussion of the various pieces of this definition, and focus on what must be done to produce an expr_type satisfying this equation. First we must define the type operator over which we wish to take the fixpoint; then we prove it contractive which allows us to use the higher-order fixpoint operator. The equation above then follows from a straightforward use of the fixpoint equation for HORec.

Definition expr_typeF
```
(τ:pred world) (F: expr ⟶ pred world) (e : expr) : pred world :=
%ALL m:mem, mtype_valid m ⟶
   (ALL m':mem,    ALL e':expr, !!(step (m,e) (m',e')) ⟶
      ▷(diamond contractsM (mtype_valid m' && F e'))) &&
   (!!(stopped m e) ⟶ EX H:isValue e, with_val (exp_to_val e H) (%τ)).
```

Lemma expr_type_sub1 :
 ∀ τ P Q, ALL e:expr, ▷(P e ⇛ Q e)
                ⊢ ALL e:expr, expr_typeF τ P e ⇛ expr_typeF τ Q e.

Lemma expr_type_cont : ∀ τ, HOcontractive (expr_typeF τ).
Definition expr_type e τ := HORec (expr_typeF τ) e.

The proof of contractiveness is a straightforward application of facts about the various operators making up the definition of `expr_typeF`. In the end, the proof goes through because the recursive call is "guarded" by the later operator. Note that τ is a *parameter* of the recursive definition because it does not vary at each recursive call, whereas e is an *argument* that must be threaded through the recursion.

Now, to the pieces of the definition itself. Recall that the operator %P means that P holds under all extensions of the current memory typing. This operator must be applied at the outermost level of the definition in order to force expression typing to be stable under extension of memory typings. In general, implications to not preserve these sorts of closure properties, even if their subexpressions do, making this additional operator necessary.

The next major piece of the definition is the quantification over all valid memories. The predicate `mtype_valid` is defined below.

Program Definition mtype_valid (m : mem) : pred world :=
  fun w ⇒
  match w with (k, v) ⇒
   let (n,φ) := unsquash k in
    ∀ (a : addr),
      match φ a with
      | None ⇒ fst m <= a
      | Some τ ⇒ fst m > a ∧ (%▷τ) (k, deref m a)
      end
  end.
Next Obligation. ... **Qed**.

Unpacking the notation, what `mtype_valid` *m* means is that, for each address *a* in the domain of the current memory typing, the value at *a* has type $\% \triangleright \tau$, where τ is the type recorded in the memory typing at location a. Furthermore, locations not in the domain of the memory typing are unallocated. In other words, the memory m is correctly described by the current memory typing.

So, we are next ready to examine the two conjuncts in the definition of expr_type. The first says that for each valid memory m, and for each expression configuration (e', m') that can be reached from (e, m) via one step of computation, there is some extended memory typing such that, up to approximation, m' is valid for that memory typing and e' (recursively) has type τ. The operator diamond contractsM is the dual form of $\%$ and means "there exists an extended memory typing making the predicate true." It is assigned no special notation because it is used only here in the proof.

The second conjunct states that if the configuration (e, m) cannot take any further steps, then it must be that e is a value and that value has type $\% \tau$. As noted above, these two conjuncts correspond to the "preservation" and "progress" properties from standard type safety arguments.

At first, the operator that allows us to extend the memory typing may seem a bit mysterious. It is needed to account for the fact that stepping from (e, m) to (e', m') may have allocated a new reference. In order to account for this new reference, we must allow the memory typing to be extended with a new entry for that cell's type. As we shall see below, this operator gives a neat explaination for why something like the value restriction becomes necessary when we consider polymorphic types.

Now that we have defined expression typing, we are ready to define the funtion type.

Definition ty_lam (τ_1 τ_2 : pred world) : pred world :=
    EX e:expr, EX H:closed' 1 e, just (v_Lam e H) &&
    $\triangleright \%$(ALL v':value, with_val v' ($\% \tau_1$) $\longrightarrow$ expr_type (subst 0 v' e) τ_2).

As with the other operators, we begin by stating that the value must syntactically be a lambda; furthermore, the enclosed expression has exactly one free variable. The meat of the definition states that (under approximation and extension) whenever we substitute a value of type τ_1 into the body of the lambda expression, we get an *expression* of type τ_2.

With this definition made, we are now almost done with the core definitions making up our type system. All that remains is to define the typing judgment itself. The typing judgment has a similar feel to the typing definition for lambdas: informally, we say $\Gamma \vdash e : \tau$ holds if, whenever we substitute values of the types given in Γ for the free variables of e, the resulting expression is of type τ.

Definition env : Type := list value.

Fixpoint subst_env' (n : nat) (rho : env) (exp : expr) : expr :=
    match rho **with**
    | nil ⇒ exp
    | v :: vx ⇒ subst n v (subst_env' (n + 1) vx exp)
    end.

Definition subst_env (rho : env) (exp : expr) : expr :=
    subst_env' 0 rho exp.

Definition etype : Type := list (pred world).

Fixpoint etype_valid (e : env) (G : etype) : pred world :=
    match (e,G) **with**
    | (v :: es, τ :: Gs) ⇒ with_val v (%τ) && etype_valid es Gs
    | (nil, nil) ⇒ TT
    | _ ⇒ FF
    end.

Definition Typ (G : etype) (exp : expr) (τ : pred world) : Prop :=
    closed' (length G) exp ∧
    ∀ env, etype_valid env G ⊢ expr_type (subst_env env exp) τ.

In this definition (subst_env env exp) refers to the result of simultaneously substituting all the values in env into the expression exp.

FINALLY WE ARE DONE STATING THE DEFINITIONS leading up to our type system. Now we have two remaining tasks ahead of us: we must prove *soundness*—

that well-typed programs do not go wrong—and we must prove that the standard typing rules are valid. Let us examine the first task, as it is much easier. We specifically designed the typing system to prove soundness, so that property is deeply "baked-in" to the system. This proof goes in two steps. First we show that well-typed expressions are safe to run for n steps, where n is the level of the world in which the expression is safe.

Lemma expr_type_safen: $\forall$ k v e τ,
  expr_type e τ (k,v) $\rightarrow$
  $\forall$ m, mtype_valid m (k,v) $\rightarrow$ safen (level k) (m,e).

This lemma is really the core of the entire soundess proof. It is here that we do induction on the level of worlds, and it is here that the entire step-indexing strategy finally comes together. The proof itself, however, is fairly short and uneventful, consisting mostly of bookeeping. By and large, it involves unfolding the various definitions and exploiting the progress and preservation facts built into the definition of `expr_type`.

The final theorem puts all the pieces together to show that expressions typeable in the empty context are safe programs.

Theorem typing_implies_safety: $\forall$ e τ, Typ nil e τ $\rightarrow$ safe_prog e.

The key step in this proof is to show that for a program to be safe, it is sufficent for it to be safe up to n steps, for all n and for all memories m. Then, given an arbitrary n, we can construct an initial world such that expr_type e τ holds on that world, as does mtype_valid m. Then we can apply the previous lemma to complete the proof.

Thus we have shown that program safety follows from typeability in the empty context—this theorem was the aim of all the definitions occuring previously. Note that we have not yet said anything about typing rules. Unlike in a syntactic proof, where the typing rules define the judgment, here the rules are instead consequences of the definitions.

To ensure we have not defined a useless typing system, we prove the standard typing rules of the lambda calculus with references. A selection of the rules we have proved for this system are listed below; the form of these rules should be unsurprising.

Lemma T_weaken : ∀ G G' e τ, Typ G e τ → Typ (G++G') e τ.

Lemma T_Nat : ∀ G n, Typ G (Nat n) ty_nat.

Lemma T_Var: ∀ G x τ,
nth_error G x = Some τ *(* G(x) = τ *)* → Typ G (Var x) τ.

Lemma T_Abs: ∀ G σ e τ,
Typ (σ :: G) e τ → Typ G (Lam e) (ty_lam σ τ).

Lemma T_App: ∀ G e1 σ τ e2,
Typ G e1 (ty_lam σ τ) → Typ G e2 σ → Typ G (App e1 e2) τ.

Lemma T_New: ∀ G e τ,
Typ G e τ → Typ G (New e) (ty_ref τ).

Lemma T_Deref: ∀ G e τ,
Typ G e (ty_ref τ) → Typ G (Deref e) τ.

Lemma T_Update: ∀ G e1 τ e2 e3 σ,
Typ G e1 (ty_ref τ) → Typ G e2 τ → Typ G e3 σ →
Typ G (Update e1 e2 e3) σ.

By and large, these proofs break down three recognizable parts. For syntactic forms containing expressions, one has to show that typing respects the congruence rules of the operational semantics; this part of the proof is largely routine. The other two parts occur when a term resembling a redex occurs. For such terms, one must show that the reduced expression has the same type as the original and one must show that the redex is not stuck. In other words, there is a progress and a preservation aspect to each of the typing rule proofs.

ONCE THE BASIC TYPING RULES are established, the story is not yet over. Because the meaning of types and the typing jugement are given by definition, nothing prevents us from adding additional types and rules after the fact. Unlike with a syntactic proof, we need not worry that our additions will break any parts of the previous proof—there are no complicated induction hypotheses that may need to be adjusted.

As an example of this property, here we define additional type constructors related to polymorphism. In fact, for universal polymorphism, there is not much to do. The universal quantification operator we have been using in the logic over worlds serves this role! We must simply prove the characteristic rules for universal introduction and elimination.

Lemma T_UnivI : ∀ G e (X:pred world → pred world),
   openValue e → (∀ τ, Typ G e (X τ)) → Typ G e (allp X).

Lemma T_UnivE : ∀ G e (X:pred world → pred world) τ,
   Typ G e (allp X) → Typ G e (X τ).

The elimination rule for universals is totally standard: if one has a term of universal type, then one instantiates the universal type with an arbitrarily chosen instance type. The introduction rule is also standard: to prove a term has universal type, it suffices to prove it has the same type with an arbitrary type variable.

However, notice that the universal introduction rule only applies for expressions that are open values, that is, expressions that are of one of the three value forms, but that may contain free variables. This is the usual "value restriction" from ML [89]. It (or some other restriction, e.g., the "imperative" type discipline of Tofte [86]) is necessary because the rule without any restriction is unsound! It is not hard to show that unrestricted universal generalization in a calculus with references leads to an unsound type system; examples demonstrating this are well known [86].

Despite this fact, it is interesting to *attempt* to prove the unsound rule in order to understand where the proof breaks down. Unfolding the definitions far enough, one eventually finds expression typing hiding underneath. In the recursive clause of expression typing there appears the "diamond" operator that allows the memory typing to extend. Unwinding *its* definition, we find that it is basically an existential quantifier. One way of reading the unsound universal generalization rule is in terms of manipulating formulae: it says that a universal quantifier can be "pushed inside" the definition of expression typing. This works as long as all the elements of the definition commute with universal quantifiers. However, this existential quantifier blocks the universal quantifier from traveling inward. It is not sound in general to push a universal quantifier inside an existential quantifier. From the hypothesis, one knows that for each τ there exists some sound way to extend the memory typing, but you *need* the stronger fact that there is some way to extend the memory typing that is sound for every type τ. That is, the memory type extension must be uniformly chosen.

The counterexamples regarding unrestricted universal generalization attack exactly the issue raised by this quantifier inversion. They always involve setting up a reference cell with a polymorphic type and using the same reference cell at two distinct types. This makes it so that there is no uniform choice that can be made about the cell's typing and unsoundness follows.

With this understanding, it becomes easy to see why the value restriction works. By only considering values, we can discharge the recursive clause of expression typing via contradiction. This avoids the need to do unsound quantifier manipulations and allows the proof to go through. More complicated systems, such as Tofte's imperative typing discipline, essentially require that a term not allocate any new references with free variables for that term to be polymorphic. This restriction ensures that a uniform choice can be made about how to extend store typings.

Chapter 37

Higher-order Hoare logic

In an ordinary Hoare logic we have first-order assertions, and we may also have quantifiers over first-order values. For more expressive specification of programs in more expressive languages—recursive types, recursive predicates, function-pointer specifications, objects—we want higher-order features in our program logic. Such higher-order features can be difficult to construct models for, and we do want models so that we can prove soundness of the program logic.

We will make use of indirection theory's concept of an *approximation* or *aging* operator $\triangleright P$, pronounced "later P". We define $x \models \triangleright P$ if, whenever $\mathrm{age}^+(x, x')$ then $x' \models P$. Clearly, $\triangleright P$ is a more approximate predicate than P, since it looks at elements that are less informative (and if $\mathrm{level}(x) = 0$, then $\triangleright P$ is simply true).

Hoare-logic assertions operate on states containing local variables, memories, function-pointers, and mutex locks. But only some of these components of the state are associated with assertions or predicates: namely, the function-pointers and mutex locks. It is only these components that are affected by aging: the associated assertions become more approximate. Meanwhile, aging does not alter "ordinary" state components such as integer and pointer values stored in local variables and memory.

WE BEGIN A LOGIC OF AGEABLE PREDICATES with the entailment operator $\vdash$, pronounced derives:

Definition derives {A} `{ageable A} (P Q:pred A) :=   ∀ a:A, P a → Q a.

Notation "P '|--' Q" := (derives P Q) (at level 80, no associativity).

Here are some very generic lemmas that follow from the definition of derives:[1]

$$\text{equiv\_eq} \frac{P \vdash Q \qquad Q \vdash P}{P = Q} \qquad\qquad \text{derives\_cut} \frac{P \vdash Q \qquad Q \vdash R}{P \vdash R}$$

Even before we populate the logic with "interesting" operators, we can write down the basic connectives such as true, false, and, or, implication.

Program Definition TT {A} `{ageable A}: pred A := fun a:A ⇒ True.
Next Obligation. split; auto. **Qed**.

Program Definition FF {A}`{ageable A}: pred A := fun a:A ⇒ False.
Next Obligation. split; auto. **Qed**.

Program Definition orp {A} `{ageable A} (P Q:pred A) : pred A :=
    fun a:A ⇒ P a ∨ Q a.
Next Obligation. ... **Qed**.

Program Definition andp {A} `{ageable A} (P Q:pred A) : pred A :=
    fun a:A ⇒ P a ∧ Q a.
Next Obligation. ... **Qed**.

Definition necR {A} `{ageable A} : relation A := clos_refl_trans A age.

Program Definition imp {A} `{ageable A} (P Q:pred A) : pred A :=
    fun a:A ⇒ ∀ a':A, necR a a' → P a' → Q a'.

We use Coq's **Program Definition** here, because the left-hand side of each := is supposed to be a pred A, that is, a package containing a function A → Prop and a proof that the function is hereditary; but on the

---

[1]We can write $P = Q$ for the equivalence of assertions because we use Leibniz equality (the axiom of extensionality).

right-hand side of each := we write down only the function. The job of
Program Definition is to let us write tactical proof-scripts of the missing
Obligations, and then it builds the package for us.

The true (TT) and false (FF) predicates are naturally invariant under
aging, as are andp and orp. But a naive definition of implication would not
be. We define the relation "necessary" (necR) that is the reflexive-transitive
closure of the age relation, and force imp to be closed under that relation.

Now we add notation for these operators:

Infix "||" := orp (at level 50, left associativity) : pred.
Infix "&&" := andp (at level 40, left associativity) : pred.
Notation "P '-->' Q" := (imp P Q) (at level 55, right associativity): pred.
Notation "P '<-->' Q" := (andp (imp P Q) (imp Q P))
$\qquad\qquad\qquad\qquad\qquad$ (at level 57, no associativity) : pred.

One can prove the usual inference lemmas on the propositional connectives;
there is no need to show more than a couple of examples here:

$$\text{modus\_ponens}\frac{}{P\mathbin{\&\&}(P\to Q)\vdash Q}\qquad\qquad \text{andp\_right}\frac{X\vdash P\qquad X\vdash Q}{X\vdash P\mathbin{\&\&}Q}$$

OUR LOGIC IS *modal*, in that the "later" operator ▷ is a mode, and there will
be other modes as well. In fact, there is a whole system of modalities: any
relation that commutes with age can form a modality. That is, a modality is
a package of a relation plus a proof that it commutes with age.

Definition valid_rel {A} `{ageable A} (R:relation A) : Prop :=
$\qquad$ commut A age R ∧ commut A R age.

Definition modality {A} `{ageable A} := sig valid_rel.

Definition app_mode {A} `{ageable A} (m:modality) : A → A → Prop :=
$\qquad$ proj1_sig m.
Definition mode_valid {A} `{ageable A} (m:modality) := proj2_sig m.
Global Opaque modality.
Coercion app_mode : modality >-> Funclass.

Program Definition box {A}`{ageable A}(M:modality)(P:pred A): pred A
:= fun a:A ⇒ ∀a', M a a' → P a'.

We define modality over ageable types, not just any type that happens to have an age relation, because we want to ensure that age follows the laws of the ageable class. The coercion app_mode allows us to elide the projection from the modality package. Finally, for any modality M, we have a modal operator $\square_M$ such that $x \models \square_M(P)$ whenever, in all worlds x' reachable from P using the app_mode(M) relation, the assertion P holds.

The relation laterR, which is just the transitive closure of the age relation, (obviously) commutes with age, so it can form a modality that we call laterM:

Definition laterR {A} {EQ: Equiv A} `{Age A} : relation A :=
        clos_trans A age.
Lemma valid_rel_later {A} `{ageable A} : valid_rel laterR.

Definition laterM {A} `{ageable A} : modality :=
        exist _ laterR valid_rel_later.

Notation " '|>' e" := (box laterM e) (at level 30, right associativity): pred.

In fact, necR also commutes with age and therefore forms a modality, but we do not need an explicit operator for it, because every assertion would be invariant under the application of this operator. Also, age commutes with age, therefore forms a modality; but $\square_{\text{ageM}}$ turns out to be equivalent to $\square_{\text{laterM}}$, so the ageM modality adds nothing new to our system.

We write ▹P, or in Coq the notation |> P, for the mode "later P".

THE MODAL OPERATORS BUILT FROM box behave as they should in a modal logic, satisfying axioms such as these:

$$\text{axiomK} \frac{}{\square_M(P \to Q) \vdash \square_M P \ \to \ \square_M Q} \qquad \text{box\_positive} \frac{P \vdash Q}{\square_M P \vdash \square_M Q}$$

$$\text{box\_and} \frac{}{\square_M(P \ \&\& \ Q) \ = \ \square_M P \ \&\& \ \square_M Q} \qquad \text{box\_or} \frac{}{\square_M(P \ \| \ Q) \ = \ \square_M P \ \| \ \square_M Q}$$

Since ▷ is just $\Box_{\mathsf{laterM}}$, these rules all apply to the "later" operator. In addition, there are some rules specifically about ▷ itself.

$$\text{now\_later}\,\frac{}{P \vdash \triangleright P} \qquad \text{later\_commute}\,\frac{}{\Box_M \triangleright P \;=\; \triangleright \Box_M P} \qquad \text{loeb}\,\frac{\triangleright P \vdash P}{\vdash P}$$

The Loeb rule[2] is the most important thing about the ▷ operator. It is a rule for induction over recursive types. We use it in Chapters 36, 19, and 39.

Existential and universal quantifiers are modeled in the ageable Hoare logic almost exactly as they were in the ageless logic of Chapter 8. As before, we use the variable-binding machinery of the enclosing logical framework to implement binding in our embedded logic.

Program Definition allp{A}`{ageable A}{B: Type}(f: B→ pred A): pred A
    := fun a ⇒ ∀ b, f b a.
Next Obligation. ... **Qed**.

Program Definition exp{A}`{ageable A}{B: Type}(f: B→ pred A): pred A
    := fun a ⇒ ∃ b, f b a.
Next Obligation. ... **Qed**.

Notation " 'ALL' x ':' T ',' P " := (allp (fun x:T ⇒ P%pred))
                           (at level 65, x at level 99) : pred.
Notation " 'EX' x ':' T ',' P " := (exp (fun x:T ⇒ P%pred))
                           (at level 65, x at level 99) : pred.

Also as before, we define a prop operator for embedding Coq propositions into our assertion language:

Program Definition prop {A}`{ageable A}(P: Prop): pred A :=
      (fun _⇒ P).
Next Obligation. repeat intro. intuition. **Qed**.
Notation "'!!' e" := (prop e) (at level 25) : pred.

---

[2]Martin H. Löb, 1921–2006, proved *Löb's theorem* in 1955. We use $\triangleright P$ meaning "approximately P"; Löb used *Bew*($\#P$) meaning "the formula with Gödel number $\#P$ is provable."

SO FAR WE HAVE THE BEGINNINGS of Hoare logic that is *higher-order* in two distinct ways: The existential and universal quantifiers are *impredicative higher-order;* and assertions can predicate over assertions. Let's take these one at a time.

(1) First-order logic allows quantification only over base types such as the integers. Higher-order logic allows quantification over predicates, for example,[3]

$$Q(x : \text{nat}) = \forall P : (\text{nat} \to \text{Prop}). \; P(x) \vee P(x + 1).$$

A *predicative* higher-order logic stratifies the predicates, with base (quantifier-free) formulas at level 0, and formulas at level $n + 1$ can quantify only over predicates of level n or less. An *impredicative* logic does not stratify, so that any quantifier can be instantiated with any other predicate of the right type, regardless of its internal quantification.

The semantics of predicative logics are often easier to model, but for reasoning about real programming languages (such as the closures of functional languages or the instance variables of object-oriented languages) we need impredicative logics [82, §2.2]. The quantification in our Verified Software Toolchain is the more powerful kind, *impredicative*.

In fact, even the "ageless" separation logic of Chapter 8 can quantify at higher types. But that quantification becomes much more interesting and powerful when combined with *indirection*, that is—

(2) In a language with function pointers (or method-containing objects or higher-order functions), we would like to *specify* a function-pointer in an assertion by giving its pre- and postconditions (or, similarly, its type). For example, if f is a function-pointer to any of several functions that all return even numbers when passed odd numbers, then we can write approximately the following Hoare triple:

$$\{f : \{\text{odd}\}\{\text{even}\} \wedge x = 2y\} \; z := f(x + 1) \; \{\exists i. z = 2i\}$$

---

[3]The predicate Q is not meant to be *useful*, as of course it is always false.

where $f : \{odd\}\{even\}$ is a function specification with precondition $\{odd\}$ and $\{even\}$. Function specifications can and should be more expressive than the sketch shown here; see Chapters 18 and 24.

When an assertion $R = \{f : \{P\}\{Q\}\}$ can characterize the bindings of other assertions P and Q to an address f, paradoxes can appear if we are not careful, especially in the presence of recursive functions, and when a pointer to f can be passed as an argument to function f. Here the step-indexing power of indirection theory is really useful; Chapter 39 shows how to construct models of higher-order program logics from the primitives of indirection theory.

Chapter 38

Higher-order separation logic

To our higher-order Hoare logic, we can add the operators (such as $*$) of separation logic. We are working here in the semantic framework (separation algebras), so when we write the notation $P \wedge Q$ we mean that P and Q are (ageable) predicates over an element type A. A type-class instance {agA: ageable A} is implicit in this formulation.

For separation $P * Q$ there must also be (implicitly) a join relation {JA: Join A}. When a type has both a separation algebra and an age relation, these must interact according to the axioms of the Age_alg class:

Class Age_alg (A:Type) {JOIN: Join A}{as_age : ageable A} := mkAge {
    age1_join : $\forall$ x {y z x'}, join x y z $\rightarrow$ age x x' $\rightarrow$
                    $\exists$ y':A, $\exists$ z':A, join x' y' z' $\wedge$ age y y' $\wedge$ age z z'
; age1_join2 : $\forall$ x {y z z'}, join x y z $\rightarrow$ age z z' $\rightarrow$
                    $\exists$ x':A, $\exists$ y':A, join x' y' z' $\wedge$ age x x' $\wedge$ age y y'
; unage_join : $\forall$ x {x' y' z'}, join x' y' z' $\rightarrow$ age x x' $\rightarrow$
                    $\exists$ y:A, $\exists$ z:A, join x y z $\wedge$ age y y' $\wedge$ age z z'
; unage_join2 : $\forall$ z {x' y' z'}, join x' y' z' $\rightarrow$ age z z' $\rightarrow$
                    $\exists$ x:A, $\exists$ y:A, join x y z $\wedge$ age x x' $\wedge$ age y y'
}.

The axioms of Age_alg explain that the age relation must commute with the join relation in all the ways shown.

So, in order to prove that $P * Q$ is a well-behaved predicate, i.e. that it is preserved under aging, we require also that join commutes with age as specified by the Age_alg axioms. Thus we have,

Program Definition sepcon
$\qquad$ {A}{JA: Join A}{PA: Perm_alg A}{AG: ageable A}{XA: Age_alg A}
$\qquad$ (p q:pred A) : pred A :=
fun x:A $\Rightarrow$ $\exists$y:A, $\exists$z:A, join y z x $\wedge$ p y $\wedge$ q z.

Next Obligation.
$\quad$ destruct H0 as [y [z [H0 [? ?]]]].
$\quad$ destruct (age1_join2 _ H0 H) as [w [v [? [? ?]]]].
$\quad$ exists w; exists v; split; auto.
$\quad$ split.
$\quad$ apply pred_hereditary **with** y; auto.
$\quad$ apply pred_hereditary **with** z; auto.
Qed.

Notation "P '$*$' Q" := (sepcon P Q) : pred.

This is a Program Definition, not just a Definition, because there is the proof obligation that $P * Q$ is hereditary over the age relation. The proof script uses age1_join2 (from Age_alg) and pred_hereditary (from ageable).

$\quad$ Lemmas about the operators of separation logic will need all of these typeclass-instance parameters, and in addition will typically need the axioms of permission algebras or separation algebras. For example, the associativity of $*$ relies on the associativity of join, which is found in Perm_alg:

Lemma sepcon_assoc {A}{JA: Join A}{PA: Perm_alg A}{AG: ageable A}{XA: Age_alg A}:
$\qquad$ $\forall$(P Q R:pred A), $\quad$ (P $*$ Q) $*$ R $=$ P $*$ (Q $*$ R)
Proof. ... **Qed.**

$\quad$ Although in this text we will present many of these lemmas in a more "mathematical" style,

$$\text{sepcon\_assoc}\frac{}{(P * Q) * R = P * (Q * R)} \qquad \text{sepcon\_comm}\frac{}{P * Q = Q * P}$$

one must remember that they are typeclass-parametrized out the wazoo,[1]

_____

[1] to use a technical term

which will cause Coq proof-scripts to fail if the required typeclass instances do not exist.

As in the first-order case (Chapter 8), emp is sensible only in cancellative separation algebras: an element satisfies emp iff it is an identity.

Program Definition emp
$\quad$ {A}{JA: Join A}{PA: Perm_alg A}{AG: ageable A}{XA: Age_alg A}
$\qquad\qquad$: pred A $\qquad$:= identity.
Next Obligation. ... **Qed**.

The Age_alg requirement that aging must interact gracefully with separation allow us to prove these rules:

$$\text{later\_sepcon}\frac{}{\triangleright(P * Q) = \triangleright P * \triangleright Q} \qquad \text{later\_wand}\frac{}{\triangleright(P \mathbin{-\!\!*} Q) = (\triangleright P) \mathbin{-\!\!*} (\triangleright Q)}$$

THE CONSEQUENCES OF COMBINING indirection theory (ageable) with separation (Join, Perm_alg, etc.) follow straightfowardly from the commutation axioms (Age_alg). There are a few small surprises, as we will now explain.

WE CAN DEFINE MAGIC WANDS (universal and existential) in ageable separation logics. We find that wand needs explicit quantification over future worlds x', while ewand has a definition that is practically identical to the first-order case.

Program Definition wand {A}{JA: Join A}{AG: ageable A} (p q:pred A) : pred A :=
$\quad$ fun x $\Rightarrow$ $\forall$ x' y z, necR x x' $\rightarrow$ join x' y z $\rightarrow$ p y $\rightarrow$ q z.

Program Definition ewand
$\qquad$ {A}{JA: Join A}{PA: Perm_alg A}{AG: ageable A}{XA: Age_alg A}
$\qquad$ (P Q: pred A) : pred A :=
$\quad$ fun w $\Rightarrow$ $\exists$ w1, $\exists$ w2, join w1 w w2 $\wedge$ P w1 $\wedge$ Q w2.

EACH UNIT ELEMENT of an ASA, because it is an element of an ageable type, has a level; and elements with different levels are not equal. Thus, an ASA is naturally a multi-unit separation algebra.

Product operators. Because every ageable separation algebra (ASA) is also a separation algebra (SA), one can apply the SA operators such as Cartesian product (see Chapter 7). But often one wants the result to be an ASA, not just an SA. So we need some operators on ASAs. Age_prod gives the cartesian product ASA of a SA with an ASA: the age operator can applies to the ASA component while leaving the SA component alone. We have not found the product of two ASAs (with possibly different ages) useful.

The trivial ASA. Sometimes we have separation-logic formulas that are not predicates on particular elements, but behave more like modal propositions that are true on all elements of a certain level. To fit these into our framework, we treat them as assertions over the Triv ASA whose elements have no more to them than a level. Here, the join relation is join_equiv, meaning that each element joins only with itself (and is a unit for itself); the age relation is decrement; and the level of an element is itself.

The logic of ageable predicates was presented in Chapter 15 (the Indir and SepIndir classes) and Chapter 16 (the RecIndir class). The file msl/alg_seplog.v demonstrates that ageable separation algebras provide a model for this logic. The axioms of Indir are the Löb rule, plus the commutation of ▷later with universal and existential quantifiers and with implication; these laws are proved in msl/predicates_hered.v. The axioms of SepIndir are the commutation of ▷ with $*, -\!\!*, -\!\circ$; these are proved in msl/predicates_sl.v. The axioms of RecIndir concern the fash operator, written #, and its interaction with other operators; these are proved in msl/subtypes.v. Finally, the SepRec class (page 103) has one axiom showing how the unfash operator distributes over separation; this is proved in msl/subtypes_sl.v. In addition, such a model must include a Triv class (page 100) and the fash_triv axiom (that $\#P = P$ for all P in Triv); these are in msl/alg_seplog.v.

The special power of ageable separation algebras is that they can build models of quasi-self-referential *resource maps* for modeling higher-order separation logics. We will demonstrate this in the next chapter.

Chapter 39

Semantic models of predicates in the heap

Our Hoare logic of separation is quasicircular in two ways. (1) An assertion R can characterize the binding of an address to another assertion P, or even to the same assertion R (using a recursively defined predicate). (2) In proving the correctness of (mutually) recursive functions, one can assume the specifications of functions f, g in the proof that function-bodies f, g meet their specifications.

HOW DOES ONE BUILD SEMANTIC MODELS FOR SUCH LOGICS? In Part VI we will present the semantic model for the Verifiable C logic, but in this chapter we present the basic ideas in a much simpler setting. Recall the tiny continuation-language with first-class functions, and its separation logic, from Chapter 18. That Hoare judgment had rules such as,

$$\text{semax\_assign}\frac{\Delta \vdash_{\text{type}} y \qquad x, \Delta; \Gamma \vdash \{P\}c}{\Delta; \Gamma \vdash \{\triangleright P[y/x]\}\, x := y; c}$$

$$\text{semax\_func\_cons}\frac{x \notin \text{map fst } \vec{F} \qquad \text{no\_dups}(\vec{y}) \qquad |\vec{y}| = |\text{formals}(S)| \\ \vec{y}; \Gamma \vdash \{\text{call } S\ \vec{y}\}c \qquad \Gamma \vdash_{\text{func}} \vec{F} : \Gamma'}{\Gamma \vdash_{\text{func}} \langle x, \vec{y}.c \rangle :: \vec{F}\ :\ \langle x, S \rangle :: \Gamma'}$$

for the assignment statement and for a function-body, respectively.

The semax_func_cons rule concludes that the function-body $\langle x, \vec{y}.c \rangle$ satisfies the specification $\langle x, S \rangle$. The main premise is that $\vec{y}; \Gamma \vdash \{\text{call } S \; \vec{y}\} c$, that is, that $S(\vec{y})$ is an adequate precondition for the safety of the function-body, command c. Let us examine that premise more closely:

$$\vec{y}; \Gamma \vdash \{\text{call } S \; \vec{y}\} c$$

On the left-hand side we have $\vec{y}$, saying that the formal parameters $\vec{y}$ are available for c to use; and we have Γ, containing function-specifications for calls to global functions. The function-spec S is $\langle \vec{x}, P \rangle$ with formals $\vec{x}$ and precondition $P : \text{env} \to \text{pred(rmap)}$. On the right hand side, the assertion call $S \; \vec{y}$ applies P to an environment formed by binding $\vec{y}$ to $\vec{x}$, producing a precondition for the function-body c.

We use the power of indirection theory to build a semantic model, and prove soundness, for such Hoare judgments. First we will construct a semantic model of resource maps (rmap), and define assertions as ageable predicates on rmap. Then we construct a semantic model for the Hoare judgment, $\vec{y}; \Gamma \vdash \{P\} c$. (Recall that in a continuation-based language, there are no postconditions, so we have Hoare "doubles" instead of "triples.")

THE THEORY OF RESOURCE MAPS, Module Type RMAPS (Figures 39.1–39.3), has a model constructed in the file msl/rmaps.v. RMAPS is parameterized over an AV structure, which defines an address type and a kind type. Just as a *memory* maps addresses to values, an rmap maps addresses to resources of different *kinds*. In a typical application, one of the kinds will be VAL(v) with a value v (see examples/cont/model.v). But there can be other kinds as well, for function-specifications attached to function-pointers, for locks (semaphores), and so on.

Figure 39.1 shows that the theory RMAPS concerns the type rmap, over which there is a cancellative ageable separation algebra with disjointness. There is also a type resource, with the empty resource NO, a spatial resource YES, and a PURE resource. There is a disjoint cancellative ageable separation separation algebra over resource, such that NO is a unit for both NO and YES, and every PURE resource is a unit for itself. Both YES and PURE resources carry a *kind* and some *predicates*. In a typical

Module Type RMAPS.
Declare Module AV:ADR_VAL. **Import** AV.

Parameter rmap : Type.
Axiom Join_rmap: Join rmap.   **Axiom** Perm_rmap: Perm_alg rmap.
Axiom Sep_rmap: Sep_alg rmap.   **Axiom** Canc_rmap: Canc_alg rmap.
Axiom Disj_rmap: Disj_alg rmap.
Axiom ag_rmap: ageable rmap.   **Axiom** Age_rmap: Age_alg rmap.

Inductive preds : Type :=
    SomeP : ∀A : list Type, (listprod A → pred rmap) → preds.
Definition NoneP := SomeP ((Void:Type)::nil) (fun _ ⇒ FF).

Inductive resource : Type := NO : resource
                                    | YES: pshare → kind → preds → resource
                                    | PURE: kind → preds → resource.

Inductive res_join : resource → resource → resource → Prop :=
 | res_join_NO1 : res_join NO NO NO
 | res_join_NO2 : ∀ π k p, res_join (YES π k p) NO (YES π k p)
 | res_join_NO3 : ∀ π k p, res_join NO (YES π k p) (YES π k p)
 | res_join_YES : ∀ (π₁ π₂ π₃: pshare) k p, join π₁ π₂ π₃ →
        res_join (YES π₁ k p) (YES π₂ k p) (YES π₃ k p)
 | res_join_PURE : ∀k p, res_join (PURE k p) (PURE k p) (PURE k p).

Instance Join_resource: Join resource := res_join.
Axiom Perm_resource: Perm_alg resource.
Axiom Sep_resource: Sep_alg resource.
Axiom Canc_resource: Canc_alg resource.
Axiom Disj_resource: Disj_alg resource.

Figure 39.1: Module Type RMAPS, part 1

Definition preds_fmap (f:pred rmap → pred rmap) (x:preds) : preds :=
match x **with** SomeP A Q ⇒ SomeP A (f oo Q) **end**.

Definition resource_fmap (f:pred rmap→ pred rmap) (x:resource) :=
match x **with** NO ⇒ NO
       | YES π k p ⇒ YES π k (preds_fmap f p)
       | PURE k p ⇒ PURE k (preds_fmap f p)
end.

Definition valid(m: address→ resource):Prop:= AV.valid(res_option oo m).
Definition rmap' := sig valid.

Definition rmap_fmap (f: pred rmap → pred rmap) (x:rmap') : rmap' :=
match x **with** exist m H ⇒ exist (fun m ⇒ valid m)
               (resource_fmap f oo m) (valid_res_map f m H) **end**.
Axiom rmap_fmap_id : rmap_fmap (id _) = id rmap'.
Axiom rmap_fmap_comp : ∀f g,
      rmap_fmap g oo rmap_fmap f = rmap_fmap (g oo f).

Parameter squash : (nat ∗ rmap') → rmap.
Parameter unsquash : rmap → (nat ∗ rmap').

Axiom rmap_level_eq: @level rmap _= fun x ⇒ fst (unsquash x).
Axiom rmap_age1_eq: @age1 _ _=
    fun k ⇒ **match** unsquash k **with**
| (O,_) ⇒ None
| (S n,x) ⇒ Some (squash (n,x))
end.

Definition resource_at (ϕ:rmap) : address → resource :=
         proj1_sig (snd (unsquash ϕ)).
Infix "@" := resource_at (at level 50, no associativity).

Figure 39.2: Module Type RMAPS, part 2

Instance Join_nat_rmap': Join (nat * rmap') :=
   Join_prod _(Join_equiv nat) _ _.

Axiom join_unsquash : $\forall \phi 1\ \phi 2\ \phi 3$,
   join $\phi 1\ \phi 2\ \phi 3$ ↔
   join (unsquash $\phi 1$) (unsquash $\phi 2$) (unsquash $\phi 3$).

Definition rmap_unage (k:rmap) : rmap :=
   match unsquash k **with** (n,x) ⇒ squash (S n, x) **end**.

Program Definition approx (n:nat) (p: pred rmap) : pred rmap :=
   fun w ⇒ level w < n ∧ p w.
Next Obligation. ... **Qed**.

Axiom squash_unsquash : $\forall \phi$, squash (unsquash ϕ) = ϕ.
Axiom unsquash_squash : $\forall$ n rm,
      unsquash (squash (n,rm)) = (n,rmap_fmap (approx n) rm).
End RMAPS.

Figure 39.3: Module Type RMAPS, part 3

application, the VAL kind will be carried by a YES resource with the trivial predicates, NoneP. That is, we permit "predicates in the heap" but a VAL has no interesting predicates.

   YES resources *separate*—that is, YES $\pi_1 k_1 p_1$ ⊕ YES $\pi_2 k_2 p_2$ = YES $\pi_3 k_3 p_3$ if and only if $\pi_1 \oplus \pi_2 = \pi_3$ and $k_1 = k_2 = k_3, p_1 = p_2 = p_3$. Since we use   YES • (VAL v) NoneP   to model the value v in memory, this rule for ⊕ leads to the expected behavior of memory cells in separation logic. On the other hand, PURE resources join only with themselves, and do not obey the rule for separation. Since we use PURE(FUN $\vec{y}$)P to model function specifications—where $\vec{y}$ are the formal parameters and P is the function precondition—this rule for ⊕ leads to the expected behavior of "timeless, eternal" function specifications in Hoare logic. (If we wanted run-time code generation, we would have to use YES for FUN resources, which would mean more bookkeeping for user-level proofs.)

Predicates in the heap are modeled by the inductive datatype preds with a single constructor SomeP. In some applications we want a simple predicate on rmaps, of type pred rmap. In other applications, we want the predicate to have more arguments: For the *cont* language, a function-precondition predicate must also see the list of actual-parameter values. In our Verifiable C program logic, in addition to the actual parameters the precondition predicate must also see the extra "specification variables" that relate the precondition to the postcondition—for example, the variables π, σ in reverse_spec on page 198. Therefore SomeP is a dependent product: the first argument A is a list of the Types of the extra parameters, and the second argument has type listprod $A \to$ pred rmap, where listprod simply makes the cartesian product type of all the elements of A.

When no interesting predicates are desired, one can simply use $A=$(Void:Type)::nil and set the predicate itself to False; this is what the definition NoneP does.

FIGURE 39.2 EXPLAINS THAT, given a predicate-transformer f, the function resource_fmap composes f with the predicates in a resource. We define rmap': a function from address to resource, packaged with a proof that the function is *valid* according to the AV structure.[1] The resource_fmap function must preserve identities and composition, as explained at page 300.

Figure 39.2 continues with the squash and unsquash functions, explained at page 298. We define the resource_at function, which takes an rmap ϕ and an address l and looks up the (approximate) value at l in ϕ. We use @ as infix notation for resource_at.

Figure 39.3 explains how join interacts with unsquash, and how squash and unsquash form a section-retraction (page 298).

---

[1]The notion of AV.valid is a digression from our main story here: it allows the AV structure to impose some structural conditions on how resources may be joined together. In our concurrent separation logic for C, we ensure that a 4-byte word used as a semaphore is not split apart by the join relation. In our *cont*-language example, AV.valid is trivially true. In general, AV.valid must depend only on structural properties derivable from the permission-shares and the kinds, not from the levels or predicates of an rmap. Thus in Figure 39.2 the valid predicate is formed from AV.valid(res_option oo m), where res_option extracts only the share and kind from the resource m(l).

THE MODEL FOR RMAPS is built using indirection theory. Since the "paradox" is that the type rmap contains instances of the type pred which is (approximately) a predicate on rmap, we avoid the paradox by first making a *stratified model* (StratModel in file msl/rmaps.v) in which the entire construction is parameterized by an abstract type PRED instead of the circular type pred. Then we use the stratified model as the parameter to the knot construction (page 311). That is, in module Rmaps we use apply KnotHered module of indirection theory to our stratified model, and the result is the rmap type (with its axioms). We lift the squash-unsquash proofs from the "raw" knot to the rmap type. Then, from the properties of rmap, we derive the axioms of the resource type, and prove that resource maps form a separation algebra.

From the RMAPS axioms, we can derive many useful lemmas about resource maps, some of which are shown in Figure 40.1 and Figure 40.2.[2]

WE DO NOT BUILD OUR PROGRAM LOGIC *directly* on program states. We relate program states to abstract environments and resource maps, partly for reasons explained on page 58 and mainly because the rmaps contain richer specification information than is available in the concrete states. That is:

	Concrete state	Abstract state	
Functions	p: program	—	
Func. Specifications	Γ: funspecs	ϕ: rmap	(PURE(FUN) resources)
Local variables	σ': locals	σ: env	
Memory	h: heap	ϕ: rmap	(YES(VAL) resources)
Continuation	k: control	k: control	
State	(σ', h, k)	k, σ, ϕ	

The assertion funassert Γ: pred rmap is a predicate on a resource-map ϕ. It says that every address with a specification in Γ is also claimed as a FUN resource in ϕ with the same predicate—and vice versa, every FUN in ϕ is also in Γ.

---

[2] Compared to the RMAPS presented in this chapter, the C light separation logic uses a slightly different version of RMAPS in which a NO resource carries a permission share. This is to model *retainer shares* (page 365). Thus where in this chapter we would write NO, in Figures 40.1 and 40.2 we write NO ∘, with an empty share ∘.

A program state is *safe* if, in the Kleene-closure of the small-step relation, it cannot reach a *stuck* state (a nonhalted state with no successor). In our step-indexed reasoning, make a slightly smaller claim: a program is *safe for N steps* if it cannot reach a stuck state within N small-steps:

Definition safeN (p: program) (sk: state) (n: nat) : Prop :=
∃ sk', stepN p sk n = Some sk'.

We can lift this into our assertion logic as a predicate on abstract states:

Program Definition assert_safe
    (p: program) (V: varset) (k: control) (σ: env): pred rmap :=
fun φ ⇒ ∀ σ' h,
      varcompat V σ' →   locals2env σ' = σ →
      cohere h φ →   safeN p (σ', h, k) (level φ).
Next Obligation. *(∗ prove it is hereditary ∗)* **Qed.**

That is, consider a concrete state $(σ', h, k)$ with local variables $σ'$, heap h, continuation k. Suppose the resource map $φ$ coheres with h, meaning that whenever $h(x) = $ Some v then $φ@x = $ YES • (VAL, v) NoneP, and vice versa. Suppose $σ'$ corresponds to environment $σ$, and all variables in V are mapped in $σ'$. Then it is safe to execute n steps from the state $(σ', h, k)$, where n is the approximation-level of $φ$.

A predicate P guards a continuation k whenever: from any state that satisfies P, it is safe to execute k. Chapter 4 introduced this concept. Here we write it in our indirection-theory logic.

Definition guard (p: program) (Γ: funspecs) (V: varset)
                (P : assert) (k: control) : pred nat :=
  ALL σ:env, P σ && funassert Γ ⇛ assert_safe p V k σ.

That is, in program p with specification-context $Γ$ at control-point k, given any $σ, φ$ such that $Pσφ$ and funassert $Γ φ$, then the state $k, σ, φ$ is safe for level($φ$) steps. The resource-map $φ$ is implicitly quantified by the definition of ⇛ (see Chapter 16).

Next we build the model of the Hoare judgment, $V; Γ ⊢ \{P\}c$, in examples/cont/model.v. Informally it means, "assuming all the function-specifications in Γ can be believed, then P serves as an adequate precondition for the safety of executing the command c." (The variables V are permitted to be free in c and in P.) But the meaning of a specification $(f, [\vec{y}]P)$ in Γ is that $(\Gamma; \vec{y}; P)$ serves as an adequate precondition for executing f. That is, the semax judgment is defined recursively. To make such a (contravariant) recursive definition work, and we use the contravariant recursion operator HORec.

Parameter HORec: $\forall \{A\}\{NA: \text{NatDed } A\}\{IA: \text{Indir } A\}\{RA: \text{RecIndir } A\}$
        $(X: \text{Type}\} \ (F: (X \to A) \to (X \to A)), X \to A.$
Parameter HORec : $\forall \{A\} \ \{Ag: \text{ageable } A\}$
        $\{X: \text{Type}\} \ (F: (X \to \text{pred } A) \to (X \to \text{pred } A)), X \to \text{pred } A.$

The first of these definitions is the *logical* (%logic) view of HORec, described in Chapter 17 (and msl/alg_seplog.v). The second is the *semantic* (%pred) view of the same operator (in msl/predicates_rec.v). During the construction of the semax judgment, we work entirely at the semantic level; at the very end, we abstract to obtain the logical view.

The semax judgment takes parameters Γ, V, P; this triple we will call a semaxArg and it will instantiate the parameter X of HORec.

Record semaxArg : Type :=
  SemaxArg {sa_vars: varset; sa_P: env $\to$ pred rmap; sa_c: control}.

The semax judgment $V; \Gamma \vdash \{P\}c$ is akin to a proposition, a nullary predicate. Thus, where HORec demands a pred(A) on some ageable type A, we use the most trivial A possible: nat. The natural number n serves as the *level* (approximation index).

Definition semax_ (semax: semaxArg$\to$ pred nat)(a: semaxArg): pred nat :=
  match a **with** SemaxArg V P c $\Rightarrow$
      ALL p: program, ALL Γ: funspecs,
      believe_all semax Γ p Γ $\longrightarrow$ guard p Γ V P c
  end.

This says, let semax be some hypothetical model of the Hoare judgment. Then semax_(semax) is a one-level-more-accurate model: Given a program p and its specification Γ, suppose we can believe all the claims that semax makes—that all the functions in p satisfy their specifications in Γ. Then it will be the case that $(V;\Gamma;P)$ guards the safety of executing c.

Definition believe (semax: semaxArg $\rightarrow$ pred nat)
     (p: program) $((\vec{y},P)$: funspec) $(f$: adr) : pred nat :=
  EX $(\vec{x},k)$: list var $*$ control,
   !!(table_get p f = Some k $\wedge$ $|\vec{x}| = |\vec{y}|$) &&
  $\triangleright$semax (SemaxArg $\vec{x}$ (fun $s \Rightarrow$ call $(\vec{y},P)$ (map s $\vec{x}$)) k).

Definition believe_all (semax: semaxArg $\rightarrow$ pred nat) (Γ: funspecs)
                (p: program) (Γ': funspecs) : pred nat :=
  ALL v:adr, ALL $\vec{x}$: list var, ALL P: env$\rightarrow$pred rmap,
   !! (table_get Γ' v = Some $(\vec{x},P)$) $\longrightarrow$
  believe semax p $(\vec{x},$ fun $s \Rightarrow P$ s && funassert Γ) v.

Given a (hypothetical) semax, to believe that the function at address f satisfies the specification $(\vec{y},P)$ means that whenever P is satisfied in some state, it is safe to call the function body k. (The predicate call $(\vec{y},P)$ (map s $\vec{x}$) adjusts P by substituting actuals for formals.)

To believe that *all* functions in Γ' satisfy their specifications—believe_all— is to say that whenever an address v has a specification $(\vec{y},P)$ in Γ', then we can believe that specification relative to Γ. Typically we can expect Γ to be *all* the function specifications of a whole program, and Γ' to be some subset of those specifications, representing the ones proved correct "so far;" see page 122.

We prove that the function semax_ is *contractive*, then use HORec to find a fixed point. What it makes it contractive is the judicious use of $\triangleright$later in the definition of believe. We can afford the $\triangleright$ operator at just that point, because performing a function-call uses up one exection step.

Now that we have a model of the Hoare judgment, we use it to prove correctness of all the inference rules given in Figure 18.1 and on page 122. Each of these rules is derived as a **Lemma** in Coq, following from the definition of semax.

In addition, we prove the *whole-program soundness theorem,* which also follows from the definitions:

Definition program_proved (p: program) :=
   ∃ Γ, semax_func Γ p Γ ∧
      table_get Γ 0 = Some (0::nil, fun σ ⇒ allocpool (eval (Var 0) σ)).

Theorem semax_sound:
   ∀ p, program_proved p → ∀ n, run p n <> None.

The definition program_proved corresponds precisely to the description on page 122.

The proof of every inference rule for semax, and for this soundness theorem, can be found in examples/cont/model.v.

Part VI

Semantic model and soundness of Verifiable C

SYNOPSIS: *To prove soundness of the Verifiable C separation logic, we first give a model of mpred as pred(rmap), that is, predicates on resource maps. We give a model for permission-shares using trees of booleans. We augment the C light operational semantics with juicy memories that keep track of resources as well as "dry" values. We give a semantic model of the Hoare judgment, using the continuation-passing notion of "guards." We use this semantic model to prove all the Hoare rules. Our model and proofs have a modular structure, so that they can be ported to other programming languages (especially in the CompCert family).*

Chapter 40

Separation algebra for CompCert

In building a Hoare logic over a language specified by an operational semantics, we can view the assertions of the Hoare logic as predicates on the states of the operational semantics. But we do this in two layers: first, relate the operational *states* into semantic *worlds*; then, apply the Hoare assertions to the worlds. We do this for several reasons: The operational states may contain information that we want to hide from the Hoare assertions, particularly *control* information (program counter, control stack) that is not supposed to be visible to a Hoare-logic assertion. The semantic worlds may contain information that we want to hide from the operational semantics, such as step-indexes, ghost variables, predicates in the heap (for modeling first-class functions or mutex locks), and permission-shares. For convenience in reasoning, we require Liebniz equality on worlds—equivalent worlds should be equal—but operational states do not generally satisfy Liebniz equality. In our two different toy examples (Chapter 9 and Chapter 39) we have separated operational states from semantic worlds, and we do so for the VST Separation Logic for CompCert C light.

Some components of the world are subject to separating conjunction (∗), and others are not. Generally, to "heap" or "memory" or any other *addressable* component of the world, we apply separation in order to reason about antialiasing. Nonaddressable local variables (and the *addresses* of addressable local variables) do not require separation, because there is no aliasing to worry about.

The *worlds* seen by separation-logic predicates include,

ge Global environment, mapping identifiers to addresses of global (extern) variables and functions. This is extracted from the genv of the operational state, but omits the mapping of function-addresses to function-bodies.

ve Variable environment, mapping identifiers to addresses of addressable local variables, extracted from the ve of the operational-semantic state but represented instead as a function satisfying Liebniz equality. (The index-tree data structure used in the operational semantics does not have unique representations, so we cannot use the axiom of extensionality to reason about it, and we do not wish to use setoids.)

te Temp environment, mapping identifiers to values of ordinary local variables, the conversion of the operational state's ve to a function.

̸k The operational semantics' control contexts are not present in worlds.

̸m Instead of memories, we have,

φ Resource map (of type rmap), giving an enriched view of memory, including step-indexed predicates in the heap. Also, resource maps associate a permission-share (see Chapter 11, Chapter 41) with each address, giving finer distinctions than just "Readable" or "Writable."

An assertion in our Separation Logic has the form environ → mpred where the environ contains $\langle$ge, ve, te$\rangle$, and mpred = pred(rmap). That is, it is a *lifted separation logic* (Chapter 21) where the underlying separation logic has abstract formulas (type mpred) which are modeled by predicates on resource-maps (rmap).

CompCert's memory model has a permission hierarchy that is not just Writable/Readable/None. The permission Freeable is stronger than Writable, giving permission to deallocate the location. The permission Nonempty is weaker than Readable but stronger than None, and assures that no other thread can deallocate the object. In this permission system, one thread can hand off a Writable permission to another thread, while retaining a Nonempty permission that ensures the address stays allocated.

On the other hand, CompCert's Readable permission is not expressive enough to model the kind of permission accounting described in Chapter 11 and Chapter 41. This is not a *bug* in CompCert's specification, since CompCert's permission model is expressive enough for reasoning about compiler correctness—even correctness in compiling sequential threads for concurrent shared-memoryshared memory execution. The inexpressiveness is relevant to *reasoning about source programs.*

Our program logic for reasoning about source programs has a finer-grain permission-share model than does CompCert, and we relate it to the discrete CompCert permission hierarchy. Our *full share*, written as Share.top or notated as •, relates to the strongest possible permission, Freeable. Our *empty share*, Share.bot or ○, gives no permission. The left split of •, that is fst(split(top))=◖◦ models a Nonempty permission. Any nonempty subshare of ◖◦ is called a "retainer," whose purpose is to retain an object from being deallocated.

The right split of T, snd(split(top))=◦◗, models the smallest Writable permission. ("The right share is the write share.") Any share that has a nonempty overlap with ◦◗ is readable, and any share that wholly contains ◦◗ is writable. Any permission share π can be broken into two disjoint pieces, a retainer share ($\pi \sqcap ◖◦$) and a read/write share ($\pi \sqcap ◦◗$).

Any nonempty share, even if just a retainer share, permits pointer-equality tests on addresses. Requiring a nonempty share avoids the kind of undefined pointer comparisons described on page 249.

A RESOURCE-MAP ϕ has at every address, a resource. Our resource maps for CompCert are similar to those in the higher-order case study of Chapter 39. The differences are: for addresses, we use the CompCert notion of block × offset; we associate a retainer-share and an operation-share with every "YES" resource; we have LOCK resources in addition to VAL and FUN; and the FUN resources describe functions that return, not just continuations.

NO π models an address of which this share has either no permission at all (if $\pi = \circ$) or at most Nonempty permission (if $\pi \neq \circ$).

YES $\pi_r \pi$ (VAL v) NoneP models an address with retainer-share π_r and
read/write share π, containing CompCert value v. The positive-share
π cannot be empty—π belongs to the Pos_alg of lifted shares—and if
$\pi = \bullet$ then this address is Writable, otherwise just Readable. NoneP
means that there are no predicates associated with VAL addresses.

YES $\pi_r \pi$ (LK k) (SomeP R) models an address that implements a mutex
lock. The retainer-share is π_r. Holding the nonempty share π
permits a thread to (attempt to) acquire the lock. Although a mutex
(semaphore) can be implemented with a single bit, some computers
require a full k-byte word for the compare-and-swap instruction,
hence the parameter k.

The resource invariant of the lock is a separation-logic indirection-
theory predicate R.

YES $\pi_r \pi$ (CT i) NoneP is the ith byte of a k-byte mutex lock, $0 < i < k$.

PURE (FUN sig) (SomeP [A] P Q) represents a function-pointer with pa-
rameter/result type-signature sig, precondition P, and postcondition
Q. The semantics of [A] P Q is discussed in pages 165–167.

Resources form a cancellative separation algebra (Canc_alg) with the
disjointness (Disj_alg) property. The resource NO $\circ$ is the only unit for NO
or YES resources; any PURE resource is a unit for itself.

For example, the rmap $\overline{P_0}\,\overline{P_1}\,\overline{P_2}\,\boxed{3}\boxed{1}\boxed{4}\boxed{1}\boxed{5}$ indicates PURE resources
P_0, P_1, P_2 describing the specifications of functions at three different ad-
dresses in the lower part of memory, and five bytes of YES(VAL) resources
containing the values $3, 1, 4, 1, 5$. This can be divided (in many ways) into
subheaps, for example,

$$(\overline{P_0}\,\overline{P_1}\,\overline{P_2}\,\boxed{3} \qquad \boxed{1}\boxed{5}) \oplus (\overline{P_0}\,\overline{P_1}\,\overline{P_2} \quad \boxed{1}\boxed{4} \quad) = \overline{P_0}\,\overline{P_1}\,\overline{P_2}\,\boxed{3}\boxed{1}\boxed{4}\boxed{1}\boxed{5}$$

where each subheap contains the function specifications.

The join relation for resources (Join_alg resource) is inductively defined as:

$$\text{res\_join\_NO1} \frac{\pi_1 \oplus \pi_2 = \pi_3}{\text{NO}\,\pi_1 \;\oplus\; \text{NO}\,\pi_2 \;=\; \text{NO}\,\pi_3}$$

$$\text{res\_join\_NO2} \frac{\pi_1 \oplus \pi_2 = \pi_3}{\text{NO}\,\pi_1 \;\oplus\; \text{YES}\,\pi_2\,\pi\,k\,p \;=\; \text{YES}\,\pi_3\,\pi\,k\,p}$$

$$\text{res\_join\_NO3} \frac{\pi_1 \oplus \pi_2 = \pi_3}{\text{YES}\,\pi_1\,\pi\,k\,p \;\oplus\; \text{NO}\,\pi_2 \;=\; \text{YES}\,\pi_3\,\pi\,k\,p}$$

$$\text{res\_join\_YES} \frac{\pi_1 \oplus \pi_2 = \pi_3 \qquad \pi_a \oplus \pi_b = \pi_c}{\text{YES}\,\pi_1\,\pi_a\,k\,p \;\oplus\; \text{YES}\,\pi_2\,\pi_b\,k\,p \;=\; \text{YES}\,\pi_3\,\pi_c\,k\,p}$$

$$\text{res\_join\_PURE} \frac{}{\text{PURE}\,k\,p \;\oplus\; \text{PURE}\,k\,p \;=\; \text{PURE}\,k\,p}$$

For technical reasons in the construction of concurrent separation logic, we must not split a k-byte mutex lock into separate pieces. That is, in an rmap ϕ_1, any resource of the kind YES(LK k) must have all k bytes in ϕ_1, or none of them. We must not use $\phi_1 \oplus \phi_2 = \phi$ to separate a YES(CT i) resource from its base resource YES(LK k). We enforce this structural constraint relating CT to LK via the notion of AV.valid in the ADR_VAL module-type.

Since rmap is an instance of indirection theory, there are squash and unsquash functions satisfying the axioms of indirection theory. (These axioms are presented in the Module Type RMAPS in veric/rmaps.v.) That is, the type rmap' of "unpacked" resource-maps is just the function from address to resource, restricted to those functions that also satisfy the structural validity constraint AV.valid described in the previous paragraph. Then squash packs (and approximates) an rmap' into an abstract rmap, and unsquash unpacks.

Definition rmap' := {m: address → resource | AV.valid (res_option ∘ m)}.
Parameter rmap : Type.
Parameter squash : (nat ∗ rmap') → rmap.
Parameter unsquash : rmap → (nat ∗ rmap').

Along with unsquash comes the notion of level and approx_n as defined on page 302.

As an instance of indirection theory, resource maps are equipped with an fmap function to apply an arbitrary transformation to every predicate contained within an rmap (see page 300).

Definition resource_fmap (f:pred rmap → pred rmap) (x:resource): resource
  := **match** x **with**
    | NO rsh ⇒ NO rsh
    | YES rsh sh k p ⇒ YES rsh sh k (preds_fmap f p)
    | PURE k p ⇒ PURE k (preds_fmap f p)
    end.
Axiom resource_fmap_id : resource_fmap (id _) = id resource.
Axiom resource_fmap_comp :
  $\forall$ f g, resource_fmap g ∘ resource_fmap f = resource_fmap (g ∘ f).

Definition rmap_fmap (f: pred rmap → pred rmap) (x:rmap') : rmap' :=
  ... (* apply resource_fmap(f) to the resource at each address *)
Axiom rmap_fmap_id : rmap_fmap (id _) = id rmap'.
Axiom rmap_fmap_comp :
  $\forall$ f g, rmap_fmap g ∘ rmap_fmap f = rmap_fmap (g ∘ f).

The operator resource_at ϕ l, notated $\phi@l$, looks up a resource at location l in resource-map ϕ. It works by unsquashing ϕ (to extract the rmap'), then projecting (to extract the address→resource function):

Definition resource_at (phi:rmap) : address → resource :=
      proj1_sig (snd (unsquash phi)).
Infix "@" := resource_at (at level 50, no associativity).

From the axioms of indirection theory and resource maps we can prove many useful lemmas, shown in Figure 40.1.

$$\text{approx\_p} \frac{}{\text{approx}_n\, P \vdash P}$$

$$\text{approx\_lt} \frac{\text{level } w \;<\; n \qquad w \models P}{w \models \text{approx}_n\, P}$$

$$\text{approx\_ge} \frac{\text{level } w \;\geq\; n}{w \not\models \text{approx}_n\, P} o$$

$$\text{ageN\_level} \frac{\text{ageN } n\; \phi_1 \;=\; \text{Some } \phi_2}{\text{level } \phi_1 \;=\; n + \text{level } \phi_2}$$

$$\text{NO\_identity} \frac{}{\text{identity}(\text{NO}\circ)}$$

$$\text{PURE\_identity} \frac{}{\text{identity}(\text{PURE}\, k\, P)}$$

$$\text{identity\_NO} \frac{\text{identity } r}{r = \text{NO} \,\vee\, \exists k, p.\, r = \text{PURE}\, k\, p}$$

$$\text{age1\_resource\_at\_identity} \frac{\text{age } \phi\; \phi'}{\text{identity}(\phi @ l) \;\longleftrightarrow\; \text{identity}(\phi' @ l)}$$

$$\text{unage1\_resource\_at\_identity} \frac{\text{age } \phi\; \phi' \qquad \text{identity}(\phi' @ l)}{\text{identity}(\phi @ l)}$$

$$\text{make\_rmap} \frac{\text{valid } f \qquad \forall l.\; \text{resource\_fmap approx}_n\; (f\, l) \;=\; f\, l}{\{\phi : \text{rmap} \mid \text{level } \phi = n \,\wedge\, \text{resource\_at } \phi = f\}}$$

$$\text{approx\_oo\_approx}' \frac{n' \geq n}{\text{approx}_n \circ \text{approx}_{n'} = \text{approx}_n}$$

$$\text{approx\_oo\_approx}'' \frac{n' \geq n}{\text{approx}_{n'} \circ \text{approx}_n = \text{approx}_n}$$

$$\text{deallocate} \frac{\text{valid } f \qquad \text{valid } g \qquad \forall l.\, f\, l \oplus g\, l = \phi @ l}{\exists \phi_1, \phi_2.\; \phi_1 \oplus \phi_2 = \phi \,\wedge\, \text{resource\_at } \phi = f\}}$$

$$\text{unsquash\_inj} \frac{\text{unsquash } x \;=\; \text{unsquash } y}{x = y}$$

$$\text{rmap\_ext} \frac{\text{level } \phi_1 \;=\; \text{level } \phi_2 \qquad \forall l.\; \phi_1 @ l = \phi_2 @ l}{\phi_1 = phi_2}$$

Figure 40.1: Lemmas about resource maps (part 1)

$$\text{resource\_at\_join}\frac{\phi_1 \oplus \phi_2 = \phi_3}{\phi_1@l \oplus \phi_2@l = \phi_3@l}$$

$$\text{resource\_at\_join2}\frac{\text{level } \phi_1 = \text{level } \phi_2 = \text{level } \phi_3 \qquad \forall l.\ \phi_1@l \oplus \phi_2@l = \phi_3@l}{\phi_1 \oplus \phi_2 = \phi_3}$$

$$\text{resource\_at\_approx}\frac{}{\text{resource\_fmap approx}_{\text{level } \phi}\ (\phi@l) = \phi@l}$$

$$\text{necR\_resource\_at}\frac{\text{necR } \phi\ \phi' \qquad \phi@l = \text{resource\_fmap approx}_{\text{level } \phi}\ r}{\phi'@l = \text{resource\_fmap approx}_{\text{level } \phi'}\ r}$$

$$\text{all\_resource\_at\_identity}\frac{\forall l.\ \text{identity}(\phi@l)}{\text{identity } \phi}$$

$$\text{YES\_join\_full}\frac{\text{YES} \bullet n\ p \oplus r_2 = r_3}{r_2 = \text{NO}}$$

$$\text{preds\_fmap\_fmap}\frac{}{\text{preds\_fmap } f\ (\text{preds\_fmap } g\ p) = \text{preds\_fmap}(f \circ g)\,p}$$

$$\text{resource\_fmap\_fmap}\frac{}{\text{resource\_fmap } f\ (\text{resource\_fmap } g\ p) = \text{resource\_fmap}(f \circ g)\,p}$$

$$\text{necR\_YES}\frac{\text{necR } \phi\ \phi' \qquad \phi@l = \text{YES } \pi\,k\,p}{\phi'@l = \text{YES } \pi\,k\,(\text{preds\_fmap}(\text{approx}(\text{level } \phi'))\,p)}$$

$$\text{necR\_NO}\frac{\text{necR } \phi\ \phi'}{\phi@l = \text{NO } \pi \;\longleftrightarrow\; \phi'@l = \text{NO } \pi}$$

$$\text{rmap\_valid}\frac{}{\text{valid}(\text{resource\_at } \phi)} \qquad \text{core\_resource\_at}\frac{}{\widehat{\phi@l} = \hat{\phi}@l}$$

Figure 40.2: Lemmas about resource maps (part 2)

N.B. In this figure and in Figure 40.1, the $\circ$ symbol is used both for the empty share and for function composition.

Separation-logic predicates for resources

Given a separation algebra of resource maps, we want to build at a slightly higher level of abstraction a set of separation-*logic* operators.[1] A simple example is a one-byte full-permission heap-mapsto predicate: $p \mapsto v$. This is a predicate on resource-maps, pred rmap. When $\phi \models p \mapsto v$ this means that $\phi@p = \text{YES} \bullet \bullet (\text{VAL } v) \text{NoneP}$ and at all other addresses $q \neq p$, $\phi@q$ is an identity.[2] (The two bullets $\bullet \bullet$ indicate a full retainer share and a full operational share.) To put this another way, we write

$$p \mapsto v := \text{fun } \phi \Rightarrow \quad (\phi \models \text{yesat NoneP } (\text{VAL } v) \bullet \bullet p)$$
$$\wedge \; \forall q. \; q \neq p \; \rightarrow \; \phi \models \text{noat } q$$

where yesat...p means that there is a YES resource at address p, and noat q means that there is an identity resource at address q.

This pattern—one resource at a decidable set S of addresses and a different resource at all other addresses—is so common that we can make an operator for it:

$$\text{jam } (S : B \rightarrow \text{Prop}) (P \; Q : \; B \rightarrow \text{pred rmap}) : B \rightarrow \text{pred rmap} :=$$
$$\text{fun } l \; \phi \; \Rightarrow \; \text{if } Sl \text{ then } \phi \models Pl \text{ else } \phi \models Ql$$

and then we can rephrase the one-byte full-permission heap-mapsto as,

$$p \mapsto v := \text{ALL } p : \text{address. jam } (\text{eq } p) (\text{yesat NoneP } (\text{VAL } v) \bullet \bullet) \text{ noat}$$

The value v is not really a C-light value, it is a memval, which is a one-byte in-memory encoding of (part of) a C-light value. In a more useful example, the function decode_val from the CompCert specification would also need to be used in the right place.

This pattern of specification, "use a yesat at some addresses and a noat elsewhere," allows us to specify several predicate-operators in the separation logic of rmaps.

---

[1] This section describes definitions in veric/res_predicates.v.

[2] We cannot say that $\phi@q = \text{NO} \circ$, because it may be a PURE resource. For an explanation of how and why PURE resources inhabit the heap, describing function-pointer specifications, see Chapter 39.

VALspec $\pi_r\,\pi\,l$: At address l there is a byte with retainer-share π_r, operator-share π, and unknown contents; elsewhere nothing.

VALspec_range $n\,\pi_r\,\pi\,l$: At addresses $l, l+1, \ldots, l+n-1$ there is a byte with retainer-share π_r, operator-share π, and unknown contents; elsewhere nothing.

address_mapsto $ch\,v\,\pi_r\,\pi\,l$: The C-light value v is represented as a memory-chunk ch starting at address l with permissions $\pi_r\,\pi$; elsewhere nothing. A CompCert memory-chunk (such as Mint8signed, Mint32, Mfloat64) indicates a word-size and memory-representation of a C value.

LKspec $R\,\pi_r\,\pi\,l$: a mutex lock with resource invariant R is at address l; elsewhere nothing.

FUNspec $A\,P\,Q\,l$: A function with precondition P and postcondition Q is at address l; elsewhere anything. The parameter A gives the type of a logical value to be shared between precondition and postcondition. "Elsewhere anything" because function-specifications are not meant to *separate* from other resources; the appropriate conjunction to use is &&, not $*$. This is appropriate for immutable objects such as functions.

The definition of address_mapsto conveys an idea of the complexity of the C semantics:

Definition address_mapsto (ch: memory_chunk) (v: val)
$\qquad\qquad$ (rsh sh: Share.t) (l: AV.address) : pred rmap :=
EX $\vec{b}$: list memval,
!! (length $\vec{b}$ = size_chunk_nat ch $\wedge$
$\qquad$ decode_val ch $\vec{b}$ = v $\wedge$ (align_chunk ch | snd l)) &&
allp (jam (adr_range_dec l (size_chunk ch))
$\qquad\qquad$ (fun l' $\Rightarrow$ yesat NoneP (VAL (nth (nat_of_Z (snd l' -snd l))
$\qquad\qquad\qquad$ $\vec{b}$ Undef)) rsh sh l')
$\qquad\qquad$ noat).

That is, location l is the beginning of an n-byte in-memory value. The memory-type-description ch (such as Mint16signed or Mint32) describes the size (n) and signedness; the n-byte list $\vec{b}$ describes the bytes in memory that decode into value v; the address l is aligned to the appropriate multiple as specified by the align_chunk rules for ch. Then, at each byte in the range $l \leq l' < l + n$, there is a YES resource with retainer-share rsh and read/write-share sh, containing the $(l' - l)$th byte of $\vec{b}$; and outside that range there is an empty resource.

From this definition, we can construct the umapsto predicate ("untyped maps-to") visible to the user of the separation logic:

Definition umapsto (π: share) (τ: type) (v_1 v_2 : val): pred rmap :=
   match access_mode τ **with**
| By_value ch $\Rightarrow$
   match v_1 **with**
   | Vptr b z $\Rightarrow$
      address_mapsto ch v_2 (unrel Lsh π) (unrel Rsh π) (b, Int.unsigned z)
   | _ $\Rightarrow$ FF
   end
| _ $\Rightarrow$ FF
end.

The type τ must be an access-by-value type such as integer or pointer. Then its memory-type-description (memory_chunk) is ch, which is used as an argument to address_mapsto. The value v_1 must be a pointer type (Vptr b z); then z is converted from a 32-bit unsigned representation into a mathematical integer for the construction of the address (b, Int.unsigned z). Finally, the share π is decomposed into a retainer-share and a read/write share for separate arguments to address_mapsto. This is "untyped" in that it does not enforce that value v_2 belongs to type τ; but it is type-dependent insofar as it depends on the size of τ.

THE RELATION OF SEMANTIC rmaps TO OPERATIONAL MEMORIES is discussed in Chapter 42.

Chapter 41

Share models
by Robert Dockins[1]

An important application of separation algebras is to model Hoare logics of programming languages with mutable memory. We generate an appropriate separation logic by choosing the correct semantic model, that is, the correct separation algebra. A natural choice is to simply take the program heaps as the elements of the separation algebra together with some appropriate join relation.

In most of the early work in this direction, heaps were modeled as partial functions from addresses to values. In those models, two heaps join iff their domains are disjoint, the result being the union of the two heaps. However, this simple model is too restrictive, especially when one considers concurrency. It rules out useful and interesting protocols where two or more threads agree to share *read* permission to an area of memory.

There are a number of different ways to do the necessary permission accounting. Bornat et al. [27] present two different methods; one based on fractional permissions, and another based on token counting. Parkinson, in chapter 5 of his thesis [74], presents a more sophisticated system capable of handling both methods. However, this model has some drawbacks, which we shall address below.

Fractional permissions are used to handle the sorts of accounting

---

[1]This chapter is adapted from the second half of Dockins *et al.* [40].

situations that arise from concurrent divide-and-conquer algorithms. In such algorithms, a worker thread has read-only permission to the dataset and it needs to divide this permission among various child threads. When a child thread finishes, it returns its permission to its parent. Child threads, in turn, may need to split their permissions among their own children and so on. In order to handle any possible pattern of divide-and-conquer, splitting must be possible to an unbounded depth.

The token-counting method is intended to handle the accounting problem that arises from reader-writer locks. When a reader acquires a lock, it receives a "share token," which it will later return when it unlocks. The lock tracks the number of active readers with an integer counter that is incremented when a reader locks and decremented when a reader unlocks. When the reader count is positive there are outstanding read tokens; when it is zero there are no outstanding readers and a writer may acquire the lock.

Here we will show how each of the above accounting systems arises from the choice of a "share model," and we present our own share model which can handle both accounting methods and avoids a pitfall found in Parkinson's model.

SUPPOSE WE HAVE A SEPARATION ALGEBRA $\langle S, J_S \rangle$ of *shares*. If L and V are sets of addresses and values, respectively, we can define a SA over heaps as follows:

$$ H \;\equiv\; L \;\rightarrow\; (S \times V_=)_\perp \tag{41.1} $$

This equation is quite concise but conceals some subtle points. The operators in this equation are the operators on SAs defined in Chapter 7. We let $V_=$ be the "discrete" SA over values (i.e., values V with equality for the join relation) and $S \times V_=$ is the SA over pairs of shares and values. Next we construct the "lowered lifted" SA $(S \times V_=)_\perp$, which removes the unit values and adds a new, distinguished unit $\perp$. This requires values to be paired only with nonunit shares. Finally, $L \;\rightarrow\; (S \times V_=)_\perp$ builds the function space SA. Thus, heaps are partial functions from locations to pairs of nonunit shares and values.[2]

Now we can define the points-to operator of separation logic as:

$$\ell \mapsto_s v \quad \equiv \quad \lambda h. \, h(\ell) = (s, v) \wedge (\forall \ell'. \ell \neq \ell' \rightarrow h(\ell') = \bot) \tag{41.2}$$

Here, $\ell \in L$ is an address, $v \in V$ is a value, and $s \in S^+$ is a nonunit share. In English, $\ell \mapsto_s v$ means "the memory location at address ℓ contains v, I have share s at this location, and I have no permission at any other locations." Now the exact behavior of the points-to operator depends only on the share model S.

An important property of this definition is that the separation algebra on shares lifts in a straightforward way through the separation logic:

$$s_1 \oplus s_2 = s \quad \longleftrightarrow \quad (\ell \mapsto_s v \; \longleftrightarrow \; \ell \mapsto_{s_1} v * \ell \mapsto_{s_2} v) \tag{41.3}$$

Thus we can use properties of our share model in the separation logic.

A traditional separation logic, in which each heaplet has either full ownership or no ownership of address a, can be achieved by choosing S to be the SA over Booleans with the smallest join relation such that "false" is the unique unit:

THE BOOLEAN SHARE MODEL is $\langle \{\circ, \bullet\}, J \rangle$ where J is the least relation satisfying $J(\circ, x, x)$ and $J(x, \circ, x)$ for all $x \in \{\circ, \bullet\}$.

Here $\circ$ and $\bullet$ stand for "false" and "true", respectively. This share model is unsophisticated: one either has unrestricted permission or no permission at all. Note that the lifting operator removes $\circ$, leaving $\bullet$ as the only legal annotation. This justifies omitting the annotation, resulting in the more familiar $\ell \mapsto v$.

Boyland proposed a model which takes shares as fractions in the interval $[0, 1]$ as shares [28]. Although Boyland works in the reals, the rationals suffice.

---

[2]Our heaps are quite similar those defined by Bornat et al. [27]. Their "partial commutative semigroup" of shares arises here from the nonunit elements of a SA.

THE FRACTIONAL SHARE MODEL is $\langle [0,1] \cap \mathbb{Q}, + \rangle$ where $+$ is the restriction of addition to a partial operation on $[0,1]$.

The main advantage of the fractional share model is that it is infinitely splittable. The splitting function is simple: to split a share s, let $s_1 = s_2 = s/2$. The fractional share model satisfies the positivity axiom but not the disjointness axiom, which leads to the problems noticed by Bornat et al. [27].

Bornat et al. also examined the *token factory* model, where a central authority starts with total ownership and then lends out permission tokens. The authority counts the outstanding tokens; when the count is zero, all have returned. A slight modification of Bornat's construction yields a suitable model:

THE COUNTING SHARE MODEL is $\langle \mathbb{Z} \cup \{\perp\}, J \rangle$ where J is defined as the least relation satisfying:

$$J(\perp, x, x) \quad \text{for all } x \in \mathbb{Z} \cup \{\perp\} \tag{41.4}$$

$$J(x, \perp, x) \quad \text{for all } x \in \mathbb{Z} \cup \{\perp\} \tag{41.5}$$

$$(x < 0 \vee y < 0) \wedge ((x + y \geq 0) \vee (x < 0 \wedge y < 0)) \to J(x, y, x + y) \tag{41.6}$$
$$\text{for all } x, y \in \mathbb{Z}.$$

This definition sets up the nonnegative integers as token factories and negative integers as tokens. To absorb a token back into a factory, the integers are simply added. The token factory has collected all its tokens when its share is zero. Like the fractional model, the counting model satisfies positivity but not disjointness.

This share model validates the following logical axioms:

$$\ell \mapsto_n v \quad \leftrightarrow \quad (\ell \mapsto_{n+m} v * \ell \mapsto_{-m} v) \quad \text{for } n \geq 0 \text{ and } m > 0 \tag{41.7}$$

$$\ell \mapsto_{-(n+m)} v \quad \leftrightarrow \quad (\ell \mapsto_{-n} v * \ell \mapsto_{-m} v) \quad \text{for } n, m > 0 \tag{41.8}$$

$$(\ell \mapsto_0 v * \ell \mapsto_n v) \quad \leftrightarrow \quad \text{false} \tag{41.9}$$

Equation (41.7) says that a token factory with n tokens outstanding can be split into a token (of size m) and a new factory, which has $n + m$ tokens outstanding. Furthermore the operation is reversible: a token and its factory can be recombined to get a factory with fewer outstanding tokens. Equation (41.8) says that the tokens themselves may be split and merged. Finally, equation (41.9) says that it is impossible to have both a full token factory (with no outstanding tokens) and any other share of the same location (whether a factory or a token).

If one only utilizes tokens of size one, then equations (41.7)–(41.9) describe the sorts of share manipulations required for a standard reader-writer lock. Other token sizes allow more subtle locking protocols where, for example, one thread may acquire the read tokens of several others and release them all at once.

In his thesis, Parkinson defines a more sophisticated share model that can support both the splitting and the token counting use cases.

PARKINSON'S NAMED SHARE MODEL is given by $\langle \mathscr{P}(\mathbb{N}), \uplus \rangle$, where $\mathscr{P}(\mathbb{N})$ is the set of subsets of the natural numbers and $\uplus$ is disjoint union.[3]

This model satisfies the disjointness axiom, and thus positivity. It also satisfies the cross-split axiom: the required subshares are calculated by set intersection.

In order to support the token-counting use case, Parkinson considers the finite and cofinite subsets of $\mathbb{N}$. These sets can be related to the counting model given above by considering the cardinality of the set (or set complement, for cofinite sets). We will see the details of this embedding later.

Unfortunately, this share model is not infinitely splittable, since there is no way to split a singleton set into two nonempty subsets. Therefore we cannot define a total function which calculates the splitting of a share in this model, and this makes it difficult to support the parallel divide-and-conquer use case.

We can fix this problem by restricting the model to include only the *infinite* subsets of $\mathbb{N}$ (and the empty set). We can split an infinite set s by enumerating its elements and generating s_1 from those in even positions and s_2 from the those in odd positions. Then s_1 and s_2 are infinite, disjoint, and partition s.

---

[3]That is, the union of disjoint sets rather than discriminated union.

Unfortunately, restricting to infinite subsets means that we cannot use finite and cofinite sets to model token counting. This problem can be solved, at the cost of some complication, with an embedding into the infinite sets [74].

The problem with *that* solution is that the infinite subsets of $\mathbb{N}$ are also not closed under set intersection, which means the share model no longer satisfies the cross split axiom. To see why this axiom fails, consider splitting $\mathbb{N}$ into the primes/nonprimes and the even/odd numbers. All four sets are infinite, but the set $\{2\}$ of even primes is finite and thus not in the share model.

Hobor suggested further restricting the model by reasoning about equivalence classes of subsets of $\mathbb{N}$, where two subsets are equivalent when their symmetric difference is finite; but developing this model in Coq was difficult [49].

We will present a new model with all the right properties: disjointness axiom, cross-split axiom, infinitely splittable, supports token counting, and is straightforward to represent in a theorem prover. As a bonus, we also achieve a decidable test for share equality.

Binary tree share model

Before giving the explicit construction of our share model, we shall take a short detour to show how we can induce a separation algebra from a lattice.

LATTICE SEPARATION ALGEBRA. [4] Let $\langle A, \sqsubseteq, \sqcap, \sqcup, 0, 1 \rangle$ be a bounded distributive lattice. Then, $\langle A, J \rangle$ is a separation algebra where J is defined as:

$$J(x, y, z) \equiv x \sqcup y = z \wedge x \sqcap y = 0 \tag{41.10}$$

Disjointness follows from the right conjunct of the join relation; cross split follows from the existence of greatest lower bounds. 0 is the unique unit for a lattice separation algebra.

---

[4]msl/boolean_alg.v

It is interesting to note that all of the share models we have examined thus far that satisfy the disjointness axiom are instances of this general construction.[5] The Boolean share model is just the lattice SA derived from the canonical 2-element Boolean algebra, and Parkinson's model (without the restriction to infinite subsets) is the separation algebra derived from the powerset Boolean algebra. Restricting Parkinson's model to infinite sets as described above buys the ability to do infinite splitting at the price of destroying part of the structure of the lattice. Below we show that paying this price is unnecessary.

If the structure is additionally a Boolean algebra, then we can make the following pleasant connection:

$$x \preceq y \leftrightarrow x \sqsubseteq y \tag{41.11}$$

That is, the SA order coincides with the lattice order. (Recall that $x \preceq y$ means $\exists u. \, x \oplus u = y$.) The forward direction holds for any bounded distributive lattice. The backward direction relies on the complement operator to construct the witness ($\neg x \sqcap y$) for the existential quantifier in the definition of $\preceq$. Furthermore, any bounded distributive lattice satisfying (41.11) is a Boolean algebra; the witness of $\preceq$ gives the complement for x when $y = 1$. Therefore (41.11) holds iff the lattice is Boolean.

TREES.[6] Now we can restate our goal; we wish to construct a bounded distributive lattice which supports splitting and token counting. This means we must support a splitting function and we must be able to embed the finite and cofinite subsets of the naturals. We can build a model of shares supporting all these operations by starting with a very simple data structure: the humble binary tree. We consider binary trees with Boolean-valued leaves and unlabeled internal nodes.

$$\tau ::= \circ \mid \bullet \mid \widehat{\tau \, \tau} \tag{41.12}$$

We use an empty circle $\circ$ to represent a "false" leaf and the filled circle $\bullet$ to represent a "true" leaf. Thus $\bullet$ is a tree with a single leaf, $\widehat{\circ \bullet}$ is a tree with one internal node and two leaves, etc.

---

[5]This is not *necessarily* so. There exist disjoint SAs which are not distributive lattices.
[6]msl/tree_shares.v, msl/shares.v

We define the ordering on trees as the least relation $\sqsubseteq$ satisfying:

$$\circ \ \sqsubseteq \ \circ \tag{41.13}$$

$$\circ \ \sqsubseteq \ \bullet \tag{41.14}$$

$$\bullet \ \sqsubseteq \ \bullet \tag{41.15}$$

$$\circ \ \cong \ \overset{\frown}{\circ\,\circ} \tag{41.16}$$

$$\bullet \ \cong \ \overset{\frown}{\bullet\,\bullet} \tag{41.17}$$

$$x_1 \sqsubseteq x_2 \ \rightarrow \ y_1 \sqsubseteq y_2 \ \rightarrow \ \overset{\frown}{x_1\,y_1} \sqsubseteq \overset{\frown}{x_2\,y_2} \tag{41.18}$$

Here, $x \cong y$ is defined as $x \sqsubseteq y \wedge y \sqsubseteq x$. The intuitive meaning is that $x \sqsubseteq y$ holds iff x has a $\circ$ in at least every position y does once we expand leaf nodes using the congruence rules until the trees are the same shape. The congruence rules allow us to "fold up" any subtree which has the same label on all its leaves.

This relation is reflexive and transitive; however it is not antisymmetric because of the structural congruence rules. We can get around this by working only with the "canonical" trees. A tree is canonical if it is the tree with the fewest nodes in the equivalence class generated by $\cong$. Canonical trees always exist and are unique, and the ordering relation is antisymmetric on the domain of canonical trees. Therefore we can build a partial order using the canonical Boolean-labeled binary trees with the above ordering relation.

The details of canonicalization are straightforward but tedious, so we will work informally up to congruence. In the formal Coq development, however, we give a full account of canonicalization and show all the required properties. The short story is that we normalize trees after every operation by finding and reducing all the subtrees which can be reduced by one of the congruence rules.

Our next task is to implement the lattice operations. The trees $\circ$ and $\bullet$ are the least and greatest element of the partial order, respectively. The least upper bound of two trees is calculated as the pointwise disjunction of Booleans (expanding the trees as necessary to make them the same shape). For example, $\overset{\frown}{\bullet\,\overset{\frown}{\circ\,\circ}} \sqcup \overset{\frown}{\circ\,\overset{\frown}{\bullet\,\circ}} \cong \overset{\frown}{\overset{\frown}{\bullet\,\bullet}\,\overset{\frown}{\circ\,\circ}} \sqcup \overset{\frown}{\overset{\frown}{\circ\,\circ}\,\overset{\frown}{\bullet\,\circ}} \cong \overset{\frown}{\overset{\frown}{\bullet\,\bullet}\,\overset{\frown}{\bullet\,\circ}} \cong \overset{\frown}{\bullet\,\overset{\frown}{\bullet\,\circ}}$.

Likewise, the greatest lower bound is found by pointwise conjunction, so that $\langle tree \rangle \sqcap \langle tree \rangle \cong \langle tree \rangle \sqcap \langle tree \rangle \cong \langle tree \rangle \cong \langle tree \rangle$. Finally, this structure is a Boolean algebra as well as a distributive lattice, and the complement operation is pointwise Boolean complement: $\neg \langle tree \rangle \cong \langle tree \rangle$. The Boolean algebra axioms can be verified by simple inductive arguments over the structure of the trees.

We can also define a decidable test for equality by simply checking structural equality of trees. Trees form a lattice, and thus a decision procedure for equality also yields a test for the lattice order. In contrast, Parkinson's model over arbitrary subsets of $\mathbb{N}$ lacks both decidable equality and decidable ordering.

In addition to the lattice operations, we require an operation to split trees. Given some tree s, we wish to find two trees s_1 and s_2 such that $s_1 \sqcup s_2 \cong s$ and $s_1 \sqcap s_2 \cong \circ$ and both $s_1 \not\cong \circ$ and $s_2 \not\cong \circ$ provided that $s \not\cong \circ$. We can calculate s_1 and s_2 by recursively replacing each $\bullet$ leaf in s with $\langle tree \rangle$ and $\langle tree \rangle$ respectively.

We can usefully generalize this procedure by defining the "relativization" operator $x \bowtie y$, which replaces every $\bullet$ leaf in x with the tree y. This operator is associative with identity $\bullet$. It distributes over $\sqcup$ and $\sqcap$ on the left, and is injective for non-$\circ$ arguments.

$$x \bowtie \bullet = x = \bullet \bowtie x \tag{41.19}$$

$$x \bowtie \circ = \circ = \circ \bowtie x \tag{41.20}$$

$$x \bowtie (y \bowtie z) = (x \bowtie y) \bowtie z \tag{41.21}$$

$$x \bowtie (y \sqcup z) = (x \bowtie y) \sqcup (x \bowtie z) \tag{41.22}$$

$$x \bowtie (y \sqcap z) = (x \bowtie y) \sqcap (x \bowtie z) \tag{41.23}$$

$$x \bowtie y_1 = x \bowtie y_2 \;\rightarrow\; x = \circ \lor y_1 = y_2 \tag{41.24}$$

$$x_1 \bowtie y = x_2 \bowtie y \;\rightarrow\; x_1 = x_2 \lor y = \circ \tag{41.25}$$

Given this operator, we can more succinctly define the split of x as returning the pair containing $x \bowtie \langle tree \rangle$ and $x \bowtie \langle tree \rangle$. The required splitting properties follow easily from this definition and the above properties of $\bowtie$.

If this were the only use of the relativization, however, it would hardly be worthwhile to define it. Instead, the main purpose of this operator is to allow us to glue together arbitrary methods for partitioning permissions. In particular, we can split or perform token counting on any nonempty permission we obtain, no matter how it was originally generated. In addition, we only have to concentrate on how to perform accounting of the full permission • because we can let the $\bowtie$ operator handle relativizing to some other permission of interest.

Following Parkinson, we will consider finite and cofinite sets of the natural numbers to support token counting. This structure has several nice properties. First, it is closed under set intersection, set union and set complement and it contains $\mathbb{N}$ and $\emptyset$; in other words, it forms a sub-Boolean algebra of the powerset Boolean algebra over $\mathbb{N}$. Furthermore the cardinalities of these sets can be mapped to the integers in following way:

$$[\![p]\!]_{\mathbb{Z}} = \begin{cases} -|p| & \text{when } p \text{ is finite and nonempty} \\ |\mathbb{N} \setminus p| & \text{when } p \text{ is cofinite} \end{cases} \tag{41.26}$$

The cardinalities of disjoint (co)finite sets combine in exactly the way defined by the counting share model (equation 41.6).

We can embed the (co)finite subsets of $\mathbb{N}$ into our binary tree model by encoding the sets as right-biased trees (where the left subtree of each internal node is always a leaf). Such trees form a list of Booleans together with one extra Boolean, the rightmost leaf in the tree. Then the ith Boolean in the list encodes whether the natural number i is in the set. The final terminating Boolean stands for all the remaining naturals. If it is ∘, the set is finite and does not contain the remaining naturals, and if it is • the set is infinite and contains all the remaining naturals. This interpretation is consistent with the congruence rules that allow you to unfold the rightmost terminating Boolean into a arbitrarily long list of the same Boolean value.

For example, the finite set $\{0, 2\}$ is encoded in tree form as ⬩⟋⟍.

The coset $\mathbb{N} \setminus \{0, 2\}$ is encoded as ⟋⟍.

And, of course, ⬩⟋⟍ $\oplus$ ⟋⟍ $=$ •.

This encoding is in fact a Boolean algebra homomorphism; GLBs, LUBs, complements and the top and bottom elements are preserved.

This homomorphism allows us to transport the token counting results on (co)finite sets to binary trees. We write $[\![p]\!]_\tau = s$ when s is the tree encoding the (co)finite set p.

Now we can define a more sophisticated points-to operator which allows us to incorporate token counting along with permission splitting.

$$\ell \mapsto_{s,n} v \equiv \lambda h.\ \exists p.\ h(\ell) = (s \bowtie [\![p]\!]_\tau, v) \wedge [\![p]\!]_z = n \wedge \forall \ell'.\ell \neq \ell' \rightarrow h(\ell') = \bot \tag{41.27}$$

Then $\ell \mapsto_{s,n} v$ means that ℓ contains value v and we have a portion of the permission s indexed by n. If n is zero, we have all of s. If n is positive, we have a token factory over s with n tokens missing, and if n is negative, we have a token of s (of size $-n$).

This points-to operator satisfies the following logical axioms:

$$(\ell \mapsto_{s,0} v * \ell \mapsto_{s,n} v) \quad \longleftrightarrow \quad \text{false} \tag{41.28}$$

$$s_1 \oplus s_2 = s \quad \rightarrow \quad ((\ell \mapsto_{s_1,0} v * \ell \mapsto_{s_2,0} v) \quad \longleftrightarrow \quad \ell \mapsto_{s,0} v) \tag{41.29}$$

$$n_1 \oplus n_2 = n \quad \rightarrow \quad ((\ell \mapsto_{s,n_1} v * \ell \mapsto_{s,n_2} v) \quad \longleftrightarrow \quad \ell \mapsto_{s,n} v) \tag{41.30}$$

$$\ell \mapsto_{s,n} v \quad \rightarrow \quad \exists! s'.\ \ell \mapsto_{s,n} v \quad \longleftrightarrow \quad \ell \mapsto_{s',0} v \tag{41.31}$$

Equation (41.28) generalizes both the disjointness axiom from Parkinson and the disjointness axiom for token factories (41.9). Likewise, equation (41.29) generalizes the share axiom (41.3). Essentially, if we fix $n = 0$ we get back the simpler definition of the points-to operator from above as a special case. In equation (41.30), $n_1 \oplus n_2 = n$ refers to the token counting join relation on integers defined in equation (41.6), and this axiom generalizes the token factory axioms (41.7) and (41.8). Both of those axioms follow as a special case when we fix $s = \top$. Finally, equation (41.31) allows one to project a tokenized share into a nontokenized share (one where $n = 0$). This might be useful if one needs to perform share splitting on a share which was derived from a token factory, for example.

These axioms allow fluid reasoning about both the token-counting and splitting use cases, which enables a unified way to do flexible and precise permission accounting.

Chapter 42

Juicy memories
by Gordon Stewart and Andrew W. Appel

Indirection theory is a powerful technique for using step-indexing in modeling higher-order features of programming languages. Rmaps (Chapters 39 and 40), which figure prominently in our model of Verifiable C, rely heavily on indirection theory to express self-reference.

When reasoning in a program logic, step indexes are unproblematic: the step indexes can often be hidden via use of the ▷ operator, and therefore do not often appear explicitly in assertions. Indirection theory provides a generic method for constructing the underlying step-indexed models.

More problematic is how to connect a step-indexed program logic like Verifiable C to a certified compiler such as CompCert. CompCert's model of state is not step-indexed, nor would it be reasonable to make CompCert step-indexed. To do so introduces unnecessary complication into CompCert's correctness proofs. It also complicates the statement of CompCert's correctness theorem: naively requiring the compiler to preserve all step indexes through compilation makes it difficult to reason about optimizations that change the number of steps.

Previous chapters of this book outlined one way in which this difficulty can be resolved, by stratifying our models into two layers: operational *states* corresponding to states of the operational semantics used by CompCert, and semantic *worlds* appearing in assertions of the program logic. Chapter 40 in particular gave some motivation for why this stratification makes sense: We may not want all the information found in operational states to be visible to Hoare logic assertions (in particular, control state should be hidden). Likewise, some information used only for static reasoning—lock invariants, function specifications, and the step indexes that facilitate the encoding of this higher-order data—should be hidden from the compiler.

In this chapter, we describe the particulars of how stratification is achieved for the specific case of Verifiable C and CompCert. The stratification relies on a technique we call *juicy memories* (veric/juicy_mem.v).

To a first approximation, a juicy memory j defines what it means for an rmap ϕ to *erase* to a CompCert memory m. By erasure, we mean the removal of the "juice" that is unnecessary for execution (as in Curry-style type erasure of simply typed lambda calculus). The "juice" has several components: *permission shares* controlling access to objects in the program logic; *predicates in the heap* describing invariants of objects in the program logic; and the classification of certain addresses as values, locks, function pointers, and so on.

In the soundness proof of the program logic, we erase the predicates in the heap, but we do not completely erase the permission shares: we abstract them into the coarser-grain permissions present in CompCert memories. Only after compilation to machine code will it be appropriate to erase the CompCert permissions.

Our program logic has a system of ownership shares (Chapter 11, Chapter 41) permitting detailed accounting of "fractional" permissions. A permission share on some memory location can be split into smaller pieces, given to a set of concurrent threads for shared read-only access, and then later reassembled for exclusive write access by one thread. Of course, such splitting and reassembly is in the *proof* about a program; it does not need to occur at execution time.

CompCert has a much simpler permission model (page 252) that does not distinguish one Readable permission from another. These "dry" permissions are too coarse for our program logic, but they are sufficient for compiler-correctness proofs.

CompCert can survive with a less expressive permission model than the program logic, for this combination of reasons: (1) Permissions do not change during core-language execution.[1] (2) The compiler correctness proof is tolerant of permissions changing at external function calls. Synchronization operations (such as lock acquire/release) are modeled as external function calls, and it is at those points that a thread might give away some of its ownership-share to some addresses, leaving it with read permission or no permission; or a thread with only a read-share might give away some fraction of its share, leaving it with a smaller fraction that corresponds to the same coarse-grain CompCert permission. Ownership shares do not change at ordinary instructions.

So in the semantic model that relates the program logic to the operational semantics, we use a simple function perm_of_res that translates *resources* (ownership-shares) to CompCert *permissions*. The function follows the lattice at right, where the top share Tsh corresponds to CompCert's Freeable permission. The right-half share of the top share (or any

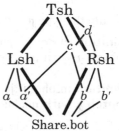

share containing it such as d) is sufficient to grant Writable permission to the data: "the right share is the write share." A thread of execution holding only Lsh—or subshares of it such as a, a'—has only Nonempty permission: the thread cannot read or write the object, but other threads are prevented from deallocating the object. Any nonempty subshare b of Rsh, in fact any share such as c that overlaps Rsh, grants Readable permission to the object. Overlap can be tested using the glb (greatest lower bound) operator.

In our model of the C-light Hoare judgment presented in Chapter 43, we maintain two views of the state *simultaneously*: the "rmap" view, for reasoning in the program logic, and the "CompCert" view, for connecting assertions and judgments in the Hoare logic to operational facts about program executions.

---

[1]Except that stack frames may be allocated and deallocated at procedure call/return; but this exception does not change the basic point.

In veric/juicy_mem.v, we define juicy memories as pairs of a memory m and an rmap ϕ. The rmap and memory must be *consistent with each other*, in a way we will make precise in a moment. In the code, we represent this pair with the following inductive type.

Inductive juicy_mem: Type :=
  mkJuicyMem: $\forall\,(m\colon$ mem) ($\phi\colon$ rmap)
    (JMcontents: contents_cohere $m\,\phi$)
    (JMaccess: access_cohere $m\,\phi$)
    (JMmax_access: max_access_cohere $m\,\phi$)
    (JMalloc: alloc_cohere $m\,\phi$),
  juicy_mem.

We equip the type juicy_mem with accessor functions of the form

Definition m_dry (j: juicy_Mem) :=
  match j **with** mkJuicyMem m _ _ _ _ _ $\Rightarrow m$ **end**.

Definition m_phi (j: juicy_Mem) :=
  match j **with** mkJuicyMem _ϕ _ _ _ _ $\Rightarrow \phi$ **end**.

The four proof objects beginning JM... enforce the four consistency requirements:

Contents. If $\phi@l = (\text{YES } \pi_r\ \pi\ (\text{VAL } v)\ pp)$ then $m\,l = v$ and $pp = \text{NoneP}$. That is, a VAL in the rmap must have no "predicates in the heap" associated with it, and the v in the rmap must match the v in the CompCert memory. Predicates will only occur in PUREs, to give function specifications, and in locks (YES $\pi_r\ \pi$ (LK k) (SomeP R)) to give resource invariants.

Access. For all locations l, $m\,l = \text{perm\_of\_res } (\phi@l)$. The fractional share $\phi@l$ must "erase" to that location's CompCert memory permission.

Max Access. For all locations l,

max_access_at $m\,l \sqsupseteq$ perm_of_sh $\pi_r\ \pi$	when $\phi@l = \text{YES } \pi_r\ \pi$
max_access_at $m\,l \sqsupseteq$ perm_of_sh $\pi_r\ \bot$	when $\phi@l = \text{NO } \pi_r$
fst $l <$ nextblock m	when $\exists f\ pp$.
	$\phi@l = \text{PURE } f\ pp$.

Alloc. For all locations l, if fst $l \geq$ nextblock m then $\phi @ l = \text{NO} \perp$. CompCert treats addresses whose abstract base pointer is beyond nextblock as not-yet-allocated. Here we ensure that ϕ makes no claim to those addresses.

The juicy-memory consistency requirements are mostly straightforward. **Max Access** is a bit more complicated. It does case analysis on the resource $\phi @ l$, ensuring that the *maximum* permission in m at a given location is greater than or equal to the permission corresponding to the pair of shares (π_r, π) or $(\pi_r, \perp)$. Maximum permissions are a technical device used in CompCert's memory model to express invariants useful for optimizations like constant propagation (see page 253). The *current permission* in m at location l, or just *permission*, is always less than the maximum permission. When $\phi @ l$ contains a PURE resource, **Max Access** just ensures that l is a location that was allocated at some point (fst $l <$ nextblock m). Here nextblock m is the next block in CompCert's internal free list.

THE CONSISTENCY REQUIREMENTS together ensure that assertions expressed in the Hoare logic on the ϕ portion of the juicy memory actually say something about the CompCert memory m. For example, suppose we know—perhaps because ϕ satisfies the assertion $l \mapsto_\pi v$—that ϕ contains the value v with share π at location l. Then, in order to prove that a load from m at location l will succeed, we would also like to be able to show that m contains v at l, with at least readable permission.

To validate that the consistency requirements described above satisfy laws of this form, we prove such a lemma for each of the basic CompCert memory operations: load, store, alloc, and free. For example, here is the lemma for mapsto with writable share.

Lemma mapsto_can_store: $\forall ch\ v\ \pi_r\ b\ ofs\ j\ v'$,
   (address_mapsto $ch\ v\ \pi_r\ \top\ (b, ofs) * \top\top$) (m_phi j) $\rightarrow$
   $\exists m'$, Mem.store ch (m_dry j) $b\ ofs\ v' = \text{Some } m'$.

This lemma relies on the consistency requirements to prove that the store in m_dry j will succeed. The lemmas for the other memory operations differ in the predicate on m_phi j but are otherwise similar.

In addition to "progress" lemmas of the form mapsto_can_store, we prove "preservation" lemmas for juicy memories. That is, we would like to know that after each CompCert memory operation on m_dry j, yielding a new memory m', it is possible to construct a new juicy memory j' such that m_dry $j' = m'$. The intuition here is that memory operations on m_dry j never touch the *hidden* parts of m_phi j, e.g., the function specifications and lock invariants appearing in Hoare logic assertions. Thus it is possible to construct j' generically from m' and m_phi j, by copying hidden data unchanged from m_phi j to m_phi j', and by updating m_phi j' at those locations that were updated by the memory operation.

For example, the function after_alloc' defines the map underlying the new m_phi j' after an allocation Mem.alloc (m_dry j) lo hi.

Definition after_alloc'
  (*lo hi*: Z) (*b*: block) (ϕ: rmap)(*H*: $\forall$ *ofs*, ϕ @ (*b,ofs*) = NO $\bot$)
  : address $\rightarrow$ resource := fun l $\Rightarrow$
    if adr_range_dec (*b*, *lo*) (*hi* - *lo*) l
      then YES $\top$ pfullshare (VAL Undef) NoneP
      else phi @ l.

Then the lemma

Lemma juicy_mem_alloc_at:
  $\forall$ j *lo hi* j' b,
    juicy_mem_alloc j *lo hi* = (j',b) $\rightarrow$
    $\forall l$, m_phi j' @ l =
      if adr_range_dec (*b*, *lo*) (*hi* - *lo*) l
        then YES $\top$ pfullshare (VAL Undef) NoneP
        else m_phi j @ l.

gives an extensional definition of the contents of the juicy memory j' that results. Here juicy_mem_alloc uses after_alloc' to construct the new juicy memory j' resulting from the allocation.

WE HAD MODULARIZED EVERY OPERATIONAL SEMANTICS of the CompCert family into a *core* semantics and an *external specification* (see Chapter 33). Based on *any* core semantics that uses "dry" CompCert memories m, now we can construct a "juicy" operational semantics that uses juicy memories (m, ϕ)—see veric/juicy_ext_spec.v. We prove the program logic sound with respect to this juicy semantics.

Chapter 43

Modeling the Hoare judgment

We model[1] the C-light Hoare judgment $\Delta \vdash \{P\}\, c\, \{Q\}$ using the *continuation-passing* style explained in Chapter 4 (pages 29–32). There we defined $\{P\}\, c\, \{Q\}$ to mean that for any continuation κ, if Q guards κ then P guards $c; \kappa$. We say Q *guards* κ, written $\{Q\}\kappa$, if from any state σ that satisfies Q, then it is safe to execute forward from κ.

In C it's more complicated: the C language has control flow, so Q is not just a single postcondition but covers all the ways in which c might exit. Our program logic is step-indexed (using indirection theory) so we can weaken P. Our operational states do not *directly* satisfy separation-logic assertions; the operational states use the CompCert model of environments and memories, whereas our assertions use a more abstract semantic model of environments and rmaps.

Each C-light thread executes in the context of an external world, which we can call an *oracle* (see Chapter 33). Both the thread and its oracle have access to the same CompCert memory m. An external function may be a separately compiled module, or an operating system-call, or (in a concurrent setting) a synchronization lock-acquire that permits other threads to run on the shared memory. Any of these kinds of external

---

[1]This chapter describes definitions in veric/semax.v.

functions may modify memory before returning, and we wrap up all these external mechanisms in the oracle. When the thread makes an external function call, the oracle can modify m before returning, and the oracle can also modify its own internal state, which is the *external state* from the point of view of the C-light thread. The *type* of the oracle's internal state is an abstract type; that is, the semantic model of our Hoare logic must not make any assumptions about how the oracle represents its internal state.

We interact with the oracle by means of calls to specifically enumerated *external functions*. Different oracles may have different external functions; each oracle comes with a *specification* of the behavior of these external functions. That is, an oracle comes with a structure of type OracleKind characterizing the internal representation of oracle states and the preconditions and postconditions of external functions (how they interact with the memory and the oracle-state). We parameterize the semax judgment (and other predicates) by (Espec:OracleKind).

THE NOTION OF *guards* RESTS ON THE DEFINITION OF *safety*. An operational state is safeN(n) if it cannot get stuck within n small-steps:

$$\text{safeN } (ge : \text{genv}) \ (n : \text{nat}) \ (z) \ (\sigma : \text{state})(m : \text{juicy\_mem}) \ : \ \text{Prop}$$

This means, in global environment ge we cannot get stuck within n steps starting from the the oracle state z, the local state $\sigma = \langle ve, te, \kappa \rangle$, and juicy memory m. Page 276 explains this in detail.

We model safety as an assertion in our separation logic:

$$\text{assert\_safe Espec } ge \ ve \ te \ \kappa \ : \ \text{environ} \ \rightarrow \ \text{pred rmap}$$

Given a *semantic state* with environment ρ and rmap ϕ we can write, $\phi \models \text{assert\_safe Espec } ge \ ve \ te \ \kappa \ \rho$ to mean: If the abstract environment ρ corresponds to the CompCert environment $\langle ge, ve, te \rangle$ (global-env, var-env, temp-env); and if ϕ is the rmap part of some juicy memory m, and **if** the approximation level of ϕ is n, **then** it is safe to execute n operational steps:[2] safeN $ge \ n \ z \ \langle ve, te, \kappa \rangle \ m$.

---

[2]The oracle-state z is left unspecified here. Thus the definition is oblivious to the state of the external world. Consequently, it will not be possible to reason explicitly about the

With safety defined as an assertion we can now define "P guards κ", $\{P\}\kappa$, as $P \longrightarrow \text{safe}(\kappa)$. The formal definition is,

Definition guard (Espec : OracleKind)
  (gx: genv) (Δ: tycontext) (P : assert) (κ: cont) : pred nat :=
ALL tx : Clight.temp_env, ALL vx : env,
   let ρ := construct_rho (filter_genv gx) vx tx **in**
   !! (typecheck_environ ρ Δ = true) && P ρ && funassert Δ ρ
    $\Rrightarrow$ assert_safe Espec gx vx tx κ ρ.

That is, we write $n \models$ guard gx Δ P κ to mean that, to approximation level n, in program gx, in type-context Δ, the assertion P guards the continuation κ. We call gx the *program* because it contains a mapping from function addresses to function bodies.

The essence of *guards* (pages 29–32) is, "for all data-states σ, $P\sigma$ implies that $\langle\sigma,\kappa\rangle$ is safe". Here our definition of guard quantifies over all tx and vx; together the temp-environment and the var-environment comprise CompCert's local data state. From these we construct ρ, a semantic environ; this together with the juicy memory m comprises our notion of state σ.

The assertion P (on the next-to-last line of the definition) takes the explicit argument ρ and the implicit argument m. The m argument is implicitly quantified in the predicate-subtyping operator $\Rrightarrow$, of which both the left and right sides are pred rmap.

So "P guards κ:" on the left side we have $P\rho(m)$ and a few other things, and on the right we have assert_safe Hspec gx vx tx κ ρ (m). What are the "few other things?" First, that the semantic environment ρ comports with the type-checking context Δ; second, that all the function-specifications in Δ are actually present (as "predicates in the heap") in m.

---

state of the oracle (such as the history of I/O events) inside the separation logic itself. Instead, we can adapt our predicates-in-the-heap mechanism to implement dependently typed ghost variables; core-language (C light) function specifications can interact with the ghost variables (see veric/ghost.v). The specifications of external functions (and therefore, oracle state) can also interact with the same ghost variables, thus connecting the specifications of internal and external functions. This is an interesting topic for future research.

This is a step-indexed definition. That is, we have the subtyping operator $\rightarrowtail$ instead of the entailment $\vdash$. The difference is that entailment quantifies over *all* juicy memories, and subtyping quantifies only over those at approximation level less than n.

Guarding a statement exit. In our simplified summary explanation of the Hoare triple (at the beginning of the chapter) we wrote, "$\{P\}\,c\,\{Q\}$ means that if Q guards κ then P guards $c;\kappa$." But because the command c can fall-through, continue, break, or return—and because (therefore) Q is really four different postcondition assertions—it's a bit more complicated. These ways of exiting are called an exitkind:

Inductive exitkind := EK_normal | EK_break | EK_continue | EK_return.

Definition exit_cont (ek: exitkind) (v: option val) (κ: cont) : cont :=
    match ek **with**
    | EK_normal $\Rightarrow$ κ
    | EK_break $\Rightarrow$ break_cont κ
    | EK_continue $\Rightarrow$ continue_cont κ
    | EK_return $\Rightarrow$ ... (* elided *)
    end.

Exiting into κ using EK_normal yields just κ; using EK_break throws away items from the head of κ up to and including a loop-control; exiting using EK_continue throws away items from the head of κ up to but not including a loop-control; and using EK_return throws away the top of the control stack down to a function-call frame, and at that point inserts the optional return-value v into the local-variable environment of the caller. For other than EK_return, v must be None.

    We define rguard (for "return guard") as the relation between Q and κ that takes into account the different ways that c can return. This is just like guard except that: (1) The type-context Δ is parameterized by ek, since we might have a stronger type-context after a fall-through than after a break, if the command c unambiguously initializes a variable. (2) The guarded continuation is not just κ, it is the continuation obtained by exiting into κ

using the exit-kind ek (and optional value v); (3) The guarding assertion R is parameterized by ek and the optional function-return-value v.

Definition rguard {Z} (Hspec : juicy_ext_spec Z)
    (gx: genv) (Δ: exitkind$\rightarrow$ tycontext) (R: ret_assert) (κ: cont): pred nat :=
    ALL ek: exitkind, ALL v: option val,
        ALL tx: Clight.temp_env, ALL vx : Clight.env,
    let ρ := construct_rho (filter_genv gx) vx tx **in**
    !! (typecheck_environ ρ (Δ ek) = true) &&
    (R ek v ρ && funassert (Δ ek) ρ) $\Longrightarrow$
        assert_safe Hspec gx vx tx (exit_cont ek v κ) ρ.

In the Hoare triple semax Δ P c Q, the command c may call a global function (or grab the address of a global function), using the rule semax_fun_id shown on page 165. In that case we use the *specification* of that function contained in Δ. The type/proof context Δ incorporates (in addition to types of local variables) the list of global function-specifications claimed by the user, such as Γ_{prog} shown on page 199. But just because the user *claims* that functions meet their specifications, why should we *believe* this? After all, none of these function-bodies have yet been proved!

Definition believepred {Z} (Hspec: juicy_ext_spec Z)
           (semax: semaxArg $\rightarrow$ pred nat)
           (Δ Δ': tycontext) (gx: genv) : pred nat :=
  ALL v:val, ALL fsig: funsig,
        ALL A: Type, ALL P: A $\rightarrow$ assert, ALL Q: A $\rightarrow$ assert,
    !! claims gx Δ' v fsig A P Q $\longrightarrow$
  (believe_external Hspec gx v fsig A P Q
    || believe_internal_ semax gx Δ v fsig A P Q).

The predicate believepred says that every function specification in Δ' is satisfied by the actual function-body in the program, at least to an approximation. That is, if the type-context Δ' *claims* a function specification for the function at address v, then you can *believe* it. In particular, v might be an external function—so you can believe_external its specification, or it might be an internal function.

To *believe* a specification means that the function-body of *v* satisfies the Hoare triple of the function's pre- and postcondition. But that Hoare triple takes Δ as a parameter (in case the function calls itself or other functions). To avoid circularity and paradox, believepred takes both Δ and Δ′, and says: if Δ′ claims something, then you can believe it about Δ.

We will use believepred in the definition of the Hoare judgment, semax. But the meaning of believe_internal refers to semax—also a potential circularity. Here we just take a semax as a parameter; we will close the loop using step-indexing.

Definition believe_internal_
  (semax:semaxArg → pred nat) (gx: genv) (Delta: tycontext)
  v (fsig: funsig) A (P Q: A → assert) : pred nat :=
  (EX b: block, EX f: function,
  prop (v = Vptr b Int.zero ∧ Genv.find_funct_ptr gx b = Some (Internal f)
    ∧ list_norepet (map fst f.(fn_**params**) ++ map fst f.(fn_temps))
    ∧ list_norepet (map fst f.(fn_vars)) ∼∧ ∼fsig = fn_funsig f)
  && ALL x : A, ▷semax (SemaxArg (func_tycontext′ f Delta)
    ((bind_args f.(fn_**params**) (P x) * stackframe_**of** f)
    && funassert (func_tycontext′ f Delta))
    f.(fn_body)
    (frame_ret_assert (function_body_ret_assert (fn_return f) (Q x))
      (stackframe_**of** f)))).

The definition of believe_internal *v* fsig *A P Q* says that the address *v* points to a function-body whose calling-convention is the function-signature fsig, whose precondition is $[x : A]P$, and whose postcondition is $[x : A]Q$. The prop conjunct is concerned with the existence of the function-body f and the well-formedness of its formal-parameter list. The ALL x conjunct says that the body f.(fn_body) meets its specification ▷later, to a slightly weaker approximation.

WERE IT NOT FOR THE CIRCULARITIES inherent in predicates-in-the-heap and mutually recursive functions, we would define the semax semantically as shown on page 30, something like,

$$\{P\}\,c\,\{Q\} := \forall k.\, \{Q\}k \to \{P\}(c;k).$$

But now, the very notion of *guards*, $\{Q\}k$, refers to the definition of the Hoare triple $\{P\}c\{Q\}$. So instead of a direct definition we will establish an *equation*. The equation that characterizes semax is:

semax Hspec Δ P c $R =$
ALL gx: genv, ALL Δ': tycontext,
   !!($\Delta \sqsubseteq \Delta'$) $\longrightarrow$
   believe_ Hspec semax Δ' gx Δ' $\longrightarrow$
   ALL κ: cont, ALL F: assert,
     (!! (closed_wrt_modvars c F)
     && rguard Hspec gx (exit_tycon c Δ') $(R * F)$ κ) $\longrightarrow$
     guard Hspec gx Δ' $(F * P)$ (Kseq c :: κ).

To paraphrase—the meaning of Hoare triple $\Delta \vdash \{P\}c\{R\}$ for a program run in an operating system Hspec is: For all programs gx, forall Δ' that is an extension of Δ, assume that all the functions in gx obey their specifications in Δ' to a slightly weaker approximation. Then for all control-continuations κ and all separation-logic *frames* F that are closed w.r.t. the modified variables of c, if $R * F$ guards κ then $P * F$ guards $c \cdot \kappa$.

The semax is defined in terms of a ▷weaker version of itself. We solve this recursive definition using the indirection-theory Löb rule, as explained in Chapter 39 and implemented in veric/semax.v.

ONCE THE semax JUDGMENT IS DEFINED, each of the Hoare-logic inference rules is proved as a derived lemma. The proofs are straightforward, though the complexities of the C operational semantics make the inference-rule proofs rather complex in places. Mostly it's a matter of unfolding the definitions and blundering around until Coq responds with "No more subgoals." These proofs are in veric/semax_straight.v (straight-line instructions such as assignment, load, and store), veric/semax_loop.v (control flow such as if-then-else, loops and loop-exit, and semicolon-sequencing), veric/semax_call.v (function call and return).

AN IMPORTANT PROPERTY OF THIS SEMANTIC METHOD for defining the program logic is that it is *not inductive* over the syntax of commands, nor on the operational-semantic small-step relation. That means new commands could be added to the language without touching all the existing proofs of the Hoare rules.

However, some rules do not fit comfortably into this paradigm. The seq_assoc rule (see page 158) says,

$$\frac{\Delta \vdash \{P\} (c_1; (c_2; c_3)) \{Q\}}{\Delta \vdash \{P\} ((c_1; c_2); c_3) \{Q\}} \qquad \frac{\Delta \vdash \{P\} ((c_1; c_2); c_3) \{Q\}}{\Delta \vdash \{P\} (c_1; (c_2; c_3)) \{Q\}}$$

We prove these (with some difficulty) by induction on the small-step relation (see the corestep_preservation_lemma in veric/semax_lemmas.v). If new commands were added to the language, more cases would need to be proved in this lemma.

THE DEFINITION OF semax IS COMPLICATED—HOW DO WE KNOW IT'S RIGHT? Each of the inference rules (in Chapter 24) is a derived lemma in CiC, checked by the Coq kernel. Thus, when we use those rules to prove a program, we have at least correctly *produced* a semax judgment. But we still need to know that the semax tells us something useful; how do we *consume* a semax judgment?

The *whole-program sequential* semax *safety theorem for C light* says that if we have semax judgments for every function in a program, then the program runs safely in the operational semantics of C light.

Theorem whole_program_sequential_safety:
$\forall p \ V \ \Gamma \ m,$
semax_prog $p \ V \ \Gamma \rightarrow$
Genv.init_mem $p = $ Some m $\rightarrow$
$\exists b, \exists q,$
   Genv.find_symbol (Genv.globalenv p) (prog_main p) = Some b $\wedge$
   make_initial_core cl_core_sem
          (Genv.globalenv p) (Vptr b Int.zero) nil = Some q $\wedge$
   $\forall$ n, safeN cl_core_sem dryspec (Genv.globalenv p) n tt q m.

Let p be a C light program, let V be a global-variable specification (describing the types of global variables), let Γ be a list of function-specifications. Suppose we have proved that all the function bodies in p satisfy their specifications in Γ, that is, semax_prog $p \vee \Gamma$. Now suppose[3] that the initializers of all the global variables succeed, yielding a CompCert memory m.

Then there *will* exist a block-number b that is the address of the main function of p; and there *will* be an initial core-state q that is the start state of the program running main; and for any n, it *will* be safe to run n steps starting at the state (q, m).

This statement is proved in veric/SequentialClight.v, relying on semax_prog_rule in SeparationLogicSoundness.v.

In later chapters we discuss generalizations of this soundness theorem for separately compiled modules and for concurrent programs.

---

[3]It should be possible to prove that for any program compiled by CompCert's front-end phase into C light, the global initializers *will* succeed, yielding a memory m.

Chapter 44

Semantic model of CSL

Dijkstra presented semaphore-based mutual exclusion as an extension to a sequential language [37]. Posix threads present Dijkstra-Hoare concurrency as an extension to a sequential language [55]. O'Hearn presented concurrent separation logic (CSL) as an extension to separation logic, in which all the rules of sequential separation logic still hold [71].

Can we really model concurrency as an extension to sequentiality? Boehm explains why it is very tricky to explain shared-memory concurrency as an extension to a sequential language [24]. But we have taken great care to specify our language's external-interaction model (Chapter 33), in order to do this soundly.

Therefore we do something ambitious: we present the semantic model of CSL, for the C language, in the presence of an optimizing compiler and weak cache coherency, as a modular extension to our semantic model for sequential separation logic. This chapter is based on Aquinas Hobor's PhD thesis [49, 51] and on current work by Gordon Stewart.

Concurrent separation logic with first-class locks. O'Hearn's presentation of CSL had several limitations, most importantly a lack of first-class locks (locks that can be created/destroyed dynamically, and in particular can be used to control access to other locks). Hobor *et al.* [51] and Gotsman *et al.* [44] independently extended CSL to handle first-class locks as well as a number of other features.

Chapter 30 explains our CSL with first-class locks. Acquiring a lock allows a thread access to additional resources (e.g., memory), and releasing a lock relinquishes said resources. The "shape" of the resource acquired or relinquished—and the invariant it satisfies—is described by a predicate in separation logic.

So, certain addresses in the heap (the locks) are associated with resource invariants that are assertions of separation logic. As new locks are created, the associated lock invariants must be attached to those addresses—in other words, the heap must be updated to "contain" the invariants. But each assertion is a predicate over program-states that contain heaps—that is, the resource invariant of one lock can describe the binding of a resource invariant to another lock. The intuitive model for this contains a circularity:

$$
\begin{aligned}
\text{res} &\equiv \text{VAL of (share} \times \text{value)} + \text{LK of (share} \times \text{bool} \times \text{pred)} \\
\text{pred} &\equiv \text{(heap} \times \text{locals)} \to \mathbb{T} \\
\text{heap} &\approx \text{address} \rightharpoonup \text{res}
\end{aligned}
$$

Heaplets (heap) are partial functions mapping locations to *resources* (res): either regular data (VAL) or locks (LK). Regular data locations contain *values*. Since multiple threads can each own part of a lock, each lock is associated with a *share*, which tracks how much of the lock is visible. Locks also have a boolean, which is true if *this thread* holds the lock (more precisely, if this thread has the right to unlock the lock); and a predicate (pred) specifying the lock's resource invariant. Predicates (pred) simply judge pairs of heap and locals (local variables). We set

$$
\begin{aligned}
F(X) &\equiv \text{address} \rightharpoonup (\text{VAL of (share} \times \text{value)} + \text{LK of (share} \times \text{bool} \times X)) \\
O &\equiv \text{locals,}
\end{aligned}
$$

and then can use indirection theory to construct the approximation

$$
\begin{aligned}
\text{res} &\equiv \text{VAL of (share} \times \text{value)} + \text{LK of (share} \times \text{bool} \times \text{pred)} \\
\text{pred} &\equiv \text{(heap} \times \text{locals)} \to \mathbb{T} \\
\text{heap} &\preceq \mathbb{N} \times (\text{address} \rightharpoonup \text{res)}.
\end{aligned}
$$

We can apply indirection theory, because F is *covariant*.

We will define the assertions points-to "$a \overset{\pi}{\mapsto} v$" and is-a-lock "$a \overset{\pi}{\boxdot\!\!\rightarrow} P$". The points-to assertion is standard (but with permission shares); is-a-lock has a share π that indicates how much of the lock is visible and a predicate P that is the lock's resource invariant. Both of these assertions depend on the structure of $F(X)$.

The intuition for points-to is that if a points to v ($a \overset{\pi}{\mapsto} v$), then the heaplet ϕ contains $\mathsf{VAL}(\pi, v)$ at location a and nothing else:

$$a \overset{\pi}{\mapsto} v \equiv \lambda(k, \rho). \text{ let } (n, \phi) = \text{unsquash } k \text{ in} \qquad (44.1)$$
$$\phi(a) = \mathsf{VAL}(\pi, v) \wedge \mathsf{domain}(\phi) = \{a\}.$$

Defining the is-a-lock assertion starts with the idea of looking up the address in ϕ: (35.17):

$$a \overset{\pi}{\boxdot\!\!\rightarrow} P \equiv \lambda(k, \rho). \text{ let } (n, \phi) = \text{unsquash } k \text{ in} \qquad (44.2)$$
$$\exists P', b. \ \phi(a) = \mathsf{LK}(\pi, b, P') \wedge \mathsf{domain}(\phi) = \{a\} \wedge P =_n P'.$$

Location a is a lock with share π and resource P if the resource map ϕ contains a $\mathsf{LK}(\pi, b, P')$ for some boolean b and predicate P' at location a, ϕ is empty everywhere else, and P is approximately equal to P'. The invariant P' will have been squashed down to level n, whereas the "query" P may make finer distinctions. The clause $P =_n P'$ means that P is approximately equal to P' (at level n), meaning that is-a-lock can only enforce the resource invariant to a level of accuracy commensurate with the current age.

RESOURCE MAPS containing locks (with resource invariants) and ordinary values fit straightforwardly into the *juicy memory* construction shown in Chapter 42. Then we can construct a concurrent operational semantics based on the CompCert sequential operational semantics. Where a sequential state has a *core* (containing local variables and control-stack of a thread), a *juicy memory*, and an *oracle* (which models the external world), a concurrent state has many cores—each representing one thread—but all cores share the same memory and external oracle.

But the Hoare judgment of separation logic—semax—treats only a single thread. So, following Hobor [49, 51] we create an *oracle semantics*, an operational semantics for a single thread that sweeps all the other threads into the oracle. When thread A performs a lock-acquire, *we* know that this may cause thread A to block, that the scheduler may suspend execution of A and run other threads until the lock is available for A to acquire; then resume A. But from A's point of view, the lock-acquire simply succeeds. That is, the call to the external function acquire returns, having made some changes to the shared memory. This fiction is the essence of oracle semantics, and it allows us to use the Hoare triples of separation logic in (seemingly) sequential reasoning.

Hobor proved that if the (pseudosequential) oracle semantics is safe, then the underlying concurrent machine is safe. Our sequential soundness proof for semax (Chapter 43), with respect to a juicy operational semantics, proves that if one carries out a verification in separation logic then the operational execution really is correct. Hobor showed that the composition of these two results demonstrates the soundness of CSL.

But there was still a subtle gap, between "juicy" resource maps and "dry" CompCert memories.

ANGELIC NONDETERMINISM FOR CONCURRENT SEPARATION LOGIC. A juicy memory (Chapter 42) contains an rmap ϕ and a CompCert memory m. We need the juice—information in ϕ that is not present in m—to understand how permissions transfer in concurrent separation logic. That is, the lock-release rule (page 224) transfers permissions away from the current thread. For a lock at address l, the transferred permissions are exactly the footprint of the resource invariant R located in the rmap ϕ at address l—it is a predicate in the heap. The juicy operational semantics looks up $\phi@l$ to get R, then (nonconstructively!) finds the unique subheap of (m, ϕ) that satisfies R. If the user has managed to prove any property of the program using the Verifiable C program logic, then we know that this step is safe, not stuck—that this subheap exists.

That is all very well—but the CompCert compiler-correctness proof is with respect to the "dry" operational semantics using CompCert memories m, not with respect to our juicy semantics. We need to perform *erasure*, converting executions of the juicy semantics to executions of the dry semantics. But the dry execution has memory permissions that must be altered at lock-synchronization points, to accomplish the transfer of permissions. We cannot fully erase all notion of memory permission, or else the optimizing compiler will have too little information to know which load-store hoisting optimizations are permitted.

Therefore we will use a form of *angelic nondeterminism* in the dry semantics: we prove that at each lock-release point in the execution, there will exist some choice of what permissions to release, such that the whole execution will be safe. Concretely, we determinize the semantics by equipping it with an *angel*—a stream of permission-sets. In the dynamic execution, at every lock-release, the next element of the angel stream will determine the set of permissions to transfer out of the executing thread.

Because permissions never change at core-language instructions—only at external function calls to such things as synchronization operators—the angel never needs to be consulted in core-language steps. In fact, the core-language semantics does not even know it is there: the angel is contained entirely within the external-specification (ext_spec) that gives an execution context for the core semantics.

From the Hoare-logic (concurrent separation logic) proof of a program, we derive that the juicy semantics executes safely, using methods described in the next chapter. From the safe execution of the juicy semantics, we prove that an angel exists that justifies the safe execution of the dry semantics. From the safe execution of the dry C light semantics, the CompCert correctness proof guarantees the corresponding safe execution of the angelic assembly language. By the time we get to assembly language, we have finished all those optimizing transformations that depended on (dry) permissions, so we can erase those permissions (and the angel). And finally, in a sufficiently expressive Hoare logic, safety implies correctness (page 30).

Chapter 45

Modular structure of the development

The Verified Software Toolchain has many components, put together in a modular way:

msl. The *proof theory and semantics of separation logics and indirection theory* is independent of any particular programming language, independent of the memory model, independent of particular theories of concurrency.

compcert. The *CompCert verified C compiler* is independent of any particular program logic (such as separation logic), of any particular theory of concurrency, and of the external-function context (such as an operating system-call setup). CompCert incorporates several programming languages, from C through C light to C minor and then (in various stages) to assembly languages for various target machines. The CompCert family may also include source languages such as C++ or ML. These various operational semantics all use the same memory model, and the same notion of external function call.

sepcomp. The *theory of separate compilation* explains how to specify the compilation of a programming language that may make shared-memory external function calls, shared-memory calls to an operating system, and shared-memory interaction with other threads. This depends on CompCert's memory model, but not on any particular one of the CompCert languages. Eventually, parts of the sepcomp theory will migrate into CompCert itself.

Some parts of the separate-compilation system concern modular program verifications of modular programs. We may even want to link program modules—and their verifications—written in different languages (C, ML, Java, assembly). This system requires that each language have a program logic that uses the same mpred (memory predicates) modeled using resource maps (rmap). But these languages will have different forms of Hoare judgment, that is, the separate compilation system is independent of semax.

veric. The Verifiable C program logic is a higher-order impredicative separation logic. It and its semantic model depend on CompCert memories and the theory of separate compilation. Many parts of VeriC (such as memory predicates mpred and their model, rmap) are independent of any particular CompCert language. If we wanted to build a program logic for a different language in the CompCert family, all these parts would be re-usable.

The model of semax and the Hoare inference rules for semax) depend specifically on the syntax and semantics of CompCert C light. But the semax, its semantic model, and its rules for the C language should be independent of any particular *instance* of a separate-compilation context. Thus we parameterize semax by the Espec:OracleKind as described in Chapter 33 and Chapter 43.

The semantic model of semax is even independent of whether the programming language is sequential or concurrent. Just as the proof theory of concurrent separation logic [71] incorporates all of the sequential rules of separation logic (as if they were oblivious of operating in a concurrent setting), our model of semax and all our sequential proof rules for C light are still valid in the concurrent setting.

However, to achieve first-class threads and locks, we need the illusion of "predicates in the heap"—that is, we want to create a new mutex lock at address l, with a binding $l : \text{lock}(R)$ that binds l to a resource invariant R that is a predicate in separation logic; and yet R itself predicates over the very heap that it lives in. We need a sufficiently powerful notion of rmap (resource map) in the semantic model that can handle such quasicircularity. It is for this reason that we took the trouble to use indirection theory to build our resource maps.

We present the program logic in two stages. First, definitions for the various assertion operators, all based on the two primitives, address_mapsto (for addresses containing data values) and func_ptr (for addresses pointing to function bodies). Second, the semax judgment and its proof theory.

veric proof theory. The proof theory of Verifiable C is specified in the Module Type CLIGHT_SEPARATION_LOGIC in veric/SeparationLogic.v. This depends on the *syntax* of C light but not (directly) on the operational semantics of C light, nor on the CompCert memory model, nor on resource maps (rmap). That is, the semax judgment is presented with a sealed abstraction: the module SoundSeparationLogic has an opaque module type, presenting the client with an abstract (proof-theoretic) view of the CLIGHT_SEPARATION_LOGIC rules for semax.

On the other hand, the expression-evaluation component of the semax proof theory is quite concrete and computational, not abstract; this is presented in veric/expr.v. This allows us to reason about expression evaluation efficiently via unfolding and simplification. Expression evaluation does not have the complexities (such as step-indexing and predicates in the heap) that impel us to keep the semax abstract.

floyd. The proof automation lemmas and tactics depend on semax's proof theory, but not its model. Thus they depend on the *logical* view of separation logics (Chapter 12), not the separation-algebra model (Chapter 6).

progs. Our case studies (such as reverse.c, sumarray.c, queue.c) depend on the floyd proof-automation system. As part of our case studies we present the general theory of list segments, progs/list_dt.v. Although we could just as well have made this lseg theory a part of the floyd system, we want to emphasize that our separation logic is expressive enough for users to be able to construct their own theories of data structures, such as lists, trees, trees with cross-edges and back edges, DAGs, graphs, hash tables, and so on.

concurrency. Our concurrent separation logic will be an extension to the program logic, proved sound w.r.t. an extension of the operational semantics. In both cases, the extensions will be accomplished by using extensibility features already in the specifications of the operation semantics and the program logic, using the *oracle semantics* approach along with *angelic erasure* (Chapter 44). Every rule of the sequential program logic is (therefore) still valid in the concurrent setting, and all proofs of sequential program modules are (therefore) still valid as part of concurrent programs.

Verifications of individual programs do not depend on the particular operational semantics used for C, nor on the semantic model used to prove soundness of the program logic, as long as the operational- and program-logic- semantics combine to justify the proof rules.

Part VII

Applications

SYNOPSIS: *In Part III we showed how to apply a program logic interactively to a program, using tactics. Here we will show a different use of program logics: we build automatic static analyses and decision procedures as efficient functional programs, and prove their soundness using the rules of the program logic.*

Chapter 46

Foundational static analysis

A *static analysis* is an algorithm that checks (or calculates) invariants of a program based on its syntactic (static) structure, in contrast to a *dynamic analysis* which observes properties of actual program executions. Static analysis can tell us properties of all possible executions, while dynamic analysis can only observe executions on particular inputs.

A *sound* static analysis is one with a proof that any invariants checked by the analysis will actually hold on all executions. A *foundationally* sound analysis is one where the soundness proof is (ideally) machine-checked, (ideally) with respect to the machine-language instruction-set architecture specification—not the source language—and (ideally) with no axioms other than the foundations of logic and the ISA specification.

Some of the first foundationally sound static analyses were proof-carrying code systems of the early 21st century [5, 45, 35, 3]. It was considered impractical (at that time) to prove the correctness of compilers, so these proof-carrying systems transformed source-language typechecking (or Hoare logic [14]) phase by phase through the compilation, into an assembly-language Hoare logic.

With the existence of foundationally correct compilers such as CompCert, instead of proof-carrying code we can prove the soundness of a static analysis from the source-language semantics, and compose that proof with the compiler-correctness proof. See for example the value analysis using abstract interpretation by Blazy *et al.* [22]

SOME KINDS OF STATIC ANALYSIS may be easier to prove sound with respect to a program logic than directly from the operational semantics. We will show this for *shape analysis*, a category of static analysis that analyzes the program's use of pointer variables to determine the shape of the data structures that these variables are creating and traversing. By *shape*, we mean questions such as, "is it a tree, a DAG, or a cyclic graph?" [42] By answering such questions, shape analysis can guarantee that a pointer dereference in the program is not fetching a null-pointer or uninitialized pointer; can guarantee certain anti-aliasing properties useful to other analyses, and can guarantee other safety properties of the program.

Shape analysis (and static analysis in general) does not require interactive verification effort of the kind described in Chapter 27—the analysis is fully automatic. Shape/static analysis may require the user to provide certain invariants—pre/postconditions of functions, or loop invariants—or the analysis may even infer those invariants automatically. But shape analysis does not concern itself with the semantic contents of the data structure, so there are many correctness properties that it cannot prove automatically. We demonstrated an example of this on page 18: a shape analysis of the list-reverse program can prove that it takes one list segment as input, and returns one list segment as output; but does not prove that if the *contents* of the input list is σ, then the contents of the output is rev(σ). The former is a shape property, the latter is a correctness property. Even though shape analyses prove "shallow" properties, their full automation makes them very useful in practice.

THE **SMALLFOOT** STATIC ANALYSIS ALGORITHM [18, 19] is a shape analysis based on separation logic. Shape analysis was invented in the early 1990s, but after the invention of separation logic in 2000/2001 it is obvious[1] that the simple way that separating conjunction keeps track of antialiasing makes it natural for expressing the action of a shape analysis.

Smallfoot analyzes list and tree data structures, but here we will show only lists. The inductive presentation of list segments (page 123) is not directly suitable for the Smallfoot analysis—it makes for easy reasoning

---

[1] It is obvious *now*, after the publication of the Smallfoot papers [18, 19].

about the head end of the segment, but not about the tail end. Therefore Smallfoot uses the Berdine-Calcagno proof theory of lists (see page 124), which is provable from the inductive presentation (and also provable from our indirection-theory description of list segments, see Chapter 19).

The Berdine-Calcagno rules form a *decidable fragment of separation logic*, meaning that there is an algorithm for finding a proof or counterexample of any entailment $P \vdash Q$ that uses only the operators $*, \wedge, \mathrm{emp}, =, \neq, \rightsquigarrow$ and next . The Smallfoot algorithm uses this by calling upon an *entailment checker* as a subroutine.

Smallfoot's user annotates the program with function pre/postconditions and loop invariants that are shape assertions in separation logic. Subsequent work that builds on Smallfoot shows how the shape analyzer can infer many of those assertions automatically, so the user has even less work to do [31, 20].

We illustrate with the canonical example: list reversal.

```
assert(v ⤳ 0)
w=0;
while (v != 0) invariant (v ⤳ 0 * w ⤳ 0)
    {t = v.next; v.next = w; w = v; v = t; }
assert(w ⤳ 0)
```

The job of Smallfoot is to prove that the program comports with these assertions. What does that mean? Berdine *et al.* [19] demonstrate that whenever the Smallfoot algorithm runs successfully on an annotated program, then there exists a separation-logic proof of that program with those annotations.

Not only is Smallfoot proved correct with respect to a program logic, it is even *explained* by using the program logic. Figure 46.1 shows *operational symbolic execution rules*. Here we assume the program is using a linked-list data structure with fields data and link. Berdine's notation $\Pi|\Sigma$ means the conjunction of pure conjuncts Π with spatial conjuncts Σ; in Chapter 26 we would write this as $\mathrm{LOCAL}(\Pi)\mathrm{SEP}(\Sigma)$.

The algorithmic interpretation is this: given a current symbolic state $\{\Pi|\Sigma\}\, c\, \{Post\}$, match the current goal against this state. This will yield hypotheses to be solved by repeating this algorithmic interpretation; or

$$\text{skip}\frac{\Pi|\Sigma \vdash \Pi'|\Sigma'}{\{\Pi|\Sigma\}\,\{skip\}\Pi'|\Sigma'}$$

$$\text{set}\frac{\{x = e[x'/x] \wedge (\Pi|\Sigma)[x'/x]\}\,c\,\{\Pi'|\Sigma'\}}{\{\Pi|\Sigma\}\,x = e;\,c\,\{\Pi'|\Sigma'\}}\,x'\text{ fresh}$$

$$\text{load}\frac{\{x = e_1[x'/x] \wedge (\Pi|\Sigma * e \rightarrow \text{link} \mapsto e_1)[x'/x]\}\,c\,\{\Pi'|\Sigma'\}}{\{\Pi|\Sigma * e \rightarrow \text{link} \mapsto e_1\}\,x = e \rightarrow \text{link};\,c\,\{\Pi'|\Sigma'\}}\,x'\text{ fresh}$$

$$\text{store}\frac{\{\Pi|\Sigma * e \mapsto e_2\}\,c\,\{\Pi'|\Sigma'\}}{\{\Pi|\Sigma * e \rightarrow \text{link} \mapsto e_1\}\,e \rightarrow \text{link} = e_2;\,c\,\{\Pi|\Sigma\}}$$

$$\text{if}\frac{\{\Pi \wedge e|\Sigma\}\,c_1;\,c\,\{\Pi'|\Sigma'\} \qquad \{\Pi \wedge \neg e|\Sigma\}\,c_2;\,c\,\{\Pi'|\Sigma'\}}{\{\Pi|\Sigma\}\,\text{if}\,e\,\text{then}\,c_1\,\text{else}\,c_2;\,c\,\{\Pi'|\Sigma'\}}$$

$$\text{assert}\frac{(\Pi|\Sigma) \vdash A \qquad \{A\}\,c\,\{\Pi'|\Sigma'\}}{\{\Pi|\Sigma\}\,\text{assert}\,A;\,c\,\{\Pi'|\Sigma'\}}$$

$$\text{while}\frac{\{\Pi \wedge e|\Sigma\}\,c_1\,\{\Pi|\Sigma\} \qquad \{\Pi|\Sigma \wedge \neg e\}\,c\,\{\Pi'|\Sigma'\}}{\{\Pi|\Sigma\}\,\text{while}\,(e)\,c_1;\,c\,\{\Pi'|\Sigma'\}}$$

Figure 46.1: Smallfoot operational symbolic execution rules.

in the case of skip will check the entailment $(\Pi|\Sigma) \vdash Post$. Note that each *while* statement must be preceded by an *assert* statement bearing its loop invariant. The user also annotates functions with their pre- and postconditions, which gives us the initial $(\Pi|\Sigma)$ and $(\Pi'|\Sigma')$ with which to start the algorithm. The full Smallfoot algorithm also has operational rules for new, dispose, and function call, which we do not show here.

Each one of these operational rules is easy to prove as a derived lemma in separation logic, using the primitive command rules, plus the frame rule and the rule of consequence.

Running the algorithm is not *quite* as easy as matching a rule's conclusion to the current goal: in both the load rule and the store rule, the precondition of the left-hand side must take the form $P = (\Pi | \Sigma * e \to f \mapsto e_1)$. If the current symbolic state has a precondition *equivalent* but not identical to this form, then we must apply an algorithm to *rearrange* the precondition to match. lookin There are several cases:

- We examine every conjunct of Σ, looking for the pattern $(\_ \to \text{link} \mapsto \_)$. When Σ is $A * e' \to \text{link} \mapsto e_1' * B$, we try to prove the entailment $P \vdash e = e' \wedge e_1 = e_1'$. If this succeeds, then we use the rule of consequence with $(A * B) * e \to \text{link} \mapsto e_1$, which matches the goal; otherwise we look at the next conjuncts.

- Suppose $\Sigma = A * e' \rightsquigarrow r * B$. Then if $P \vdash e = e' \wedge e' \neq r$, we can use the rule, $e \neq r \wedge e \rightsquigarrow r \vdash \exists d, q. e \to \text{data} \mapsto d * e \to \text{link} \mapsto q * q \rightsquigarrow r$ to derive $P \vdash (A * B * e \to \text{data} \mapsto d * q \rightsquigarrow r) * e \to \text{link} \mapsto q$, which has the desired form; otherwise we look at the next conjuncts.

- The *spooky disjunction* is this case: Σ is $A * e' \rightsquigarrow r * B * e'' \rightsquigarrow s * C$ where $P \vdash e = e' \wedge e = e'' \wedge r \neq s$. Then it cannot be that both list-segments are empty, for then $e = r$ and $e = s$ leading to a contradiction; and it cannot be that both are nonempty, otherwise the conjuncts $e' \rightsquigarrow r * e'' \rightsquigarrow s$ would overlap. Therefore $P \vdash Q_1 \vee Q_2$, where

$$Q_1 = \exists d, q. \Pi \wedge e = e' \wedge e = e'' \wedge e = s$$
$$| (A * B * C * e \to \text{data} \mapsto d * q \rightsquigarrow r) * e \to \text{link} \mapsto q$$

$$Q_2 = \exists d, q. \Pi \wedge e = e' \wedge e = e'' \wedge e = r$$
$$| (A * B * C * e \to \text{data} \mapsto d * q \rightsquigarrow s) * e \to \text{link} \mapsto q$$

Instead of making an entailment checker that can handle disjunctions, we consider the cases $P \vdash Q_1$ and $P \vdash Q_2$ as two separate symbolic executions. We do forward symbolic execution for Q_1 (until we reach the end of the function body, or the next loop invariant) *and* do forward symbolic execution for Q_2, and only if both succeed do we know the program is safe in all cases. Then we look at the rest of the conjuncts of Σ to see if there are other matches, and for each we do forward symbolic execution.

The rearrangement algorithm relies on the ability to test an entailment $P \vdash Q$ for validity—that is it relies on a decision procedure for this decidable fragment of separation logic. See Chapter 47.

The rules for set and load are annotated with (x' fresh), meaning that variable x' is not free in Π, Σ, x, e, e_1. Operationally this means we keep track of a positive integer, a variable name, that is greater than the names of all variables used so far in the program or in its specification.

WE CAN MAKE SMALLFOOT *foundational*.[2] Where Berdine *et al.* write an ML program and explain its principles with respect to an algorithm presented in Latex, we write a Gallina program automatically extracted into ML. Where their algorithm is proved correct informally with respect to a Latex presentation of operational rules, our program is proved correct with a machine-checked proof in Coq with respect to the VST separation logic. Where they prove soundness of their operational rules by a model of an ideal language presented in Latex, we prove the VST separation logic (our semax judgment) sound with respect to CompCert's operational semantics.

None of this means that there's something wrong with the original Smallfoot; it means that we view the presentation of Smallfoot via axiomatic separation-logic rules as a description of the foundational implementation and proof that we can build in Coq.

WE WANT A SHAPE ANALYZER THAT RUNS FAST. Since it can be slow to manipulate propositions and lambda-terms in a general-purpose proof assistant such as Coq, instead we write a special-purpose program in ML. Actually we write in Gallina (the functional programming language inside Coq) and *extract* an ML program. *Our algorithm completely avoids using Coq*

---

[2] This chapter describes *VeriSmall* [8], a verified implementation of Smallfoot. Our original VeriSmall implementation was a static analysis for the CompCert C minor programming language and operational semantics. C minor is a lower-level intermediate language, below C light in the phases of CompCert. The formal verification was done with respect to our foundational separation logic (semax) for C minor, which in turn is built and verified on similar principles to the program logic for C light described in this book.

variables, Coq propositions, Coq tactics. So we need a syntactic encoding of separation-logic expressions, formulas, and assertions:

Definition var := positive.
Inductive expr := Nil: expr | Var: var → expr.
Inductive pure_atom := Eqv : expr→ expr→ pure_atom
                            | Neqv : expr→ expr→ pure_atom.
Inductive space_atom := **Next**: expr → expr → space_atom
                            | Lseg: expr → expr → space_atom.
Inductive assertion :=
   Assertion: ∀ (Π: list pure_atom) (Σ: list space_atom), assertion.
Inductive entailment := Entailment : assertion → assertion → entailment.

In our syntactic separation logic fragment, variable-names are represented by positive numbers. An expression is either Nil or a variable. A pure (nonspatial) atom is of the form $e_1 = e_2$ or $e_1 \neq e_2$; an assertion contains (the conjunction of) a list Π of pure atoms, and the separating conjunction of a list of *space atoms*. Each space atom describes either a list cell or a list segment **Next** e1 e2 represents a cons cell at address e_1 whose tail-pointer contains the value e_2. Lseg e1 e2 represents a list segment $e_1 \rightsquigarrow e_2$.

Fixpoint exorcize (e: expr) Π Σ_0 Σ (x: var) : option(list assertion) :=
  match Σ **with**
  | nil ⇒ **if** incon (Assertion Π (rev Σ_0)) **then** Some nil **else** None
  | Lseg f f' :: Σ_1 ⇒
      if oracle (Entailment (Assertion Π (rev Σ_0 ++ (Lseg f f') :: Σ_1))
                  (Assertion (Eqv e f :: nil) (rev Σ_0 ++ Lseg f f' :: Σ_1)))
      then match exorcize e (Eqv f f' :: Π) (Lseg f f' :: Σ_0) Σ_1 x **with**
            | Some l ⇒ Some (Assertion Π
                (Next e (Var x) :: Lseg (Var x) f' :: rev Σ_0 ++ Σ_1) ::l)
            | None ⇒ None
            end
      else exorcize e Π (Lseg f f' :: Σ_0) Σ_1 x
  | a :: Σ_1 ⇒ exorcize e Π (a :: Σ_0) Σ_1 x
  end.

We factor Berdine *et al.*'s *rearrangement* algorithm into an exorcize function which eliminates spooky disjunctions, and isolate which does everything else (calling upon exorcize). These functions call the incon decision procedure to test the inconsistency of a separation-logic entailment.

Fixpoint isolate' (e: expr) Π Σ_0 Σ (x: var) (count: nat)
$$: \text{option(list assertion)} :=$$
match Σ **with**
| nil $\Rightarrow$ **if** count < 2 **then** None
    else if incon (Assertion (Eqv e Nil :: Π) (rev Σ_0))
      then exorcize e Π nil (rev Σ_0) x
    else None
| **Next** e1 e2 :: Σ_1 $\Rightarrow$
  if eq_expr e e1
  then Some [Assertion Π (**Next** e e2 :: rev Σ_0 ++ Σ_1)]
  else if oracle(Entailment(Assertion Π (rev Σ_0 ++ (**Next** e1 e2)::Σ_1))
    (Assertion (Eqv e e1 :: nil) (rev Σ_0 ++ (**Next** e1 e2) :: Σ_1)))
    then Some [Assertion Π (**Next** e e2 :: rev Σ_0 ++ Σ_1)
   else isolate' e Π (**Next** e1 e2 :: Σ_0) Σ_1 x count
| Lseg f f' :: Σ_1 $\Rightarrow$
  if oracle (Entailment (Assertion Π (rev Σ_0 ++ (Lseg f f') :: Σ_1
    (Assertion (Eqv e f :: Neqv f f' :: nil)
      (rev Σ_0 ++ (Lseg f f') :: Σ_1)))
  then Some [Assertion Π
   (**Next** e (Var x) :: Lseg (Var x) f' :: rev Σ_0 ++ Σ_1)]
  else if oracle (Entailment (Assertion Π (rev Σ_0 ++ (Lseg f f') :: Σ_1))
    (Assertion (Eqv e f :: nil) nil (rev Σ_0 ++ (Lseg f f') :: Σ_1)))
    then isolate' e Π (Lseg f f' :: Σ_0) Σ_1 x (S count)
  else isolate' e Π (Lseg f f' :: Σ_0) Σ_1 x count
end.

Definition isolate (e: expr) (P: assertion) (x: var): option(list assertion) :=
 match P **with** Assertion Π Σ $\Rightarrow$ isolate' e Π nil Σ x 0 **end**.

The variable x is the *freshness counter*, the lowest-numbered fresh variable. We we need to introduce a new variable (such as q in the description of spooky-disjunction-elimination, page 415), we use x. The oracle function is the decision procedure for entailments, returning a boolean. What exorcise returns is a list of all the ways that $e \rightarrow \text{next} \mapsto \_$ can match, each in the context of a larger assertion. Σ_0 accumulates the conjuncts we have already seen.

The isolate' function walks through the list Σ, accumulating conjuncts it has already seen in Σ_0. If it finds Next e_1 e_2, meaning $e_1 \rightarrow \text{next} \mapsto e_2$, then it tests $P \vdash e = e_1$; if so, it has found the unique match. (No other conjunct could overlap, or the original assertion would be inconsistent.) Otherwise, it finds candidates $f \rightsquigarrow f'$ for unfolding. For each one, if it can prove $f \neq f'$ then it unfolds, using x as the free variable for the intermediate link. Otherwise, it adds to the count of spooky-disjunction candidates.

By the time isolate' reaches the end of Σ, if the count≥ 2 (*and if P is inconsistent with $e = \text{nil}$*) it is worth trying exorcize.

TO PROVE SOUNDNESS OF isolate, we first give a model of syntactic assertions in our semantic separation logic.

Definition expr_denote (e : expr): environ$\rightarrow$ val :=
    match e **with** Nil $\Rightarrow$ `nullval | Var x $\Rightarrow$ (eval_id x) **end**.

Definition pure_atom_denote (a : pure_atom) : mpred :=
  match a **with** Eqv e1 e2 $\Rightarrow$ `eq (expr_denote e1) (expr_denote e2)
            | Neqv e1 e2 $\Rightarrow$ `neq (expr_denote e1) (expr_denote e2)
  end.

Definition space_atom_denote (a : space_atom) (ρ: environ) : mpred :=
  match a **with**
  | **Next** x y $\Rightarrow$ `(field_mapsto_ Tsh tlist _data) (expr_denote x) *
                `(field_mapsto_ Tsh tlist _next) (expr_denote x) (expr_denote y)
  | Lseg x y, State _h $\Rightarrow$ `(lseg tlist Tsh) (expr_denote x) (expr_denote y)
  end.

Definition assertion_denote (f : assertion) : spred :=
match f **with** Assertion Π Σ ⇒
     fold_right andp TT (map pure_atom_denote Π)
     ∧ fold_right sepcon emp (space_atom_denote Σ)
end.

GHOST VARIABLES. Throughout Part III of this book, when we write (eval_id x) the variable x is a variable from the source program. When we neet to talk about intermediate values (e.g., in the unfolding of a list) we use a Coq variables y of type val; then it would make no sense (nor would it typecheck) to write (eval_id y).

But our implementation of Smallfoot is purely syntactic, and as such when we choose a "fresh variable" it comes out of the same syntactic space as x. We simply the augment the environment ρ by binding ghost variables.

Our function freshmax_expr finds the highest-numbered variable in an expression; we write fresh freshmax_expr e x to mean that x's name is greater than any name in e. We write existsv x A to mean that there is a value v such that the assertion $A[v/x]$ holds

With this, we can state the soundness theorem for exorcize.

Lemma exorcize_sound: $\forall e\ \Pi\ \Sigma\ x$,
    fresh freshmax_expr e x →
    fresh freshmax_assertion (Assertion Π Σ) x →
    $\forall l$, (exorcize e Π nil Σ x) = Some l →
(assertion_denote (Assertion Π Σ) ⊢
  fold_right orp FF (map (fun P ⇒ existsvx (assertion_denote P)) l) ∧
    ($\forall$ Q, In Q l →
           match Q **with**
           |Assertion _(**Next** e_0 _:: _) ⇒ $e = e_0$
           | _⇒ False
           end ∧ fresh freshmax_assertion Q (Psucc x)).

Assuming x is fresh for e and for the assertion $(\Pi|\Sigma)$, suppose exorcize returns a list $l = l_0 :: l_1 :: \ldots :: l_n ::$ nil of assertions. Let $l' = (\exists v.l_0[v/x]) \vee$

$(\exists v.l_1[v/x]) \vee \ldots \vee (\exists v.l_n[v/x]) \vee \bot$. Then the denotation of $(\Pi|\Sigma) \vdash l'$. Furthermore, the *first* spatial conjunct of each assertion in l has the form **Next** e _, and the next variable after x is fresh for every assertion in l.

The soundness theorem for isolate is like the one for exorcize. Both are proved by applying the rules and definitions of our separation logic, by induction over the execution of the **Fixpoint** functions.

Lemma isolate_sound: $\forall e$ P x l,
  isolate e P x = Some l $\rightarrow$
  fresh freshmax_expr e x $\rightarrow$ fresh freshmax_assertion P x $\rightarrow$
  assertion_denote P $\vdash$
    fold_right orp FF (map (fun Q $\Rightarrow$ (existsv x (assertion_denote Q))) l) $\wedge$
  $\forall$ Q, In Q l $\rightarrow$
      match Q **with**
      |Assertion _(**Next** e_0 _:: _) $\Rightarrow$ $e = e_0$
      | _$\Rightarrow$ False
      end $\wedge$ fresh freshmax_assertion Q (Psucc x).

THE SYMBOLIC EXECUTION ALGORITHM is our functional-program implementation of the operational rules shown in Figure 46.1. It uses some auxiliary functions: Cexpr2expr translates a C expression to an expr of our syntactic fragment of separation logic; getSome extracts a value from an option.

Symbolic execution is flow-sensitive, and when interpreting an **if** statement, "knows" in the **then** clause that the condition was true, and in the **else** clause that the condition was false. For this purpose we define a function Cexpr2assertions e a f that takes C expression e and assertion $a = (\Pi|\Sigma)$, generates two new assertions equivalent to $(\Pi \wedge e|\Sigma)$ and $(\Pi \wedge \neg e|\Sigma)$, and applies the continuation f to both of these assertions.

Symbolic execution relies on functions subst_expr x e e', subst_pures x e Π, and subst_spaces x e Σ that substitute expression e for the variable x in (respectively) an expression e', a pure term Π, or a space term Σ.

Definition getSome {A} (x: option A) (f: A $\rightarrow$ bool):=
  match x **with** Some y $\Rightarrow$ f y | None $\Rightarrow$ false **end**.

Definition Cexpr2assertions(e:Clight.expr)(a:assertion)
                    (f:assertion→ assertion→ bool):=
match a **with** Assertion Π Σ ⇒
  match e **with**
  | Ebinop Oeq a b ⇒
      getSome (Cexpr2expr a) (fun a' ⇒ getSome (Cexpr2expr b) (fun b' ⇒
        f (Assertion (Eqv a' b' ::Π) Σ) (Assertion (Neqv a' b' ::p) Σ)))
  | Ebinop One a b ⇒
      getSome (Cexpr2expr a) (fun a' ⇒ getSome (Cexpr2expr b) (fun b' ⇒
        f (Assertion (Neqv a' b' ::Π) Σ) (Assertion (Eqv a' b'::Π) Σ)))
  | _⇒ getSome (Cexpr2expr e) (fun a' ⇒
        f (Assertion (Neqv a' Nil ::Π) Σ) (Assertion (Eqv a' Nil ::Π) Σ))
end end.

Smallfoot symbolic execution uses a restricted form of assertion without disjunction. Therefore when a disjunction would normally be needed, Smallfoot does multiple symbolic executions over the same commands. For example, for

$$(\text{if } e \text{ then } c1 \text{ else } c2); c3; c4; \text{assert } Q$$

with precondition P, Smallfoot executes the commands c1;c3;c4 with precondition $e \wedge P$ and then executes c2;c3;c4 with precondition $\sim e \wedge P$. Because Berdine et al.'s original Smallfoot used only simple "if and while" control flow, this re-execution was easy to express.

C has break and continue commands to exit from loop bodies or from loops. One branch of an **if** statement might exit, while the other might continue normally. To handle this notion, the parameters of the check function include not only a precondition P but a break-condition list BR that gives exit-postconditions for break, continue, and return. For simplicity of presentation, we omit BR and breaks from the check function in this chapter.

In order to handle re-execution mixed with breaks, we write the symbolic execution function in continuation-passing style. The argument

Fixpoint check (P: assertion) (c: stmt) (x': positive)

                        (cont: assertion → positive → bool) : bool :=
if incon P **then** true
else **match** c **with**
 ({P} skip {_} *)*
 | Sskip ⇒ cont P x'

 ({P} assert(Q) {_} *)*
 | Sassert Q ⇒ oracle (Entailment P Q) && cont Q x'

 ({P} x=i {_} *)*
 | Sset x (Etempvar i _) ⇒
    match P **with** Assertion Π Σ ⇒
    let P':=Assertion(Eqv (Var x) (subst_expr x (Var x') (Var i))
                     :: subst_pures x (Var x') Π)
                   (subst_spaces x (Var x') Σ)
    in cont P' (Psucc x')
    end

 ({P} x=i↦ next {_} *)*
 | Sset x (Efield (Ederef (Etempvar i _) _) f _) ⇒
    eq_id f _next &&
    getSome (isolate (Var i) P x') (**fun** l ⇒
     forallb(**fun** P' ⇒
        match P' **with**
        | Assertion Π' (**Next** _f :: Σ') ⇒
          cont (Assertion (Eqv (Var x) (subst_expr x (Var (Psucc x')) f)
                      :: subst_pures x (Var (Psucc x')) Π')
              (subst_spaces x (Var (Psucc x')) (**Next** (Var i) f ::Σ')))
                   (Psucc (Psucc x'))
        | _⇒ false
       end)
     l)

```
(* check (P: assertion) (c: stmt) (x': positive)
                        (cont: assertion → positive → bool) := *)
  (* {P} e1→ next=e2 {_} *)
  | Sassign (Efield (Ederef e1 _) f _) e2 ⇒
      eq_id f _next &&
      getSome (Cexpr2expr e1) (fun e1' ⇒
      getSome (Cexpr2expr e2) (fun e2' ⇒
      getSome (isolate e1' P x') (fun I ⇒
      forallb(fun P' ⇒
              match P' with
              | Assertion Π' (Next _f :: Σ') ⇒
                  cont (Assertion Π' (Next e1' e2' :: Σ')) (Psucc x')
              | _⇒ false
              end)
          I)))


  (* {P} while (e) c {_} *)
  | Swhile e c ⇒
      Cexpr2assertions e P (fun P1 P2 ⇒
          check P1 c x' P && cont P2 x')


  (* {P} if (e) c1; else c2 {_} *)
  | Sifthenelse e c1 c2 ⇒
      Cexpr2assertions e P (fun P1 P2 ⇒
          check P1 c1 x' cont && check P2 c2 x'cont)


  (* {P} c1; c2 {_} *)
  | Sseq c1 c2 ⇒ check P c1 x' BR (fun P' y' ⇒
check P' c2 y' BR cont)


  | _⇒ false
end.
```

cont is the check function's continuation. Once check has computed the postcondition Q for a given statement, it calls cont with Q. If it needs to call cont more than once, it may do so. For example, in the clause for Sifthenelse notice that cont is passed to two different recursive calls to check, each of which will perhaps call cont.

THE MIRACLE OF TERMINATION. In Coq, a **Fixpoint** function must have a structurally inductive parameter, such that in every recursive call the actual parameter is a substructure of the formal parameter. Here the structural parameter is the statement c. Most of the recursive calls are buried in continuations (lambda-expressions passed to the cont parameter)—and may not actually occur until much later, inside other calls to check. The miracle is that Coq still recognizes this function as structurally recursive.

AT THE START OF THE SYMBOLIC EXECUTION, the check0 function computes the first fresh variable x for the given program by taking the max of all variable names in use:

Definition check0 (P: assertion) (c: stmt) (Q: assertion) : bool :=
  let x := Pmax (Pmax (freshmax_assertion P) (freshmax_stmt c))
                    (freshmax_assertion Q)
  in check P nil c x (fun Q' _⇒ oracle (Entailment Q' Q)).

Theorem check_sound: ∀ Δ P c Q,
    check0 P c Q = true →
    semax Δ (assertion_denote P) (erase_stmt c)
    (normal_ret_assert (assertion_denote Q)).

SOUNDNESS OF SYMBOLIC EXECUTION.   If the symbolic executor checks a Hoare triple (check0 P c Q) then that triple is semantically sound, according to our axiomatic semantics semax. Since check0 takes syntactic assertions and semax takes semantic assertions, the statement of this theorem must take assertion-denotations. The function erase_stmt removes the assert statements from the program.

Chapter 47

Heap theorem prover

by Gordon Stewart, Lennart Beringer, and Andrew W. Appel

VeriStar is the *machine-verified* theorem prover for separation logic that lies at the core of the Smallfoot-style program analyzer of Chapter 46. To decide heap entailments, VeriStar implements an algorithm (cf. Navarro Pérez and Rybalchenko [69]) based upon the *paramodulation* calculus, a variant of resolution specialized for equality. The system is proved sound in Coq with respect to an axiomatization of separation logic, instantiated by the CompCert C model.

The VeriStar fragment of separation logic, which includes the usual separation logic connectives such as $\mapsto$ *(maps-to)* and $*$ *(separating conjunction)* as well as inductively defined list segments *(lseg)*, corresponds quite closely to the fragment used by Smallfoot and similar tools. The main limitations of this fragment with respect to the more expressive separation logics described in previous chapters of this book is that it is first-order and it does not allow arbitrary nesting of pure and spatial terms. These restrictions are necessary for efficiency but are usually not prohibitive when verifying shape properties.

FIGURE 47.1 presents the main components of the VeriStar theorem prover. To build an intuition for how the pieces fit together, consider the following

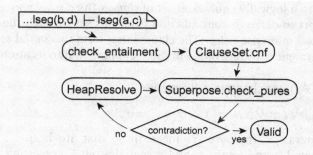

Figure 47.1: The main components of the VeriStar system. Superpose and HeapResolve form the heart of the heap theorem prover, performing equational and spatial reasoning respectively. The ClauseSet module defines the clausal embedding of assertions as well as the prover's clause database using a tuned red-black tree implementation of the Coq MSets interface.

(valid) VeriStar entailment

$$a \neq c \wedge b = d \wedge a \mapsto b * \mathsf{lseg}(b,c) * \mathsf{lseg}(b,d) \vdash \mathsf{lseg}(a,c) \qquad (47.1)$$

which consists of two assertions separated by a *turnstile* ($\vdash$). The first assertion states that program variable a does not equal c, b equals d and the heap contains a pointer from a to b and two list segments with heads b and tails c and d, while the assertion to the right of the turnstile states that the heap is just the list segment with head a and tail c. The task of the theorem prover is either to show that this entailment is *valid*—that every model of the assertion on the left is a model of the assertion on the right—or to return a counterexample in the process.

Most theorem provers for separation logic (e.g., Smallfoot [18], SLAyer [20]) attack the entailment problem *top-down*, exploring proof trees rooted at the goal. Each step of a top-down proof is an entailment-level deduction justified by a validity-preserving inference rule.

VeriStar, by contrast, is *bottom-up* and *indirect*. Instead of exploring proof trees rooted at the goal, it first decomposes the *negation* of the goal (hence indirect) into a logically equivalent set of *clauses* (its *clausal normal form*), then attempts to derive a contradiction from this set through the application of clausal inference rules. The clauses that form this initial set are a logically equivalent encoding of the original entailment into its atomic parts.

In particular, a VeriStar clause is a disjunction

$$(\pi_1 \vee \ldots \vee \pi_m) \vee (\overline{\pi'_1} \vee \ldots \vee \overline{\pi'_n}) \vee (\sigma_1 * \ldots * \sigma_r)$$

of positive pure literals π (by *pure* we mean those that are heap-independent), negated pure literals $\overline{\pi'}$ and a spatial atom Σ consisting of the star-conjoined simple spatial atoms $\sigma_1 * \ldots * \sigma_r$. The atom Σ may be negated or may occur positively but not both: we never require clauses containing two atoms Σ and Σ' of different polarities. We write positive spatial clauses (those in which Σ occurs positively) as $\Gamma \to \Delta, \Sigma$, where Γ and Δ are sets of pure atoms and Σ is a spatial atom, and use analogous notation for pure and negative spatial clauses. For example, in negative spatial clauses, Σ appears to the left of the arrow ($\Gamma, \Sigma \to \Delta$), and in pure clauses Σ does not appear at all ($\Gamma \to \Delta$). The *empty clause* $\emptyset \to \emptyset$ has no model because on the left, the conjunction of no clauses is True, and on the right, the disjunction of no clauses is False. Clauses such as $\Gamma \to a = a, \Delta$ and $\Gamma, a = b \to a = b, \Delta$ are tautologies.

ClauseSet.cnf (Figure 47.1) expresses the negation of the entailment as a set of clauses, taking advantage of the fact that it can encode any positive atom π as the positive unit clause $\emptyset \to \pi$ and any negative atom π' as the negative unit clause $\pi' \to \emptyset$. It can do the same for negative and positive spatial atoms. Since the negation of any entailment $F \vdash G$ is equivalent, classically, to $F \wedge \neg G$, the original entailment becomes:

$$a = c \to \emptyset \tag{47.2}$$

$$\emptyset \to b = d \tag{47.3}$$

$$\emptyset \to a \mapsto b * \mathsf{lseg}(b, c) * \mathsf{lseg}(b, d) \tag{47.4}$$

$$\mathsf{lseg}(a, c) \to \emptyset \tag{47.5}$$

Here the spatial atom $\mathsf{lseg}(a, c)$ appears to the left of the arrow in clause (47.5) since it appears in the right-hand side of the original entailment.

Likewise, the spatial atom $a \mapsto b * \mathsf{lseg}(b,c) * \mathsf{lseg}(b,d)$ appears to the right of the arrow in clause (47.4) since it appears in the left-hand side of the original entailment.

After encoding the entailment as a set of clauses, VeriStar enters its main loop (VeriStar.main_loop in Figure 47.1). First, it filters the *pure* clauses from the initial clauseset (clauses (47.2) and (47.3) above), then passes these clauses to Superpose.check_pures, the pure prover. Superpose attempts to derive a contradiction from the pure clauses by equational reasoning. In this case, however, Superpose is unable to derive a contradiction, or indeed, any new clauses at all from the set, so it constructs a model of the pure clauses by setting b equal to d (completeness of the superposition calculus guarantees that this model exists) and passes the model, along with the current clauseset, to HeapResolve for spatial normalization and unfolding.

HeapResolve uses the fact that b equals d in the model as a hint to normalize the spatial clauses (47.4) and (47.5) by clause (47.3), resulting in the new spatial clause

$$\emptyset \to a \mapsto d * \mathsf{lseg}(d,c) * \mathsf{lseg}(d,d) \tag{47.6}$$

in which b has been rewritten to d and therefore no longer appears. But now the spatial prover recognizes that since list segments are acyclic, $\mathsf{lseg}(d,d)$ can hold only if it denotes the empty heap. Thus $\mathsf{lseg}(d,d)$ can be simplified to emp, resulting in the new clause

$$\emptyset \to a \mapsto d * \mathsf{lseg}(d,c). \tag{47.7}$$

This new clause can almost be resolved against clause (47.5) using *spatial resolution*—an inference rule allowing negative and positive occurrences of spatial atoms in two different clauses to be eliminated—but only if clause (47.5) is unfolded to accommodate the next atom $a \mapsto d$ in clause (47.7). Unfolding $\mathsf{lseg}(a,c)$ to $a \mapsto d * \mathsf{lseg}(d,c)$ is sound, in turn, only when $\mathsf{lseg}(a,c)$ is nonempty, i.e., when $a \neq c$. To encode this fact, HeapResolve generates the new clause

$$a \mapsto d * \mathsf{lseg}(d,c) \to a = c. \tag{47.8}$$

$$a = c \rightarrow \emptyset$$
$$\emptyset \rightarrow b = d$$
$$\emptyset \rightarrow a \mapsto b * \mathsf{lseg}(b,c) * \mathsf{lseg}(b,d)$$
$$\mathsf{lseg}(a,c) \rightarrow \emptyset$$
$$\emptyset \rightarrow a \mapsto d * \mathsf{lseg}(d,c) * \mathsf{lseg}(d,d)$$
$$\emptyset \rightarrow a \mapsto d * \mathsf{lseg}(d,c)$$
$$a \mapsto d * \mathsf{lseg}(d,c) \rightarrow a = c$$
$$\emptyset \rightarrow a = c$$
$$\emptyset \rightarrow \emptyset$$

Figure 47.2: VeriStar-style resolution proof of Entailment (47.1)

Clause (47.8) can then be resolved with clause (47.7) to produce the positive unit clause

$$\emptyset \rightarrow a = c. \tag{47.9}$$

Superpose resolves clause (47.9) with clause (47.2) to derive the empty clause $\emptyset \rightarrow \emptyset$, which is unsatisfiable. Since the inference rules of the HeapResolve and Superpose systems preserve all models, the original set of clauses (encoding the negation of the entailment VeriStar set out to prove) is unsatisfiable; the entailment is therefore valid. Figure 47.2 presents the completed proof.

Atomic assertions in VeriStar (Figure 47.3) denote equalities and inequalities of program variables, singleton heaps and acyclic list segments. The assertion emp denotes the empty heap. The assertion $a \mapsto b$ (**Next** a b in VeriStar syntax) denotes the heap containing just the value of variable b at the location given by a (and is empty everywhere else), while Lseg a b denotes the heap containing the acyclic list segment with head pointer a and tail pointer b. Equalities and inequalities of variables are *pure* asser-

Expressions a, b
Nil	null pointer
Var x	Program variable

Pure Atoms π (pn_atom)
Equ a b	Expression a equals b.
Nequ a b	Expression a does *not* equal b.

Spatial Atoms σ (space_atom)
emp	Empty heap
Next a b	Singleton heap with $a \mapsto b$
Lseg a b	Acyclic list segment from a to b

Assertions F, G
Assertion Π Σ	Pairs of pure atoms Π and spatial atoms Σ

Entailments *ent*
Entailment F G	Assertion F implies G.

Figure 47.3: VeriStar syntax

tions because they make no reference to the heap, whereas $a \mapsto b$ and Lseg are *spatial* assertions.

A complex assertion $\Pi \wedge \Sigma$ is the conjunction of the pure atoms Π with the *separating conjunction* of the spatial atoms Σ. The separating conjunction $\sigma_1 * \sigma_2$ of two assertions—a notion from separation logic—is satisfied by any heap splittable into two disjoint subheaps satisfying σ_1 and σ_2, respectively. The assertion $\Pi \wedge \Sigma$ is satisfied by any environment e and heap h such that e satisfies all the assertions in Π and the pair (e, h) satisfies the separating conjunction of the assertions in Σ. Entailments $F \vdash G$ are valid whenever all the models satisfying F also satisfy G, i.e.: $\forall(e, h).\ F(e, h) \rightarrow G(e, h)$.

SEMANTICS. To ensure VeriStar can be retargeted to separation logics for a variety of languages and compiler frameworks, we proved the system sound with respect to an *abstract model* of separation logic. We first defined a generic separation algebra Interface (described in a companion technical paper [85]) with a join relation $\oplus$, a linked-list maps-to $\mapsto$ operator, and so on, that serves as a model for the Smallfoot fragment of separation logic. We then constructed an abstract model of separation logic generically for any concrete implementation satisfying the interface. This interface can be instantiated by any reasonable programming model, such as CompCert C light (we demonstrated it using CompCert C minor). The interface, and hence VeriStar's soundness proof, is general enough to be widely applicable.

THE INTERFACE axiomatizes the types of locations loc and values val; the special values nil_val, corresponding to the null pointer, and empty_val, corresponding to undefined (i.e., not in the domain of a given heap); an injection val2loc from values to locations; the types of variable environments env and heaps (heap) and a points-to operator on heaps (rawnext).

We assume a separation algebra on values, meaning that in addition to the operators on values specified in the interface (e.g., val2loc) we may use the *join* operator, written $\oplus$, to describe the union of two disjoint values.

The heap parameter gives the type of program memories. We require a separation algebra on heaps. We also require two operators on heaps, rawnext, a low-level version of the $\mapsto$ predicate of separation logic, and emp_at $(l{:}loc)$ $(h{:}heap)$, which defines when a heap h is empty at a location l. The behavior of these operators is defined by axioms [85].

THE ABSTRACT MODEL of separation logic is defined with respect to the interface we just described. States are pairs of environments e and heaps h.

Inductive state := State: $\forall$ $(e{:}env)$ $(h{:}heap)$, state.

The Coq keyword **Inductive** declares a new inductively defined datatype with, in this case, a single constructor named State. State takes as parameters an environment e and a heap h. In more conventional ML-like notation, this type is equivalent to the product type State **of** (env $*$ heap). Predicates on states, called spreds, are functions from states to Prop.

Notation spred := (state $\rightarrow$ Prop).

Prop is the type of truth values True and False, except that predicates in Prop need not be decidable and are erased during program extraction. Thus, we use Prop in our proofs, but bool in the verified code. A Coq **Notation** simply defines syntactic sugar. The interpretations of expressions (expr_denote), expression equality (expr_eq) and pure atoms (pn_atom_denote) are standard so we do not describe them here.

List segments are defined by an inductive type with two constructors.

Inductive lseg : val $\rightarrow$ val $\rightarrow$ heap $\rightarrow$ Prop :=
| lseg_nil : $\forall x\ h$, emp $h \rightarrow$ nil_or_loc $x \rightarrow$ lseg $x\ x\ h$
| lseg_cons : $\forall x\ y\ z\ l\ h_0\ h_1\ h$,
    $x \neq y \rightarrow$ val2loc $x =$ Some $l \rightarrow$ rawnext $l\ z\ h_0 \rightarrow$
    lseg $z\ y\ h_1 \rightarrow$ join $h_0\ h_1\ h \rightarrow$ lseg $x\ y\ h$.

The lseg_nil constructor forms the trivial list segment whose head and tail pointers are equal and whose heap is emp. The lseg_cons constructor builds a list segment inductively when x does not equal y, x is injected to a location l such that $l \mapsto z$, and there is a sub-list segment from z to y.

The function space_atom_denote maps syntactic spatial assertions such as Lseg $x\ y$ to their semantic counterparts (i.e., lseg $x\ y$).

Definition space_atom_denote $(a$: space_atom$)$: spred :=
  match a **with Next** $x\ y \Rightarrow$ fun $s \Rightarrow$
    match val2loc (expr_denote $x\ s$) **with**
    | None $\Rightarrow$ False
    | Some $l \Rightarrow$ rawnext l (expr_denote $y\ s$) (hp s) $\wedge$
                    nil_or_loc (expr_denote $y\ s$)
  end
  | Lseg $x\ y \Rightarrow$ (fun $s \Rightarrow$ lseg (expr_denote $x\ s$) (expr_denote $y\ s$) (hp s))
  end.

For **Next** $x\ y$ assertions, it injects the value of the variable x to a location l and requires that the heap contain just the location l with value v (that is, the heap must be the singleton $l \mapsto v$), where v is the interpretation of variable y. Coq's **match** syntax does case analysis on an inductively defined value (here the space atom a), defining a distinct result value for each constructor.

An Assertion Π Σ is the conjunction of the pure atoms $\pi \in \Pi$ with the separating conjunction of the spatial atoms $\sigma \in \Sigma$.

Definition assertion_denote (f :assertion) : spred :=
   match f **with** Assertion Π Σ $\Rightarrow$
      fold pn_atom_denote andp (space_denote Σ) Π
   end.

The function space_denote interprets the list of spatial atoms Σ as the *fold* of space_atom_denote over the list, with unit emp. Thus (space_denote Σ) is equivalent to

$$\left(\circledast_{\sigma \in \Sigma} \text{space\_atom\_denote}(\sigma) \right) * \text{emp}$$

(where $\circledast$ is iterated separating conjunction) and the denotation of Assertion Π Σ is

$$\bigwedge_{\pi \in \Pi} \text{pn\_atom\_denote}(\pi) \wedge \left(\circledast_{\sigma \in \Sigma} \text{space\_atom\_denote}(\sigma) \right)$$

if one simplifies $P *$ emp to P (recognizing that emp is the unit for $*$). Here space_denote Σ is the unit of the fold. Entailments from F to G are interpreted as the semantic entailment of the two assertions.

THE VERISTAR ALGORITHM. A key strength of the Navarro Pérez and Rybalchenko algorithm is that it splits the theorem prover into two modular components: the equational theorem prover for pure clauses (Superpose) and the spatial reasoning system HeapResolve, which calls Superpose as a subroutine in between rounds of spatial inference. This modular structure means well-studied techniques from equational theorem proving can be applied to the equational prover in isolation, while improving the performance of the heap theorem prover as a whole.

In this section, we describe our verified implementation of the algorithm of Navarro Pérez and Rybalchenko and give an outline of its soundness proof in Coq.

Listing 47.4 defines the main procedures of the VeriStar system, in slightly simplified form (we have commented out the termination proof for

```
Function main_loop                                                    1
  (n: positive ) (Σ: list space_atom) (ncl: clause) (S: M.t)          2
  {measure nat_of_P n} :=                                             3
  if Coqlib. peq n 1 then Aborted (M.elements S) else                 4
  match Superpose.check_pures S with                                  5
  | (Superpose.Valid, units, _, _) ⇒ Valid                            6
  | (Superpose.C_example R sel, units, S*, _) ⇒                       7
    let Σ' := simplify_atoms units Σ in                               8
    let ncl' := simplify units ncl in                                 9
    let c := norm sel (PosSpaceClause nil nil Σ') R in                10
    let S₁ := incorp (do_wellformed c) S* in                          11
    if isEq (M.compare S₁ S*)                                         12
    then if is _model_of_Π (List.rev R) ncl'                          13
         then let c' := norm sel ncl' in                              14
              let us := pures (unfolding c c') in                     15
              let S₂ := incorp us S₁ in                               16
              if isEq (M.compare S₁ S₂) then C_example R              17
              else main_loop (Ppred n) Σ' ncl' S₂ c                   18
         else C_example R                                             19
    else main_loop (Ppred n) Σ' ncl' S₁ c                             20
  | (Superpose.Aborted l, units, _, _) ⇒ Aborted l                   21
  end.                                                                22
Proof. (∗Termination proof here, that n decreases∗)                  23
Defined.                                                              24
                                                                      25
Definition check_entailment (ent: entailment) :=                     26
  let S := pure_clauses (map order_eqv_clause (cnf ent)) in           27
  match ent with                                                      28
  | Entailment (Assertion Π Σ) (Assertion Π' Σ') ⇒                    29
      match mk_pureR Π, mk_pureR Π' with                              30
      | (Π₊, Π₋), (Π'₊, Π'₋) ⇒                                        31
          main_loop m Σ (NegSpaceClause Π'₊ Σ' Π'₋)                   32
            (clause _ list2set S)                                     33
      end                                                             34
  end.                                                                35
```

Figure 47.4: The main VeriStar procedures

main_loop, line 24). The first step is to encode the entailment, *ent*, as a set of clauses (its *clausal normal form*, line 28). The algorithm then enters its main loop, first calling Superpose.check_pures (line 5) on the current set of pure clauses S, a subset of the clauses that encode *ent*, and checking whether the equational prover was able to derive the empty clause from this set. If it was, the algorithm terminates with Valid (line 6). Otherwise, Superpose returns with a model R of the set of pure clauses (line 7) and a list of unit clauses *units* derived during superposition inference (also line 7). VeriStar first rewrites the spatial atoms Σ and spatial clause *ncl* by *units* (lines 8-9), then normalizes the rewritten positive spatial atom Σ' using the model R (line 10). It then adds any new pure clauses implied by the spatial wellformedness rules to the pure set (line 12). This process repeats until it converges on a fixed point (or the prover aborts abnormally; see [85] for details). Once a fixed point is reached, more normalization of spatial atoms is performed (line 14), and unfolding of lsegs is attempted (line 15), possibly generating new pure clauses to feed back into the loop. If no new pure clauses are generated during this process, the algorithm terminates with a counterexample.

VeriStar divides spatial reasoning (lines 10-15 in Figure 47.4) into four major stages: normalization of spatial atoms, wellformedness inference, unfolding of list predicates and spatial resolution.

Normalization rules perform substitutions into spatial atoms based on pure facts inferred by the superposition system, as well as eliminate obviously redundant list segments of the form $\mathsf{lseg}(x, x)$.

Wellformedness rules generate new pure clauses from malformed spatial atoms. Consider, for example, the clause

$$\Gamma \to \Delta, \mathsf{lseg}(x, y) * \mathsf{lseg}(x, z)$$

which asserts that Γ implies the disjunction of Δ and the spatial formula $\mathsf{lseg}(x, y) * \mathsf{lseg}(x, z)$. Since the separating conjunction in the spatial part requires that the two list segments be located in disjoint subheaps, we know that the list segments cannot both start at location x unless one of the list segments is empty. However, we do not know which one is empty (see *spooky disjunction*, page 415). To formalize this line of reasoning, VeriStar generates the clause $\Gamma \rightarrow x = y, x = z, \Delta$ whenever it sees a clause with two list segments of the form given above. This new clause states that Γ implies either Δ (the positive pure atoms from the original clause) or $x = y \lor x = z$. The other wellformedness rules allow VeriStar to learn pure facts from spatial facts in much the same way.

The spatial *unfolding* rules formalize the notion that nonempty list segments can be unfolded into their constituent parts: a points-to fact and a sub-list segment, or in some cases, two sub-list segments. List segments should not be unfolded *ad infinitum*, however—it would be sound to do so, but our algorithm would infinite-loop. VeriStar performs unfolding only when certain other spatial facts are present in the clause database. These *hints* or triggers for rule application make the proof procedure tractable.

As an example, consider Navarro Pérez and Rybalchenko's inference rule U3

$$\frac{\Gamma \rightarrow \Delta, \mathsf{lseg}(x, y) * \Sigma \qquad \Gamma', \mathsf{lseg}(x, \mathsf{nil}) * \Sigma' \rightarrow \Delta'}{\Gamma', \mathsf{lseg}(x, y) * \mathsf{lseg}(y, \mathsf{nil}) * \Sigma' \rightarrow \Delta'}$$

which states that list segments $\mathsf{lseg}(x, \mathsf{nil})$ in negative positions should be unfolded to $\mathsf{lseg}(x, y) * \mathsf{lseg}(y, \mathsf{nil})$, but only when there is a positive spatial clause somewhere in the clause database that mentions $\mathsf{lseg}(x, y)$. In this rule, the left-hand side clause $\Gamma \rightarrow \Delta, \mathsf{lseg}(x, y) * \Sigma$ is unnecessary for soundness but necessary operationally for limiting when the rule is applied.

Our Coq implementation of this rule follows the declarative version rather closely.

Definition unfolding3 (sc1 sc2:clause) :=
  match sc1, sc2 **with**
  | PosSpaceClause Γ Δ Σ, NegSpaceClause Γ' Σ' Δ' $\Rightarrow$
    let l_0 := unfolding3' nil Σ Σ' **in**
    let build_clause Σ_0 := NegSpaceClause Γ' Σ_0 Δ' **in**
      map build_clause l_0
  | _, _ $\Rightarrow$ nil
  end.

Here unfolding3' is an auxiliary function that searches for and unfolds list segments from variable x to Nil in Σ' with counterpart lists of the appropriate form in Σ.

Finally, VeriStar performs *spatial resolution* of spatial atoms that appear both negatively and positively in two different clauses.

$$\frac{\Gamma, \Sigma \to \Delta \qquad \Gamma' \to \Delta', \Sigma}{\Gamma, \Gamma' \to \Delta, \Delta'}$$

Like the wellformedness rules, spatial resolution makes it possible to infer new pure facts from clauses with spatial atoms, in the special case in which Σ occurs both positively and negatively in two different clauses.

To facilitate VeriStar's soundness proof, we divided the prover into the following major components:

- Clausal normal form encoding of entailments;
- Superposition;
- Spatial normalization;
- Spatial wellformedness inference rules;
- Spatial unfolding rules; and
- Model generation and selection of clauses for normalization.

We then proved each of these components sound with respect to a formal interface (Module Type in Coq).

As an example of one such interface, the main soundness theorem for the clausal normal form encoding states that the negation of the clausal normal form of an entailment is equivalent to the original entailment before it was encoded as a clauseset.

Theorem cnf_correct: $\forall\,(e{:}\text{entailment})$,
    entailment_denote $e \longleftrightarrow$
    $\forall\,(s{:}\text{state})$, $\neg$(fold clause_denote andp TT (cnf e) s).

Here the notation fold f andp TT l s means $\bigwedge_{x \in l} (f\,x\,s)$. TT is the *always true* predicate. The function clause_denote defines our interpretation of *clauses*, i.e., disjunctions of pure and spatial atoms. Theorem cnf_correct is

the only theorem about the clausal normal form encoding that we expose
to the rest of the soundness proof, thus limiting the exposure of the rest of
the proof to isolated updates to the cnf component.

Likewise, the main soundness theorem for the superposition system
states that if Superpose.check_pures was able to derive the empty clause
from a set of clauses *init*, then the conjunction of the clauses in *init* entails
the empty_clause.

Theorem check_pures_Valid_sound: ∀ *init units g u*,
    check_pures *init* = (Valid, *units*, *g*, *u*) →
    fold clause_denote andp TT (M.elements *init*)
        ⊢ clause_denote empty_clause.

We need an additional theorem for Superpose, however, since the pure
prover may return C_example for some clausesets, in addition to those for
which it returns Valid. In the counterexample case, VeriStar constructs
a model for the pure clauses, then uses this model to normalize spatial
ones. Any clauses inferred by the pure prover while it was searching for the
empty clause must therefore be entailed by the initial set of clauses.

Theorem check_pures_Cexample_sound:
    ∀ *init units final empty R sel*,
    check_pures *init* = (C_example R *sel*, *units*, *final*, *empty*) →
    fold clause_denote andp TT (M.elements *init*)
        ⊢ fold clause_denote andp TT (M.elements *sel*) &&
            fold clause_denote andp TT (M.elements *final*) &&
            fold clause_denote andp TT *units*.

To prove the soundness of VeriStar.check_entailment, the main function
exported by the prover (Listing 47.4), we made each of the components
described above a functor over our abstract separation logic model,
VERISTAR_MODEL. As we described earlier in this chapter, our abstract
model is itself a functor over modules satisfying the VERISTAR_LOGIC
interface. VERISTAR_MODEL—and by extension, our soundness proof—is
therefore entirely parametric in the low-level details of the target separation
logic implementation (e.g., the definition of the *maps-to* operator).

In the main soundness proof for VeriStar.check_entailment, we imported the soundness proof for each component, instantiated each of the functors by Vsm:VERISTAR_MODEL, then composed the soundness theorems exported by each component to prove the main correctness theorem, check_entailment_sound.

```
Module VeriStarSound (Vsm:VERISTAR_MODEL).
    Module SPS := SP_Sound Vsm. (*Superposition*)
    Module NS := Norm_Sound Vsm. (*Normalization*)
    ...
    Module WFS := WF_Sound Vsm. (*Wellformedness*)
    Module UFS := UF_Sound Vsm. (*Unfolding*)

    Theorem check_entailment_sound: ∀ (ent:entailment),
        VeriStar . check_entailment ent = Valid →
        entailment_ denote ent.
End VeriStarSound.
```

check_entailment_sound states that if the prover returns Valid, the original entailment is semantically valid in the Vsm model. Because of VeriStar's modular design, the proof of this theorem goes by a straightforward application of the soundness lemmas for each of the subcomponents.

To target the soundness proof to CompCert, we built an implementation of the VERISTAR_LOGIC interface for C minor[1] addresses, values, local variable environments and heaps (CminLog). We instantiated our abstract separation logic by this module

```
Module Cmm:VERISTAR_MODEL:=VeriStarModel CminLog.
```

then applied VeriStarSound to Cmm,

```
Module Vss : VERISTAR_SOUND := VeriStarSound Cmm.
```

---

[1] C minor is a CompCert intermediate language two levels below C light. At the time we built VeriStar (2011), our Verified Software Toolchain targeted the C minor language. Since then, we have ported the VST to the C light language.

yielding an end-to-end proof. Here the module CminLog defines the operators and predicates on environments and heaps (env_get, env_set, rawnext, etc.) required by our soundness proof, and proves all of the required properties for these operators and predicates.

As the VeriSmall static analyzer calls on VeriStar to check separation-logic entailments, VeriSmall's soundness theorem (page 425) relies on Vss for the semantic validity of those entailments.

What we have achieved here is a *foundational* static analyzer. The ML program extracted from VeriSmall and VeriStar runs efficiently over (the abstract syntax of) C programs. Where the C program manipulates only data structures within the "Smallfoot fragment" of separation logic, VeriSmall accepts the program, implicitly making claims about the safety of the program and the *shape* of its data structures. The foundational soundness proof for those claims relies on the proofs of correctness (in Coq) for the Gallina programs from which the ML program is extracted. These correctness proofs are done with respect to the axioms of the VST program logic, which is proved sound (in Coq) with respect to the operational semantics of CompCert. Then the correctness proof (in Coq) of the CompCert compiler ensures that the behavior of the assembly-language program comports with the safety property claimed by the source-level static analyzer. The toolchain is verified from top to bottom.

Bibliography

[1] Sarita V. Adve and Hans J. Boehm. Memory models: A case for rethinking parallel languages and hardware. *Communications of the ACM*, 53(8):90–101, 2010.

[2] Amal Ahmed. *Semantics of Types for Mutable State*. PhD thesis, Princeton University, Princeton, NJ, November 2004. Tech Report TR-713-04.

[3] Amal Ahmed, Andrew W. Appel, Christopher D. Richards, Kedar N. Swadi, Gang Tan, and Daniel C. Wang. Semantic foundations for typed assembly languages. *ACM Trans. on Programming Languages and Systems*, 32(3):7:1–7:67, March 2010.

[4] Amal Ahmed, Andrew W. Appel, and Roberto Virga. An indexed model of impredicative polymorphism and mutable references. http://www.cs.princeton.edu/~appel/papers/impred.pdf, January 2003.

[5] Andrew W. Appel. Foundational proof-carrying code. In *16th Annual IEEE Symposium on Logic in Computer Science (LICS'01)*, 2001.

[6] Andrew W. Appel. Tactics for separation logic. http://www.cs.princeton.edu/~appel/papers/septacs.pdf, 2006.

[7] Andrew W. Appel. Verified software toolchain. In *ESOP 2011: 20th European Symposium on Programming, LNCS 6602*, pages 1–17, 2011.

[8]   Andrew W. Appel. VeriSmall: Verified Smallfoot shape analysis. In *First International Conference on Certified Programs and Proofs (CPP'11), LNCS 7086*, pages 231–246, 2011.

[9]   Andrew W. Appel and Sandrine Blazy. Separation logic for small-step C minor. In *20th International Conference on Theorem Proving in Higher-Order Logics*, pages 5–21, 2007.

[10] Andrew W. Appel and David McAllester. An indexed model of recursive types for foundational proof-carrying code. *ACM Trans. on Programming Languages and Systems*, 23(5):657–683, September 2001.

[11] Andrew W. Appel, Paul-André Melliès, Christopher D. Richards, and Jerôme Vouillon. A very modal model of a modern, major, general type system. In *34th Annual Symposium on Principles of Programming Languages (POPL'07)*, pages 109–122, January 2007.

[12] Andrew W. Appel, Neophytos G. Michael, Aaron Stump, and Roberto Virga. A trustworthy proof checker. *J. Automated Reasoning*, 31:231–260, 2003.

[13] Le Xuan Bach, Cristian Gherghina, and Aquinas Hobor. Decision procedures over sophisticated fractional permissions. In *APLAS: 10th Asian Symposium on Programming Languages and Systems, LNCS 7705*, 2012.

[14] Gilles Barthe, Benjamin Grégoire, César Kunz, and Tamara Rezk. Certificate translation for optimizing compilers. *ACM Trans. on Programming Languages and Systems*, 31(5):18:1–18:45, 2009.

[15] Ricardo Bedin França, Denis Favre-Felix, Xavier Leroy, Marc Pantel, and Jean Souyris. Towards optimizing certified compilation in flight control software. In *Workshop on Predictability and Performance in Embedded Systems (PPES 2011)*, volume 18 of *OpenAccess Series in Informatics*, pages 59–68. Dagstuhl Publishing, 2011.

[16] Jesper Bengtson, Jonas Braband Jensen, and Lars Birkedal. Charge! A framework for higher-order separation logic in Coq. In *Third International Conference on Interactive Theorem Proving (ITP'12)*, *LNCS 7406*, pages 315–331. Springer, August 2012.

[17] Josh Berdine, Cristiano Calcagno, and Peter O'Hearn. A decidable fragment of separation logic. *FSTTCS 2004: Foundations of Software Technology and Theoretical Computer Science*, pages 110–117, 2005.

[18] Josh Berdine, Cristiano Calcagno, and Peter W. O'Hearn. Smallfoot: Modular automatic assertion checking with separation logic. In *Formal Methods for Components and Objects, LNCS 4709*, pages 115–135. Springer, 2005.

[19] Josh Berdine, Cristiano Calcagno, and Peter W. O'Hearn. Symbolic execution with separation logic. In *APLAS'05: Third Asian Symposium on Programming Languages and Systems, LNCS 3780*, pages 52–68, 2005.

[20] Josh Berdine, Byron Cook, and Samin Ishtiaq. SLAyer: Memory safety for systems-level code. In *Computer Aided Verification (CAV'11), LNCS 6806*, pages 178–183. Springer, 2011.

[21] Lars Birkedal, Bernhard Reus, Jan Schwinghammer, Kristian Støvring, Jacob Thamsborg, and Hongseok Yang. Step-indexed kripke models over recursive worlds. In *POPL'11: 38th ACM SIGPLAN-SIGACT Symposium on Principles of Programming Languages*, 2011.

[22] Sandrine Blazy, Vincent Laporte, Andre Maroneze, and David Pichardie. Formal verification of a C value analysis based on abstract interpretation, 2013.

[23] Sandrine Blazy and Xavier Leroy. Mechanized semantics for the Clight subset of the C language. *Journal of Automated Reasoning*, 43(3):263–288, 2009.

[24] Hans-J. Boehm. Threads cannot be implemented as a library. In *PLDI '05: 2005 ACM SIGPLAN Conference on Programming Language Design and Implementation*, pages 261–268, 2005.

[25] S. Boldo and G. Melquiond. Flocq: A unified library for proving floating-point algorithms in Coq. In *20th IEEE Symposium on Computer Arithmetic (ARITH)*, pages 243–252. IEEE, 2011.

[26] Richard Bornat. Proving pointer programs in Hoare logic. In *MPC'00: International Conference on Mathematics of Program Construction, LNCS 1837*, pages 102–126. Springer, 2000.

[27] Richard Bornat, Cristiano Calcagno, Peter O'Hearn, and Matthew Parkinson. Permission accounting in separation logic. In *POPL'05: 32nd ACM Symposium on Principles of Programming Languages*, pages 259–270, 2005.

[28] John Boyland. Checking interference with fractional permissions. In *10th Static Analysis Symposium (SAS'03), LNCS 2694*, pages 55–72. Springer, 2003.

[29] James Brotherston and Cristiano Calcagno. Classical BI: Its semantics and proof theory. *Logical Methods in Computer Science*, 6(3), 2010.

[30] Rod Burstall. Some techniques for proving correctness of programs which alter data structures. *Machine Intelligence*, 7:23–50, 1972.

[31] Cristiano Calcagno, Dino Distefano, Peter O'Hearn, and Hongseok Yang. Compositional shape analysis by means of bi-abduction. In *POPL'09: 36th Annual ACM SIGPLAN-SIGACT Symposium on Principles of Programming Languages*, pages 289–300, January 2009.

[32] Cristiano Calcagno, Peter W. O'Hearn, and Hongseok Yang. Local action and abstract separation logic. In *LICS'07: 22nd Annual IEEE Symposium on Logic in Computer Science*, pages 366–378, 2007.

[33] Adam Chlipala. Mostly-automated verification of low-level programs in computational separation logic. In *PLDI'11: Proceedings 2011 ACM SIGPLAN Conference on Programming Language Design and Implementation*, pages 234–245, 2011.

[34] Adam Chlipala. *Certified Programming with Dependent Types: A Pragmatic Introduction to the Coq Proof Assistant.* MIT Press, 2013.

[35] Karl Crary. Toward a foundational typed assembly language. In *POPL'03: 30th ACM Symposium on Principles of Programming Languages*, pages 198–212, 2003.

[36] Maulik A. Dave. Compiler verification: A bibliography. *SIGSOFT Softw. Eng. Notes*, 28(6):2–2, November 2003.

[37] Edsger W. Dijkstra. Cooperating sequential processes. In F. Genuys, editor, *Programming Languages*, pages 43–112. Academic Press, New York, NY, 1968.

[38] Robert Dockins. *Operational Refinement for Compiler Correctness.* PhD thesis, Princeton University, Princeton, NJ, August 2012.

[39] Robert Dockins and Aquinas Hobor. A theory of termination via indirection. In Amal Ahmed et al., editors, *Modelling, Controlling and Reasoning About State*, number 10351 in Dagstuhl Seminar Proceedings, Dagstuhl, Germany, 2010.

[40] Robert Dockins, Aquinas Hobor, and Andrew W. Appel. A fresh look at separation algebras and share accounting. In *APLAS: 7th Asian Symposium on Programming Languages and Systems, LNCS 5904*, pages 161–177, 2009.

[41] Philippa Gardner and Mark Wheelhouse. Small specifications for tree update. In *6th International Conference on Web Services and Formal Methods, LNCS 6194*, pages 178–195, 2010.

[42] Rakesh Ghiya and Laurie J. Hendren. Is it a tree, a DAG, or a cyclic graph? A shape analysis for heap-directed pointers in C. In *POPL'96: 23rd ACM SIGPLAN-SIGACT Symposium on Principles of Programming Languages*, pages 1–15, 1996.

[43] Jean-Yves Girard. Linear logic. *Theoretical computer science*, 50(1):1–101, 1987.

[44] Alexey Gotsman, Josh Berdine, Byron Cook, Noam Rinetzky, and Mooly Sagiv. Local reasoning for storable locks and threads. In *5th Asian Symposium on Programming Languages and Systems (APLAS'07)*, 2007.

[45] Nadeem Hamid, Zhong Shao, Valery Trifonov, Stefan Monnier, and Zhaozhong Ni. A syntactic approach to foundational proof-carrying code. In *17th Annual IEEE Symposium on Logic in Computer Science (LICS'02)*, pages 89–100, July 2002.

[46] Robert Harper. A simplified account of polymorphic references. *Information Processing Letters*, 51:201–206, 1994.

[47] Robert Harper. *Practical Foundations for Programming Languages*. Cambridge, 2012.

[48] C A. R. Hoare. Monitors: An operating system structuring concept. *Communications of the ACM*, 17(10):549–57, October 1974.

[49] Aquinas Hobor. *Oracle Semantics*. PhD thesis, Princeton University, Princeton, NJ, November 2008.

[50] Aquinas Hobor. Improving the compositionality of separation algebras. http://www.comp.nus.edu.sg/~hobor/Publications/2011/psepalg.pdf, 2011.

[51] Aquinas Hobor, Andrew W. Appel, and Francesco Zappa Nardelli. Oracle semantics for concurrent separation logic. In *ESOP'08: 17th European Symposium on Programming, LNCS 4960*, pages 353 – 367, 2008.

[52] Aquinas Hobor, Robert Dockins, and Andrew W. Appel. A theory of indirection via approximation. In *37th Annual ACM Symposium on Principles of Programming Languages (POPL'10)*, pages 171–185, January 2010.

[53] Aquinas Hobor and Jules Villard. The ramifications of sharing in data structures. In *POPL'13: 40th Annual Symposium on Principles of Programming Languages*, pages 523–536, 2013.

[54] Michael R. A. Huth and Mark D. Ryan. *Logic in Computer Science: Modelling and Reasoning About Systems*. Cambridge, 2nd edition, 2004.

[55] IEEE and The Open Group. IEEE Standard 1003.1-2001, 2001.

[56] Samin Ishtiaq and Peter O'Hearn. BI as an assertion language for mutable data structures. In *POPL 2001: The 28th ACM SIGPLAN-SIGACT Symposium on Principles of Programming Languages*, pages 14–26. ACM Press, January 2001.

[57] ISO. International standard ISO/IEC 9899:1999, Programming languages – C, 1999.

[58] Jonas Braband Jensen and Lars Birkedal. Fictional separation logic. In *ESOP'12: European Symposium on Programming, LNCS 7211*, 2012.

[59] Achim Jung and Jerzy Tiuryn. A new characterization of lambda definability. In M. Bezem and J. F. Groote, editors, *Typed Lambda Calculi and Applications*, volume 664 of *Lecture Notes in Computer Science*, pages 245–257. Springer Verlag, 1993.

[60] Gerwin Klein and Tobias Nipkow. A machine-checked model for a Java-like language, virtual machine and compiler. *ACM Trans. on Programming Languages and Systems*, 28:619–695, 2006.

[61] D. Leinenbach and E. Petrova. Pervasive compiler verification – from verified programs to verified systems. *ENTCS*, 217:23–40, July 2008.

[62] Xavier Leroy. A formally verified compiler back-end. *Journal of Automated Reasoning*, 43(4):363–446, 2009.

[63] Xavier Leroy. The CompCert verified compiler, software and commented proof, March 2011.

[64] Xavier Leroy and Sandrine Blazy. Formal verification of a C-like memory model and its uses for verifying program transformations. *Journal of Automated Reasoning*, 41(1), 2008.

[65] David MacQueen, Gordon Plotkin, and Ravi Sethi. An ideal model for recursive polymophic types. *Information and Computation*, 71(1/2):95–130, 1986.

[66] Andrew McCreight. Practical tactics for separation logic. In *TPHOL: International Conference on Theorem Proving in Higher Order Logics*, LNCS 5674, pages 343–358. Springer, 2009.

[67] J. S. Moore. A mechanically verified language implementation. *Journal of Automated Reasoning*, 5(4):461–492, 1989.

[68] Hiroshi Nakano. A modality for recursion. In *LICS'00: 15th IEEE Symposium on Logic in Computer Science*, pages 255–266, 2000.

[69] Juan Antonio Navarro Pérez and Andrey Rybalchenko. Separation logic + superposition calculus = heap theorem prover. In *PLDI'11: Proceedings 2011 ACM SIGPLAN Conference on Programming Language Design and Implementation*, pages 556–566, 2011.

[70] Michael Norrish. *C Formalized in HOL*. PhD thesis, University of Cambridge, 1998. Tech. report UCAM-CL-TR-453.

[71] Peter W. O'Hearn. Resources, concurrency and local reasoning. *Theoretical Computer Science*, 375(1):271–307, May 2007.

[72] Peter W. O'Hearn. A primer on separation logic (and automatic program verification and analysis). In *Software Safety and Security*, pages 286–318. IOS Press, 2012.

[73] Jonghyun Park, Jeongbong Seo, and Sungwoo Park. A theorem prover for boolean BI. In *POPL'13: 40th Annual Symposium on Principles of Programming Languages*, pages 219–232, 2013.

[74] Matthew J. Parkinson. *Local Reasoning for Java*. PhD thesis, University of Cambridge, 2005.

[75] Benjamin C. Pierce. *Types and Programming Languages*. MIT Press, Cambridge, Mass., 2002.

[76] Benjamin C. Pierce et al. Software Foundations. http://www.cis. upenn.edu/~bcpierce/sf/, 2012.

[77] Gordon D. Plotkin. Lambda-definability and logical relations. Technical Report Memorandum SAI-RM-4, University of Edinburgh, 1973.

[78] François Pottier. Syntactic soundness proof of a type-and-capability system with hidden state. *Journal of Functional Programming*, 23(1):38–144, January 2013.

[79] John Reynolds. Separation logic: A logic for shared mutable data structures. In *LICS 2002: IEEE Symposium on Logic in Computer Science*, pages 55–74, July 2002.

[80] John C. Reynolds. An introduction to separation logic. http://www.cs.cmu.edu/afs/cs.cmu.edu/Web/People/jcr/copenhagen08.pdf, 2008.

[81] John C. Reynolds. Readable proofs in Hoare logic and separation logic. Unpublished slides for an invited talk at ETAPS 2009. http://www.cs.cmu.edu/~jcr/etaps.pdf, March 2009.

[82] Christopher D. Richards. *The Approximation Modality in Models of Higher-Order Types*. PhD thesis, Princeton University, Princeton, NJ, June 2010.

[83] Moses Schönfinkel. Über die Bausteine der mathematischen Logik. *Mathematische Annalen*, 92:305–316, 1924.

[84] Dana S. Scott. Data types as lattices. *SIAM Journal on Computing*, 5(3):522–587, 1976.

[85] Gordon Stewart, Lennart Beringer, and Andrew W. Appel. Verified heap theorem prover by paramodulation. In *ICFP'12: 17th ACM SIGPLAN International Conference on Functional Programming*, pages 3–14, 2012.

[86] Mads Tofte. Type inference for polymorphic references. *Information and Computation*, 89:1–34, November 1990.

[87] Harvey Tuch, Gerwin Klein, and Michael Norrish. Types, bytes, and separation logic. In *POPL'07: 34th Annual Symposium on Principles of Programming Languages*, pages 97–108, 2007.

[88] Thomas Tuerk. A formalisation of Smallfoot in HOL. In *TPHOL'09: Theorem Proving in Higher Order Logics, LNCS 5674*, pages 469–484. Springer, 2009.

[89] Andrew K. Wright. Simple imperative polymorphism. *Lisp and Symbolic Computation*, 8(4):343–355, December 1995.

Index